# Estate & Trust Administration

## FOR DUMMIES®

A Wiley Brand

## 2nd Edition

## by Margaret Atkins Munro, EA, and Kathryn A. Murphy, Esq.

**Estate & Trust Administration For Dummies®, 2nd Edition**

Published by
**John Wiley & Sons, Inc.**
111 River St.
Hoboken, NJ 07030-5774
www.wiley.com

Copyright © 2013 by John Wiley & Sons, Inc., Hoboken, New Jersey

Published by John Wiley & Sons, Inc., Hoboken, New Jersey

Published simultaneously in Canada

For general information on our other products and services, please contact our Customer Care Department within the U.S. at 877-762-2974, outside the U.S. at 317-572-3993, or fax 317-572-4002.

For technical support, please visit www.wiley.com/techsupport.

Wiley publishes in a variety of print and electronic formats and by print-on-demand. Some material included with standard print versions of this book may not be included in e-books or in print-on-demand. If this book refers to media such as a CD or DVD that is not included in the version you purchased, you may download this material at http://booksupport.wiley.com. For more information about Wiley products, visit www.wiley.com.

Library of Congress Control Number: 2013934913

ISBN 978-1-118-41225-1 (pbk); ISBN 978-1-118-41226-8 (ebk); ISBN 978-1-118-41227-5 (ebk); ISBN 978-1-118-41228-2 (ebk)

Manufactured in the United States of America

10  9  8  7  6  5  4  3  2

# About the Authors

**Margaret Atkins Munro, EA,** is a tax consultant, advisor, writer, and lecturer with more than 30 years of experience in various areas of finance and taxation. She's an Enrolled Agent, licensed by the federal government to represent clients in the areas of tax and tax-related issues, and currently operates a widely diverse private practice that specializes in trust and estate accounting and income taxation, among other areas. A classic example of living a life that doesn't follow the plan set out in college, Peggy received a BA in history from The Johns Hopkins University, in addition to attending University College in Cork, Ireland, and the Pontifical Institute of Mediaeval Studies in Toronto, Canada. She resides with her family in Vermont.

Peggy is the author of *529 & Other College Savings Plans For Dummies* and the coauthor of *Taxes (2005, 2006, 2007, 2008,* and *2009) For Dummies.* She writes a biweekly column on anything and everything to do with money for *The Montpelier* [Vermont] *Bridge* and has lectured extensively about taxes and tax-related issues. She's been interviewed on numerous financial and tax-related topics by a variety of national media outlets, including CNN Radio, Fox Business, *The Wall Street Journal, Family Circle Magazine, U.S. News and World Report, USA Today, Parents Magazine,* and the Associated Press.

**Kathryn A. Murphy, Esq.,** is an attorney with more than 20 years' experience in the fields of estate planning and administration, including drafting of sophisticated estate plans and prenuptial agreements for high net worth individuals. She has also administered many estates and trusts, both large and small, and prepared more than her fair share of estate and gift tax returns.

She graduated from The University of Michigan with an AB in English Language and Literature, received her Juris Doctor from Harvard Law School, and is a member of the Massachusetts Bar. Kathy, her daughter, Ana, and their poodle, Danny Boy, have recently returned to her home state of Michigan after more than 20 years in New England. Kathy is the coauthor of *Taxation of Estates and Trusts* (Michigan Continuing Legal Education) and *Estate and Trust Administration* (Michigan Continuing Legal Education). She has also lectured on these topics for Michigan Continuing Legal Education. She's been interviewed by the national media on financial and trust topics. Her writing is an outgrowth of two of her loves: literature and the law.

# Dedication

To my dear friend Howard, who gave me the idea for this book, even though he didn't know it at the time, and to the memory of his parents, Harry and Molly. And to Colin and Jacob, who supported me wholeheartedly as I worked on it.

—Margaret Atkins Munro

To my daughter, Ana, who inspires me in many ways. And to my friend, Peggy, for asking me to join her in this adventure.

—Kathryn A. Murphy

# Authors' Acknowledgments

First and foremost, our thanks to Mike Baker, Joyce Pepple, and Diane Steele at Wiley, who really listened to this idea one afternoon at lunch and then ran with it. Without them, this book would still be a figment of our imaginations. And many thanks as well to our technical editor Diane Hubbard Kennedy, our copy editor Nancy Reinhardt, and, most especially, to our project editors, Alissa Schwipps and Jennifer Tebbe, and assistant editor David Lutton, who were patience personified as we had to tell them, repeatedly, that we still really needed to see the results of the "fiscal cliff" negotiations in order to finalize this edition of the book.

We've both had many mentors over the years, among them Palmer Worthen and Frederick R. Keydel, who were responsible for steering us into our careers in trust and estate administration and planning. And we must, of course, thank all our friends in the Private Client and Trust Group and the Trust Administration & Investment Services Department at Goulston & Storrs, PC, where the two of us met 23 years ago and began our long friendship.

Last, but certainly not least, our gratitude to Melinda Haskins and Sean Siemen, who assisted us in so many important ways. This book is as much a testament to their efforts as it is to our own.

## Publisher's Acknowledgments

We're proud of this book; please send us your comments at http://dummies.custhelp.com. For other comments, please contact our Customer Care Department within the U.S. at 877-762-2974, outside the U.S. at 317-572-3993, or fax 317-572-4002.

Some of the people who helped bring this book to market include the following:

*Acquisitions, Editorial, and Vertical Websites*

**Senior Project Editor:** Alissa Schwipps

   *(Previous Edition: Chad Sievers)*

**Acquisitions Editor:** Erin Calligan Mooney

**Copy Editor:** Nancy Reinhardt

   *(Previous Edition: Megan Knoll)*

**Assistant Editor:** David Lutton

**Editorial Program Coordinator:** Joe Niesen

**Technical Editors:** Diane Hubbard Kennedy, Mark Friedlich

**Editorial Manager:** Christine Meloy Beck

**Editorial Assistants:** Rachelle S. Amick, Alexa Koschier

**Cover Photo:** © DNY59 / iStockphoto.com

*Composition Services*

**Project Coordinator:** Katherine Crocker

**Layout and Graphics:** Carrie A. Cesavice, Melanee Habig, Joyce Haughey

**Proofreaders:** Lauren Mandelbaum, Bonnie Mikkelson

**Indexer:** Ty Koontz

*Special Help*
Jennifer Tebbe

**Publishing and Editorial for Consumer Dummies**

   **Kathleen Nebenhaus,** Vice President and Executive Publisher

   **David Palmer,** Associate Publisher

   **Kristin Ferguson-Wagstaffe,** Product Development Director

**Publishing for Technology Dummies**

   **Andy Cummings,** Vice President and Publisher

**Composition Services**

   **Debbie Stailey,** Director of Composition Services

# Contents at a Glance

*Introduction* ..................................................... *1*

*Part 1: Getting Started with Estate and Trust Administration* ................................................. *7*

Chapter 1: Operating in a Fiduciary World.................................................9
Chapter 2: Exploring the Ins and Outs of Estates .....................................19
Chapter 3: Identifying Different Types of Trusts ......................................31
Chapter 4: Assembling Your Team Members
and Knowing When to Use Them .........................................................57

*Part 11: Administering an Estate* ..................... *73*

Chapter 5: Taking the First Steps after Death .........................................75
Chapter 6: Navigating the Probate Process..............................................91
Chapter 7: Marshalling and Liquidating Assets ......................................109
Chapter 8: Paying the Debts, Expenses, Bequests,
and Devises from the Estate .............................................................133
Chapter 9: Closing the Estate ................................................................147

*Part 111: Operating a Revocable or Irrevocable Trust...* *157*

Chapter 10: Understanding the Trustee's Duties ....................................159
Chapter 11: Funding the Trust ...............................................................171
Chapter 12: Investing the Trust's Assets and Paying Its Expenses .........183
Chapter 13: Paying Trust Beneficiaries..................................................203
Chapter 14: Creating and Keeping Trust Records ...................................217
Chapter 15: Terminating the Trust.........................................................231

*Part 1V: Paying the Taxes* ................................ *241*

Chapter 16: Preparing the Estate Tax Return, Part 1 ..............................243
Chapter 17: Preparing the Estate Tax Return, Part 2 ..............................263
Chapter 18: Filing Income Tax Returns for a Decedent, Estate, or Trust ..............287
Chapter 19: Weighing Income Tax Implications ......................................311
Chapter 20: Reporting Tax Info on Schedule K-1 ....................................321

## Part V: The Part of Tens ........................................... 333

Chapter 21: Ten Pitfalls for the Unwary...........................................335
Chapter 22: Ten Types of Taxes You May Have to Pay ............................343

## Appendix A: Glossary ............................................... 349

## Appendix B: State-by-State Rules of Intestacy and Estate or Inheritance Tax ..................................... 359

## Index ....................................................................... 379

# Table of Contents

*Introduction* ........................................................ *1*

About This Book .................................................... 1
Conventions Used in This Book.................................. 2
What You're Not to Read ......................................... 3
Foolish Assumptions............................................... 3
How This Book Is Organized .................................... 3
    Part I: Getting Started with Estate and Trust Administration ........ 4
    Part II: Administering an Estate ........................... 4
    Part III: Operating a Revocable or Irrevocable Trust ........ 4
    Part IV: Paying the Taxes ................................. 4
    Part V: The Part of Tens .................................. 5
Icons Used in This Book .......................................... 5
Where to Go from Here............................................ 6

*Part 1: Getting Started with Estate*
*and Trust Administration* ....................................... *7*

**Chapter 1: Operating in a Fiduciary World** ................ 9

Identifying the Players ............................................ 9
    Determining an estate's fiduciaries ...................... 10
    Knowing who the trustees are ............................ 11
    Lining up your team of advisors ......................... 13
Estate of Change: Delving into Estates ....................... 13
    Altering the status quo.................................... 14
    Probating an estate........................................ 14
    Collecting the estate's assets ............................ 14
    Paying expenses and making distributions .............. 15
    Tying up the estate's loose ends ......................... 15
Operating a Trust ................................................. 15
    Understanding your duties as trustee..................... 15
    Putting assets into trust.................................. 16
    Putting the trust to work.................................. 16
    Discovering the purpose of the trust ..................... 16
    Compiling and organizing trust records .................. 17
    Bringing the trust to its conclusion...................... 17
Paying Uncle Sam ................................................ 17
    Compiling the estate tax return ........................... 17
    Figuring out the income taxes............................. 18

Planning an income tax strategy ....................................................... 18
Whipping together Schedule K-1 ..................................................... 18

**Chapter 2: Exploring the Ins and Outs of Estates . . . . . . . . . . . . . . . . .19**

Defining the Estate for Probate Administration Purposes ...................... 19
Will Power: Understanding How a Will (Or No Will) Affects an Estate ... 21
Dying testate ................................................................................. 21
Dying intestate .............................................................................. 22
Taking a Look at Who Can Inherit .................................................... 23
Surviving spouse ........................................................................... 23
Individuals omitted from the decedent's will
(including intentional disinheritance) ......................................... 25
The other players: Devisees and legatees ....................................... 26
Heirs-at-law .................................................................................. 26
Defining the Estate for Tax Purposes ............................................... 26
Transfer taxes ............................................................................... 27
Other taxes ................................................................................... 29

**Chapter 3: Identifying Different Types of Trusts . . . . . . . . . . . . . . . . . .31**

Differentiating for Income Taxes: Grantor versus
Non-Grantor Trusts .......................................................................... 31
Grantor trusts ............................................................................... 32
Non-grantor trusts ........................................................................ 32
Intentionally defective grantor trusts ............................................ 33
Creating Trusts during Lifetime and after Death ............................... 34
Trusts created during lifetime ....................................................... 34
Trusts created under a last will ..................................................... 35
Grasping Revocable Trusts .............................................................. 35
Still breathing: Living trusts .......................................................... 36
Tackling Totten Trusts ................................................................... 37
Going incognito: Nominee trusts ................................................... 38
Understanding Irrevocable Trusts .................................................... 38
Making gifts to an irrevocable trust ............................................... 39
Getting the maximum tax benefit out of dying: Marital trusts ....... 40
Protecting the estate tax exemption: Credit shelter trusts ............ 43
Grandpa (or Grandma) knows best: Grandchildren's trusts ......... 46
Better safe than sorry: Insurance trusts ........................................ 46
It's only a name, not a description: Crummey trusts ...................... 47
Keeping a finger in the pie: Grantor-retained interest trusts ......... 48
Exploring Charitable Trusts .............................................................. 50
Split-interest charitable trusts ....................................................... 51
Non-operating charitable foundations ............................................ 52
Owning Subchapter S Shares in Trust ............................................... 53
Qualified Subchapter S Trusts (QSSTs) .......................................... 54
Electing Small Business Trusts (ESBTs) ......................................... 55

**Chapter 4: Assembling Your Team Members and Knowing When to Use Them** ............................. **57**

Finding What You Need to Go It Alone ...................................... 57
Finding an Attorney ................................................................... 59
   Knowing where to look ..................................................... 59
   Asking the right questions ................................................ 61
   Discussing payment options ............................................ 62
   Finalizing your decision ................................................... 63
   Working with your attorney ............................................. 63
Hiring a Tax Professional ........................................................... 64
   Discovering where to look ............................................... 65
   Discussing payment options ............................................ 65
Considering Help from Other Pros ............................................ 66
   Determining whether you need an investment advisor ....... 66
   Obtaining appraisers where necessary ............................ 69
   Consulting with other miscellaneous pros ...................... 70
Recognizing Malpractice ............................................................ 70
   Surveying why malpractice occurs .................................. 71
   Covering your ass . . . ets ................................................ 72

**Part II: Administering an Estate** ....................... **73**

**Chapter 5: Taking the First Steps after Death** ...................... **75**

Addressing the Immediate Concerns When Someone Dies ....... 75
   Honoring anatomical gifts ................................................ 76
   Having an autopsy performed .......................................... 76
Arranging the Funeral ................................................................ 77
   Making important decisions ............................................. 77
   Obtaining copies of the death certificate ....................... 82
Understanding How Death Changes Everything about
   the Decedent's Assets ......................................................... 83
   Bank accounts and the need for funds ............................ 83
   Powers of attorney ........................................................... 84
Locating the Estate-Planning Documents .................................. 84
   The Last Will and testament (The Will) ......................... 84
   Trust agreements and amendments ................................ 84
   Letters of intent ............................................................... 85
   Other documents that dispose of property ..................... 86
Notifying Those Who Need to Be Notified ................................. 86
Creating Calendars and Files ...................................................... 88
   Eyeing what kind of calendar to create ........................... 89
   Setting up a filing system ................................................. 89

**Chapter 6: Navigating the Probate Process** . . . . . . . . . . . . . . . . . . . . .**91**

    Filing the Last Will with the Probate (Or Equivalent) Court....................92

    Figuring Out Whether Administration Is Necessary ...............................93

        Do you need a temporary executor?................................................93

        Do you need a special administrator?..............................................95

        Determining domicile ......................................................................95

        Accessing ancillary administration ................................................97

    Deciding What Shape Your Probate Procedure Should Take................98

        Taking small estate shortcuts .........................................................99

        Traveling the traditional probate route.........................................101

    Taking Important First Steps after Your Appointment........................105

    Eyeing the Surviving Spouse's Rights and Decisions

        Regarding Property.........................................................................106

        Exercising rights ahead of the provisions of the will...................107

        Electing against the will ................................................................107

        Claiming dower ..............................................................................108

**Chapter 7: Marshalling and Liquidating Assets** . . . . . . . . . . . . . . . . .**109**

    Understanding Why You Need to Determine

    What the Decedent Owned...................................................................110

    Observing the Obvious: Big-Ticket Items ...........................................110

        The bricks and mortar: Real estate ...............................................111

        Things that move: Cars, boats, and cycles....................................112

        Small (and closely held) businesses .............................................112

    Tracking Down All the Other Assets ...................................................113

        Reading the mail ...........................................................................114

        Perusing other personal papers .....................................................115

        Finding the hiding places...............................................................116

        Emptying the safe deposit box.......................................................117

        Sleuthing for digital assets and info .............................................118

        Checking over prior tax returns.....................................................119

    Listing Personal and Household Effects ..............................................120

    Appraising the Property .......................................................................121

        Tangibles........................................................................................121

        Intangibles .....................................................................................122

        Real estate......................................................................................124

    Contacting the Employer about Employee Benefits ............................125

    Locating and Collecting Insurance Proceeds......................................127

    Ascertaining Any Other Death Benefits ..............................................128

    Preparing and Filing the Probate Inventory.......................................129

    Liquidating Assets ...............................................................................130

        Selling stocks, bonds, and other securities...................................131

        Disposing of real estate.................................................................131

**Chapter 8: Paying the Debts, Expenses, Bequests, and Devises from the Estate**.................................**133**

    Determining and Paying Debts of the Decedent
      and Administration Expenses .................................. 133
        Finding out how and when to pay claims ........................ 134
        Prioritizing payment ........................................ 136
        Declaring the estate insolvent .............................. 137
    Informing Potential Beneficiaries of Their
      Right to Consider Disclaimer .................................. 138
    Segregating and Distributing Specific Property ..................... 139
        Treading slowly before distributing ........................... 140
        Making the distributions .................................... 140
        Considering tangible property ............................... 141
        Looking at intangible property .............................. 142
        Fulfilling bequests of specific dollar amounts ................. 143
    Dividing Other Personal Property Equitably ...................... 143
        Basing division on letter of intent ........................... 144
        Creating a system for heirs to choose ......................... 144
        Disposing of unwanted personal property ..................... 145
    Slicing Up the Residue ........................................ 145

**Chapter 9: Closing the Estate**.................................**147**

    Obtaining Tax Closing Letters .................................. 147
    Acquiring Releases of Lien for Real Estate ....................... 148
    Paying Final Administration Expenses ........................... 149
    Making Final Distributions to Residuary Beneficiaries ............ 150
    Preparing and Filing Final Estate Income Tax Returns ............ 151
    Readying Accounts for Allowance by the Probate Court .......... 151
        Using the appropriate form of accounting .................... 152
        Following the proper probate procedures .................... 153
        Remembering filing fees .................................... 155
        Appointing a guardian ad litem, if needed ................... 155
        Filing a military affidavit, if necessary ....................... 156
        Notifying the surety ........................................ 156

**Part III: Operating a Revocable or Irrevocable Trust.... 157**

**Chapter 10: Understanding the Trustee's Duties**.................**159**

    Getting Acquainted with the Trust Instrument ................... 160
        Creating a plan based on the trust's terms .................... 160
        Identifying the players ...................................... 161
        Reforming the trust ........................................ 163

Empowering the Trustee .................................................... 163
    Buying and selling assets ............................................... 163
    Determining distributions to beneficiaries ..................... 164
    Hiring and firing advisors ............................................. 166
Coloring Inside the Lines: Understanding Fiduciary
  Duty and Limitations ...................................................... 166
    Exercising discretion ..................................................... 166
    Obtaining errors and omissions insurance ..................... 167
Protecting the Trust's Assets ............................................... 168
    Diversifying the assets .................................................. 168
    Asking for help ............................................................. 169
Preparing and Filing Annual Income Tax Returns and Accounts .......... 169

**Chapter 11: Funding the Trust . . . . . . . . . . . . . . . . . . . . . . . . . . . . .171**
Putting Assets in Trust during Life ...................................... 171
Signing It Over: Giving the Trust Asset Ownership ................. 172
    Cash and securities ...................................................... 172
    Privately held stocks, promissory notes,
      and limited partnership interests ............................... 175
    Real estate ................................................................... 176
    Life insurance policies .................................................. 178
    Personal and household property in trust ...................... 180
Rolling Property into Trust after Death ................................. 182

**Chapter 12: Investing the Trust's Assets and Paying Its Expenses . . . 183**
Appreciating the Importance of Income and
  Principal in Trust Administration ...................................... 184
    Defining principal and income ....................................... 184
    Distinguishing between the two ...................................... 185
Using Investment Advisors Effectively ................................. 186
Holding and Diversifying Assets .......................................... 188
    Stocks ......................................................................... 188
    Bonds .......................................................................... 189
    Mutual funds ............................................................... 192
    Cash needs .................................................................. 192
    Real estate .................................................................. 193
    Small business stocks ................................................... 194
Going Green in a Trust ...................................................... 195
    Socially conscious ....................................................... 195
    Politically aware .......................................................... 196
Looking to the Beneficiaries' Needs ..................................... 196
    Age ............................................................................. 197
    Purpose of trust .......................................................... 197

Paying the Trust's Expenses ....................................................... 199
    Trustee's fees .................................................................... 200
    Investment advice............................................................. 200
    Accounting fees................................................................. 200
    Taxes .................................................................................. 201

## Chapter 13: Paying Trust Beneficiaries .......................203

Notifying Beneficiaries of the Trust ......................................... 203
    Obtaining addresses and Social Security numbers...................... 204
    Verifying dates of birth ................................................... 204
Determining Scheduled Distributions........................................ 205
    Figuring out how much to pay ........................................ 205
    Creating a payment schedule......................................... 208
Distributing When the Beneficiary Reaches a Specific Age ................... 209
When Beneficiaries Request More Money:
    Paying Out Extra Distributions ..................................... 210
Making the Decision to Distribute Discretionally:
    Eyeing the Trust's Terms................................................ 212
    Ensuring health and well-being...................................... 212
    Paying for education........................................................ 213
    Buying a home.................................................................. 213
    Starting a business.......................................................... 214
    Using trustee discretion ................................................. 215

## Chapter 14: Creating and Keeping Trust Records................217

Creating a Filing System............................................................. 217
    Getting started: Organizing the right way ..................... 218
    Keeping the trust instrument handy .............................. 220
    Compiling correspondence ............................................. 220
    Filing financial records................................................... 221
    Preserving annual accounts ........................................... 221
    Referencing tax returns.................................................. 222
Preparing an Initial Inventory and Valuing the Assets ........... 223
    Arriving directly from the donor .................................... 223
    Coming from the donor's estate ..................................... 224
Compiling Records of All Transactions ..................................... 224
    Knowing the difference between income and principal .............. 224
    Filing income tax returns annually ................................ 225
Producing Annual Trust Accounts ............................................. 226
    Assembling the desired information ............................... 226
    Obtaining assents of beneficiaries................................. 228
    Filing with the probate court.......................................... 228

**Chapter 15: Terminating the Trust**...........................231

Distributing All Assets According to the Trust Instrument ................. 231
Calculating final income distributions ..................... 232
Holding back funds for final taxes and fees ................. 233
Paying the remaindermen ................................. 234
Submitting the Final Income Tax Returns ......................... 236
Determining any final tax liability ........................ 236
Filing a short-year return ............................... 237
Preparing Final Accounting and Obtaining
Assents of All Remaindermen ............................ 238
Finally finishing a non-probate trust ..................... 238
Polishing off a probate trust ............................ 239
Dealing with Outliers after the Trust Terminates ................ 240

*Part 1V: Paying the Taxes*............................... *241*

**Chapter 16: Preparing the Estate Tax Return, Part 1** ............243

Figuring Out Which Estates Must File ........................... 244
Who must file .......................................... 244
Who actually files Form 706 and when ..................... 245
Obtaining a Release from Personal Liability .................... 246
Understanding Some of the Nitty-Gritty Rules for Filing Form 706 ....... 246
Where and how to file .................................. 247
How to pay the tax ..................................... 247
Penalties for late filing, late payment,
and understatement of valuation ....................... 248
Signature and verification .............................. 248
Extensions of time to file and pay tax ................... 249
Supplemental documents ............................... 250
Completing the Form 706, Pages 1–4 ......................... 252
Part 1: Decedent and Executor ......................... 252
Part 2: Tax Computation ............................... 252
Signature of executor(s) .............................. 254
Signature of preparer other than the executor ........... 254
Part 3: Elections by the executor ...................... 254
Part 4: General Information ............................ 257
Part 5: Recapitulation ................................. 260
Part 6: Portability of Deceased Spousal
Unused Exclusion (DSUE) ............................. 260
Being Ready for and Handling an Audit ....................... 261
Getting an Estate Tax Closing Letter ........................ 262

## Chapter 17: Preparing the Estate Tax Return, Part 2 .............263

Tackling the Most Common Schedules...................................263
  Focusing on real estate: Schedule A..............................264
  Identifying stocks and bonds: Schedule B.......................265
  Addressing mortgages, notes, and cash: Schedule C.............269
  Considering life insurance: Schedule D..........................270
  Eyeing jointly owned property: Schedule E.......................271
  Considering other property: Schedule F..........................273
  Touching on funeral and administration expenses: Schedule J....275
  Recording debts, mortgages, and liens: Schedule K..............278
  Listing net losses and such: Schedule L.........................279
  Covering bequests to a surviving spouse: Schedule M............280
  Recording charitable, public, and similar
    gifts and bequests: Schedule O................................282
Knowing When to Ask for Help............................................283
  Listing transfers during life: Schedule G........................284
  Exercising powers of appointment: Schedule H....................284
  Considering annuities: Schedule I................................285
  Claiming a credit for foreign death taxes: Schedule P...........285
  Getting a credit for tax on prior transfers: Schedule Q.........285
  Generation-Skipping Transfer tax: Schedule R....................286
  Electing a qualified conservation easement exclusion:
    Schedule U....................................................286
  Filing a protective claim for refund: Schedule PC...............286

## Chapter 18: Filing Income Tax Returns for a Decedent, Estate, or Trust .................................287

Before You Begin: What You Need to Do ...............................287
  Obtain a federal tax ID number..................................288
  Choose a tax year-end...........................................289
Calculating the Income.................................................290
  Interest........................................................290
  Dividends.......................................................290
  Business income.................................................291
  Capital gains and losses........................................292
  Income from rents, royalties, partnerships,
    and other estates and trusts..................................295
  Farm income or loss.............................................295
  Ordinary gain or loss...........................................296
  Other income....................................................297
Deducing Deductions....................................................297
  Interest........................................................298
  Taxes...........................................................299
  Fiduciary fees..................................................299
  Charitable deductions...........................................300

Attorney, accountant, and preparer fees...................................301
Miscellaneous itemized deductions ...............................301
The Income Distribution Deduction (Schedule B) ......302
The estate tax deduction ..............................................304
Taxes owed...................................................................304
Credits .........................................................................308
Additional taxes ..........................................................309
Answering the Questions on the Back of Page 2 (Form 1041) .....309

**Chapter 19: Weighing Income Tax Implications** ................**311**

Timing Payments In and Out of an Estate ...........................312
Benefitting from the estate's fiscal year.........................312
Balancing the estate's taxable income
against the beneficiary's .........................................313
Timing the receipt of income .......................................313
Paying the ongoing expenses of the estate ...................315
Investing to Minimize Income Taxes....................................315
Limiting the fiduciary's income taxes ...........................317
Protecting the beneficiary ............................................317
Introducing the Unearned Income Medicare
Contribution (UIMC) Tax ...............................................318
Calculating the tax .......................................................319
Lessening the tax's impact ...........................................320

**Chapter 20: Reporting Tax Info on Schedule K-1** ............**321**

Understanding Schedule K-1 ...............................................321
General information.......................................................322
Income items ................................................................325
Deductions and credits .................................................326
Alternative minimum tax information............................327
Allocating Types of Income on the K-1 ................................328
Preparing Supplements to Schedule K-1 .............................329
Showing foreign tax allocations ...................................330
Providing state tax information ....................................330
Creating Nominee Form 1099s .............................................330

*Part V: The Part of Tens*............................................... *333*

**Chapter 21: Ten Pitfalls for the Unwary** ........................**335**

**Chapter 22: Ten Types of Taxes You May Have to Pay** ...........**343**

*Appendix A: Glossary*..................................................... *349*

*Appendix B: State-by-State Rules of Intestacy and Estate or Inheritance Tax*..................................... *359*

*Index*........................................................................ *379*

# Introduction

$T$his country is aging. Fewer babies are being born, and people are living longer and longer. They're also managing to accumulate more and more wealth. Wealth is relative; two generations ago, a middle-income family owned a house and maybe a car and perhaps even had a little money in the bank. Today, that scenario has become much more complicated. Many who would never consider themselves wealthy now own more than one home and have investments in the stock market, retirement accounts that continue on after death, and debt up to their eyeballs.

With this increased complexity in financial affairs comes a parallel complexity in transferring all these accumulated assets to the next generation(s), either at death or before. In the past, heavy-duty trusts were only for the very wealthy; today, they've become part of the legal landscape for ordinary Americans. And because ours is a do-it-yourself society in so many aspects, that I-can-do-it-myself attitude has carried over into trust and estate administration. Why, many people ask, should they pay someone else to do work that they themselves can perform just as well for a fraction of the cost?

And that's why we wrote the second edition of this book. Between the two of us, we have more than 60 years of estate and trust administration experience. In that time, we've come across some unusual situations in our careers and devised ways to avoid standard pitfalls that await the unwary. We wrote this book to share with you some of this accumulated wisdom — and to help you avoid the mistakes that we've made (or narrowly avoided).

## About This Book

*Estate & Trust Administration For Dummies,* 2nd Edition, is the practical reference for those who find themselves appointed as executor, administrator, or personal representative of an estate, or as trustee of a trust. In these pages, you can find advice on what to do — and what to avoid — as you acquire, manage, and dispose of assets that belong to the estate or trust you're administering.

The world of estate and trust administration is one that can baffle you before you ever get out of the starting gate. You're asked to make decisions literally before you've had the opportunity to process that your friend or family member has died. In those first days after a death, when so much of the world seems like it's at sixes and sevens, you need to decide about the funeral, collect house keys, find the decedent's last will — the list seems endless, and so are the opportunities to have seemingly innocuous items fall through the cracks.

That's where this book comes in. We designed it to explain how you can administer an estate or trust by yourself. It gives you guidelines on what aspects of the work you can undertake on your own and which areas you really want to ask for an expert to help you.

Simply put, this book allows you to create and follow a road map toward successfully completing your appointed task without ripping out your hair and running into the streets screaming. You can use this book in a couple of ways:

- ✓ **As a reference:** Everything's here, whether you have questions about probate, taxes, or how to plan a funeral. The world of trusts and estates can seem complicated, but it's all governed by common sense and rules (and plenty of them).

- ✓ **As an advisor:** Some problems may seem unsolvable when you first confront them, but rarely is that truly the case. This book can help you find what questions you need to ask and who you should look to for answers. It gives you solid advice that you can literally take to the bank and lets you know when you would be better served by seeking professional advice.

We try to give you as complete information as possible, but trust and estate administration covers a lot of ground, much of it very complex. Still, we have to warn you that every situation is different, and periodically having a professional check your progress in administering any estate or trust is never a bad idea. At best, he or she will confirm that you're doing a brilliant job; at worst, the pro will catch any mistakes you may be making before they have a chance to become really serious.

# Conventions Used in This Book

To help you navigate this book, we use the following conventions:

- ✓ *Italic* highlights words or terms that are being defined. (We also use it occasionally for emphasis.)

- ✓ **Boldface** indicates keywords in bulleted lists or the action parts of numbered steps. It also flags the names of specific tax documents so you can find them easily in any discussion.

- ✓ Monofont tells you that you're looking at a Web address.

# What You're Not to Read

We'd love for you to read every single word we wrote, but we're also realistic and understand that you probably only have time for just the need-to-know information. If you're overwhelmed and want just the essentials, you can skip anything marked with a Technical Stuff icon; all you'll miss is some overly technical gibberish.

# Foolish Assumptions

The world of estates and trusts is rife with assumptions, foolish and otherwise. Here are some of the assumptions we made about you:

- ✓ You're not a professional trustee or executor, or a trust or estate administrator already (although even if you are, you should still find the information in this book helpful).

- ✓ You probably have no idea what you bit off when you agreed to act as either an executor or trustee, but you're eager to find out.

- ✓ You're not scared of hard work, both physical and mental, and you're not afraid to delegate. You can do much of what needs to be done in administration yourself, whether it's prying up floorboards in search of the secret money stash or creating a probate account, but you recognize that sometimes paying someone else to do a task you feel unprepared to tackle makes perfect sense.

# How This Book Is Organized

It really wasn't difficult to organize this book because it naturally split itself into its component parts: defining a whole lot of terms and types of trusts you may not be familiar with, estate administration, trust administration, and finally transfer tax and income tax issues. The following sections outline the contents of each part.

# Part I: Getting Started with Estate and Trust Administration

What we both discovered when we first landed in law offices and started administering estates and trusts was that lawyers, judges, and just about everyone else involved spoke in code. Not only did they use words such as *whereas* and *hereunder* in general conversation, but they also threw around terms such as administratrix, CRATs, CRUTs, GRITs, and QPRTs like confetti at a wedding. In this part, not only do we give you the terminology that any executor or trustee worth his or her weight knows but we also explain who all the players are in estates and trusts (and, in the case of trusts, exactly what games are being played).

# Part II: Administering an Estate

Administering an estate is a multistep — sometimes simultaneous-step — operation that requires an eye for detail and sometimes a great deal of patience. In this part, we take you from soup to nuts: figuring out what the decedent owned (and owed), locating the necessary documents, figuring out who inherits, shepherding the estate through the probate process (if necessary), distributing what's left after everyone who has a claim against the estate has been paid, and closing the estate for good. It may seem like a monumental task, but taking it one step at a time, even if those steps go in directions you don't want them to, inevitably leads you to your desired conclusion.

# Part III: Operating a Revocable or Irrevocable Trust

Your duties as a trustee are different from the duties of an executor, and the scope of the work is generally less intense, although it takes longer. In this part, we acquaint you with what powers you have as trustee and what duties you're expected to perform. We explore your relationship to the trust's beneficiaries and how to keep it cordial. Plus, we explain how to keep the necessary records and how to terminate the trust after its job is done.

# Part IV: Paying the Taxes

Because the IRS considers trusts and estates separate entities, you have the enviable task of making sure that you file all necessary tax returns on time. We walk you through preparation of a simple estate tax return (**Form 706**) and through the annual income tax returns for trusts and estates (**Form**

**1041**). We also explain what you need to know to prepare the decedent's final **Form 1040.** Finally, we show you how to report to beneficiaries any income you may have distributed to them so they in turn can declare that information on their **Form 1040.**

## Part V: The Part of Tens

What would a *For Dummies* book be without the Part of Tens? In this part, we reveal ten mistakes that are easy to make but even easier to avoid with just a little planning, as well as the ten different types of taxes a trust or estate may be liable for. And, in case that wasn't enough, we've also included two appendixes. The first is a glossary. The second is a state-by-state list of basic rules of *intestacy* (dying without a valid last will), plus current state estate tax rules (and where you can find more information and forms, if necessary). Just a quick note of caution: The intestacy rules are far more complex than what we were able to include in the appendix. If you're administering an intestate estate, be sure to consult with the probate court or a qualified attorney as to the disposition of that particular estate.

## Icons Used in This Book

The little pictures in the margins are icons. Here's what they mean:

So much to remember, so little time: This icon alerts you to important information you really don't want to ignore.

Of course, you want to manage all the administration tasks yourself. But some you're just not qualified for, and others — take our word for it — you really do want to have someone who knows cast a hairy eyeball over. When you see this icon, you've just come across an item we suggest you don't attempt without assistance.

Estate and trust administration can get pretty technical. This icon points out specific information regarding rules, regulations, and especially Internal Revenue Code references.

We've picked up lots of techniques through hard experience, and we're happy to share them with you. This icon points out administration gems that will make your life easier. Remember, though, that not every trust or estate will need every tip that comes your way; make sure that a tip applies to your situation before you use it.

This icon tells you what to avoid when administering a trust or estate.

# Where to Go from Here

This book isn't intended as a must-read-cover-to-cover sort of tome, nor will you be able to pass a trusts and estates course in law school just because you read it. You may choose to read only what interests you and ignore the rest. You can get in and get out wherever and whenever you choose. If important information relating to a particular topic is located elsewhere, the text will send you there, so you never need to worry that you're missing basic information because you skipped a portion of the book. Of course, you may discover that it's just a page turner, and every topic fascinates you, in which case you may want to apply to law school posthaste (after you finish the book, of course).

# Part I
# Getting Started with Estate and Trust Administration

# In this part . . .

✔ Find out what's involved in being an executor, administrator, personal representative, or trustee, including the terminology, who's who, and the basics of your responsibilities.

✔ Discover the difference between what constitutes an estate for probate and for estate tax purposes, what to do if there is — or isn't — a will, and how to figure out who can inherit.

✔ Get up to speed on the different kinds of trusts, how to identify them, and their purposes.

✔ Start assembling your administration support team, if necessary, including attorneys, accountants, and other experts.

# Chapter 1

# Operating in a Fiduciary World

*In This Chapter*

▶ Becoming comfortable with the terminology surrounding estates and trusts

▶ Encapsulating estates and taking care of trusts

▶ Preparing and filing tax returns for trusts, estates, and decedents

*Y*ou may have known for a while that someone close to you has named you as the executor of his or her will, as the trustee of a trust he or she's created, or even as both. That knowledge may make you feel extremely honored while that person's alive and kicking and still able to look after his or her assets.

Those warm and fuzzy feelings may come crashing to a halt, though, the day you hear that your friend has passed away, and you're now in charge of the show. All eyes will be on you as you pick up the reins and try to keep this buggy called an estate or trust moving along at a steady clip, while keeping all the promises written down during your friend's lifetime. The responsibility is huge, but so is your potential satisfaction, as you honor his wishes after he is no longer around to appreciate your actions.

This chapter is a jumping-off point for understanding what an estate administrator or trustee actually does: assumes control of someone else's affairs in a way that's both sensitive to family dynamics and responsive to family needs. Mishandled, estate and/or trust administration can cause permanent family rifts; on the other hand, competent and careful management helps keep family memories happy and purpose intact.

## Identifying the Players

Administering a trust or estate isn't rocket science, but it does have its own language. One of the biggest stumbling blocks you run across, especially as you're beginning in your new role, is figuring out who all the players are and what roles they all play. The following sections point out some important basic lingo you need to know as you start your journey. Refer to the other chapters in Part I for more on your responsibilities as an administrator or trustee.

# Determining an estate's fiduciaries

Several kinds of *fiduciaries* (people or organizations who hold and administer assets of one person, either living or deceased, for the benefit of that person or another) may be involved in estate administration, depending upon whether a will exists and who the heirs are. You may not even be the only fiduciary; in that case, you and the other(s) must act in unison. And one person or group can fulfill multiple fiduciary roles, such as when one person is named both executor and trustee. The following are types of fiduciaries you may be named:

- **Executor:** The *executor* is the person named in the will to "execute" the will — to carry out the wishes of the person making the will, including disposing of the property according to the will. A female executor is sometimes referred to as an *executrix,* although we don't make that distinction in this book. A named executor may decline to act, although we hope this book gives you the confidence to embrace the role.

- **Administrator:** The *administrator* is a person appointed by the probate court to administer the decedent's estate when the decedent left no valid will. A female administrator may be referred to as an *administratrix.*

- **Personal representative:** The *personal representative* is a general term for both the executor and the administrator. In some states, this term is used in place of executor or administrator.

- **Guardian:** A *guardian* is the person appointed by the probate court to take care of the person and the property of another person who is considered incapable of taking care of his or her own affairs because of his or her age (often a minor) or for other reasons such as mental disability, physical incapacity, or illness.

- **Conservator:** A *conservator* is similar to a guardian, but with less restrictive rules than those for a guardian. For example, the probate court may appoint a conservator for someone who can't properly care for his or her property due to mental disability or physical incapacity, or for a person missing in action or a prisoner of war.

A probate court rarely appoints a conservator for an estate, especially if you've already been appointed as executor or administrator; however, you may find yourself dealing with an already-appointed conservator of an estate beneficiary. Remember, just because you're all working with the same set of assets doesn't mean that you belong to the same team. As executor or administrator, you're only responsible for the property owned by the decedent; a beneficiary's conservator is responsible for that beneficiary's interest.

# Knowing who the trustees are

A trust, just like an estate, must have a fiduciary heading up its team: in this case, a *trustee*. The trustee of a trust is charged with the task of investing the trust's assets and balancing the desires of the trust's creator (the *grantor,* also referred to as the *settlor*) with the needs of the *beneficiary of the present interest* (the person or organization entitled to receive the income earned by the trust's assets and, depending on the terms of the trust, perhaps some or all of the trust assets themselves) and the wants of the *remainderman* or *remainder beneficiary* (the person or organization who receives what's left of the trust's assets after the trust period ends). It may sound daunting, but when done properly, everyone should go home happy.

Because balancing these competing interests can be complicated, many grantors choose two or more individuals and/or corporations to act together as co-trustees, jointly filling these roles, assigning general powers to all and sometimes specific additional powers to certain trustees. In order to differentiate between the trustees, trustees often are designated as either *independent* or *family*. This section discusses these two types of trustees. Chapter 3 goes into more depth about the different types of trusts.

## All by themselves: Independent trustees

*Independent trustees*, or fiduciaries who aren't named in the trust as either grantor, beneficiary, or remaindermen, can be an important cog in keeping the wheels of a trust running smoothly. Whether they're trusted friends of the grantor or are banks, trust companies, lawyers, or accountants, independent trustees owe their primary allegiance to the grantor, who is relying on them to make decisions that best serve the interest of the trust, rather than that of any present interest beneficiary or remainderman.

Frequently, grantors direct an independent trustee to make all decisions regarding discretionary distributions to beneficiaries, especially if one of the trust beneficiaries is also a trustee. And, in the case of testamentary trusts, the probate court often delegates the power to make discretionary distributions to the independent trustee alone so as to remove any semblance of self-serving from a trustee who also has a beneficial or remainder interest in the trust.

For example, one of us acts as trustee for a testamentary trust where the decedent's widow (who is the income beneficiary) and two children (the remaindermen) are also trustees. Only the independent trustee may make decisions regarding distributions of principal to the widow or the children. Distributions to the children prior to their mother's death require either the consent of the independent trustee or the probate judge.

No independent trustee assumes the responsibilities lightly. As a result, expect to pay for their services, unless the independent trustee is a close friend of the grantor, who may be willing to perform this service out of long friendship and the goodness of his heart. Banks and trust companies most likely have pamphlets that list how they calculate their fees; because they probably have active custody of the trust assets, they usually collect their fees automatically from the trust. Non-institutional professional trustees such as attorneys and accountants bill you for their services. They may charge based on their normal hourly rates, but they're more likely to calculate their fees based on a percentage of the market value of the assets of the trust, as well as a percentage of income collected.

Trusts that mandate an independent trustee typically also include a *line of succession* so that if one trustee is no longer able to act, another is in line to take his or her place. If the trust requires an independent trustee, make sure that any vacancies are filled promptly because it's next to impossible for the trust to function efficiently without one in place.

### All in the family: Family trustees

Trust grantors often feel that using only professional trustees (as efficient as they may be) may not account for special family circumstances. In these cases, the grantor may choose to also have a *family trustee*, or a trusted member of his or her family, who knows the players (the present interest beneficiaries and the remaindermen) well and has no difficulty making decisions based on the grantor's wishes.

Family trustees usually have most of the same powers as independent trustees (such as investment powers and the authority to prepare and sign income tax returns and to make scheduled distributions to present interest beneficiaries), but their powers over discretionary distributions are often limited if they have a vested interest in the trust as a present interest beneficiary or remainderman.

It's possible for trusts to exist with only a family trustee, although the results are sometimes messy. Somehow, wherever money is concerned, perceptions of appropriate behavior on all sides tend to skew; in our opinion, you're far better off to limit opportunities for self-serving during trust administration by never allowing a family trustee to serve alone. With the addition of an independent trustee, everyone concerned — from the grantor to the present interest beneficiary to the trust remaindermen — can be confident that all the competing interests were considered throughout administration and that the trustees made appropriate and fair decisions.

Another bad idea: having family members be sole trustees of a trust established for their benefit. Unless the trustee/beneficiary is only entitled to mandatory distributions of all the income annually (and principal distributions made under very limited circumstances), the assets of the trust can be included in the trustee/beneficiary's taxable estate at the time of his or her death, even though the trust property would never be included in the probate estate. If there's also an independent trustee, the grantor can give far more flexibility to that trustee to make distributions of income and principal to the beneficiary, and the trust assets still won't be included in that beneficiary's taxable estate upon his or her death.

And, even though the surviving spouse may be the sole trustee of a marital trust for his or her benefit (after all, the property in the marital trust at the time of the surviving spouse's death will be included in his or her taxable estate anyway), in practice, we've seen few trusts where there isn't also an independent trustee, if only for ease of administration. If the surviving spouse is the beneficiary of a trust other than the marital trust, an independent trustee can provide more flexibility in distributions to the surviving spouse without having the trust assets included in his or her estate.

## Lining up your team of advisors

No matter whether you've just been named as the fiduciary, or you're the fiduciary's trusted advisor, you'll probably have times when you really want someone else to explain your options to you or set out the potential pros and cons of a decision you must make. Creating a team of professional advisors before you need the advice is the best way to ensure that, when the time comes to make those decisions, you're able to ask for the advice and move forward in a clear and measured manner. Chapter 4 lists the types of advisors you may want to employ and explains how they can help you administer a trust or estate without your surrendering all the fun to them.

# Estate of Change: Delving into Estates

The day a person dies, you're sure to have more on your mind than the fact that you've just assumed a new role — that of the person designated to wrap up the decedent's affairs. And yet even while you're wrestling with your personal feelings about the loss, you're somehow supposed (and expected) to start tossing all the various balls in the air. You may find yourself planning a funeral at the same time that you're creating the estate's calendar, collecting keys to the residence (if the decedent has no surviving spouse), buying the food for the after-funeral *collation* (light meal), and figuring out what the decedent owned and owed.

In the next sections, we walk you through all the steps of administering an estate. Just remember, when all the advice begins to leave you breathless, prioritizing can mean the difference between keeping your sanity and running screaming into the sunset. (Check out Part II for more info.)

## Altering the status quo

Although losing a friend or loved one may be difficult, you need to realize that the person's status is static. Your loved one is dead; your status, as administrator or executor has also been altered, but that alteration will continue to evolve through the process. You're now responsible for the estate and the decedent's assets and liabilities.

Chapter 5 walks you through the first steps in your legal role. We help you dive into the decedent's affairs. You gain a sense of what the decedent owned and how he held title to it (and thus whether it flows through the probate estate), who he or she owed money to, and who inherits what's left. You create a calendar with all the estate's important deadlines listed, and you discover the documents — both ones that were created before the decedent's death and others that you obtain after death — that you need in order to start moving this estate forward.

## Probating an estate

*Probate* is a fairly straightforward process of providing court supervision to your administration of an estate. Probate exists for your protection as executor as much as to protect the interests of the estate's heirs and legatees. With the probate court judge standing between you and the heirs, you have the opportunity to do your job unmolested. And, as you do that job, the judge and the court staff check your steps and help you when you need it, making sure that you're doing everything you should. As the executor of the estate, you'll start the process by filing the decedent's last will, if there is one, and applying for administration. You can't finish until the court tells you that you can, when you file the final account, and it's allowed.

In Chapter 6, you work your way through the probate process, including getting appointed as executor, administrator, or personal representative; filing the last will, if one exists; notifying heirs and creditors; and completing the legal documents you're required to file with the court.

## Collecting the estate's assets

Most of the fun in administering an estate (at least, we think so) is digging for buried treasure. Without accurately knowing what's there, you won't know if you'll be required to file an estate tax return, or what kind of probate administration you'll need to do. Chapter 7 tells you where and how to dig, including in some fairly unusual places, and what to do with those assets after you find them. You also discover how to value property, including when you can do it yourself and when you're better served to have an expert help you.

# Paying expenses and making distributions

Just because the decedent isn't living doesn't mean that he or she doesn't still have expenses. After all, the electricity in the house wasn't turned off at the moment of death, and any mortgage on the residence still needs to be paid. In addition, the estate begins accumulating its fair share of costs, whether for accounting and investment services, or for lawn mowing. In fact, the estate expenses may look similar to the decedent's before death. As the executor, you're responsible for making sure that the decedent's and estate's bills are paid. Chapter 8 takes you through the expenses you may run across, including the funeral; the first expense most people think about in relation to death.

After you pay all the estate's bills, you're free to pay off everyone the decedent listed in his or her last will (or the heirs-at-law if he or she died without a valid last will). In Chapter 8, you also discover how to slice up what remains of the pie, in what order you make payments, how to transfer property other than cash, and how to mathematically make divisions of property when the dividing line isn't entirely clear.

## Tying up the estate's loose ends

Even after you've paid everyone, you still need to tidy some odds and ends before you can close the estate. Chapter 9 guides you through all the necessary final steps. You find out what you need to file with the probate court, the IRS, and the decedent's state tax authority to obtain the letters releasing you from further responsibility. You also discover all the final flourishes that will bring the estate to its natural conclusion.

# Operating a Trust

Unlike an estate, which only exists for a relatively short period of time (we hope), trusts can continue on for decades, depending on the terms of the trust and the ages of all the participants. Because you're involved for the long haul, the lists of what you need to do in the short term and on an ongoing basis are different. The following sections highlight some of your main tasks as trustee. Whether you've just been appointed or you've been a trustee for a while but still have questions, you can check out Part III for complete answers.

## Understanding your duties as trustee

When you agree to act as a trustee, more is involved than just signing on the dotted line and then walking away. You're now obligated to do your best for the grantor in carrying out his or her wishes as set forth in the trust instrument, which clarifies and specifies your duties. Chapter 10 discusses these duties. You grapple with the limits of fiduciary responsibility and discover what it means to honor the grantor's intent. And you explore how to invest the trust assets so that you not only protect the trust principal but also produce the income that the income beneficiary has a right to expect.

## Putting assets into trust

If you've finally reached the stage where it's time to transfer assets into a trust, either your own or someone else's, you need to know and follow certain rules in order to make a smooth transition from individual ownership to trust ownership. Chapter 11 explains how to smoothly make those transfers, whether during the grantor's lifetime or after his or her death.

## Putting the trust to work

After you transfer the assets into the trust, you, as trustee, have to create an investment plan that balances income production and growth against risk. Remember, the money in the trust isn't yours to play with, so you can't make any ridiculous gambles with it. Still, taking a keep-it-safe-and-in-the-bank approach isn't smart either because the income beneficiary has a right to (and will) expect income from the trust.

Chapter 12 gives you the pros and cons of a variety of investment options, as well as clueing you in to some current investment theories. It also shows you how to factor in beneficiary needs when determining how best to invest trust assets. Finally, it gives you a heads-up as to what sorts of fees the trust will incur — fees that you have to factor into your calculations when you determine how much, if anything, you can pay to the beneficiaries.

## Discovering the purpose of the trust

A trust's purpose, and your mission, is to balance income generation for the benefit of the current income beneficiary (and principal distributions, when permitted) with principal protection for the remainder interest. Chapter 13 is where you unearth the extra information you may want to consider as you handle this balancing act, such as the beneficiary's health, education, or other extraordinary circumstances. Figuring out which life events warrant additional distributions may be the trickiest part of trust administration. In Chapter 13, you also discover why many trustees are likened to kindly relatives, as you attempt to uncover all that you can about the income, or the current beneficiary (without being accused of stalking).

## Compiling and organizing trust records

You've done all the tricky stuff, but you still must track the activity correctly. Keeping records, although not difficult, isn't particularly fun or exciting, so many people get sloppy about it. Our advice to you: Keep 'em neat! Staying on top of your recordkeeping means never finding yourself buried in an avalanche of paper you're not quite sure what to do with. Chapter 14 tells you how to maintain the trust's records with a minimum of fuss and bother.

## Bringing the trust to its conclusion

Trusts sometimes seem to go on forever, but the day eventually comes when all trusts must come to an end. When that day comes, you need to know how to tie up all the loose ends neatly, like preparing and filing the final tax returns and accounts and making the final distributions of the remaining income and assets. You've done a great job up until now — it would be a shame to ruin your track record at this late date. Chapter 15 explains how to terminate a trust with a minimum of fuss and bother. And call us crazy, but for us, life doesn't get much better than when we've received the last assent to that final trust account, the one on which the ending balance is zero!

# Paying Uncle Sam

Taxes in estates and trusts can be pretty involved. Why? Because you're not only dealing with income taxes (and we know how much everyone loves income taxes), but you may also be responsible for preparing **Form 706, United States Estate (and Generation-Skipping Transfer) Tax Return.** Part IV gives an overview of **Form 706,** the estate and trust income tax return (**Form 1041**), as well as the decedent's final **Form 1040.**

## Compiling the estate tax return

Not every estate is required to file **Form 706,** but if you must file, dive right into Chapter 16, which takes you on a stroll through the lengthy estate tax return. Although the blank return may seem formidable, you may find that with the help of this chapter and the **Form 706** instructions you're able to prepare all, or at least large chunks, of the return yourself. Chapter 17 goes into more depth and walks you through many of the schedules associated with **Form 706.** Give yourself some credit and take a stab at **Form 706;** you'll probably be surprised by how far you get. Even if you do end up taking this return to a professional, you gain a much better handle on all the assets and expenses of the estate by first attempting it yourself.

If your decedent held title to property, whether in his name alone, as a joint tenant, or in the name of his revocable trust, all the decedent's property is subject to the federal estate tax. But of course, that's after the whopping exclusion amount of $5.25 million in 2013, indexed annually for inflation.

## Figuring out the income taxes

Whether you are administering a trust or are involved in an estate, you have to file annual income tax returns as long as either entity owns assets that are producing income. If you're the executor of an estate, you may also be responsible for filing the decedent's final income tax return (or maybe even his or her final two years of income tax returns, depending on when he or she died). We have you covered.

Discover how fiduciary income taxes differ from personal income taxes in Chapter 18, and find out what quirks exist for the decedent's final return(s). Armed with a **Form 1041, U.S. Income Tax Return for Estates and Trusts,** in one hand, and Chapter 18 in the other, you can work your way through trust or estate return preparation on a line-by-line basis.

## Planning an income tax strategy

There is rarely just one way to skin a cat, and the same can be said of preparing tax returns. With a little forethought and scheming, you can minimize the amount of income taxes paid by both the trust or estate and the income beneficiary. In Chapter 19, we discuss how to legally reduce the amount of income tax you pay to the IRS.

## Whipping together Schedule K-1

Tax forms can be intimidating, especially unfamiliar ones. And **Schedule K-1, Beneficiary's Share of Income, Deductions, Credits, etc.,** may seem overwhelming. But it's really not. In Chapter 20, see how the information from **Form 1041** translates to **Schedule K-1** when you've made distributions to a beneficiary from either a trust or estate. After you figure out how to make the calculations, it almost becomes fun (well, at least for us, but then we're an accountant and an attorney.)

# Chapter 2

# Exploring the Ins and Outs of Estates

## In This Chapter

▶ Classifying the estate differently for probate administration and tax purposes

▶ Knowing what to do regardless of whether the decedent left a will

▶ Determining who inherits

▶ Figuring out how to define the estate for tax purposes

*W*hen you're named as executor or administrator of an estate for the first (or second or third) time, you may have some questions as to what, exactly, an estate is, and about the whole probate estate and estate tax process in general. Before you can administer an estate, you need to have a firm grasp of what an estate is. Don't worry, though — you don't have to become an estate and trust attorney. We provide you with the ABCs of estates right here. Consider it your entry-level course to understanding the basics on estates.

This chapter defines many of the terms associated with estates, lays out the process of determining who inherits, and explains the difference between the estate as it's defined for probate purposes and for estate tax purposes. So read on, dip your toe in, or take the plunge — we think you'll end up with a firmer grasp on estates.

## Defining the Estate for Probate Administration Purposes

In order to administer an estate, you want to know what you're administering. Although an estate may appear to be a confusing legal entity, you don't need to be concerned about all the technicalities. All you need to know about *a probate estate* is all the assets a person owns at his or her death that are subject to *probate administration* (proving to a probate court that the will is genuine). Chapter 6 walks you through the specific stages of the probate process.

So what types of assets comprise a probate estate? Check out the following:

- ✔ All assets held in the *decedent's* (deceased person's) name alone.

- ✔ All assets the decedent owned as a tenant in common with one or more other persons. A *tenant in common* holds property together with other tenants in common, but none of the tenants automatically inherit the shares of a tenant who dies. Each tenant holds an equal share of the property unless the property title specifies otherwise. Upon the decedent's death, his or her share becomes subject to probate, even though in some states actual title to real estate (if that is what they're holding) passes to the heirs as of the decedent's death.

- ✔ All assets payable to the estate because either the estate is the designated beneficiary or the asset has no designated beneficiary, such as life insurance on the deceased and employee benefits.

- ✔ Amounts owed to the decedent before death but paid after death, such as the decedent's last paycheck, and other amounts due to the decedent's estate by reason of his or her death, such as an award from a wrongful death lawsuit.

- ✔ Household items, jewelry, and other items that don't usually have title (unless the decedent has, in writing, declared them to belong to his or her revocable living trust during life; see Chapter 3 for more on revocable living trusts).

Chapter 7 includes a complete list of assets to look for as executor or administrator, many of which end up in the probate estate for one of these reasons.

If an asset is in the decedent's name alone for convenience only but really belongs to another individual (for instance, if the decedent was holding it for a relative who is incapacitated), the person claiming ownership of the property must furnish proof that it actually belongs to him or her. The asset then goes to the actual owner (or his or her representative) instead of becoming part of the decedent's estate for administration or estate tax purposes. For example, Mary is listed as the only signer on her disabled daughter Sue's checking account, which is funded solely by Sue's monthly disability payments. If Mary dies, Sue (or someone acting for her if she is unable to act for herself), must provide documentation that the account and the money in it actually belong to Sue and not Mary. This proof may be in the form of a letter between Sue and Mary, mentioning the arrangement, check stubs from the disability payments, and bank statements. After that documentation is in order, you have the proof you need to exclude this particular bank account from Mary's estate, both for probate and tax purposes.

Most assets that are subject to probate administration come under the supervision of the probate (or equivalent) court in the place where the decedent lived at death. The one exception to this rule is real estate. You must probate real estate in the county and state in which it's located. If the estate you're responsible for has real estate in another jurisdiction, including out-of-state real estate, you need to have *ancillary* administration (separate probate of the property in the jurisdiction where it's located), in addition to probate in the decedent's state of residence. See Chapter 6 for more on determining domicile.

# Will Power: Understanding How a Will (Or No Will) Affects an Estate

Whether or not the decedent left a will determines what form of probate you undertake, and this section gives you a look at the effect of having and not having a will. A will requires you to file a petition with the probate court to have it admitted to probate. The will probably names you as executor, so you don't have to worry about applying for the job. If the decedent didn't leave a will, you file a petition to administer the intestate estate, and other folks who feel that they're just as qualified may file a petition as well. If more than one person applies to be administrator, the court decides who gets the privilege. Whether the decedent left a will also determines whether the decedent's wishes (with a will) or state laws in the decedent's state of domicile (with no will) determine whom the assets will go to.

*Domicile* is the decedent's legal home. It's decided by a combination of factors, including where the decedent lived for more than half of the calendar year, was registered to vote and registered any cars, plus the address he or she used on income tax returns, and many other supporting factors. See Chapter 6 for a complete discussion of domicile.

## Dying testate

A decedent dies *testate* if he or she leaves a valid will. The will then undergoes probate according to the laws of the decedent's domicile at the time of death. The purpose of probate is for the court to rule on the validity of the will and supervise the administration of the estate.

What determines the validity of a will? It's based on individual state law. For instance, in most, if not all, states, a will writer must be at least 18 years old and of sound mind (know as *having testamentary capacity*). The will must (usually) be in writing (typed or handwritten), and signed by the decedent or another at the decedent's direction and in his or her presence. The following list gives you an overview of some common types of wills:

- **Holographic:** A *holographic* will is written in the decedent's own handwriting, dated, and signed, but may or may not be witnessed. It's valid in some, but not all jurisdictions. However, people are more likely to challenge it, and if questions come up about the decedent's intentions (which won't be as clear as in a lawyer-crafted document), the probate court interprets those intentions.

- ✔ **Attested:** An *attested* will is usually prepared and typed by an attorney's office and signed by the decedent and two (or in some states, three) witnesses who receive no benefit under the will. This is the most typical kind of will.

- ✔ **Oral:** An *oral* will (also known as a *nuncupative* will) is a will spoken orally to another person and not written down. A few states recognize them in extreme circumstances, such as imminent death.

Other issues affecting validity are whether the testator was under undue influence from another in making the will, whether fraud was committed against the testator, whether he or she had knowledge of the contents of the will, and whether the will is a forgery. If you as executor are aware of any issues affecting the validity of the will, or have any doubts as to its validity, you should bring this to the attention of the probate court.

## Dying intestate

A decedent dies *intestate* if he or she leaves no will. The laws of intestacy also apply if a will turns out to be invalid and the decedent had no prior valid will. (Reasons a will may be declared invalid include forged wills, wills not properly witnessed, a decedent who wasn't of sound mind when he or she signed the will, and fraud or undue influence on the decedent during the writing of the will.) If the decedent died intestate, the laws of the decedent's state of domicile govern both how the estate is administered and who inherits the estate. Check out the next section, "Taking a Look at Who Can Inherit," for more info on how intestacy affects the estate.

We've both administered estates where the decedent died intestate and we've experienced challenges to the will. Intestacy can be an unfortunate situation because the laws of intestacy frequently don't follow what would have been the decedent's wishes. For example, depending on the decedent's state of domicile, if one spouse dies without a will, the surviving spouse won't inherit everything unless the decedent has no children and, in some cases, other blood relatives with claims to the estate. If minor children are involved, a court-appointed guardian must hold their shares, with the assets supervised by the court until the child reaches adulthood. Of course, that arrangement works out best for the court-appointed guardian, who may not have even known the decedent or the family, and who is well paid by the estate to manage those assets and the expenses of raising that child.

The court also decides who will be the guardian of the child's person (who will raise the child) if both parents are deceased, or if the court considers the surviving parent to be unfit. Note that one person can be guardian of both the person and the property of a child, if the court deems that appropriate.

Sometimes more than one family member (or family friend) feels strongly that he or she is the best person to raise the child, in which case, things can get messy. Most parents prefer to make that choice themselves, and the court will honor their wishes if the court finds it's in the child's best interest. But we actually know several people who have delayed creating wills because they don't want to face the guardianship question, either because they don't want to offend family members or because they feel they have no good choices for guardians.

# Taking a Look at Who Can Inherit

If you're serving as executor or administrator of an estate, one of the first things you need to do is determine who inherits the estate's assets. If the estate has a valid will, determining who gets what is usually straightforward because the will sets out who the assets go to. However, wills can be fuzzy if they're not well drafted, and sometimes beneficiaries can be hard to track down. If the decedent left no valid will, you have to rely on the laws of intestacy to figure out who gets what.

The following sections walk you through the people who can potentially inherit something from an estate.

## Surviving spouse

If the decedent was married at the time of his or her death, his or her surviving spouse becomes a major player in the eventual disposition of the estate whether or not the decedent had a valid will. If the estate is will-less, the surviving spouse is entitled to a share of the decedent's estate as dictated by the intestacy laws of the decedent's state of residence. When there is a valid will, the surviving spouse has a choice:

- He or she can choose to take any inheritance stated under the will.

- He or she can elect to *take against the will* — that is, to receive the share that he or she is entitled to by statute, known as the *statutory share*, rather than the amount he or she stands to inherit under the will. Generally, the spouse's statutory share isn't as generous as the spouse's *intestate share* (the share he or she would receive if the decedent died without a will), and they are definitely two different animals.

The next sections take a closer look at these choices. Appendix B shows you the rules for intestate shares, state by state.

In certain instances, such as when the surviving spouse's own estate is taxable without any additions from the decedent's estate, it may not be in the surviving spouse's best interest for estate tax purposes to accept any inheritance from the decedent. In this case, the surviving spouse should *disclaim,* or refuse by a legal document, any part of either what the decedent left him or her under the will or the spousal portion of the estate determined by the intestate statute. See Chapter 8 for details on disclaimers.

### Inheriting under the will

In the most common scenario we see, the surviving spouse chooses to inherit whatever the will provides for him or her in accordance with the decedent's wishes. Most spouses plan their estates together and execute their wills at the same time. They typically have a common purpose in mind: to take care of the survivor during his or her lifetime (along with any children if they're minors). Their plans typically mirror each other's. These sorts of wills are often referred to as *reciprocal*, where each will gives everything (except for bequests of specific personal property) to the other and only after the second death does the property pass out into the wider family.

### Taking against the will

Each spouse has the right to leave his or her property by will to whomever he or she wants. To offset that right, the surviving spouse has the right to take an amount allowed by statute rather than the amount, if any, left to that spouse under the will. For a variety of reasons (such as a second marriage where the decedent wants to favor children from a first marriage in his or her will, or if the spouses aren't amicable before the decedent's death), the surviving spouse may get less under the will than he or she would receive by taking his or her statutory share. That's when the surviving spouse may decide to take against the will. See Chapter 6 for a fuller discussion of the spouse's decision of whether to take against the will. Don't forget, this spousal statutory share is not the same beast as the intestate statutory share. Though every state has a spousal statutory share, any *prenuptial agreement* (an agreement signed before marriage — think movie stars, billionaires, and second marriages) or *postnuptial agreement* (an agreement signed after marriage) that the surviving spouse signed that set out or limited the amount he or she would inherit upon the decedent's death, will govern (and it no doubt waives the statutory share).

### Surviving spouse's allowance

Most states have a provision for a surviving spouse's allowance. For instance, under the new Massachusetts Probate Code, enacted in 2012, the surviving spouse has the right to live in the home of the decedent for six months, plus "a reasonable allowance in money out of the estate" during the administration of the estate for the maintenance of the surviving spouse and the decedent's minor and dependent children. These amounts are intended to help the surviving spouse and/or children through the estate administration period. See Chapter 6 for more on this provision.

## No such thing as a free ride: Goodbye, dower and curtesy

Although the surviving spouse's statutory share has largely replaced the old concepts of dower and curtesy, they're worth mentioning. Dower and curtesy (defined in the following paragraphs) have now been abolished in most states, or replaced by dower for both surviving spouses; under the old laws of dower and curtesy, the widower's share was far greater than the widow's.

The definition of *dower* may vary from state to state, but typically it's a provision that gives a widow (now usually defined as any surviving spouse) a *life estate* (the use of, for the rest of his or her life) in a portion of all real estate owned by the decedent at death. Dower has been abolished in many states and greatly altered in others.

*Curtesy*, on the other hand, is generally defined as the widower's right to a life estate in all the real estate his deceased wife owned at death. Curtesy has been abolished or greatly altered in most states, and replaced in some by dower for both widow and widower. See Chapter 6 for information on dower and curtesy.

# Individuals omitted from the decedent's will (including intentional disinheritance)

Another group of individuals not included in a will may have a right to inherit some assets in an estate. These individuals, called *pretermitted heirs*, are usually children or *issue* of a deceased child (all persons who have descended from that child, like a grandchild of the decedent). If the will doesn't include them, they may elect to take the share they would have received under intestacy, unless the decedent provided for them during his or her lifetime or it's shown that the omission was intentional. The purpose of this policy is to avoid the unintentional disinheritance of a child or other issue of the decedent.

For example, Robert Kennedy's youngest child, daughter Rory, was born after his death. If in his will he left bequests to all his children by name, not naming Rory, she could argue that she was left out by mistake and thus was a pretermitted heir entitled to her intestate share. Of course, the Kennedys had good estate planners, so they would never have named specific children without allowing for ones to be born later, and they used trusts for privacy, so this example is just a what if. See Chapter 6 for more on pretermitted heirs.

Intentional omissions, including disinheritance, are generally fairly obvious because most competently prepared wills have a provision stating whether the person making the will (the *testator*) intended to provide for children born after the will was made or for any children or other issue or other relatives not mentioned in the will. Typically, where there's been a family falling-out, you find language in the will stating that this or that child or other relative has been intentionally left out (or has been left $1). Sometimes a will contains language stating that a child or other family member was left out because he or she has been adequately provided for in his or her lifetime or by other means.

## The other players: Devisees and legatees

Other people may have a claim to inheriting the assets in a decedent's estate. The decedent may name anyone to inherit under his or her will, subject to the rights of the surviving spouse and/or minor and dependent children. The following are a few technical names for you to ponder while you figure out who all the players are in the estate you're administering.

- ✔ **Residuary devisee:** A person or entity named to receive all the real property not specifically *devised* (left by will)

- ✔ **Specific devisee:** A person or entity named to receive specific *real property* (real estate) under a will

- ✔ **Residuary legatee:** A person or entity named to receive all the personalty not specifically disposed of under a will

- ✔ **Specific legatee:** A person or entity named to receive *a legacy* (*personalty*, or personal property disposed of by will)

## Heirs-at-law

*Heirs-at-law* are those people who inherit a person's estate under state statutes of descent and distribution if he or she died intestate (without a will). For example, Massachusetts resident John Doe dies without a will, survived only by his wife, Mariah (no children) and Great Aunt Ophelia, from whom he is estranged. Under the intestacy statute, his surviving wife inherits the first $200,000 of assets, and the rest are split ½ to his wife and ½ to Great Aunt Ophelia. If John had children, his estate would have gone as follows: everything split ½ to his wife and ½ to his children. If John Doe is survived by his wife and no other relatives of any degree, his wife receives everything. Statutes vary from state to state, and we lay out the results of all of them in Appendix B.

## Defining the Estate for Tax Purposes

The probate process is intended to ensure the smooth transfer of property from the decedent to a beneficiary where no other means of transferring the property is in place. However, federal and state tax authorities are much more concerned with how much of the decedent's property they can tax and accordingly allow for a much broader definition of what the decedent owned at the time of his or her death. Although the probate estate includes only property in the decedent's name alone or payable to the estate, for estate tax purposes all property owned by the decedent in any form, including jointly held or in a revocable trust, and any property payable to any person or the probate estate as a result of the decedent's death, is includible in the taxable estate. And, you may have to deal with more than one type of tax; each tax on the decedent's estate also has a specific purpose. The following sections take a closer look at the types of taxes an estate may need to pay. (Part IV expands on the specifics and what you need to do as an executor with these taxes.)

## Transfer taxes

*Transfer taxes* are taxes on a person's right to transfer property and are levied on the value of property as it passes from one person to another through gift or inheritance. Although the following taxes go by different names (gift tax, estate tax, and generation-skipping transfer tax), they're all part of the same umbrella system of taxing the transfer of property.

Some transfers that are *not* considered taxable gifts include

- **Annual exclusion gifts:** Gifts that are limited to the *annual exclusion amount* (the amount which can be transferred per donee without incurring gift tax per year). The annual exclusion amount in 2013 is $14,000 per donee and is reviewed annually, with periodic increases to deal with inflation. In addition, a husband and wife can split gifts from either of them, so together they can give away $28,000 per donee (or two times the annual exclusion amount) in 2013 without using any of their lifetime exemptions.

- **Gifts to a spouse:** You may give an unlimited amount to your spouse, provided your spouse is a U.S. citizen. If your spouse isn't a citizen, the exclusion amount in 2013 is $143,000. This amount also adjusts periodically for inflation.

- **Tuition and medical expenses paid for someone else:** Just make sure that you write the checks directly to the school, the hospital, or the doctor. If you make a mistake and write the check to your deserving niece or nephew directly, even if he or she turns right around and pays tuition, that gift isn't unlimited, and you may find you've just made a gift that requires a gift tax return (**Form 709**), or even worse, a gift tax return and a gift tax.

- **Gifts to political organizations**.

- **Gifts to qualified charities:** *Qualified charities* have obtained tax-exempt status from the IRS.

There is also a lifetime *unified credit* that can be applied against any gift tax. Any use of this unified credit during life reduces the use of the unified credit against the federal estate tax upon death. Check out the explanation of the unified credit and how it works in Chapter 16.

### Federal gift tax

The *federal gift tax* is a tax on the transfer of property from one person (the *donor)* to another (the *donee*) with no payment (or less than full payment) in return. Watch it, because the gift tax is triggered whether the person transferring the property intended to make a gift or not!

### Federal estate tax

The *federal estate tax* (sometimes mistakenly referred to as the "death tax") is a tax on the transfer of property at death. All property the decedent owns or has an interest in at death, in whatever form it's held, is subject to the tax.

Only about 2 percent of estates are actually subject to the estate tax because of an exemption amount (based on the unified credit; see Chapter 16 for an explanation of how the unified credit is determined), which is $5.12 million for 2012. See Chapter 16 for more in-depth information about the federal estate tax and what you need to do as the executor.

### Generation-skipping transfer tax

The generation-skipping transfer (GST) tax is a relatively new invention, intended to ensure that the federal government gets its slice of the pie each and every time assets move from one generation to the next. As a result of more and more people discovering that they may be able to pay less overall transfer tax by bypassing their children and giving property directly to grandchildren (or even better, great-grandchildren), Congress plugged this particular loophole so that the gift tax and estate tax can no longer be evaded at any generational level by skipping a generation on the transfer. And so now, rules trigger the GST tax any time a transfer is made that skips a generation, with the exception of transfers made into *irrevocable trusts* (trusts that can't be amended) created before September 25, 1985, which are "grandfathered" from the GST tax.

The GST tax doesn't apply to gifts that aren't subject to the gift tax.

*Note:* A transfer of property to a grandchild is normally considered a *direct skip* and is subject to the GST tax. However, if that grandchild's parent has already died at the time of the transfer, the transfer is not subject to the GST tax.

If property is left in trust for life for a child, at the child's death, there will be one of the following:

- ✔ An estate tax payable because the child had enough control over the trust that it is considered to be owned by him or her and is included in his or her taxable estate

- ✔ A GST tax payable because the terms of the trust are restrictive enough that the property is not considered to be owned by the child, so the GST tax is triggered because a generation has been skipped

The GST tax is also applied to transfers to or for an unrelated person who is 37½ or more years younger than the transferor — what the IRS has determined to be the equivalent of skipping a generation.

As you can see, there's just no getting around it — a transfer tax is going to be paid at every generation after you pass the exemption threshold.

### State estate, inheritance, and other transfer taxes

State transfer taxes are in a state of flux due to fairly recent changes in federal estate tax law. Until 2005, there was a credit against estate tax due on the federal estate tax return for state death taxes paid, with the limit on the amount of the credit based on the size of the taxable estate. That credit was abolished as of 2005.

Unfortunately, state death taxes paid may now be taken only as a deduction against the amount of the federal taxable estate, and deductions are never worth as much in your pocket as credits.

Many states had (or still have) an estate tax system which is variously known as a *pick-up, sponge,* or *slack-tax* system, because it is designed to collect tax only on the amount allowed as a state tax credit on the federal estate tax return. Of course, when the federal credit was eliminated, the state estate tax source was also eliminated for the states with this system, causing loss of significant tax revenues. Understandably, a lot of states were unhappy with this result, and some enacted new estate tax laws to make up for the disappearance of their estate tax and the resulting lost revenue. However, other states are choosing not to impose a tax or to raise the amount which is exempt from estate tax. Some states have an *inheritance tax*, which taxes the amount inherited by a particular beneficiary, rather than the estate as a whole. The tax rate depends upon the relationship of the beneficiary to the decedent, and the tax is payable by the beneficiary, although some decedent's wills may provide that the estate is to pay all inheritance taxes.

Overall, slightly less than half of all states currently have an estate or inheritance tax, and there are movements afoot in several states to eliminate the estate or inheritance tax.

## Other taxes

No, you're not out of the tax woods yet, but at least these taxes should be somewhat more familiar to you from your personal tax life.

- ✔ **Federal income tax for decedent and estate:** You must prepare and file the decedent's final federal income tax return, as well as an income tax return for the estate for every year it's in existence. The estate income tax return does have some differences from the individual return, all of which are explained fully in Chapter 18.

✓ **State income tax for decedent and estate:** If the decedent was domiciled (had his or her legal place of residence; see Chapter 6 for more on determining domicile) in a state that has an income tax, you must also prepare and file a final state income tax return for the decedent and an estate state income tax return for each year the estate is in existence. Try saying that three times fast!

✓ **State intangibles tax:** If your decedent was domiciled in a state which has an *intangibles tax* (a tax on certain intangible assets owned by the decedent, such as stocks and bonds), and if he or she had assets subject to the tax, you must prepare and file the final intangibles tax return for the decedent, as well as returns for the estate (if required). You may also find that prior year returns for the decedent were never filed (this is surprisingly common) and must be filed in order to close the decedent's estate. You can check with your local probate (or equivalent) court to see whether this is a requirement in your jurisdiction.

# Chapter 3

# Identifying Different Types of Trusts

### In This Chapter

▶ Understanding the difference between grantor- and non-grantor-type trusts

▶ Deciding when the trust will start

▶ Defining various types of revocable and irrevocable trusts

▶ Grasping charitable trusts

▶ Qualifying a trust as a Subchapter S corporation shareholder

**T**rusts come in every size, shape, color, and variety. There are enough different types of trusts for every day of the week and every month of the year. Trusts can give money away, save money, pay only certain expenses, or buy the moon. Trusts can contain almost any type of property for almost any length of time, so long as it's not forever (although *almost* forever certainly works).

In fact, the sheer number of different types of trusts makes the possibilities for their use almost endless. Not to worry though. You don't need to memorize all this information. Just know that this chapter takes you on a tour of some of the more popular types of trusts and trustees and shows you how to determine what type of trust you're holding, and what sorts of administration you may be asked to undertake.

## Differentiating for Income Taxes: Grantor versus Non-Grantor Trusts

You can slice and dice trusts in any number of ways, depending on the terms and provisions of a particular trust. But however they may be categorized, all *funded* trusts (trusts that hold assets) are divided into two main types for income tax purposes: *grantor* and *non-grantor*. You must determine what manner of beast the trust you're administering is in order to prepare and file the correct income tax returns in the correct way each year. Remember, funded trusts are taxable entities, and you must make the decision either to file a **Form 1041** for the trust, or to declare all items of income and deduction on the *grantor*'s (the person who created the trust) **Form 1040.** And watch out! Although it's not common, you may come across a third type of trust: the *intentionally defective grantor trust*, which contains elements of both grantor and non-grantor trusts.

All trusts have the following participants: *grantors* (sometimes referred to as *donors* or *settlors*), trustees, beneficiaries, and remaindermen. (If you're not sure who these folks are, we define them all in Chapter 1.) The determination of whether a trust is grantor or non-grantor depends on the relationship of each of the participants to the grantor. The following sections spell out these types of trusts and help you know how to differentiate between them so you can be sure that you're administering them correctly and reporting the income on the correct income tax return.

## Grantor trusts

*Grantor trusts* allow the person who creates the trust to retain certain powers over the administration of the trust, often up to and including the power to revoke the trust and regain ownership of trust property while that person is living. If, for example, the grantor names him- or herself, or his or her spouse during the grantor's lifetime, as trustee, you're looking at a grantor trust. Likewise, if the grantor or the grantor's spouse is an income beneficiary, the trust is grantor. The key to identifying a true grantor trust doesn't necessarily rest on the grantor's power to revoke the trust but rather on the grantor's keeping control, however tenuous, over the property inside the trust.

In a grantor trust, the grantor is typically not only grantor but also a trustee; he or she is usually beneficiary of not only the trust's income but also as much of the *principal* (the property funding the trust) as he or she needs at any given time. (To understand the complete distinction between principal and income, check out Chapter 12.) Generally, in a grantor trust, the existence of the trust is ignored for income tax purposes, and the grantor declares all items of income and deduction on his or her income tax return. In most cases, the trust doesn't even have its own Tax Identification Number (TIN, the trust equivalent of a Social Security number) because the trust doesn't need to file its own tax return.

## Non-grantor trusts

*Non-grantor trusts* are trusts over which the grantor has given up all right, title, and interest in the property funding the trust. Although the trust may be *revocable* (can be dissolved), at least during the grantor's lifetime, the grantor may not terminate the trust; only the trustee, who must be someone other than the grantor, may. In a non-grantor trust, the grantor (and the grantor's spouse), in addition to not being a trustee, also may not be named as a present interest beneficiary or as a *remainderman* (a person or entity who receives what's left of the trust's property when the trust terminates or ends).

Even though a trust, when it's first established, may begin as a grantor trust or an intentionally defective grantor trust (see the next section), at the grantor's death, all trusts become non-grantor trusts. If you haven't obtained a Tax Identification Number for the trust prior to the grantor's death, you should take care of that now. See Chapter 18 for how to obtain a TIN. Remember, come December 31 of the year of the grantor's death, you're responsible for filing a **Form 1041** for the non-grantor trust that succeeds the grantor trust in existence up until the date of death.

## Intentionally defective grantor trusts

In an *intentionally defective grantor trust* (IDGT), the grantor creates a trust that looks like a non-grantor-type trust: The grantor makes an irrevocable gift of property into the trust, sets up the trust for the benefit of his or her children or grandchildren, and names someone other than himself or herself as trustee. The difference is that the grantor retains the right to substitute other property of equal value for the property he or she initially funds the trust with, in order to intentionally create a defect; the income tax treatment for this trust changes into something that's not entirely a grantor trust but not really a non-grantor trust, either.

In fact, when you're administering an IDGT, you must obtain a TIN and file a **Form 1041** every year. On the face of the **Form 1041,** you get to write the following: "Under the terms of the trust instrument, this is a grantor trust. In accordance with Sections 671-678 IRC, 1986, all income is taxable to the Grantor. Statements of income, deduction, and credits are attached." How's that for lively prose? Before you file the **Form 1041,** make sure that you attach those required statements. The grantor then includes all those items on his or her personal return.

An intentionally defective grantor trust is frequently used to hold real estate and closely held businesses. Why on earth would anyone want a defective grantor trust? It's an estate-planning strategy that, among other purposes, "freezes" the value of property transferred into the trust for estate tax purposes; having the grantor be liable for the income tax removes the income tax paid from the grantor's estate for estate tax purposes. That's because, unlike the grantor trust income tax rules that make the income includible on the grantor's **Form 1040,** the property is effectively transferred out of the decedent's estate for estate and gift tax purposes at the time it's transferred to the trust. Gift tax, if any, is paid on the value of the property on the date it's transferred into the trust. No estate tax is due when the grantor dies.

Using an intentionally defective grantor trust is a fairly nifty technique, but not one to be undertaken by amateurs. If you think this might be a route that makes sense for you, please find a qualified estate and trust attorney to help you draft the trust and do the initial funding.

# Creating Trusts during Lifetime and after Death

Grantors' reasons for establishing trusts vary, from protecting certain pieces of property to providing an income stream for heirs to trying to establish a framework within which a messy family situation may become manageable. Whatever the reason, a grantor may set up a trust that begins functioning during his or her lifetime, or trusts may be created upon the grantor's death.

By the time you start administering the trust, the distinction between a trust created during the grantor's lifetime or after his or her death is probably moot. Still, you need to know whether the trust is *inter vivos* or *testamentary*. The following sections explain the difference between these two options.

## Trusts created during lifetime

As they craft their estate plans, many people want to retain the greatest amount of control possible over their estates during their lives and after their deaths. In order to do so, many create *inter vivos* trusts, which are trusts governed by a legal document other than their last wills. As their Latin names suggest, these trusts are created "among the living" during the grantor's lifetime. So basically because an *inter vivos* trust is governed by an instrument other than the will, its provisions remain private, unlike the will, which becomes public knowledge after it's filed for probate administration. That's why *inter vivos* trusts are important to families who have substantial assets or who are in the public eye and don't want everyone knowing what they're worth.

A grantor may fund *inter vivos* trusts either during his or her life or after his or her death. If funded during the grantor's lifetime, you, the trustee, need to check the instrument carefully to see if the trust falls under the grantor trust rules explained earlier in the "Grantor trusts" section, or under the intentionally defective grantor trust rules to determine whether to report the income on the grantor's **Form 1040** or on a **Form 1041** for the trust. *Inter vivos* trusts may be revocable (often referred to as *living trusts*) or irrevocable; after the grantor's death, they're all irrevocable.

A grantor often uses *inter vivos* trusts to remove property from his or her estate, at least for probate purposes (check out Chapter 6 for more on probate), and in other cases, for both probate and estate tax purposes. For example, if the trust was treated as a non-grantor or intentionally defective grantor trust during the grantor's lifetime (see the previous sections). If, however, the trust was treated as a grantor-type trust during the grantor's lifetime, be sure to include all property inside the trust when making estate tax calculations.

## Trusts created under a last will

Although the idea of a trust for which no probate court supervision is necessary may seem attractive to you, having the court keeping its beady eyes on a rancorous family isn't always the worst idea. And, in our experience, nothing can turn a family situation uglier in a hurry than the death of a wealthy parent or grandparent. In cases where a grantor suspects that life may become unpleasant for his or her trustees after his or her death, choosing a *testamentary trust,* or a trust whose provisions are contained in, and a part of, the decedent's last will, over an *inter vivos* trust, can be a wise decision. Testamentary trusts are only funded after the grantor's death and are therefore always non-grantor-type trusts.

Unlike *inter vivos* trusts, where accounting standards are sometimes lax, testamentary trusts must usually provide the probate court with an annual account, depending on what state you're probating the estate in. Check with the probate court involved to be sure of its requirements because trustees who fail in their duty to prepare and file these annual accounts when required may be sanctioned by the probate court, usually with just a slap on the wrist, but sometimes with a fine or in very rare circumstances a contempt-of-court citation.

Probate accounts are a matter of public record, and anyone with the time and energy to go looking for them, from trust beneficiaries, disinherited heirs, or even newspaper reporters nosing around for some dirt, may access them.

# Grasping Revocable Trusts

Like their names suggest, *revocable trusts* are ones that the grantor can *revoke,* or terminate, at any time prior to his or her death. Whether the grantor creates the trust to avoid probate (a so-called *living trust*) or to shelter the true ownership of property behind an opaque curtain, the terms of the trust remain open to revision, reinterpretation, and outright dissolution by the grantor up to the day he or she dies.

Revocable trusts of all flavors serve as estate-planning tools, so you may run across them because you've set up one yourself, you've been named as a trustee on a living trust, or you're administering an estate, and find one or more different types as part of the decedent's estate plan. The next sections point out the most common revocable trusts you may encounter.

## Still breathing: Living trusts

*Living trusts*, or trusts created and funded during the grantor's lifetime, are an estate-planning technique designed to remove assets from the grantor's estate, either directly to his or her heirs upon the grantor's death or into his or her trust *without* ever setting foot in a probate court. These probate-avoidance trusts almost always begin their lives as revocable trusts and are usually treated as grantor trusts for income tax purposes. Most living trusts are clearly identifiable because the grantor fills all the roles during his or her lifetime: grantor, trustee, and beneficiary.

If you've created a living trust, your goal should be to transfer as many of your assets as you can into the trust during your lifetime. You may not be able to shift every asset, such as those items you hold jointly with someone else. If the joint owner is your spouse, and you both really want that specific property to be held in trust, you may opt to transfer full ownership to one or the other of the owners, or split it into two separate pieces, with each of you retaining half. After ownership is vested in only one name, you may then proceed to transfer the property into the name of the trust.

Either the grantor or someone given the grantor's power of attorney can transfer assets into a living trust. Living trusts also have provisions that handle the incapacity of one trustee and the appointment of a predetermined successor, or a procedure for determining a successor. This means that in the case of the grantor's mental or physical incapacity, provisions in a living trust instrument can enable a trusted friend, relative, or advisor whom the grantor has selected in advance to assume the trusteeship and take over control of the grantor's assets without the probate court having to appoint a guardian or conservator (see Chapter 2 for more information on guardianship and conservatorship).

Many living trust instruments are written in such a way that, upon the grantor's death, the trust instrument governing the trust remains the same, but new provisions regarding the trust's administration come into force. A trust designed to continue beyond the grantor's death becomes *irrevocable* at death, and the provisions contained in the trust instrument can no longer be changed or revoked. This now-irrevocable trust will have new trustees and new beneficiaries (remember, while it was a living trust, the grantor was probably also the trustee and the beneficiary) and it will require a new TIN.

## Joint revocable living trusts

A joint revocable living trust is sometimes used when the combined assets of the husband and wife are expected to be less than the amount exempt from federal estate tax. You'll recognize this trust because both the husband and wife are grantors. However, administration of these trusts can be fraught with gift and estate tax implications, and there are a number of pitfalls that can arise in creating them, funding them, and allocating assets to separate trusts within them. If you find yourself as the trustee of a joint trust, seek expert professional advice regarding its administration.

## *Tackling Totten Trusts*

Although it's much simpler than a living trust (and involves much less documentation), a *Totten Trust* (some states call it a *payable-upon-death account*) is still an estate-planning technique designed to move assets from the grantor's estate, either directly to his or her heirs upon his or her death, or into his or her trust *without* ever setting foot in a probate court, only this time there's no trust instrument. Instead, with the Totten Trust, the grantor opens a specific bank or brokerage account by using specific, formulaic language, and filling out specific paperwork that the bank or brokerage firm provides. For example, Sue Smith may have $10,000 she wants to give to her niece, Ellen Smith, at Sue's death and not a moment sooner. To do this, she can put the $10,000 into a bank account entitled "Sue Smith, in trust for Ellen Smith." For as long as Sue Smith lives, she can add to this account, take money out of it, or even close it entirely. When she dies, any money still in the account now belongs to Ellen Smith.

With this type of trust, the income earned is taxed to the grantor, and these accounts use the grantor's Social Security number to report any earnings. No separate tax returns are necessary. Upon the grantor's death, no probate is necessary for the assets contained in the account.

Because a Totten Trust doesn't have a trust instrument, each Totten Trust account a grantor opens has its own paperwork.

Not all states recognize Totten Trusts, and many that do have restrictions and regulations for them. If you're thinking of setting up one or more yourself, check with the bank or brokerage firm beforehand to make sure that your state honors the payable-upon-death designation and to see what restrictions, if any, apply to this type of account in your state. If your state doesn't honor the payable-upon-death designation, the person you name as the successor will still inherit the property, but only after it passes through the probate court.

## Going incognito: Nominee trusts

One reason grantors use living trusts to transfer ownership of assets from themselves to their heirs is to maintain privacy and keep that transfer from becoming a matter of public record in the probate court. However, placing real estate into that same trust may negate that purpose. Many states require that real property held in trust record not only the deed but also the trust instrument at the registry of deeds. If you live in one of those states, don't fear! You may still own property in the name of a trust — you just need a different type of trust.

*Nominee trusts* are a type of trust designed to hold real estate and only real estate. The trustee for the trust has very limited powers; instead, the beneficiaries actually control what happens in the trust (including whether to sell the property). To prevent the world from knowing who the beneficiaries are, a *Schedule of Beneficial Interest,* which lists the names and percentage ownership of each of the beneficiaries, is attached to the original nominee trust instrument but not to the copy recorded at the registry of deeds. That way, although the names of the nominee trust, its trustee, and the property that's in trust are all matters of public record, the names of the people who actually control the property aren't.

Because nominee trusts are disregarded entities for income tax purposes and don't require separate tax returns, the beneficiaries actually claim any income or deductions that the real estate produces on their personal income tax returns. If the real estate in question is property that the transferor ideally would have liked to place in his or her living trust, he or she can name the trustees of the living trust as the beneficiary of the nominee trust in states that recognize nominee trusts. In other states, a nominee partnership is used instead; the partners are typically the trustees of the living trust.

# Understanding Irrevocable Trusts

When it comes down where the action is as far as administration is concerned, the real meat and potatoes of trusts are the *irrevocable trusts,* or trusts that grantors have created to hold property where the trust instrument may not be revoked or changed. So what is an irrevocable trust?

- ✔ The grantor has given up all right, title, and interest to the assets held in an irrevocable trust, and has also given up any right to terminate the trust.

- ✔ The property held by the trust is used for the benefit of the named beneficiaries (or unascertained interests who are defined by the trust instrument).

> ✔ The *remainder interests* (those people or organizations who are entitled to receive what's left of the trust property, if anything, when the trust terminates) in the trust property are clearly spelled out in the trust instrument.

That's what all irrevocable trusts have in common. But because a person can draft trust instruments in many different ways and for many different circumstances, a wide variety of types of trusts fall into this category. The following sections highlight the reasons why grantors use irrevocable trusts and some of the most common types.

## Making gifts to an irrevocable trust

When a grantor funds an *irrevocable trust* (a trust that the grantor can't change or terminate) with property during his or her lifetime, and the grantor is neither a trustee nor beneficiary of the trust, he or she is giving up all right, title, and interest to that property — the legal definition of a *gift*. Depending on the size of the gift, the grantor may have gift tax and/or generation-skipping transfer tax (see Chapter 17) consequences as a result of the transfer.

If the grantor is making a taxable transfer to an irrevocable trust (and by taxable, we mean any amounts over and above the amount of the annual exclusion, which is $14,000 in 2013 and is adjusted annually for inflation), he or she will have to complete a **Form 709, United States Gift (and Generation-Skipping Transfer) Tax Return**, giving the name and taxpayer ID number of the trust, and showing the size of the gift. Unless the amounts involved are huge, the grantor probably won't actually pay a tax on the transfer; this **Form 709,** however, becomes part of his or her permanent tax records. Together with any other taxable transfers the grantor makes during his or her lifetime, this gift will be included when calculating the grantor's taxable estate which, in turn, will be used to determine the total estate tax due upon the grantor's death.

Married couples may opt to minimize gift tax consequences by so called *gift-splitting,* where the two spouses each show one-half of the gift on their **Forms 709** (you're not allowed to file a joint **Form 709**), even if they didn't own the gifted property jointly. Splitting gifts between husbands and wives doubles the amount of annual exclusion gifts available to the grantor and reduces the amount of any taxable transfer. For instance, in 2013 the two spouses could transfer $28,000 (2 × the $14,000 exclusion amount), no matter whose assets actually were transferred.

If the transfer is to a trust for the benefit of a *skip person* (your grandchild, a more distant relative, or a nonrelated person who is more than 37½ years younger than the grantor), you also have to complete the generation-skipping part of **Form 709.**

Property the grantor gifts irrevocably into a trust keeps the same *basis,* or acquisition cost and acquisition date, as it had in the grantor's hands unless the asset is worth less on the date of the gift than the grantor's original basis. In this case, the basis will be the lower of cost or market value at the time of transfer. This information is crucial in determining whether there's a taxable gain or loss when the trustee disposes of the property. It's best to give these records to the trustee at the time the gift is made, and then the trustee should be certain to maintain good and complete records going forward.

## Getting the maximum tax benefit out of dying: Marital trusts

Leaving a trust (or more than one, in many cases) behind for your husband or wife after you die isn't a sign that you don't think he or she can handle your money; instead, it's a crafty tax technique designed to minimize the taxes paid on your estate at your death and also those due and payable after your spouse's death. Welcome to the world of marital trusts, where a funded trust means that the grantor has already died and his or her spouse is still alive.

No matter what type of marital trust you're administering, the value of that trust on the surviving spouse's date of death is included in his or her estate tax calculations after he or she dies. Even though you may have avoided paying estate taxes on it after the first spouse's death, you probably won't avoid paying taxes the second time if the surviving spouse's estate, including this trust, is large enough.

All marriages aren't alike; neither are all marital trusts. You may encounter a variety of options depending on a number of factors, like the size of the estate, whether the surviving spouse is a U.S. citizen, or whether the spouse surviving is from a second or subsequent marriage.

### Giving the surviving spouse free rein: Unlimited marital trusts

In an unlimited marital trust, the surviving spouse is entitled not only to all the net income but also as much of the principal as he or she desires. *Net income* includes interest, dividends, rents, business income, income from other trusts or estates, and state tax refunds (to name several types), but excludes capital gains and the expenses paid from income for administering the trust (like the trustee's and tax preparer's fees).

Unlimited marital trusts, sometimes also referred to as *power of appointment* trusts, contain one of two types of power of appointment:

- ✔ **A general power of appointment:** The trust beneficiary may name anyone he or she designates, including himself or herself, at any time during his or her lifetime or upon his or her death, as the recipient of the trust property.

- ✔ **A limited power of appointment:** The grantor designates a group of acceptable appointees (such as the couple's children, grandchildren, or charities).

You typically find powers of appointment buried deep within the actual trust instrument. If a single trust instrument contains the governing provisions for several different trusts, the power of appointment for each trust will be stated with the provisions that are specific to that particular trust. For example, the spouse's power of appointment will be contained in the marital trust. Powers of appointment can be exercised in the will of the power holder (if it's to be effective upon death) or in a separate document.

If a power of appointment isn't exercised, the trust instrument will contain provisions for distributing the assets after the death of the trust beneficiary, so never fear, the assets don't just sail off into the sunset if the surviving spouse forgets to exercise the power or otherwise ignores it.

### Deferring estate taxes for a noncitizen spouse: Qualified domestic trust

The unlimited marital trust is the norm, but it only works if the surviving spouse is a U.S. citizen. If the surviving spouse is a citizen of another country, you have to find a different way to skin this particular cat. And that way is the *QDOT,* or the *qualified domestic trust.*

The quick-and-easy description of a QDOT is that it's a type of trust that allows a non-US citizen surviving spouse to defer, but not avoid, the estate taxes due upon the first spouse's death until after his or her own death. Unlike the unlimited marital trust, though, you can't make the assumption that all the assets will still be in the U.S. when the second spouse dies. And that's what makes qualifying a trust for QDOT treatment special.

For a trust to qualify as a QDOT, it must meet the following conditions:

- ✔ At least one trustee must be a U.S. citizen or a U.S. or state registered bank or trust company.

- ✔ The estate's executor must make an irrevocable QDOT election to qualify for the marital deduction on the federal estate tax return within nine months of the decedent's date of death.

- ✔ If the QDOT's assets are $2 million dollars or less, no more than 35 percent of the value can be held in real property outside of the U.S. unless

- The trustee is a U.S. or state regulated bank.

- The individual U.S. trustee furnishes a bond for 65 percent of the QDOT's asset value (based on the values at the decedent's date of death).

- The U.S. trustee furnishes an irrevocable letter of credit from a banking institution to the U.S. government for 65 percent of the value.

✔ If the QDOT's assets are more than $2 million dollars, then either

- The U.S. trustee must be a U.S. or state regulated bank or trust company.

- The individual U.S. trustee is required to furnish a bond of 65 percent of the QDOT's asset value as of the decedent's date of death.

- The individual U.S. trustee must furnish an irrevocable letter of credit issued by a banking institution to the U.S. government for 65 percent of the value.

The easiest way around the QDOT regulations is for the surviving spouse to become a U.S. citizen before the filing deadline (nine months after date of death) for the **Form 706, Estate Tax Return.** If that's not an option because the surviving spouse doesn't want to become a citizen or because there's not enough time to become a citizen in that nine-month window, a QDOT election can be made by the decedent's executor within that same nine months if there is no QDOT provision in the decedent's will or trust.

### Keeping tighter control: Marital estate trust

The *marital estate trust* may be funded with almost all the deceased spouse's (the grantor's) estate, just like the unlimited marital trust. However, unlike the unlimited marital trust, the terms of a marital estate trust are typically less freewheeling. You as the trustee may have the discretion to distribute income as well as principal. At the death of the surviving spouse, who is also the trust beneficiary, the assets are paid directly into his or her estate, where they're included for estate tax purposes.

### Reining in the surviving spouse: Qualified terminable interest property trust QTIP)

This trust has nothing to do with cotton swabs. Instead, the *qualified terminable interest property trust* (QTIP) beneficiary (the surviving spouse) receives the net income (paid at least annually) but is *not* required to receive any of the principal, during lifetime. Unlike the unlimited marital trust, where the trust beneficiary designates where the principal goes during his or her lifetime or after his or her death, the grantor of a QTIP trust makes that determination in the trust instrument. The trust beneficiary, the surviving spouse, has no say.

## Understanding the unified credit

The unified credit is the lynchpin of the combined gift, generation-skipping transfer, and estate tax system. Although the amount isn't the same for all three types of transfers, the theory behind this credit is.

Unlike deductions, which are subtracted from taxable amounts before you calculate the tax owed, credits are subtracted from the actual tax that's been calculated. So, in the case of the unified credit, you first calculate the tax due on the transfer being made and then subtract the credit from the tax. If the tax you calculate doesn't use up the whole credit, the remaining credit carries forward to a subsequent year in the case of gift and generation-skipping transfer taxes. In the case of estates, if the tax doesn't require the entire credit, the estate won't owe any estate tax.

The unified credit is a cumulative credit. During lifetime, any amounts the decedent doesn't use carry forward; after death, you subtract whatever amounts the decedent previously used from the total amount of the credit available to the estate. So if Flo gave away taxable gifts that used $250,000 of her unified credit during life, at her death her executor or administrator must subtract $250,000 from the total unified credit available to her estate. If she had an estate of $5 million (including her taxable gifts, which are added back for this calculation) when she died in 2009, the total tax on that amount would be $2,130,800, and the amount of unified credit available for all transfers in her year of death was $1,455,800 (or the equivalent of $3,500,000 of assets in 2009). Because she gave gifts during her lifetime that used up $250,000 of unified credit, her remaining credit would be $1,205,800 ($1,455,800 total unified credit available — $250,000 amount of credit used), and her estate would pay $925,000 ($2,130,800 total tax — $1,205,800 remaining unified credit), not the $675,000 it would have paid if she hadn't used any of her unified credit during her lifetime. In addition, in certain circumstances, the surviving spouse can now use a deceased spouse's unused exemption amount on the surviving spouse's later death.

Where it gets tricky is that the unified credit doesn't remain a static amount. As Congress adjusts the amount at which transfers begin to be taxed, the credit rises, falls, or on occasion, even disappears. Because it's a moving target, if you're planning on making large gifts, or even dying, you may want to consult a competent tax advisor to see what rules are currently in place.

## *Protecting the estate tax exemption: Credit shelter trusts*

Under the transfer tax system in the United States, a person can transfer part (sometimes all, depending on size) of his or her estate without paying any tax on that transfer. During life, you're allowed to make annual gifts (sometimes referred to as *annual exclusion gifts* — $14,000 in 2013, adjusted annually for inflation in $1,000 increments) that fly under the transfer tax system radar without counting against this nontaxable portion. But at death, all the decedent's assets are added up (including property transferred in excess of annual exclusion gifts) and subjected to estate tax. At this point, whatever portion of that allowable tax-free transfer (also called the *applicable exclusion amount*) the decedent didn't use during lifetime is subtracted from the total estate. This portion of the estate funds the *credit shelter trust* (sometimes referred to as the *bypass trust* or *family trust*), or the trust that holds the amount of assets equal to the remaining *applicable exclusion amount*. Not coincidentally, this is the same value of assets on which the corresponding tax would equal the amount of the unified credit available to the estate if those assets were to be taxed. (For a more in-depth discussion of unified credit, see the "Understanding the unified credit" sidebar.)

Before funding the credit shelter trust, obtain copies of the decedent's most recent gift tax return, which should show how much, if any, of the unified credit the decedent used while alive. If the decedent wasn't too generous during lifetime, you have the full amount ($5,250,000 in 2013, adjusted annually for inflation). If the return does include taxable gifts, subtract the total gifts (not the credit assigned to the tax assessed on those gifts) from the total amount of the estate that's exempt from taxation to arrive at the amount you can use to fund this trust.

---

# Lower your estate tax (and make your kids and grandkids really happy)

Funding children's and grandchildren's trusts during lifetime with annual gifts equal to the current *annual exclusion amount* (gifts not subject to the gift tax — $14,000 in 2013, adjusted annually for inflation in $1,000 increments) is a great way to remove assets from the grantor's estate, especially if that estate may be taxable at death. We once shared a wealthy client who religiously gave all the annual exclusion gifts she could to each of her children's and grandchildren's trusts. When she died, all those $10,000 gifts (the amount of the annual exclusion at the time she made the transfers) had been invested for years, and the total value that was sitting pretty in these trusts far exceeded the size of her taxable estate (which was still huge). Had she waited to fund these trusts until after her death, the available pot of money would have been much smaller because her estate would have paid 55 percent in estate tax.

# Skipping generations

Probably the least likely answer to the question "What kind of tax do you think of when someone mentions taxes?" is the generation-skipping transfer (GST) tax. It is, as its name suggests, a tax based on the transfer of assets between generations that bypasses at least one generation along the way. Whenever a grandparent transfers property to a grandchild, for example, if the intervening child (that is, the donor's child and grandchild's parent) is still alive, a generation has just been skipped, and you need to pay attention to this tax. Likewise, if a person makes a gift to an unrelated friend and there's more than a 37½-year age gap between the two, the IRS considers that the transfer has skipped a generation.

The GST tax rules are Byzantine. The concept of GST tax came about because some wealthy people were avoiding transfer taxes by moving their wealth to their grandchildren and great-grandchildren rather than their children. Instead of having their wealth pass *step-wise* (from generation to generation) with either a gift or estate tax being collected at every step along the way, these skip transfers had taxes (either gift or estate) collected only every second, or even third, generation. Like the big one that got away, Congress looked at the lost tax revenue and came up with a system to make sure that it assessed tax on every available step on the generational staircase, even if the assets never came to rest on each of them in turn.

GST taxes are calculated and assessed in addition to gift and/or estate taxes on transfers made to *skip persons* (the grandchildren or other recipients in the skip transfers). As with the annual gift tax exclusion, you can exclude a set amount each year from the tax if you meet the rules for qualifying for the exclusion, which are different from those for qualifying for the gift tax exclusion. You are also allowed to exclude a certain amount over the course of your lifetime and after your death. It would be awfully easy if that amount stayed the same, year in and year out. Unfortunately, it doesn't. Some years the GST exemption amount is the same as the overall gift and estate amount that can transfer without paying a tax; other years, the amounts are different. But just like the gift and estate taxes, the amount of generation-skipping transfers you make is tracked cumulatively over the course of your lifetime, not just from year to year.

Small and moderate-sized estates can usually avoid the GST tax altogether, even if they make transfers to grandchildren and the like. In larger estates, it becomes a question of getting the most bang for your exclusion bucks. For example, large estates often apply GST tax exemptions to trusts funded with life insurance policies. The grantor applies the GST tax exemption against only the transfer of cash to pay the insurance premiums. When he or she dies and the face value of the policy is paid into the trust, the new value of the trust far exceeds the amount of GST tax exemption the grantor used to fund it, but all those proceeds are now GST tax exempt.

## Grandpa (or Grandma) knows best: Grandchildren's trusts

If you're not sure whether your children are ready to handle large sums of money, chances are good you're even more convinced that your grandchildren aren't ready. *Grandchildren's trusts* are like children's trusts in almost every respect except one: Transfers made into trusts created for grandchildren are subject to the generation-skipping transfer (GST) tax. (Check out Chapter 17 and the nearby sidebar, "Skipping generations," for more on this tax.) And remember, any GST tax you pay is in addition to any gift taxes or estate taxes owed on the transfer.

Grantors often create these trusts to provide funds for a specific purpose, such as education or the purchase of a home. These trusts often allow the trustee a great deal of discretion when choosing to make a distribution for another purpose. As with children's trusts, the grantors often create them with an end plan in place so the principal is distributed to the beneficiary at specific ages.

## Better safe than sorry: Insurance trusts

Many grantors hold assets, such as a company they own or the family farm, that can't readily go into a trust. But those items still have real value and are part of the total estate when calculating estate taxes. Of course, if that type of asset represents the bulk of the decedent's estate, the estate may not have enough cash to pay the tax man when the time comes. Enter the insurance trust, a type of irrevocable trust funded during the grantor's lifetime. An *insurance trust* uses insurance policies (plus a small amount of cash) as the only type of asset. The trust owns the insurance policies on the life of the grantor, and the trust is the sole beneficiary. In fact, insurance trusts are a reasonably inexpensive way to make sure that adequate funds are available to pay the cash needs of a decedent's estate that may be otherwise short of cash, without forcing a fire sale of other assets that may not be readily marketable.

When the grantor dies, the proceeds from the insurance policies are paid into the trust. Money is then available to pay the debts of the decedent and the estate, including any estate taxes due. If the trust is structured correctly and the premiums have been paid by using the grantor's annual exclusion from gift tax or some of his or her lifetime annual exclusion, the face value of the life insurance policies on the grantor's death isn't included in the grantor's estate for estate tax purposes.

# It's only a name, not a description: Crummey trusts

In a *Crummey trust,* creating the illusion that the beneficiaries have the right to use the gift at the time it's given (a *present interest*) is the key. Without a present interest, the grantor can't use the annual exclusion to eliminate any gift tax consequences.

Crummey trusts are named for *Crummey v. Commissioner,* a court case decided in the U.S. Ninth Circuit Court of Appeals in 1969. The case enabled a grantor to make a gift into trust of a *present interest* in property that wasn't really a present interest gift, while claiming an annual gift tax exclusion for it at the same time.

In a Crummey trust, the grantor transfers money equal to or less than the annual exclusion amount into a trust set up for the benefit of his or her children and/or grandchildren. When the gift is made, the trustee sends a letter to all the named beneficiaries informing them of the gift and telling them they have a right to withdraw some or all of that gift within a specified period of time, usually 30, 45, or 60 days. When the beneficiaries fail to take the money out of the trust during this period (and the grantor, trustee, and beneficiaries all understand that the beneficiaries won't be asking for their money), their ability to do so lapses, and the money now remains inside the trust and is available to pay life insurance premiums. This ability to withdraw the contributions at the time they're made, even though no one ever exercises their right to do so, creates the present interest required for annual exclusion gifts and is called a *Crummey power.*

In a Crummey trust, the trustee is responsible for investing the cash, allowing it to grow over time. At some date far in the future, distributions may be made to the beneficiaries, many times to pay for education or the purchase of a new home. In some cases, the trust terminates at a specific date or when the beneficiaries reach certain ages, with the principal being paid out to the beneficiaries. In others, the trust may operate long after the contributions have been made to it, paying income and/or principal to the beneficiaries according to their needs.

Many grandparents have paid for their grandchildren's college educations by funding Crummey trusts for them. Although these trusts aren't afforded any income tax breaks (unlike specifically designated college savings accounts such as Section 529 plans or Coverdell Education Savings Accounts), Crummey trusts may be far more flexible than either of those accounts. With a Crummey trust, the principal doesn't have to be used to pay for education, and the distributions are discretionary. So the grandchild who may land a

four-year free ride for whatever reason won't have a mountain of unnecessary college savings, and the grandchild who may otherwise qualify for outright grant or scholarship money won't be penalized because of money that
has been explicitly set aside for his or her education.

## Keeping a finger in the pie: Grantor-retained interest trusts

Sometimes, grantors want to put specific property into trust but aren't sure
that they're ready to lose the benefit from that property yet. Welcome to the
world of *grantor-retained interest trusts,* where the grantor makes the gift of
property into trust but holds back an interest, either in the income from the
property or the use of the property for a specified period of time.

Because the grantor hangs onto an interest in the property transferred for
a period of time, you may be tempted to view these trusts as grantor trusts,
discussed earlier in this chapter, so that no gift tax returns would be required
because the grantor didn't give up complete control of the property in question. Grantor-retained interest trusts are more of a hybrid, though — although
the grantor keeps an interest, that interest is finite, and the transfer of property
into one of these trusts constitutes a gift that requires filing **Form 709.** But
the value of the taxable gift isn't the same as the value the property had in the
hands of the grantor. Instead, the gift tax value is the value of the property at
the date of the gift, less the value of the grantor's retained interest.

Why bother with grantor-retained interest trusts? To reduce taxes. Using
these trusts can substantially reduce the transfer tax value of property by
using today's values instead a higher value years down the road, which will
result in a higher tax. This isn't foolproof: Sometimes values shrink rather than
expand. But, while you should never make any estate planning decision purely
based on the tax consequences, we've both been involved with plenty of these
trusts where large potential transfer tax bills were almost entirely eliminated
because the grantor created a grantor-retained interest trust.

Grantor-retained interest trusts come in many varieties. Among the most
popular are the following:

✓ **Grantor-retained Annuity Trusts (GRATs):** The grantor transfers property into trust and receives a regular, fixed payment from it, based on a
percentage of the initial value of the transfer, for a period of years.

✔ **Grantor-retained Income Trusts (GRITs):** The grantor transfers property into this trust but holds onto the income earned by the trust for a period of years. At the end of the period, the property either distributes out to the beneficiaries, or remains in trust, but now the beneficiaries receive the income.

✔ **Grantor-retained Unitrusts (GRUTs):** The grantor transfers property into trust, and like with a GRAT, retains the right to receive an annual payment from the trust for a period of years. Instead of a fixed annuity amount determined when the trust is initially funded, the unitrust payment changes annually, and is calculated based on an asset valuation done on a specific day each year. In many cases, that date is the second business day of the calendar year. (Don't ask — we're just responsible for telling you the rules, not for making them.)

✔ **Qualified Personal Residence Trusts (QPRTs):** The grantor transfers his or her home into the trust, retaining the right to live there, rent free, for a period of years. After the specified period ends, the property now belongs to the named beneficiaries (usually the children but sometimes the grandchildren), and it's up to those beneficiaries whether to allow the grantor to remain in the residence. It's very important, though, that the grantor now pays the new owners market rent for that house if he or she continues to live in the home. Otherwise, the IRS may decide that the grantor never actually made the gift and therefore still owns the house.

The rules for structuring a grantor-retained interest trust, and for determining the gift tax value of the property transfers into the trust, aren't for the weak of heart. If not done correctly, the IRS may come along at any time and disallow the gift. Unlike income tax returns, which have a specified statute of limitations beyond which time the IRS may not question the return unless they suspect fraud, gift tax returns remain open items with the IRS until the taxpayer's death. The IRS can still question gifts made 30 years ago, changing valuations or even disallowing them entirely. If you're thinking of setting up one of these trusts for yourself, find an expert estate planner with plenty of experience to draft the necessary documents and prepare the gift tax returns. And if you've been named as trustee of one, get a second opinion and have a professional of your choice review the trust instrument. That way, if the document is fine, and the valuations are dandy, you're only out a relatively small fee. But if you do have a problem, your expert will, hopefully, find it and correct it before the IRS catches on.

## The rule against perpetuities: Property 101

The law historically didn't like property to be tied up in trust forever. In states that follow the traditional rule against perpetuities, a trust must be structured so that it terminates no later than 21 years after the death of a specific living person or persons referenced by name or relationship in the trust document. For example, the document may end the trust "no later than 21 years after the death of the last to die of the now-living descendants of my grandparents and my spouse's grandparents." Note that those descendants needn't be beneficiaries of the trust; referencing them merely gives the trust the possibility of a longer life. In states where this rule still applies, all well-crafted trusts contain a *fail-safe* provision which provides that, whatever the other provisions of the trust, it won't violate the rule against perpetuities.

Nowadays, about half the states follow a uniform law that provides that an interest in a trust must vest within 90 years of when the trust was created or the trust will be reformed by the court to meet this requirement. Some states actually have repealed or are repealing their rule-against-perpetuities laws to take advantage of a tax loophole that was created regarding dynasty trusts. These states hope to attract more trust business (or at least keep trust business from going elsewhere) by eliminating the rule against perpetuities.

# Exploring Charitable Trusts

Whether you've been extraordinarily fortunate during your lifetime or you prefer that your assets go to charity rather than to your family (whom you may feel you've already given enough to), establishing and funding charitable trusts are increasingly popular elements of estate plans. The days when only the extremely wealthy created private foundations and other types of charitable trusts have disappeared — now, even people with more modest means are discovering that instead of gifting money directly from your personal account to a particular charity, you can be charitable and reduce your taxable estate at the same time.

Charitable trusts allow you to transfer assets out of your estate, with the goal of using all, or a substantial part of that property, and the income earned from it, to act charitably. What better feeling can you have than seeing your money be used for worthy causes?

Of course, because charitable gifts carry with them tax consequences, and because most people have come to rely on tax consequences when making major decisions, giving to charity is rarely as simple as dropping a few coins in a bucket or mailing a check to a worthy recipient. By funding a charitable trust, you not only enable yourself to give a current gift but also provide the means, from the same assets, to make future gifts. And you aren't only entitled to remove these assets permanently from your estate, reducing your taxable estate, but you also get a healthy income tax deduction, upfront, for the transfer. In many ways, it's a win-win situation.

The next sections discuss the two major types of charitable trusts that grantors may create.

## Split-interest charitable trusts

*Split-interest charitable trusts* are trusts where the grantor retains an interest in the trust property. The grantor may create a trust enabling him or her to receive payments during his or her lifetime, or for a period of years, after which the remaining trust property is given to charity (so-called *charitable remainder trusts*). Or the trust may permit set payments to charity from the income and principal for a period of years (the *charitable lead interest*). After that period expires, the remaining trust principal is distributed to the *remaindermen,* or to the people entitled by the trust instrument to receive whatever's left after the charitable lead interest expires (so-called *charitable lead trusts*). The four major types of split interest trusts are

- **Charitable Lead Annuity Trusts (CLATs):** Charity receives a fixed annual payment every year. Payments are calculated as a percentage of asset value as of the date the grantor gifts the property into the trust.

- **Charitable Lead Unitrusts (CLUTs):** Charity receives annual payments, calculated on a percentage of the assets (valued as of the second business day of the year) for a fixed number of years.

- **Charitable Remainder Annuity Trusts (CRATs):** The grantor receives payments for life, based on a percentage of the value of the assets on the date the trust is funded.

- **Charitable Remainder Unitrusts (CRUTs):** The grantor receives payments for life that are fixed annually, based on a percentage of the value of the assets (which are usually valued on the second business day of each year).

All CLATs, CLUTs, CRATs, and CRUTs must file annual income tax returns. What makes this an interesting exercise is that these forms aren't typically fiduciary income tax returns like the ones described in Chapter 18. Instead, **Form 5227, Split-Interest Trust Information Return** is your form of choice. Note that **Form 5227** is an information return only; no tax is ever due. If the trust you're administering is a remainder trust, you have to give a **Schedule K-1** from the trust return to the income beneficiary, who will then be responsible for including on his or her personal **Form 1040** all items of income and deduction shown on the **K-1**. We discuss how to complete **Schedule K-1** in Chapter 20.

Don't fail to file your tax returns, including any required state returns. Just because you're not paying any tax doesn't mean that the IRS doesn't want to see what's happened during the year. Failure to file the **Form 5227** carries a hefty filing penalty, calculated on the number of days it's late, and maxing out at a whopping $50,000 per return, and the IRS very rarely abates it. It figures if you're swift enough to figure out the positive estate and income tax consequences of setting up one of these trusts, you're also swift enough to make sure that you file the tax returns on time. Although ignorance on other tax matters may sometimes earn you some IRS sympathy, it doesn't here.

## Non-operating charitable foundations

You may have heard of the Ford Foundation, the Rockefeller Foundation, and (more recently) the Gates Foundation. These are *non-operating charitable foundations* (sometimes also referred to as *family foundations*), which are established by some very philanthropic folks in order to further their charitable goals. Although these foundations may be incorporated and be run by the full gamut of corporate officers and directors, they may also be governed by a trust instrument and trustees. For many smaller foundations, the trust route is the way to go because the tax reporting requirements are the same and they don't have any corporate filing obligations.

### Supercharging your charitable giving by setting up a foundation

Creating a charitable foundation gives new scope to charitable giving. Now, in exchange for the rather hefty charitable donation you can claim on your income tax return each time you transfer assets into the foundation, charitable giving is no longer optional for you. The knowledge that you're required to give at least 5 percent of the average value of the assets in the foundation each and every year turns you, and other members of your family, into much more committed and inventive charitable givers.

There's a cost to be paid, though, in making a large gift into a charitable foundation you've established: establishing the foundation's tax-exempt status and annual tax reporting. In order for you to take charitable deductions for gifts you make to the foundation, you must obtain an IRS determination letter, stating that your foundation is a qualified charity.

### Filing for tax-exempt status

To do so, file **Form 1023, Application for Recognition of Exemption under Section 501(c)(3) of the Internal Revenue Code.** Expect that your application will be rejected at least once, but know that this is a situation of "if at first you don't succeed, keep trying." The IRS will give you explicit reasons why it has kicked back your application. Fix up those problematic sections and resend it. Obtaining tax exemption is a key element for your foundation; without it, you may as well not have one.

After you've filed your application, you also have to file an annual **Form 990-PF, Return of Private Foundation.** Don't wait until you've received your determination letter before you begin filing annual **Form 990-PFs;** instead, assume you'll eventually receive your exemption. **Form 990-PF,** although not an income tax return, is an excise tax return, and you'll be required to pay either 1 or 2 percent of your net income as excise tax. Unlike most other types of trusts, family foundations are allowed to use a *fiscal year-end* (ending the tax year on the last day of any month, not just December) for tax reporting purposes. If you choose a fiscal year-end for your foundation, **Form 990-PF** is due 4½ months after the end of the fiscal year.

Filling out the **Form 990-PF** can charitably be called a nightmare. Chances are good that you won't ever prepare this return on your own, and neither will most professionals. Not to fear — some professional preparers do prepare these returns, but you may have to do some homework to find one. Don't just accept a preparer's word that he or she can do this work; ask to see some evidence. **Form 990-PF** is open to public inspection, and you're well within your rights to ask to see one he has prepared.

In these days of easy identity theft, be aware that **Form 990-PF** is a matter of public record and anyone can ask to see it. In fact, all **Form 990-PFs** are now available online at www.guidestar.org. Be sure when you're completing the return that you limit the amount of personal information you provide. You may want to use a business address and phone number, not just for yourself as trustee, but also for the foundation; if you don't have a business address, renting a post office box makes a great deal of sense.

# Owning Subchapter S Shares in Trust

In a simple world, the only assets owned by trusts would be publicly traded stocks, bonds, and cash. But this isn't a simple world, and many grantors have less traditional sorts of property that they want to transfer into their trusts. One of these assets is often shares the grantor owns in a small business corporation, commonly known as a Subchapter S corporation.

In exchange for a significant tax break over larger C corporations, Subchapter S corporations are governed by rules limiting the number of shareholders (no more than 75), and who, exactly, may own shares. Trusts usually may not own shares, except for grantor trusts, where the grantor declares all trust income on his or her **Form 1040.** However, if a trust instrument contains appropriate language and the IRS is notified in a timely manner, trusts may own S corporation shares. This section explains the options.

# Qualified Subchapter S Trusts (QSSTs)

In a Subchapter S corporation, the shareholders (not the corporation) pay the income tax on income the corporation earns. The corporate income tax return (**Form 1120S, U.S. Income Tax Return for an S Corporation**) shows all the income for the year, and then splits it among all the shareholders on **Schedule K-1.** Each shareholder than declares his or her portion of the income on **Form 1040.** Because trusts, in general, don't fall under the list of approved shareholders, if a trust wants to become a qualified shareholder, it must be certain to pass all the income out to its income beneficiary. Welcome to the world of *Qualified Subchapter S Trusts,* or QSSTs.

In order for a trust to be a QSST, it must meet the following conditions:

- ✔ The Subchapter S income must be distributed 100 percent to the trust's income beneficiary because that income must be declared on individual tax returns, not on trust tax returns. So in order for a trust to own S shares, it must pay out all its income to its income beneficiary. Or, if the trust is a grantor trust and doesn't have a separate tax return, the grantor declares all items of income on his or her **Form 1040.**

- ✔ A QSST may only have one income beneficiary, who must be a U.S. citizen or resident, during the lifetime of that beneficiary. If the trust beneficiary is a *nonresident alien* (a citizen of another country who doesn't live in the U.S.) or a corporation, that trust can't be a QSST.

One trust instrument may create multiple QSSTs. If a trust instrument creates these so-called *separate shares,* each of the shares may qualify as a Subchapter S shareholder, provided, of course, that the mandatory income beneficiaries fulfill the other requirements for S shareholders.

If only it were as easy as knowing that the trust and the beneficiary are qualified S shareholders. Unfortunately, you have to let the IRS know. Seek advice sooner rather than later from a qualified professional (attorney, CPA or Enrolled Agent) to make sure that the QSST election is filed on time (typically 2½ months after the S corporation's year-end). Failure to file these elections jeopardizes not only the trust's election but also the entire S corporation's existence as an S corporation. Remember, an S corporation that has even one disqualified shareholder stands to lose its S designation, leaving it liable for double taxation, first on corporation income and then on the dividends paid to the shareholders.

# Electing Small Business Trusts (ESBTs)

Although QSSTs must have one mandatory income beneficiary who is a U.S. citizen or resident (see the preceding section), *Electing Small Business Trusts* (ESBTs) may have multiple income beneficiaries, and the trust doesn't have to distribute all income. Instead, in an ESBT, the following apply:

- ✔ All beneficiaries must be individuals, estates, or charitable organizations.
- ✔ The S stock may not be purchased by the trust.
- ✔ The trust may not be a QSST or a tax-exempt trust.
- ✔ Each potential income beneficiary counts toward the total allowable number of shareholders any S corporation may have.

In an ESBT, the trustee (not the beneficiary) makes the election, notifying the IRS where the corporation files its tax return of the name, address, and TIN for each trust beneficiary. Usually, you must file ESBT elections within 2½ months of the corporation's year-end.

Like QSSTs, ESBTs are tricky beasts best not attempted on your own, at least while you're getting going. Making a mistake here jeopardizes not only the status of the trust's election but also of the corporation's S election. And if you think messing up a trust tax return is bad, just wait until you have a bunch of angry former S shareholders hunting you down because they now have to pay more taxes due to your error.

# Chapter 4

# Assembling Your Team Members and Knowing When to Use Them

*In This Chapter*

▶ Identifying what you can and can't do yourself

▶ Locating an attorney

▶ Assessing accountants

▶ Finding other experts and assistants

▶ Considering the facts about malpractice

The universe of trusts and estates is quite unlike any other and has its own sets of rules and conventions that may seem completely foreign. In the fiduciary (trust and estate) cosmos, accounting rules are different, and so are many of the tax laws.

Navigating these new waters by yourself isn't impossible, but it's also not uncommon to want expert advice and assistance along the way. In this chapter, we tell you about different types of advisors you may want to consult, from attorneys and accountants to investment advisors, appraisers, and other assorted professionals.

## Finding What You Need to Go It Alone

We both know lots of people who have successfully maneuvered their way through the world of estate or trust administration unassisted. Many of these were folks whose professional lives touched on this area, so they had some idea of where to start and how to proceed. We also know plenty others whom we met midway through the administration process, after the executor, administrator, or trustee finally threw up his hands in defeat.

You can find a middle ground. Administering a trust or estate without professional help is entirely possible, but you shouldn't assume that you'll be able to do it without doing some homework. The fact that you're reading this book is a great starting point, but we'd be remiss if we didn't point you to some other resources as well, such as:

- ✓ **IRS Publication 559, Survivors, Executors, and Administrators:** Although reading this publication may not be your idea of a good time, it's a key resource and highlights important issues you need to be aware of. It gives you tax advice for the *decedent's* (deceased person's) final **Form 1040,** the estate's (or trust's) **Form 1041,** and the estate's **Form 706** (see Chapters 16 and 17). It also gives general administration advice, comprehensive income tax return examples, and a valuable checklist of forms and due dates.

- ✓ **Instructions for tax forms:** We'd love to say that we never read the tax form instructions, but we'd be lying. They seem dense and intimidating, especially if you're not sure where to look. Fortunately, most give instructions line by line, and very often terms and concepts are introduced either at the beginning of the instructions or at the start of a particular chapter within the instructions. If you're afraid of losing the information after you've located it, make a photocopy of the appropriate page, highlight the pertinent text, and keep it together with your copy of the return and any supporting documents.

- ✓ **Your local probate court (or its equivalent in your state):** In addition to being the best place to locate all the probate forms you need, most courts also have pamphlets available that explain the probate process in your locale. Making friends with clerks or assistant registrars at the probate court never hurts. Many of them have been there longer than the furniture, and what they *don't* know about probate probably isn't worth knowing.

- ✓ **Your state department of taxation or revenue:** Every state has specific requirements for trusts and estates, and many have publications available to help guide you through the process. In addition, if you have questions, call the state tax department and ask to be transferred to the fiduciary (or trust and estate) section. Every state tax department has at least one person in that area. Make sure that you get her contact info and keep it handy. If you run into trouble down the road, having a person who is familiar with your situation is invaluable.

We don't suggest that you ever phone the IRS for fiduciary tax advice. The IRS doesn't focus its training on fiduciary tax, and its telephone support is spotty, at best. What's worse, you don't know whether the person on the other end of the phone actually knows what she is talking about. If you can't find the answer you're looking for in writing, you may want to ask the question of a private practice tax expert who specializes in trust and estate returns. She may be willing to answer your question for free if it's a simple one, or at least point you in the right direction. See the section "Hiring a Tax Professional," later in this chapter.

# Finding an Attorney

If the prospect of estate or trust administration leaves you cold, or you've already begun delving into the administration and realize that you're in over your head, you may want to consider hiring an attorney to either shepherd the process from beginning to end or to help you with only certain aspects of administration. For example, you may want help with the probate process and with preparation of the estate and income tax returns, but you feel you should be the one to go through the house and figure out what the decedent owned. Even doing this much yourself can save you a pretty penny in fees, and the experts are usually happy to have you do as much fact gathering as possible.

Whatever the extent of the work you want an attorney to perform, finding one you can work with for a reasonable fee isn't impossible. Before you start, though, make sure that you have some idea of the scope of work you want the attorney to undertake for you. A common pitfall in estate and trust administration is not having a grasp of who's responsible for what duties. Although any attorney worth his weight will have a comprehensive things-to-do list that covers most scenarios, the only sure thing about estates and trusts is that no two estates or trusts are alike. When working with an attorney (or any professional, for that matter), make sure that everyone knows what they're supposed to be doing and every job is covered. Nothing should ever fall through the cracks.

The following sections can help you not only locate an attorney but also choose one after careful investigation. After you hire an attorney, you also need to know how to pay him, so we cover payment options as well.

## Knowing where to look

When searching for an attorney to help you with your estate or trust, you may be wondering, where's the best place to look? Unfortunately, you can't rub a magic lamp and ask for an attorney to appear, but you can do some investigative work on your own to uncover one that's a good match for you. Check out the following resources when searching for an attorney:

✔ **Phone directory or search engine:** Your first thought may be to rush to your phone directory and start flipping through the listings, or turn on your computer and begin a search. Chances are good you'll see pages and pages of attorneys listed. You'll probably notice multiple display ads touting this or that firm's expertise with various types of law.

Although we certainly don't think you should ignore the phone book (or any other form of advertising) when finding an attorney to assist you, we don't think you should rely on this information entirely. No one is checking the validity of the claims being made in advertising, and anyone with a law degree can hang out a shingle stating that she concentrates in this area. Just because someone says they're competent doesn't mean that they are.

✔ **Martindale-Hubbell:** This database lists most lawyers in the United States, as well as many of those in foreign countries; we're not sure that we'd consider using an attorney who wasn't listed in Martindale-Hubbell. You can find attorneys all over the country by using their free website, www.martindale.com. Not only can you search for attorneys and law firms by practice type (and the practice type you want is either *Trusts and Estates* or *Wills and Probate*) and location, but you can also check out the peer rankings (other attorneys' opinions of this attorney's expertise). (A rating of CV is very good, BV is even better, and AV means the attorney is one of the greats in that area.)

✔ **Local, county, and state bar associations**: Bar associations all have lawyer referral services, which match you with an attorney in your region whose law practice focuses on the area you request. Referrals are free and made on a rotating basis. Your first half-hour appointment with the attorney is typically billed at a much-reduced rate.

✔ **Personal references:** You may already know someone who's been in charge of someone's estate or trust, but you're just not aware of it. Ask people you trust where you work, within your family, or at your place of worship if they've personally worked with an attorney on estate or trust matters and whether they were satisfied with the service they received.

✔ **Referrals from other professionals or within law firms:** You may already be working with a tax pro or an investment advisor who may have the name of an attorney whom they know to be competent and reasonable. Or you may be the client of a large firm that practices in many areas, even if the attorney you usually employ doesn't do trust and estate work. Generally, referrals from other professionals are good ones — after all, the professional reputation of the person who makes the referral is as much on the line as that of the person being recommended. Referring a nonqualified person doesn't benefit anyone.

In order to double-check an attorney's credentials, check out the following:

✔ **His law firm's website:** Before you actually speak to him, visit the firm's website. Often, websites include abbreviated resumes, lists of articles written, or professional and charitable organizations the attorney is involved with. Because you may find yourself working closely with this person for a period of months or years, this relationship is an important one. The more info you can gather up front, the happier you may be with your final selection.

✔ **Your state's licensing and oversight agency for attorneys:** Particularly if the attorney you select isn't personally known to you or to someone you trust, you can check with a Board of Bar Overseers or the like to make sure that the attorney hasn't had any complaints or malpractice suits filed against him — or at least none with any merit. (You can consider overlooking nuisance lawsuits, but you would want these explained away very thoroughly.)

# Asking the right questions

Finding a competent attorney is only the first step in crafting an effective partnership between you (as the executor, administrator, or trustee) and your new attorney. Now you must establish lines of communication and determine whether you and this attorney are compatible.

Although working with an attorney isn't really like a marriage, two people with completely different work styles and ethics will be sure to rub each other the wrong way. Before you get too involved in the whole administration process, you may want to interview the attorney to get a sense of whether you'll be able to work efficiently with this person. Among the questions you may want to ask are

- ✔ How much experience do you have in administering trusts and estates?
- ✔ How often do you check in with your clients?
- ✔ How long does it typically take you to respond to requests from clients?
- ✔ Who actually performs the work — you or a paralegal, trust or estate administrator, or legal secretary? Of course, if a subordinate is actually preparing the work (with the advisor simply reviewing it and being ultimately responsible for it), the arrangement can be very cost effective for you because the hourly rates for junior staff members are always lower than those for more senior attorneys.
- ✔ How do you prefer to communicate with clients — via phone, written correspondence, e-mail, or in person?
- ✔ What are your privacy policies?

Only after you have answers to these and whatever other questions you may come up with can you be fully prepared to decide whether to hire this attorney or not. If you choose to, great! Your search is over. If you find the little hairs on the back of your neck stand at attention, though, you may want to continue looking. You probably kissed a lot of frogs before you met your life partner; this choice, although not the stuff dreams are made of, can turn into a nightmare if the attorney you hire is actually a toad. And remember, if you decide at a later date that the attorney you've chosen is no longer someone you'd want to bring home to meet your family, you can change. An estate or trust attorney works for you, the executor or trustee, and not for the estate or trust. If you're not happy, keep searching until you find the right person.

## Discussing payment options

One of the biggest questions, and one that most attorneys are very happy to discuss, is the manner and size of the payment. Attorneys involved in estates may charge fees in one of three ways (plus they all charge for miscellaneous disbursements, which are almost always additional):

- ✔ **Hourly fee:** The most common type of fee arrangement, attorneys bill you for the number of hours (or partial hours) they spend on your estate or trust. They'll tell you up front how much they charge per hour. Don't be shocked at some of the numbers you'll hear, some of which now exceed $1,000 per hour in major cities. Remember, high hourly rates don't always equate to the best legal help money can buy.

  Large firms charge more because their overhead is greater, and single practitioners who hang out their shingles in the town square charge less. Keep in mind, though, that the overall fees charged by the large firm are often comparable to those of the single practitioner because the large firm has staff such as trust and estate administrators who actually perform the bulk of the work. These estate and trust experts work under the supervision of an attorney, but their hourly rates are much lower. Attorneys bill hourly fee arrangements periodically, sometimes as often as monthly.

- ✔ **Flat fee:** Usually calculated as a percentage of the value of the estate. If the attorney manages to efficiently administer the estate, you know in advance how much the fee is, and the attorney usually walks away very happy. Flat fees are normally paid on a schedule or in partial payments whenever the attorney bills you. This sort of fee arrangement is most common in small- to medium-sized estates, rather than larger estates, because not only the probate court but also the IRS must approve the fees an estate attorney charges if an estate tax return is filed.

- ✔ **Contingency fee:** Although rare in the world of trusts and estates, in certain circumstances an attorney may accept an estate on a *contingency fee* basis, or a percentage of the amount collected by the estate. If a trust or estate is suing another party in a lawsuit and stands to potentially receive a substantial cash award in the future, a lawyer may agree to represent it (and you, as fiduciary) in exchange for the chance of receiving a hefty piece of that award.

- ✔ **Miscellaneous disbursements:** No discussion of attorneys' fees is complete without alerting you to the fact that all the attorney's fee covers is her time. Everything else is extra. Expect an itemized breakdown on every invoice of things like postage, photocopying, delivery services, filing fees, and even the sandwich you ate when you met the attorney for a lunchtime conference.

Fees aren't typically negotiable. An attorney presents you with her terms before you decide to do business. You can usually ask an attorney who normally charges a flat fee to bill you on an hourly basis, but those who charge hourly or on a contingent basis probably won't change, although you may convince one to give you some sort of discount (perhaps you're friends with her great-aunt?) Even a discounted rate will cost you plenty if the attorney is doing everything. The best, and surest, way to keep fees low is to do as much of the work as you can yourself.

## Finalizing your decision

Whether you meet with one attorney or with several, you'll eventually find one that fits your personality and wallet. Remember, your choice isn't irrevocable. You may change attorneys at any time and for any reason. Unhappiness with your choice, even without professional misconduct or shady dealings, is reason to try again.

In order to formalize the arrangement between client and attorney, the attorney may require that you sign an *engagement letter,* outlining the scope of the work to be performed, and each of your responsibilities. For example, you may be responsible for providing the attorney with all relevant information, and she may undertake to provide necessary forms and documents to be filed. Generally, these letters are formulaic, but you should still take the time to read through them carefully. Anything you don't agree with can be crossed out and additions can be manually inserted, provided that both you and the attorney initial the changes. Ask questions if anything in the letter is unclear. After all, it's your decedent's money.

## Working with your attorney

Hiring an attorney (or other professional) you like is only the first step. Now you have to work with him or her, and the success or failure of your new relationship rests on how responsive each of you is to the other.

Good communication is the key. When you receive requests for info, you should try to respond within a reasonable length of time. If you're not able to give him or her a complete answer reasonably quickly, you should make a phone call or send an e-mail outlining where you are in the process and how soon you anticipate having a complete answer.

## Choosing where to look for a professional advisor

Strange as it may seem, looking in your hometown for the advisors you need to assist you in administering a trust or estate may not be the best choice. Because the estate must go through probate in the county in which the decedent lived when he or she died, choosing an attorney or Certified Public Accountant licensed in that state is usually best. That attorney or accountant will be up-to-date on all the specific rules for that state and will be able to more efficiently help you through whatever probate and/or tax issues you may have than an attorney or accountant from a different state can. As a matter of fact, if the attorney will be appearing or filing documents in the probate court on your behalf, he or she must be licensed to practice law in that state.

On occasion, the decedent will have owned property in more than one state, and probate must be established in each state where he or she owned real estate. In that case, your attorney may encourage you to hire attorneys in the other jurisdictions. In fact, attorneys who specialize in estate and trust work often have reciprocal arrangements with attorneys in states such as Florida and Arizona where many people own second homes. If you're happy with the work your attorney is doing, odds are you'll also be happy with the services of someone she recommends.

The location of your advisor makes no difference when your major concern is investing, although you do want to make certain that the advisor is aware of the estate or trust's state of residence. This knowledge often affects the investments the advisor suggests to you. When probating an estate, be sure that any advisor you select is licensed to do business in the estate's state of domicile.

Finally, if your expert of choice is an Enrolled Agent, or someone who is licensed by the U.S. Treasury specifically to deal with tax and tax-related issues, you may comfortably hire one from any state in the country. Enrolled Agents are licensed by the federal government, so they may practice in any of the states, territories, possessions, or commonwealths of the United States.

# Hiring a Tax Professional

In the process of administering the estate or trust, you may find that the tax and accounting requirements are beyond what you're happy or comfortable doing. If this describes you, having a tax professional, like a Certified Public Accountant (CPA) or an Enrolled Agent (EA) on your team, can help ensure that the trust or estate is always in compliance with tax and accounting rules.

You're not alone if you're not sure of the difference between a CPA and an EA. CPAs are qualified in all areas of public accounting, including taxation and auditing. EAs, on the other hand, specialize only in taxation. Because public accounting rules don't apply to trusts and estates, both EAs and CPAs, if experienced in this type of work, can competently perform any of the accounting functions required, such as account preparation or figuring out how much, and what, property will roll from the estate to the trust after the estate terminates and trusts assume ownership of the decedent's assets.

Whether you choose a CPA or an EA, both are subject to rigorous regulation and are required to participate annually in continuing education. Provided the person you choose has experience with trusts and/or estates, either is well qualified to assist you. The next sections can help you make the right choice.

## Discovering where to look

Unlike looking for an attorney where you can search a database, no single place exists for finding CPAs or EAs. If you're searching for a CPA, you can check with the state board of accountancy in the state where you want to hire one, or with that state's CPA professional association. You can locate EAs through their national professional organization, the National Association of Enrolled Agents (NAEA), or through their state or regional organizations.

In addition to assessing state licensing boards and state and federal professional organizations, you may also request referrals from family, friends, and other professionals, such as attorneys or investment advisors, who may keep lists of CPAs and EAs with whom they've dealt with in the past.

It's common practice for CPAs or EAs to have you sign an engagement letter when you hire them, which outlines the scope of the work to be done, who is responsible for obtaining necessary information, and the level of review they will use to determine the accuracy of that info.

Hiring an accounting pro who will provide you with the service you need is really no different from hiring an attorney — you need to know that your work styles complement each other and that you won't drive each other nuts during administration. You should ask any CPA or EA you're considering employing the same questions you ask the attorney (check out the earlier section, "Asking the right questions"). Don't hesitate to add any others you may think of.

Not all tax return preparers are created equal, and this is especially true in the world of estates and trusts. Only attorneys, CPAs, and EAs are licensed to practice in front of the IRS. Other tax return preparers may say they have them expertise, but they haven't been tested and they have no requirements to stay up-to-date on current laws. Before you put your faith, and your trust or estate tax returns, in the hands of any preparer, carefully check their qualifications and their expertise,.

## Discussing payment options

CPAs and EAs typically charge for their services based on the number of hours worked or the number and type of tax forms prepared. In the case of a trust or estate, most bill on an hourly basis. Costs such as photocopying, postage, and deliveries are often additional, although individual accountants may cover these incidental costs by charging slightly more per hour. Accountants' hourly fees are usually less than attorneys', but they're still in the same ballpark. Be prepared — we don't want you to suffer from sticker shock.

Be sure to establish not only the hourly rate but also what it includes *prior to* having a tax professional prepare any work for you. It's awful, both for you and your accountant, to have an initially positive relationship sour upon receipt of that first bill, purely on the basis of a misunderstanding.

Accountants, like attorneys, often have subordinates perform many of the tasks you assign to them, with Mr. or Ms. Big supervising the project and retaining the responsibility for its timely and accurate completion. Remember, the employee who actually performs the work is probably quite expert. As an added bonus, because the person doing most of the project is charging you less per hour, this practice is much more economical for you.

# Considering Help from Other Pros

Very often, executors, administrators, and trustees are thrust into situations for which they have no preparation and no experience. You may find yourself in this category as you attempt, for example, to dispose of Auntie Bess's doll collection, rent Uncle Sam's house, or invest Cousin Mercy's millions. Figuring out what you have, what its value is in the estate or trust, and maintaining that value, is often a job for the experts. The following sections highlight a few other professionals you may need to help you fulfill your duties as head of the estate or trust.

## Determining whether you need an investment advisor

Both of us are reasonably savvy investors with decades of experience in various investment strategies; we both can easily tell you the difference between stocks, bonds, and options. Despite our comfort with handling large sums of other peoples' money, we wouldn't hesitate to hire an investment advisor to advise us on investing estate or trust funds.

The unfortunate reality is that, in a world where corporations and individuals alike are sued for seemingly frivolous reasons, an executor or trustee who fails to act prudently to preserve the value of the assets is fair game for a lawsuit. If you're in charge of assets that require investing, you should protect yourself against charges that you acted improperly; hiring an investment advisor provides you with an insurance policy against such accusations.

### Doing it yourself — at your own risk

Perhaps you're leaning toward investing the money yourself. Maybe you assume that no one will else want the bother of managing the small pot of money you have to invest. But how do you even know if you have enough assets to bother with the expense of an investment advisor? If you have $600,000 or less, you may choose to use a full-service broker. He can advise you for the cost of the commission he makes on each stock or bond purchase and sale, or you may opt to invest in mutual funds (which are invested by a professional money manager), bypassing the need for a separate investment advisor. For larger amounts, or if you want to invest only in individual securities, you may want to hire a reputable advisor whom you trust. In making this decision, keep in mind that, unlike the trust assets, which may be in there for the long haul, estate assets are held for a relatively short time.

Because your duty as executor is to preserve, not grow, the estate, your investment decisions may be quite simple if your goal is to distribute the estate outright to the beneficiaries upon its termination instead of continuing it in trust. See Chapter 7 for more on making the decision whether to sell assets to protect against your liability.

### Going with an investment advisor

If you want to go with a professional to help you invest the money, you have a few options. However, unlike an attorney, CPA, or EA, who must be credentialed either by a state or the federal government in order to practice, an investment advisor doesn't have to have any specific credentials. Among the professionals who offer financial advice are the following:

- ✔ **Certified Financial Planners:** Licensed by the Certified Financial Planner Board of Standards, these individuals have completed extensive additional education in addition to their bachelor's degree.

- ✔ **Attorneys, CPAs, or EAs:** Their training isn't specifically in investments, but many of them have become quite expert in this area because of the nature of their practice. Don't assume that every attorney or tax professional is qualified to also act as your investment advisor, but don't rule out the possibility, either.

- ✔ **Stockbrokers:** Full-service brokers not only purchase and sell securities for you but also research the companies they recommend. Stockbrokers must have passed the Series 7 exam in order to qualify. Remember, an online or discount broker doesn't provide investment advice; he merely places the trades upon your instructions.

REMEMBER

Knowing where to turn isn't always easy, because no one size fits all. Be sure to ask questions, starting with those you asked when hiring an attorney or a tax advisor (refer to those two applicable earlier sections). And add this important one: Could anyone else (like the insurance company the advisor works for, for example) benefit from the advisor's recommendations? If you don't like the answers, or think the advisor is promising you the moon in order to win your business, move onto the next name on your list. Like speed-dating, if there's anything that makes you uneasy in the first few minutes of conversation, chances are good that this advisor isn't a good fit for you.

Investment advisors expect to be paid for their expertise, but their fees sometimes seem excessive. When negotiating what you're willing to pay for these services, watch for certain warning signs:

✓ **Commissions:** Stockbrokers earn commissions each time they buy or sell stocks on your behalf. When stockbrokers have complete control of an investment account, they may *churn* the account, placing trades frequently with the sole intention of earning more commissions. This practice is strongly frowned on. If you think your broker is *churning* (look for frequent trades, especially in small numbers of shares), you should question the broker and advise his supervisor. Short-term investing in a trust or estate account to capture market fluctuations is a no-no, and you, as fiduciary, shouldn't permit it. Don't forget, it's always appropriate to review predeath brokerage statements for churning, too.

✓ **Fee for service:** This method is the safest way to pay for advice because you pay only for the time the advisor works on your investments. Of course, sometimes the bill may seem high to you. If you suspect that your advisor is padding the number of hours he is billing you and you're not already receiving an itemized statement (which you may not have thought to ask for when you established this relationship), you should ask to see a breakdown of the charges. But if the advice you're receiving is good, you may sour the relationship with this advisor by questioning his charges.

✓ **Percentage fees:** You're most likely to see these fees from advisors who actively invest for you. You give them control of the investments, based on a written understanding between you as to the type of investing you desire. The advisor charges quarterly fees based on two components — a percentage of the market value of the security portfolio and a percentage of income (interest and dividends) earned by that portfolio. You may negotiate the fees at the time you and the advisor are establishing the contract. If you feel the advisor's percentages are too high based on the portfolio's size and how much work you believe will be involved, you can always ask for a lower percentage. Remember, the advisor wants your business, and his fees aren't set in stone.

No one standard regulatory board oversees all investment advisors (although the SEC regulates many of them), so official monitoring can be spotty. Because they often have almost unfettered access to the trust or estate's assets, the potential for abuse can be high. Make sure that you obtain and check references before you hire an advisor, and don't shirk your responsibility by assuming that the investments are in safe hands.

Constantly review the advisor's work, asking questions when something doesn't make sense to you. Remember, someone else placed great trust in you and your judgment when they named you as fiduciary; use that good judgment to figure out when something just doesn't smell right.

## *Obtaining appraisers where necessary*

In a perfect world, property would only enter trusts and estates as cash, as stocks and bonds, or as precious metals, the value of which is easy to determine and maintain. Unfortunately, trusts and estates rarely inhabit a simple world and often include other assets, like the house, the car, jewelry, rental real estate, early 20th-century Japanese art, or a comic-book stash. You, as executor or trustee, need to know what it's all worth. And although you may be able to rely on yard-sale values or online auction sale prices for general household goods, you need to find a reputable appraiser for larger items like jewelry, artwork, and real estate.

When searching for an appraiser, go first to the source. If you're holding Aunt Bertha's diamond ring, and it's still in the jeweler's box with the name stamped on the cover, try to find that jeweler. He may still have the original documentation and will be able to prepare an official estimate of value without too much additional work. Likewise, real estate agents often have certified appraisers in their offices (many both sell and appraise property). If you need to value a rare coin collection, go to the local rare coin dealer. In fact, people who sell specialized property are used to appraising, and it's typically one of the services they offer.

Of course, some property is one-of-a-kind and appraisals for these items can be notoriously difficult to obtain. In the case of artwork by an artist who's still living, the gallery that represents his work should be able to provide you with a written appraisal. Auctioneers from top-echelon auction houses can provide appraisals for artwork from deceased artists as well as for antique furnishings. Occasionally, you'll run across singular pieces of art or furnishings that may require you to inquire of art museum curators.

Appraisals are increasingly coming under IRS scrutiny. If you need to obtain an appraisal, make sure that the person appraising the property is an expert in that field. The appraiser will, as a rule, attach to the appraisal a resume or curriculum vitae showing his qualifications. If it's not attached to the official appraisal, ask for it. Should the IRS ever question the valuations you use on a **Form 706** (see Chapter 16), appraisals jotted down on a piece of paper will not fly, but one that documents the value of the item in question and the qualifications of the appraiser most likely will.

## Consulting with other miscellaneous pros

Every estate and trust requires different levels and sorts of advice. Some additional professionals you may want to consult include

- ✔ **Business consultants:** If an asset of the trust or estate is an operating business, don't be shy about finding someone to help you run it.

- ✔ **Charitable advisors:** If you're trustee of a charitable foundation, reputable advisors can assist you in developing the foundation's charitable direction and show you how to identify charitable organizations you may want the foundation to contribute to.

- ✔ **Doctors and other medical professionals:** As a trustee, you're often charged with providing resources to guard the health and general well-being of trust beneficiaries. Sometimes, you need to do more than just foot the bill — you actually have to make arrangements with various medical professionals for necessary services.

- ✔ **Litigators:** Even though you, as fiduciary, presumably already have an attorney, you may find you need representation in a lawsuit involving the estate or trust. Remember, the trust or estate's attorney isn't always experienced in litigation and in courtroom situations, and will probably refer you to a competent litigator in your area if you find yourself in this situation. He definitely won't be offended if you go elsewhere for representation, and in fact, should applaud the move.

# Recognizing Malpractice

Everyone makes mistakes. It's the nature of the error and what steps are taken to rectify it that determines whether or not you have a case of malpractice.

Professional malpractice covers quite a bit of ground. Among the reasons you may claim malpractice are cases where a professional has been negligent, where a professional has acted unprofessionally according to the standards set by his or her peers, and where there is a fee dispute.

We've seen many cases of malpractice over the course of our careers, and cleaned up after a variety of attorneys, accountants, and investment advisors who not only messed up, but left the mess sitting for the next person. What defines the malpractice is that, not only was the mistake preventable and the cleanup expensive, but the estate or trust has to foot the cost.

Malpractice can occur while you're administering the estate, but it also could have occurred during the decedent's lifetime, and you need to be on the lookout for potential malpractice when you first become executor or trustee. For instance, if the decedent's attorney didn't draft the will and/or trust correctly, with unintended results, that's malpractice. Although you may not have the professional expertise to know this type of malpractice when you see it, those professionals whom you hire hopefully will.

## Surveying why malpractice occurs

Malpractice happens for primarily two reasons: lack of knowledge and/or oversight, and lack of ethics. The first, lack of knowledge or oversight, causes most mistakes. Unfortunately, ignorance of the law is no excuse, so an unwitting omission is still a mistake, and may still cost you.

True professionals do everything in their power to make sure that you don't suffer for their mistakes. When an error is discovered, not only will a professional notify you of the problem but hewill also take steps to rectify it while limiting, or even eliminating, the cost to you. So, for example, an accountant who fails to file accurate income tax returns should pay for the penalties if the inaccuracy was due to his failure, and not the client's. On the other hand, it's reasonable to expect the client to pay the additional tax and interest, as the tax was owed regardless, and the client had the use of the money for the additional time the tax remained unpaid.

Malpractice due to an ethical lapse is rarer, but much more difficult to identify and fix. Face it, crooks are crooks; crooks with many letters after their names are just crooks who've been to college. They know things that you don't, they know ways to steal and hide money that you've never thought of, and they have excuses and explanations ready and waiting to hand to you when you first begin to feel uneasy.

The types of ethical malpractice are limited only by your imagination. There are numerous cases of elder abuse, of embezzlement, of fees charged for phantom work, of experts hired whose sole claim to expertise is the fact that they're Uncle Joe's nephew. The list is truly endless, and just when you think you've seen everything, something new comes along to surprise you.

 Just because you're in the dark about what someone is doing in your name doesn't mean that you're necessarily off the hook if he turns out to be shady. Remember, you hired this person, and you're supposed to know what he's doing at all times. If your radar is going off and you're not doing anything to discover why, a court may find you equally liable even though you had no knowledge of the misdeed.

 The key to finding malpractice is checking, auditing, or whatever else you'd like to call it. Don't assume that something is done just because someone has given you assurances. Check it yourself. Call the beneficiary to make sure that he or she received the distribution. Visit the elder for whom you're paying round-the-clock nursing care, and make sure that a qualified nurse is there. Insist on receiving, and then reading, your quarterly or monthly statements. If you don't understand something on them, ask. If you don't like the answer, it's time to have someone else take a look.

## Covering your ass . . . ets

Whenever you hire any professional to do work for you, be sure that person has adequate insurance. Just as you wouldn't let someone work on your roof without first being certain he carried liability insurance, don't give anyone access to your books and records without seeing proof that this person carries professional liability insurance (sometimes known as errors and omissions [E&O] insurance).

In addition, if you're acting as a trustee for a testamentary trust, as a court-appointed guardian, conservator, administrator, or executor, you will likely be required to obtain a fiduciary bond. Being bonded is a good thing; it provides you with protection in case someone decides you're doing a bad job. Unfortunately, if there is no bond required, you may have no insurance protection if someone brings a lawsuit against you. Talk with your insurance agent to see if you already have adequate coverage; if you don't, get some and charge the cost to the estate or trust.

For non-testamentary trusts (those not created under the decedent's will) or if no bond is required for a testamentary trust, you should check with your insurance agent to see if your actions as a fiduciary are covered under your own umbrella liability policy.

# Part II
# Administering an Estate

## Five Key Groups to Notify of the Decedent's Death

- Professionals hired by the decedent, including the attorney, accountant, investment advisor, and insurance agent
- Heirs-at-law and beneficiaries
- The Social Security Administration
- The Veterans' Administration
- Pension and other retirement plans

**web extras**  You can ease the burden on the administrator of your future estate by leaving a list of all your assets in advance. Head to www.dummies.com/extras/estate trustadministration for help creating this list and gaining a rough idea of what your estate is worth.

# In this part . . .

- ✔ Address the immediate concerns after death, including planning the funeral, finding the will, and creating calendars and files for the estate.

- ✔ Know how to deal with the probate court, if necessary, including filing the will, having the will admitted to probate, and appointing the executor or administrator.

- ✔ Locate everything the decedent owned and safeguard and liquidate assets where appropriate. Also find out how to secure a property appraisal and prepare the probate inventory.

- ✔ Identify all the decedent's debts and set about prioritizing and paying them. Also get advice on dividing and distributing personal property and the rest of the decedent's assets.

- ✔ Close the estate, including gathering all the necessary documentation, paying the final administration expenses, and dealing with after-discovered assets.

# Chapter 5

# Taking the First Steps after Death

*In This Chapter*

▶ Knowing what you have to take care of right off the bat

▶ Planning the funeral

▶ Treating the decedent's assets differently now that he or she has passed

▶ Locating estate planning documents and determining who inherits and how

▶ Informing those who need to know about the death and staying organized

*T*he decedent has died and you're now in charge of everything, whether that's because you advised him or her during life, you were friends, or you're the only sibling he or she ever trusted. You may know that you've been appointed as executor, or you may be the only one, in all the confusion of death, who suspects that the decedent had a Last Will and begins the search to find it. Whatever your scenario, you may have many questions, including some you don't yet know you have! Read on for the answers.

This chapter discusses the immediate issues arising after the decedent dies, everything from dealing with the decedent's physical remains to how the situation regarding the decedent's assets changes when he or she dies. From what the estate-planning documents are and how to locate them to how to identify heirs-at-law and beneficiaries, how to notify everyone who needs to be notified about the decedent's death, and how to stay organized. Although we're not the "estate whisperers," we do help you tame that not-so-bad wild mustang — estate administration.

# Addressing the Immediate Concerns When Someone Dies

After someone dies, although you may be grieving, some matters need to be addressed immediately; they may occur to you naturally, or you may just need to bear them in mind and watch out for them. Make sure that the following items are taken care of. Some of them may not be relevant to your decedent, but others are a necessity.

## Honoring anatomical gifts

As soon as someone dies, make sure that you check to see whether the decedent had a notation on his or her driver's license or a donor card, personal identification card, or other legally recognized document by which he or she indicated a desire to make an anatomical gift. Sometimes the decedent will have told loved ones of this decision as well. If the decedent's wishes regarding anatomical donation aren't clear, and the possibility exists of using his or her organs for transplant, the doctors or other hospital staff will explain the available donation options to the family or next of kin. Donation depends upon the family or next of kin's assent; if they agree to have the donation made, the organs will be harvested and the body will then be available for a funeral and burial or cremation.

Even if organ or tissue donation isn't made, the decedent may have donated his or her body to a medical school or other institution. The donation may be contained in a letter of intent located with the estate-planning documents. If the decedent donated his or her remains, contact the institution and they'll make arrangements for, and cover all costs of, transportation and eventual cremation. Most will return the cremated remains to the family, if desired.

## Having an autopsy performed

Where the decedent's death may have been the result of violence, foul play, or other unnatural causes, or for various reasons detailed in individual state laws, the state medical examiner can perform an autopsy, whether or not the family consents. In this case, the medical examiner's office bears the cost of the autopsy. On the other hand, the family may choose to request an autopsy when it suspects the possibility of medical malpractice (or for other medical reasons). If the family wants to request an autopsy, it should inform the attending physician immediately. In the unlikely event the body has been transported to a funeral home, the family should immediately inform the funeral director (who normally won't embalm the body without the consent of the family) so that embalming doesn't occur. The family bears the autopsy cost if it requests the procedure for suspected medical malpractice. If the hospital itself is concerned about a possible medical error, it sometimes requests that the medical examiner's office do an autopsy so that a disinterested third party performs it.

Some religions frown on autopsies as desecration of the body. Although not all autopsies are avoidable, if the cause of death is obvious and there was clearly no foul play, you or your funeral director can request that an autopsy not be performed. One of us, for example, recently had a friend commit suicide. Her body was removed by the medical examiner and scheduled for autopsy; fortunately, there was no question as to cause of death, the funeral director intervened, and the family was able to bury the body undisturbed.

# Arranging the Funeral

As executor, you may be asked to arrange the decedent's funeral. Be sure to consult with the decedent's family, both as a possible source for the decedent's wishes and to honor those of close family members. Sometimes, the decedent has left written wishes as to his or her funeral. Look through the decedent's personal papers, especially copies of his or her estate-planning documents, to see if he or she left anything in writing with the other documents. Less frequently (but it does happen), a decedent has also written his or her own obituary. As helping hands go, you don't get much better than that — after all, who knew more about what was important in the life just ended than the decedent?

 Funerals, like weddings, are one of those life events where everyone's nerves are on edge, and feuds ignite out of the slightest of miscues. Tread very carefully as you plan the funeral. Consult, consult, and consult again. Don't rely on the say-so of just one family member; check in with several. Remember, any hard feelings that arise now will carry through the entire course of estate administration. Invest a little extra time to get it right. One of us remembers an aunt who was buried by the wrong (also known as "the other") funeral director in town. Who knows, the funeral may have been beautiful, but all anyone remembers is that it was held in an unfamiliar chapel among — gasp — strangers who didn't know us.

## Making important decisions

From the time of the decedent's death, you make sensitive decisions that can mean as much to the family as how you manage the estate.

### Choosing a funeral director

Wherever the decedent died, unless they or their family donated organs or their cadaver, their body typically goes to a funeral home for cremation or preparation for burial. You don't need to figure out how to do this; the funeral director will make all the arrangements for transportation of the body and complete all the necessary paperwork. A few families are starting to prefer various versions of do-it-yourself funerals, without a funeral director involved, and it can be done legally in some states. If this is the case with the decedent's family, they will (hopefully) take on every aspect of planning and carrying out the funeral.

The family may have a funeral director they always use, or the decedent's church or temple, if the decedent had a connection to one, may typically use a particular funeral home. If the family or the decedent's clergyperson is unable to guide you, make sure that any funeral director you consider is a member of a state funeral directors association and/or a national association. Check with the local Better Business Bureau to see if a director has any complaints.

### Writing the death notice or obituary

You may pay to put a small death notice in the newspaper in major cities. If the decedent was very well known, the newspaper may also publish an *obituary,* which contains more information about the decedent's family and life. Frequently the funeral director will gather information from you or the family and submit it to the appropriate newspaper for write-up and publication. You may even have a decedent who writes his or her own obituary in advance, as did one of our relatives. Many families now want a more personalized obituary and submit one already written. You may assist the family in this task, or you may write it yourself. Either way, it's an important testament to the decedent's life.

If the decedent lives in a suburb or smaller town, the local newspaper will no doubt publish a submitted obituary. In many small towns, the obituary section is the first thing readers turn to when they open their newspapers. Newspapers have figured this out, and now encourage the contribution of more information about the decedent than ever before for inclusion in the obituary.

As more and more newspapers cease print publication, funeral homes are increasingly taking on the responsibility of publishing an online obituary as well as a virtual guestbook in which family and friends may write condolence notes. While this is certainly not standard operating procedure at this time, the day of print notices and obituaries may be coming to a close, and the digital model will become the norm.

### Planning the funeral or memorial service

Funerals occur anywhere from the day after death to a week or later, depending on religious and local custom, and whether family must travel to attend. Some families hold a wake, also known as calling hours or visitation, at the funeral home during set hours (usually on the day before the funeral) or a *shivah* (usually for three or seven days after the funeral). Rather than a funeral, a memorial service may be held at a later time.

If close family is available, they most likely want to be very involved in planning all funeral and memorial observances. More and more commonly, family members want to prepare photo boards, albums, or slide shows of the decedent and the family and to display mementos like framed wedding photos and photos of family groups or other significant events. You want to be sure that flowers are ordered, if appropriate for the decedent's funeral tradition, and ask the family to choose a charity to which memorial contributions can be made, or if the family prefers, to let donors choose their own charities.

You may need pallbearers, in which case the family may want to choose who has this honor. Usually, six sturdy men are necessary, but other older or frailer folks can be honorary pallbearers. Although the tradition is that men be the pallbearers, nothing says that a woman can't be one. And of course, if the decedent left specific wishes, such as the desire to be buried in a blue velour tux (and it's your grandmother, not grandfather), those wishes should be honored to the extent they're legal. If the decedent was a veteran, the family may want to have him or her buried with military honors, as described in "Understanding special burial rights for veterans."

As traveling becomes more difficult and costly, many families are finding ways to allow friends and family to attend the funeral from a distance. If you know there are people who want to attend who will not be able to, you may want to check with your funeral director or the venue where the service is being held to see if Internet streaming is available.

On the day of the funeral or memorial service, arrange for someone to watch the house — burglars read the obituaries and death notices.

### Assigning eulogies

If a clergyperson is presiding at the funeral, he will, of course, talk about the decedent. But in some cases the officiant didn't actually know the decedent personally and has gathered information and memories from family members or close friends. A personal eulogy given by one or more family members or close friends can be a meaningful addition to the service. You can ask the family who may be appropriate or want to perform this honor. The family may also opt to allow a time in some services when any who want to are offered the opportunity to speak.

Consider vetting written eulogies before the words are spoken. In our experience, funerals can be opportunities to make enemies (often unintentionally). Although we're all for freedom of speech, funerals are a time to bring families and friends together, and to remember the deceased fondly (and maybe even with some humor). They're not the appropriate forum to air dirty laundry or attempt to redress past injustices.

### Finding an appropriate clergyperson

The decedent may have had a close relationship with a clergyperson or may have rarely crossed the threshold of a place of worship. If the decedent didn't even have a place of worship, the question may even arise as to what, if any, kind of service the decedent would have wanted to have. Any information left by the decedent is helpful here, but the immediate family's wishes usually trump. The funeral home is always an appropriate setting for the funeral service, and in some religious denominations, it's the traditional setting.

### Deciding between cremation and interment

As cemeteries fill up and traditional burials become increasingly expensive, cremation is rapidly overtaking burial as the most popular way to deal with remains. If the decedent wanted to be cremated (with or without burial), he or she will typically have made his or her wishes known to a spouse or other family members or friends. The decedent's spouse or other family members may also make the decision to use cremation. If no one close to the decedent is available, or wants to make this choice, it becomes yours; either is okay.

Remember, even cremated remains may be buried in a cemetery, either in an actual plot or a *columbarium*, a wall with drawers for the ashes.

### Choosing a cemetery

Several options are available when choosing a final resting place for the decedent's remains:

- ✔ If the decedent has prepurchased a plot (frequently several plots together, for themselves and additional family members), your problem is solved: You use the prepurchased plot. If there's reason to believe the decedent purchased a plot but it can't be located, you may be able to file a petition in the Probate Court to open the decedent's safe-deposit box to look for paperwork, such as a burial deed, regarding the plot.

- ✔ If no family plot exists, most active cemeteries still have lots available for sale, either through the cemetery, or the resale by private parties of unused lots previously purchased. Choose a cemetery in a place significant to the decedent or one that you and other family members may easily visit, if you so choose.

- ✔ When the decedent has been cremated, family members frequently choose to scatter the remains in a meaningful location. In California, many services provide everything needed for a burial at sea, from the paperwork to the boat to biodegradable urns. One of us has a cousin who chose to scatter her mother's ashes in the rapids of a river near our childhood home. And another family we know of divided their father's remains among the children, with each choosing their own special location for their share of the remains.

### Picking out a headstone or grave marker

Although you don't need to order the grave marker immediately, it's an important task to take care of. If your decedent has a predeceased spouse, the plot may already have a grave marker with room for the decedent's memorial information, in which case you can simply have the appropriate information about the decedent added.

### Understanding special burial rights for veterans

If the decedent was an honorably discharged veteran, several benefits are available through the U.S. Department of Veterans Affairs (VA). The following list gives a few of these benefits; check out the VA's website (www.cem.va.gov/cem/) for more info.

- ✔ **United States flag:** Veterans are entitled to a U.S. flag to place folded in the open casket, drape the casket, or accompany the urn. The funeral home typically arranges for this, or you can go to the VA's website to obtain the flag yourself.

- ✔ **Burial in a national cemetery:** Veterans, their spouses, and their dependents may be buried at any of the national cemeteries with available space (currently 131) for no charge, including grave opening and closing and perpetual care.

- ✔ **Headstone or marker:** Whether buried in a national cemetery or not, eligible veterans are entitled to a government headstone or marker, provided by the VA, for their unmarked grave. For eligible veterans who died after November 1, 1990, the headstone is available even if the site already has a private headstone, and as of spring 2009, those whose grave is already marked have the choice of applying for either a traditional headstone or marker or a medallion which can be affixed to the private headstone.

- ✔ **Presidential Memorial Certificate:** The Presidential Memorial Certificate is an engraved paper certificate, signed by the current president, that's intended to honor the memory of honorably discharged deceased veterans. Loved ones and next of kin may apply for the certificate, and more than one may be issued. You can download the application on the VA's website.

- ✔ **Burial allowance:** Deceased veterans may be entitled to a burial allowance. For further information, call 1-800-827-1000.

- ✔ **Military funeral honors:** Upon the family's request, every veteran is entitled to a military funeral honors ceremony, with folding and presenting of the U.S. burial flag and the playing of "Taps."

## Providing a collation

In many American cultures, a *collation*, or light meal, is traditional after the funeral service. It can be held anywhere from the decedent's home, with neighbors and church members (or a catering service) supplying the food, to a church hall or restaurant. When ordering food, be aware of local and religious custom. For example, one of us has the custom of greeting the mourners as they return from the cemetery (the spouse, children, and siblings of the deceased) with hard-boiled eggs, which symbolize the continuity of life. As always, if you're not sure what to do, ask. Family members, a clergyperson, or even the funeral director may be able to give you guidance.

## Paying for funeral costs

The estate may pay for all reasonable funeral costs, to the extent that funds are available. The key word is "reasonable." A judge may disallow payment of funeral expenses found to be unreasonable. In many states, funeral expenses, expenses of last illness, and administration expenses take precedence over all other claims against the estate. But if your decedent's estate may be short of funds, keep all funeral expenses to a modest amount. Of course, funds in a decedent's funded revocable trust can be used to pay expenses, if necessary.

If the decedent had a checking account joint with his or her surviving spouse, payment can come from that account, with the amount to be repaid from other funds if the spouse doesn't ultimately receive the entire estate, minus expenses. Sometimes the funeral home will wait for payment until the executor or administrator is appointed, but it frequently adds interest to the bill after a set amount of time. You may even apply for temporary executorship to pay for the funeral.

Funeral trusts, where the decedent prepaid for his or her funeral, have become much more common as people are increasingly loathe to land a large funeral bill on the heads of their families. Be sure to check with the named funeral home if such a trust exists. If you suspect the decedent had a trust, but you're not sure with which funeral home, make all the calls before the funeral; it would be a shame to have to pay for a funeral at one home when another home already received payment.

Don't let the funeral director talk you into something that just doesn't seem right to you. Although his or her ideas may be great, they may also be an attempt to sell you additional services that you don't want or need. Making these decisions just hours after the decedent's death is difficult, and after they've had a chance to reflect on a funeral just passed, some people would have done something different. Remember, the funeral director isn't only helping you at a very stressful point but she's also running a business and always keeping an eye on her financial bottom line.

## Obtaining copies of the death certificate

You can't even begin to tackle the tasks in front of you without proof that the decedent actually died. Be sure to get a number of certified copies of the death certificate to give to anyone that may need to know about this particular death. For example, you may need copies for the probate court (if probate is necessary), for taxing authorities, for each life insurance company, and to collect other death benefits (just to name a few). You pay a small cost for each copy, but the convenience of having them on hand far outweighs that cost. Usually the funeral director obtains them for you. Otherwise, you can get them through the appropriate office in your state, which may be the county clerk's office or the state department of vital statistics.

Although death certificates are a matter of public record, they're also a minefield of information for identity thieves, who treat this information like a kid in a candy shop. You can't prevent identity thieves from obtaining this information directly from state authorities, but you don't need to make their lives easier by handing it to them. Make sure that someone asking you for a death certificate has a valid reason for needing one before you hand it over.

# Understanding How Death Changes Everything about the Decedent's Assets

When someone dies, assets owned only by him or her in individual name are essentially frozen. *Frozen assets* are simply inaccessible (that is, neither you as future executor nor anyone else has access to them or can sell, transfer, or take any other action with regard to them). Until you manage to unfreeze those assets by being appointed executor, you can't use them. A few types of jointly owned property may pass immediately to the surviving owner upon the other owner's death:

✔ Assets held in *joint names with right of survivorship* (automatically passing to the survivor or survivors on the first person's death)

✔ Real estate owned as *tenants by the entireties* (joint ownership of real estate with rights of survivorship only available to husband and wife)

✔ Assets (typically bank accounts) designated *POD* (payable on death)

The following sections explain the impact death has on a decedent's assets. They aren't available until you're appointed as executor, and that handy power of attorney that was so valuable during the decedent's life is now useless. For now, and until you're appointed as the estate's executor, you can't manage the decedent's assets and no funds are available.

## Bank accounts and the need for funds

All assets in the decedent's name alone have to go through the probate process, either according to his or her will or the laws of *intestacy* (a fancy way of saying he or she left no will); bank accounts owned by the decedent alone are no different. Money in these accounts isn't available to the family or the executor until the executor has been appointed. Only then can bank accounts be transferred into an account in the estate's name.

You may open traditional checking and/or savings accounts for an estate, or you may opt to use fiduciary services available from commercial banks, investment houses, or in some states, law firm trust departments. As we discuss in the earlier "Paying for funeral costs" section, you can request appointment as temporary executor or special administrator if the estate has an urgent need for funds. Chapter 7 discusses how to locate the decedent's bank accounts.

### Powers of attorney

*Powers of attorney* (documents appointing others to act on the grantor's behalf regarding any or all of his or her assets or financial matters) may only be used while the grantor of the power is alive; when the decedent dies, so does the power of attorney. Because the grantor's death cancels the power, don't try to act under its authority after his or her death. Any separate powers of attorney that the decedent may have executed regarding bank accounts also lose their effectiveness with the decedent's death.

# Locating the Estate-Planning Documents

When a person dies, one of your many important tasks is to locate the estate-planning documents. Frequently, the decedent has photocopies of them in a file at home or in his or her safe-deposit box. If the surviving spouse hasn't personally handed them to you, see whether you can find a home file and search the decedent's papers accordingly. You can also check with the decedent's attorney or other advisors because they may well have the originals of the will and other estate-plan documents in their will vault. At the very least, they hopefully have copies, even if the originals are elsewhere. The next sections highlight the important documents you need to find.

## The Last Will and testament (The Will)

The most important document to locate is the decedent's Last Will and testament. The decedent may have placed his or her will on file with the probate court for safekeeping. This practice isn't the same as filing the will for probate. If you find more than one will, the most recent will governs.

The decedent may also have made changes to his or her will, called *codicils*, which don't revoke the will but expressly add to, change, or remove something from the will. A person can add an unlimited number of codicils to a will. However, because interpreting many codicils is cumbersome, an entirely new will is usually written after a few codicils have been added. The original of a codicil is always kept with the original will (at least in theory).

## Trust agreements and amendments

You also want to locate any trust agreements and amendments to them that the decedent may have had. Although only one copy of a will is signed, you usually have at least two signed copies of a trust because an original copy may be needed in the transfer of assets to the trust and for other administrative purposes. At least one signed copy of the trust should be located with the original will, as should any amendments to the trust.

## Opening the safe-deposit box and locating the original will

If the safe-deposit box is in the decedent's name alone, normally no one can access it until the decedent's will has been admitted to probate. This can pose a problem if you can't locate the *original will* (although some legal documents are executed in multiples, only one will is ever signed at a time), and you think the safe-deposit box may contain the will. Some safe-deposit box contracts provide that, upon proof of the vault holder's death (such as a death certificate), a search of the box can be made for the will by an officer of the bank at the request of an appropriate party. If the box is held by the decedent as a joint tenant, the surviving joint tenant(s) may access the box,

but a representative of the estate may request to be present. As a matter of fact, the surviving joint tenant(s) would be wise to have a witness present when they open the box, to witness (in writing) what's contained in the box.

If the bank doesn't allow entrance to the safe-deposit box for a will search, some states allow you to file a petition to open the box to locate a will and burial deed (for a cemetery plot; don't remove anything else). Other states allow you to file a petition for appointment of a special administrator with the probate court so that the special administrator can open the box.

Even if the trust began its life as a *revocable living trust,* a trust designed to receive assets from the *grantor* (the trust's creator) during his or her lifetime, it becomes *irrevocable* (unable to be changed) at the grantor's death. Depending on what the will's terms are, this trust may not only continue with assets placed in it during the grantor's lifetime, but it may also stand ready to accept assets from the decedent's estate.

Just as wills may be amended by codicil, trust instruments may also be changed during the grantor's lifetime by amending the trust. An amendment must be agreed to by the trustee(s), because they signed on to administer the trust under its original terms only. But if the trustees don't want to agree to the amendment, the creator of the trust can simply change the trustees.

## *Letters of intent*

Sometimes you find a letter of intent written before the decedent's death on a subject he or she didn't want to put in his or her will (which becomes a public document when it's filed for probate) or trust. The letter of intent can be about something such as who is to get which personal and household articles (although hopefully any instructions regarding an item of great value, such as a piece of jewelry or work of art, are specifically spelled out in the will, to avoid controversy among the heirs). Letters of intent can be valuable tools in helping you carry out the decedent's wishes because they're often filled with the decedent's own words rather than language that has been legally filtered.

## *Other documents that dispose of property*

Don't forget to look for life insurance policies with beneficiary designations attached, copies of beneficiary designations as to the decedents retirement plans and individual retirement accounts, and any other assets with death benefits, all of which may be located neatly with the estate plan documents, or scattered throughout the decedent's files, or in some cases, throughout the house. Chapter 7 gives details on how best to locate all the decedent's assets.

# *Notifying Those Who Need to Be Notified*

As executor, you may feel that your job is primarily to write letters because you need to notify seemingly everyone and their uncle of the decedent's death. Some entities and individuals may be more important than others, but you should notify them all as soon as possible.

You can save yourself some time by creating your own version of a form letter that can be modified easily for each recipient. Keep it on your computer's desktop and revise it as needed. You can keep saved electronic copies of each letter sent in a folder on your desktop so you can easily identify whom you've sent letters to. The bottom line: Make sure that you organize all this correspondence. (Check out "Setting up a filing system," later in this chapter for more info.)

Make sure that you contact the following entities and individuals to inform them of the decedent's death:

- ✔ **The decedent's attorney, accountant, and so on:** At your earliest convenience, contact the decedent's attorney, accountant, investment advisor, insurance agent, and any other professional you're aware of. Each may have valuable information that can save you hours of searching for the decedent's estate-plan documents, copies of tax returns, asset information, and personal information. The surviving spouse and other family members will likely be able to give you the names of these professionals. You also may meet them at the funeral or memorial service. And you may find their names in the decedent's personal papers, so don't forget to check the papers scattered across the decedent's desk.

- ✔ **Heirs-at-law and beneficiaries:** You want to identify the *heirs-at-law* (persons who inherit if the decedent didn't have a will) and the *beneficiaries* (persons who inherit under the will) as soon as possible. If no will exists, you're required to notify the heirs-at-law of your petition for probate; if a will does exist, notify both the heirs-at-law and the beneficiaries. Be sure to get the beneficiaries' addresses, telephone numbers, and Social Security numbers, and the heirs-at-laws' addresses.

The surviving spouse and/or other family members can provide family information to help you determine the heirs-at-law. After you find the Last Will, you can determine from it who the beneficiaries are. See Appendix B for a state-by-state listing of the laws of *intestacy* (dying without a will) to help you identify the heirs-at-law.

✔ **Social Security Administration:** Call the Social Security Administration (SSA) at 800-772-1213 or contact the local SSA office (the local office is often easier to deal with) to report the decedent's death. If the decedent was receiving his or her benefits by direct deposit, notify the bank of the decedent's death and request that it return any funds it receives for the month of death and beyond to the SSA.

Don't close the bank account that's receiving direct deposits before any Social Security checks have arrived and been returned to the SSA, or the checks may be in limbo! If the decedent was receiving his or her benefits by check, don't cash any check for the month of the decedent's death or later; return them to the SSA. The estate isn't entitled to the payments made in the month of death because Social Security payments are actually made for the month ahead, and you don't get partial payments for partial months. So, if the decedent died midway through the month, that month's payment must be returned.

✔ **Veterans' Administration:** If the decedent was receiving veterans' benefits, call 800-827-1000 to report the death. You should also ask about burial and other benefits that may be available to a surviving spouse or minor children. See "Understanding special burial rights for veterans," earlier in this chapter, as well as Chapter 7, for a discussion.

✔ **Pension and other retirement plans:** Notify each of the retirement plans in which the decedent had an interest, whether the plan was sponsored by an employer or created by the decedent. See Chapter 7 for info on the different retirement plans the decedent may have.

✔ **Employer and employees:** If they aren't already aware of the decedent's death, notify the decedent's employer and/or employees as applicable.

✔ **United State Postal Service:** If no surviving spouse still lives at the decedent's residence, file a change of address form with the post office as executor, indicating where the decedent's mail should be sent. If the decedent's spouse survives, you needn't notify the post office, but ask the spouse to send along pertinent mail to you, such as bills in the decedent's name alone. The spouse may also pay them and later present the paid bills to the executor for repayment.

✔ **The decedent's landlord, if any:** Notify the landlord of the decedent's death, and if the surviving spouse doesn't want to continue the lease (or there is no surviving spouse), vacate the premises as soon as is convenient, after allowing time for proper disposition of the decedent's personal and household articles as discussed in Chapter 7. In some cases, you may find that you need to keep that home for a while until you can make appropriate distribution. Be sure to review the lease; some leases may have a provision for termination upon death. In many cases, you can reach an agreement with the landlord for early termination.

- ✓ **Creditors of the decedent, including credit card companies:** Notifying creditors of the decedent's death and the new address for statements makes them aware that you're planning to pay the bills when allowed by the court (see Chapter 8). If any debts are in both spouses' names and the surviving spouse has the funds to make the payments, he or she should make them so that his or her credit rating isn't affected. You can pay the spouse back later from estate funds if it's a debt of the decedent. Make sure that any surviving spouse has credit cards in his or her own name. Be sure to close all credit card accounts after they have been paid off, or have them retitled in the surviving spouse's name alone. And cancel those debit cards tied in with any bank accounts.

- ✓ **Utilities and cellphone companies:** Have utilities transferred to the surviving spouse's name, if applicable; if the decedent has no surviving spouse, have the utility bills mailed to you until you've cleared out the decedent's residence, at which time you may want to arrange for some of the utilities to be shut off. Cancel any contracts for telephone land lines, Internet, and/or cable TV services right away. If the decedent had a cellphone, check to see whether it's under contract and, if so, if the contract is terminable upon death. (Most cellphone service providers are willing to cancel a contract when provided with a death certificate.)

- ✓ **Membership organizations of which the decedent was a member:** Cancel the decedent's memberships in any organizations. If the surviving spouse wants to continue a membership, help to arrange it.

# Creating Calendars and Files

Administering an estate is a drawn-out process, one filled with a great deal of minutiae. Keeping organized and thorough records of all estate activity, from the decedent's date of death onward, prevents the terror of wondering whether you've missed one of those (we hate to say it) drop-dead deadlines. It also can save you hours of time as you prepare the estate inventory (see Chapter 7), estate accountings (see Chapter 9), income tax returns (see Chapter 18), federal estate tax return (see Chapters 16 and 17) and any state estate or inheritance tax returns (see Appendix B for applicable state laws). It also makes it easy to answer questions posed by probate court, estate beneficiaries, and tax auditors, to name a few. The following sections highlight the types of calendars you need, as well as how to keep everything in order.

# Eyeing what kind of calendar to create

The best way to stay organized is to create a calendar with all your estate's important dates. Whether you choose to create the calendar on your computer or on paper, make sure to insert all your estate deadlines as soon as you become aware of them, and refer to your calendar daily to keep your administration on track.

When putting your calendar together, you can devise a system to remind you of deadlines or what task you need to attend to next, even if your system consists of reviewing your calendar on a daily basis. You may refer to Chapters 6 through 9 in creating your calendar, but, of course, your specific deadlines depend on your estate, whether it's going through probate, and the decedent's state of residence.

✔ **For probate/nonprobate administration:** List all the tasks to be done with regard to both the probate and the non-probate estate in chronological order, based on your situation and the assets of your decedent. You don't want to miss an important date; for instance, if you miss your deadline to prove to the probate court that you've notified all the beneficiaries, you may have to redo the entire notice procedure to each beneficiary, greatly increasing your time spent and delaying your appointment as executor. Refer to your calendar daily; make additions as you find out about new requirements, and bask in the glow of your accomplishments as you meet each deadline in a timely manner.

✔ **Calendar for tax deadlines:** Keeping track of the many tax deadlines is very important when you're an executor of an estate. Missing a tax deadline can mean that the estate is charged penalties and interest on any tax due. And because filing tax returns and making payments on time is your duty as executor, the probate court can hold you liable (and beneficiaries can sue you) if your oversight leads to a missed deadline.

You may want to create separate calendars for each type of tax: federal estate tax, state estate or inheritance tax, estate income tax, and the decedent's final income tax return. Or you can integrate all your types of taxes into one calendar. See Part IV for information regarding taxes.

# Setting up a filing system

An organized filing system for your estate and trust means the difference between order and chaos in your administration of the estate. You may choose to organize as much as you can electronically, but you still have to deal with plenty of actual paper in administering an estate. If you don't have a file that locks, get one and keep the estate paperwork (which is, after all, confidential) safely locked away when you're not working with it.

You can create a file (legal length files are best) for the estate with separate folders within the file for each topic. Some topics may require more space than others. As a folder grows, you may find you want an entirely separate file for it. Folders within the estate file may start out with titles such as "Correspondence and memos," which may contain all general correspondence and notes, in reverse date order, with the newest on top.

Always make a note of every phone call you make or receive and meeting you have relating to the estate and file it in the appropriate folder. Be sure to date the record and note the name of the person(s) you spoke with. You don't need to craft a lovely memo. Just be sure to note every point that's covered. This practice will prove invaluable when you're following up on any estate matter.

File folders for the estate administration file may include

- ✔ Correspondence and memos.
- ✔ Federal estate tax return (**Form 706**). This one can easily become an entirely separate file, with a separate folder for each schedule of the return.
- ✔ State inheritance (or estate) tax.
- ✔ Probate pleadings (just a fancy way of labeling all the probate court paperwork).
- ✔ Life insurance.
- ✔ Retirement benefits.
- ✔ Decedent's income tax returns.
- ✔ Estate income tax returns.
- ✔ Debts of the decedent and claims against the estate.
- ✔ Estate checking account.
- ✔ Estate assets.
- ✔ Any other topics that arise in your estate.

However you choose to organize your records, keep a separate record of the decedent's debts and an ongoing record of your payment of debts. We're firm believers in to-do lists. They help keep you focused on both what you have to do today, including the best order in which to accomplish it, and what you need to accomplish long term. For more good ideas on organizing your records, check out Chapter 14.

# Chapter 6

# Navigating the Probate Process

. . . . . . . . . . . . . . . . . . . . . . . . . . . . . . . . . . . . . . . . . . . . .

*In This Chapter*

▶ Submitting the will to the court

▶ Deciding whether and what kind of probate is necessary

▶ Having the executor or administrator appointed

▶ Considering the surviving spouse's necessary decisions

. . . . . . . . . . . . . . . . . . . . . . . . . . . . . . . . . . . . . . . . . . . . .

*T*he decedent has been laid to rest and you've handled the immediate tasks after the death. (Refer to Chapter 5 for what you need to do right after the decedent has died.) Now that you've had a moment to breath, you need to take the next steps in wrapping up the decedent's affairs. Now's the time (probably within a week after the decedent's funeral) to decide whether you need probate court administration of any of the decedent's assets, and if so, how to keep probate as simple as possible. *Probate* is the process whereby the decedent's will, if any, is proved valid or invalid and the assets in the decedent's name alone, or payable to the estate, are administered in the probate estate with probate court supervision.

This chapter explains how to get the decedent's will (if any) recognized by the probate court, and how to get yourself appointed as executor(s) (the decedent may name more than one executor to act together). We point out what happens if, for whatever reason, you're the person charged with administering the decedent's estate even though he or she didn't leave a will. We also discuss how to create the probate inventory. And if the decedent has a surviving spouse, that person may have some decisions to make. Last, we discuss how a beneficiary or heir can disclaim property.

Here are a couple things to keep in mind as you navigate the probate system in your state:

✔ Probate is a state, not a federal, concept, and applicable state law will govern. As more and more states recognize same-sex marriages performed either in their state or in other jurisdictions, the probate rules contained in this chapter will apply equally to same-sex and opposite-sex spouses.

✔ Throughout this chapter, we make reference to state law and probate court rules. No two states' laws are exactly the same, no two states' probate court rules are the same, and as a matter of fact, probate court practices can differ from county to county. And not all courts that administer wills are called "probate courts." So when we discuss the procedure for probating your decedent's property, you can pretty much count on some quirk in how your decedent's county and state handle probate administration that's different from the quirkiness we describe here.

✔ We refer, in general, to the *executor.* But if there's no valid will, you're the administrator. In some states you're called the *personal representative* or some other name, but we're still referring to the person appointed to administer the estate. And the term *fiduciary* refers to all the above. That's the beauty of individual state law!

# Filing the Last Will with the Probate (Or Equivalent) Court

In most states, the person who has possession of the will is required to deliver the will to the executor or file the will with the probate court within a certain period of time (for instance, 30 days) after the decedent's death. If you're in the delicate position of knowing who has the will but hasn't filed it, you may notify the court so that the court can compel the filing. Then the probate process can begin. In practice, you file the will with the petition for probate if you decide probate is required, hopefully within that 30-day window. Most courts give you some leeway, but make sure that you know if your probate court will. If it turns out there are no assets requiring probate, simply take the will to the probate court and sign a statement to that effect.

If the decedent left a will but the estate doesn't have any assets subject to probate, the law still requires you to file the will. Just inform the probate court that, to your knowledge, no assets are subject to probate. This situation can arise when

✔ The decedent has fully funded (that is, transferred all of his or her assets into) his or her revocable trust before death.

✔ The decedent held all of his or her assets jointly with rights of survivorship with the surviving spouse or other persons or had named payable on death recipients on all of his or her assets.

✔ The decedent died penniless (which makes your job much easier).

# *Figuring Out Whether Administration Is Necessary*

Before you can decide whether probate administration is necessary, you need to get an accurate picture of all the assets in the estate. Chapter 7 explains how to uncover every asset you possibly can. You need a good idea of both the value of the assets and how the title is held. Remember, anything held in the decedent's name alone, payable to the decedent's estate, or held jointly for convenience only (but where the decedent actually acquired the property by himself or herself) is subject to probate.

To help you make an accurate determination, this section takes you through the steps involved in determining whether and what kind of probate administration is necessary.

Probating the decedent's estate through the probate court system and taxing the decedent's estate for federal estate tax and state estate or inheritance tax purposes are two entirely different animals. Just because you're not dealing with a probate estate doesn't mean that it won't owe estate or inheritance tax. Tax law isn't based on how the property was held but rather on who actually owned the property at death, and in the case of state inheritance tax, who receives it. See Chapter 16 to determine whether your decedent's estate is subject to estate tax.

## *Do you need a temporary executor?*

As soon as you receive word of the decedent's death, take a look at the estate-planning documents and start compiling the asset information. If any assets subject to probate need immediate action (either to preserve them or their value or to manage them), you may need to apply to be a *temporary executor* (can be done only if the will permits) or temporary administrator with will annexed (which can be done at the discretion of the court) because your appointment as executor may sometimes take a few weeks — or more — to accomplish. Your appointment as temporary executor or temporary administrator can be accomplished much more quickly than your appointment as executor.

You typically accomplish temporary administration through a written motion to the court where you set out the reasons it's being sought and the powers you're requesting. Some courts may have a form of petition to present. In either case, you need to present it in person to the court, along with a certified copy of the death certificate, the original will if it hasn't already been filed, and any other documents required by the local court (check with an assistant probate register). If your request is granted, your powers will be limited to those sought in the motion and approved by the court, except as set out by state law (typically to collect the personal property of the decedent and preserve it for the executor). Some instances in which you may want to apply for temporary administration:

- **To preserve the value of stocks and bonds held by your decedent.** Because of the nature of the stock market, you may want to sell these assets quickly to avoid a decrease in value. (See Chapter 18 for how to calculate any capital gain or loss, which should be minimal.)

  Your duty as executor is to preserve the estate's assets for the beneficiaries, not to increase their value. So, for example, you may want to sell all the volatile securities and convert the holdings into more-stable assets to preserve the value of the estate for ultimate distribution to the beneficiaries. Remember, any income tax consequences from the sale of these assets are small because the tax basis has stepped up to the value on the decedent's date of death. And keep in mind that you don't get credit or thanks for any gains on assets during estate administration, but you can surely be held accountable for any losses! Check your local law on this issue with an attorney experienced in local probate.

- **To continue your decedent's business.**
- **To manage real property held by your decedent.**
- **To pay expenses of last illness, funeral expenses, and taxes.**
- **To gain access to the decedent's safe deposit box to look for the decedent's will, if your state doesn't provide an alternative means of entering the box.**
- **To bury the decedent.**

One of us had the experience of going to court to seek temporary administration in order to sell stocks and bonds to preserve the estate assets, and the judge she appeared before couldn't imagine why she'd want to sell all the securities. He agreed to the temporary administration for this purpose only after his assistant found the section of the probate law regarding the duty of the executor to preserve assets and showed it to the judge. Don't be too hard on the judge here. In many instances, you're dealing with the probate and family court (with the emphasis on family). In that case the courts see an overwhelming amount of family law (divorce, guardianship) compared to their experience with probate, and many of the judges are former family law attorneys. Many more-experienced judges are expert in probate law.

You may need to file an *executor's bond* (a written promise to faithfully carry out your duties as executor), and even the temporary administrator must file an inventory and an account. The temporary appointment ends when the executor under the will or administrator (no will) is appointed.

# Do you need a special administrator?

A special administrator can be appointed whether or not there's a will. A *special administrator* (or the equivalent) is a temporary fiduciary appointed by the court in many states to marshal and preserve the assets when a delay is foreseen in appointing a permanent fiduciary, perhaps due to a will contest or problems serving notice on interested parties.

## When there's a will

In the case of a will contest, any person having an interest in the estate can file a petition for special administration in the probate court, along with a certified copy of the death certificate. The petition should name exactly what powers are being requested. Without specific court authority, the power of a special administrator is quite limited. If all interested parties assent to the petition, it can be allowed without having to publish a legal notice in a local newspaper. But, even without assents, the judge may allow the petition. Although the named executor sometimes files the petition, in the case of a will contest there may be objections, in which case a disinterested third party may be appointed. The period of appointment can be quite brief, up to 90 days, except in unusual circumstances, in which case the court may make an appointment for an indefinite period.

Check with your local court to see if special administration or its equivalent is available in your jurisdiction, and for the specific local requirements.

## When there's no will

If the decedent died intestate, special administration, or its equivalent, is the only form of temporary administration available. Temporary administration may be sought because of a delay in giving notice to all the interested parties, or because of a dispute over who is to be appointed as permanent administrator. Special administration may be asked for to administer assets, or to open a safe deposit box, if there isn't another means to do so under local law. All relevant information from the preceding section applies here also. Again, check with your local court to see what type of special administration is available to you.

# Determining domicile

Knowing where the decedent's *domicile* (where the decedent had his or her primary residence) was at date of death is key when figuring out where you must probate the assets and what state you must pay taxes to (although real estate is subject to state estate or inheritance tax, if any, in the state in which it's located). All real estate in the decedent's state of domicile and all other tangible and intangible assets located anywhere in the United States are subject to probate in the decedent's state of domicile if all other requirements for probate are met. Only after you've made that determination can you begin primary probate in the correct court and ancillary administration in any other state where the decedent owned property. (Check out the next section for more on ancillary administration.)

It may seem odd to even question where the decedent lived at the time of death, but often the decedent's official home may not have been where you thought it was and so much of estate administration rests on the decedent's legal home.

In many instances, determining domicile is as easy as can be. Uncle Jim was born on the farm, worked on the farm, and you buried him from the farm (and maybe on the farm, as one of us can bear witness to) after he died. The farm was, without question, his domicile. But in many cases, people own real property in more than one place, and even more than one state (or country), and they pay taxes in more than one state at any given time. If you're responsible for administering an estate that owns real estate located in multiple places, how do you know where to initiate probate?

The list of items used to determine domicile is long, and far from absolute. Certain items on the list may indicate one legal home, but others may show a different one. You have to make the final determination based on the weight of the evidence. Be prepared to back up your results to the state(s) that loses; for the states in question, large potential tax revenues may lie in the balance.

Evidence used to determine domicile includes the following:

- ✔ **Address of residence where the decedent lived more than 50 percent of the time.**
- ✔ **Place of religious affiliations.** Evidence of memberships in churches, synagogues, or mosques can be crucial.
- ✔ **Car registration.** People rarely register their cars in a state where they only live part time.
- ✔ **Voter registration.** You often have to show proof of residence in order to register to vote.
- ✔ **Address shown on passport.** Of course, passport addresses aren't updated when you move, but if the address matches the domicile you want to establish, so much the better.
- ✔ **Bank accounts established in local banks.** Although with the rise of interstate and Internet banking, this isn't as stellar a form of evidence as it once was.

Declarations of homestead are required in some states to protect your primary residence from creditors or to give you a lower tax rate, and if you find one attached to a tax return or stashed away in a file somewhere, it can go a long way toward supporting your argument that the decedent was domiciled in a particular state.

## Is a guardian necessary?

In some cases, the court appoints a guardian to take care of a person's affairs. We're focusing our discussion on the case where a guardian is needed because the decedent has died and the heir (usually a minor child or an otherwise legally incapacitated person) needs a guardian because he or she stands to inherit from the estate.

When the parent of a minor dies, if the parent had a will, typically he or she names the surviving spouse (or in the case of divorce, the child's other parent) as guardian, or if there is none, some other person or persons (sometimes a husband and wife). Occasionally a parent will designate one person or couple as guardian(s) of the person of his or her minor child, and another person as guardian of the property. This is likely to happen if the decedent feels that one person or couple is ideal to raise the children, but not the best person(s) to manage the child's assets.

If no guardian is named in the will, or if there is no will, the court will choose the guardian, taking into account the best interests of the child. It is always best for all involved if the decedent names a guardian in a will, as the probate judge will try to honor the decedent's wishes if at all possible. In many states, judges must follow the stated wishes in the will; in others, the judge makes the final determination based on a number of factors, of which the stated wishes of the decedent are only one.

If the decedent didn't name a guardian and there is no surviving spouse (think common accident or natural disaster, so neither parent survives), it is quite common for several relatives to come forward requesting to be appointed guardian, each claiming that he or she is the best person to take care of the minor child or children. In that case, the judge will take input from all sides and make a decision based on the child's best interests, and, if possible, taking into account the preference of the child.

## *Accessing ancillary administration*

If every decedent had only one residence or owned real estate in only one state, your life as executor would be much easier. But that's often not the case. When you're administering an estate with real estate located in a state other than the decedent's state of domicile, you have to have *ancillary* (that is, not the primary) administration in that state, but only with regard to that real property. *Ancillary administration* is an additional probate procedure in a state other than that in which the decedent was domiciled.

You usually only need to have ancillary administration if the decedent held real estate that's subject to probate (if held in decedent's name alone or as tenant in common) in another state. In that state the will is referred to as a *foreign will*, and you're a *foreign executor*. As such, you may need to appoint an agent who is a resident of that state for *service of process* (the procedure used to give legal notice). You provide the foreign court with an authenticated (by the probate court in the decedent's primary domicile) copy of your appointment as executor and of your bond, and follow that court's procedures for distribution or sale, whichever you need to accomplish, of the real estate.

All other tangible and intangible assets, whether located in the state where the decedent resided most of the year, in another state (or even country) where the decedent lived part of the year, or even in a third, nonrelated state, are subject to probate in the decedent's state of domicile.

So for example, if your decedent lived in Massachusetts but had bank accounts in Florida, the Florida bank would recognize your authority as executor appointed in Massachusetts, and deliver the contents of those accounts in accordance with your instructions.

# Deciding What Shape Your Probate Procedure Should Take

After you determine that the estate includes probate assets, you have to decide whether you want to embark on the full administration process or a special, informal form of administration. If your decedent's state of domicile (or any other state where administration required) has enacted some or all of the Uniform Probate Code, you may elect to use supervised or unsupervised administration. The procedural choices for administration and their names vary by state, as do the steps you take under the different kinds of administration. If you're lucky, your local probate court may even have checklists of what steps to take in the probate process under the different kinds of probate administration in your jurisdiction. What follows is a discussion of various procedures that may be available in a state that has enacted the Uniform Probate Code.

Don't be intimidated. Your state statutes and probate (or equivalent) court rules spell out the steps needed to probate the decedent's will in your state. But be warned that although the probate court registers and other court employees can be very helpful, if they feel that you're trying to use court staff to help you tackle a task that requires a probate attorney, their patience may wear thin. If you're administering an extensive estate, make sure that you consult an attorney who specializes in estates. Even if you use an attorney, you want to understand what's going on in the probate process, so read on.

For all probate court forms, check with your local probate court for their version. Better yet, check out your local probate court or your state court system online. There's a good chance they have posted those forms for you to download at your leisure.

## The Uniform Probate Code

The Uniform Probate Code (UPC) is a set of uniform law provisions drafted by a committee of the National Conference of Commissioners on Uniform State Laws. It's intended as a model for the various states to use in updating and reforming their own probate laws. State probate laws have historically varied widely (and we do mean widely); as states adopt the UPC, transactions between states and among citizens of different states flow more freely. The UPC is also helpful to individual states as they work to modernize their probate laws that may have become outdated. A number of states have enacted the UPC in large part (19 at last count) and many more states have enacted parts of it. Oh well, different versions of probate have only been around since the time of the Romans — it would be too much to ask for it to change uniformly and quickly.

# *Taking small estate shortcuts*

If your decedent's probate estate (assets in his or her name alone, payable to the estate, or held jointly for convenience only) is of limited size, it may qualify for one of several small estate procedures, whether or not your decedent left a will. These streamlined procedures can save you time and the estate money.

Small estate administration can be quick and reasonably painless if you're eligible to use it and using it makes sense. One of us probated her grandmother's Last Will from soup to nuts in one day by using a small estate administration procedure. It was a marathon, running from attorney to court to family members for signatures and back to court, but it only took one day. By comparison, had traditional probate been required, the entire probate process would have taken more than a year to complete.

### *Small estate procedures with some allowances taken into account*

Just about every state has some form of small estate procedure. Some of the typical small-estate procedures that may be available in your state (check with your local probate court) include the following (and don't be afraid to try to use more than one if it means that you can avoid a more lengthy probate procedure):

- **Wages and fringe benefits:** Under this type of statute, if the only assets of the estate are wages and fringe benefits from the decedent's employer, those assets are paid over to certain people as set out in the statute; for instance, the surviving spouse, children, parents, and so on, in that order, without the necessity of probate.

✔ **Automobile:** Just about every state has a statute providing for the transfer of the decedent's automobile to the heirs if there are no other assets subject to probate and the car doesn't exceed a certain value (currently $60,000 in Michigan).

✔ **Cash and wearing apparel:** In Michigan, a hospital, convalescent or nursing home, morgue, or law enforcement agency holding $500 or less and wearing apparel can deliver the same to the decedent's spouse, child, or parent. Check your state for a similar statute.

✔ **Dollar amount small estate procedures in probate court or by affidavit:** Most states have provisions for small estate procedures. The dollar amounts that qualify vary by state, but in every case, the procedure is vastly shorter and more simplified than for larger estates. For instance, in Michigan, if the decedent's gross estate after payment of funeral and burial expenses is $21,000 or less in 2012 (indexed for future years):

   • **In probate court:** The court may order that it be turned over to the surviving spouse, or, if none, to the decedent's heirs as defined by statute. To accomplish this, a Petition and Order for Assignment is filed with the probate court.

   • **By affidavit**: If there is no real estate in the probate estate, an affidavit procedure (used in a number of states) may be used instead. Under the affidavit procedure in Michigan, beginning 28 days after the decedent's death, a person possessing the decedent's property must deliver that property to a person claiming to be the decedent's successor upon being presented with a death certificate and an Affidavit of Decedent's Successor for Delivery of Certain Assets Owned by Decedent (a form obtainable from the probate court). The recipient of the property is subject to certain limitations and liabilities as set out in the statute.

### Small estate procedures with all allowances taken into account (summary administration)

Under this type of procedure, the personal representative, without giving notice to creditors, may immediately disburse and distribute the estate and may file a closing statement if it appears from the estate inventory and appraisal that the value of the entire estate, less liens and encumbrances, does not exceed:

✔ Administration costs and expenses

✔ Reasonable funeral and burial expenses

✔ Homestead allowance

✔ Family allowance

✔ Exempt tangible personal property allowance (in other words, all allowances under that state's probate laws — a total of $60,000 in Michigan in 2012, as discussed more fully later in this chapter.)

> ✔ Reasonable, necessary medical and hospital expenses of the decedent's last illness

In this case, the estate would have been started with a traditional estate administration procedure (described in "Traveling the traditional probate route"), but after it's determined that the estate qualifies for this small estate procedure (summary administration), the personal representative simply distributes the assets to the people entitled to the estate and files a closing statement instead of continuing with the formalities of full probate administration.

## Traveling the traditional probate route

In many states, traditional probate proceedings can be supervised or unsupervised, and unsupervised can be formal or informal. Consult with an attorney experienced in probate matters in your state if there is any question as to what form your probate should take.

### Unsupervised informal probate

Use unsupervised informal probate, or a similar proceeding in your state, if you don't feel the need for any extra intervention or supervision by the court at the beginning of your estate administration. There's no question that it's a timesaver, as there's no prior notice to interested persons before the will is admitted to probate and your appointment as executor. But be very sure that you have no estate issues, such as a will contest or other area of controversy, such as the decedent's domicile, determination of the decedent's heirs, or your appointment as executor (or administrator, if there is no will).

You can always ask the court to rule on specific matters later, and you probably (depending on your jurisdiction) can start with unsupervised informal or formal probate and switch to supervised probate down the road if you find it appropriate.

Consult your local probate court for the necessary forms and procedures to begin unsupervised informal probate. Here are some typical steps:

1. **File an Application for Informal Probate and Appointment of Executor (or Administrator) with the probate court along with:**

    (i) A sworn Testimony Form to Identify Heirs and, if there is a will, a sworn Supplemental Testimony Form to Identify Nonheir Devisees

    (ii) The will if there is one, and any *codicils* (supplements or additions to the will)

    (iii) A certified copy of the death certificate

    If there is anyone with a higher priority to serve as executor or administrator, you'll have to serve them with notice and file proof of service, unless you have renunciations from those persons, in which case you file those with the court. If the Probate Register sees no problems, the will is admitted to probate and you're appointed as executor, typically without having to give notice to all the interested persons (heirs-at-law and devisees under the will) or obtain waivers and consents from them.

Determining who the heirs are and who receives notice under what circumstances is the stuff of which charts are made for probate attorneys, so don't hesitate to turn to the court or your probate attorney to make sure that everyone receives notice who should. Should you give notice and inadvertently miss someone who was required to receive it, you may have to begin the entire notice procedure again.

If you're not a resident of the same state as the one where you're initiating probate, you need to check with the court to see whether you're allowed to act. Frequently, you'll be allowed to do so if you appoint a resident agent in the state of domicile before you become executor. The purpose of the agent is to be an in-state presence to receive service of process on your behalf, if necessary (think disgruntled beneficiary suing executor; not that that would ever happen to you). By the way, even though we are addressing you as executor, keep in mind that federally chartered national banks, in-state banks, and in-state trust companies can also act as executors, as can foreign (out-of-state) banks or trust companies, under certain circumstances

2. **Upon your appointment: Provide the court with**

   (i) Your proposed Letters of Appointment or Letters Testamentary for signature by an official of the court (be sure to order plenty of certified copies of the letters — they're proof that you're the executor, and you'll need them to open bank and brokerage accounts and transfer assets such as stocks and bonds and the like into your name as executor, or into new accounts in your name as executor)

   (ii) In certain situations, you'll need a Fiduciary Bond (your written pledge to guarantee your performance as executor). Whether or not you need a bond and a surety (a company that the estate pays to guarantee your bond) on the bond will depend both on state practice and on what your decedent requested in the will

   (iii) Your signed Acceptance of Appointment

   (iv) Any other requirements of your jurisdiction

3. **Serve a Notice of Appointment and Duties of Personal Representative.** Serve the notice on the heirs and devisees within 14 days of appointment, including the statement that the court won't be supervising you as executor.

4. **Send out a notice regarding attorney fees.** Whenever you retain an attorney for the estate, whether now or later in the estate proceedings, you'll want to enter into a written fee agreement and you may need to send a notice regarding any attorney fees to the interested parties.

5. **Send out a Notice of Continued Administration.** Keep in mind that, if your estate runs for more than a year, you may need to file, on a yearly basis, some kind of notice of continued administration with the court, and serve it on all the interested parties.

In some states, in certain circumstances, a *holographic* (handwritten) will is admissible. Be aware, though, that holographic wills may appear out of the blue after death from an unanticipated source and are sometimes forgeries. One of us administered an estate that had a will contest that dragged on for years, with one of the wills in question being a holographic will that the decedent had never even signed. The fact that everyone involved suspected that the will was fraudulent didn't stop it from mucking up the works on what was already a complex situation.

## Unsupervised formal probate

Use unsupervised formal proceedings if you think there may be any problems with the administration of the estate, including the validity of the will, if any, the decedent's domicile, who the decedent's heirs are, or appointment of the executor or administrator. In unsupervised formal probate, proceedings are conducted before a judge with notice to the interested parties.

Check with your local probate court for the necessary forms and procedures to begin unsupervised formal probate. We set out some typical steps here:

1. **File a petition** for probate of the will, or to set aside or prevent a will's informal probate, or for an order that the decedent died *intestate* (with no will), along with a sworn Testimony to Identify Heirs form and, if there is a will, a sworn Testimony to Identify Non-heir Devisees form. Be sure to provide the court with the original will and any codicils and a certified copy of the death certificate.

2. **Provide notice of hearing or waivers and consents:** You must then obtain a hearing date and provide a Notice of Hearing to all the interested persons either by certified mail or in person, or publish the notice in accordance with the statute, *unless* you are able to obtain waivers and consents from all the interested parties. If you obtain waivers and consents from everyone, you won't need to have a hearing or give notice. The interested parties can include

   • Heirs-at-law (those who inherit by statute in your state if the decedent left no will) and next of kin (nearest blood relatives, as defined by state law), but not beneficiaries under the will (they have no standing until the will is allowed).

   • The state attorney general if there are no heirs-at-law or if there are any charitable bequests in the will.

   • If the decedent's surviving spouse is incompetent and isn't represented by someone other than you as executor, *a guardian ad litem* (a special guardian appointed by the court) on his or her behalf needs to be a party to the petition.

- If a *pretermitted heir* — a child or descendants of a deceased child not provided for in the will (unless the omission was clearly intentional) is under a disability, such as being a minor, a guardian ad litem is required.

3. **Refer to Steps 2, 3, 4, and 5 under "Unsupervised informal probate."**

### Supervised formal probate

Supervised formal probate is rarely used and only available in limited situations. Whether it is used depends upon whether the decedent's will, if any, provides that it may or may not be used and upon the circumstances of the decedent's estate. If there might be a will contest, if the beneficiaries have conflicting interests, or if an estate is insolvent, there may be reason to request supervised formal probate, or the court may order it. It's a more time-consuming procedure, so neither you nor the court want it if it's unnecessary.

---

## Be ready in case someone ever contests the will

Just because the decedent's will names you as executor doesn't mean that the court will appoint you to act. Any of the people you've given notice to or anyone else who feels that the will isn't valid can object to its allowance, although these *will contests* aren't an everyday occurrence.

The bases on which a will may be deemed invalid include the following:

- If the decedent wasn't mentally competent or of sound mind (having *testamentary capacity,* or the ability to know and understand the will's contents or that he or she was even making a will in the first place) during the signing of the will.

- The decedent made the will in accordance with another's wishes rather than his or her own, officially known as *acting under undue influence from another.*

- The decedent's signature is shown to be a forgery.

- Evidence of a later will replacing the will in question.

- The will wasn't executed (signed and witnessed) in accordance with state law.

If you're the executor of a will that gets contested, consult an attorney with experience in will contests. Sometimes the attorney who drafted the will is best suited to defend it because he or she is most familiar with the decedent's wishes, state of mind, and the circumstances of its execution. In any event, let the attorney handle the will contest, keeping close tabs, of course, on its progress, and carry on with the estate administration after it has been settled (assuming you're still executor!). If there are pressing issues that can't wait, such as the administration of estate assets and the filing of tax returns (a will contest can drag on a long time), be sure that the court has appointed a suitable person (it may not be you, because the will is being contested) as special administrator.

Consult your local probate court for the necessary forms and procedures to begin supervised formal probate. What follow are some typical steps:

1. **File a petition for probate and its attendant documents, just as with unsupervised administration.** However, you must also say why you need supervised administration and request it on the petition.

2. **Send out a notice of hearing or waivers and consents.** Proceed just as with unsupervised formal probate.

3. **Refer to Steps 2, 3, 4, and 5 under "Unsupervised informal probate," except that the Notice of Appointment and Duties of Personal Representative won't say that the court will not supervise you as executor.**

Under supervised probate, you can't make distributions of estate assets without a court order. Other differences between supervised and unsupervised administration have to do with the number of documents you file with the court during the administration of the estate (including the number of hoops you must jump through) and the manner in which you close the estate (see Chapter 9).

# Taking Important First Steps after Your Appointment

After you've been appointed as executor, there are some important first steps every executor should take.

✔ **Adding the executor to insurance policy endorsements:**

- *Homeowner's and other real property insurance* — Add your name as executor to any policies of insurance on the decedent's real estate (and if the decedent's home is unoccupied, let the insurance company know in case a special rider is needed. Consider adding a security system if there is none and it is warranted, and see if there are any items of unusual value that must be secured). In one estate we are familiar with, the decedent hadn't insured his extensive art collection because it would have been too costly, and he had no home security system in place when he died. The executors immediately secured the art, and it eventually became a major part of a museum's collection. Also consider changing the locks on the decedent's residence if there is no surviving spouse and you aren't absolutely sure that you have collected every spare key that was ever handed out.

- *Automobile insurance* — If someone will be driving the decedent's car before the title officially transfers to them, inform the auto insurance company right away.

✔ **Obtaining a federal taxpayer identification number:** As soon as you are appointed as executor, you need to apply for a federal taxpayer identification number (also known as a TIN or EIN) for the estate. It serves the same function as a Social Security number does for an individual, and you absolutely need one before you can open any estate bank or brokerage accounts or transfer any assets to the name of the executor or the estate. You also will need it to file the estate's income tax returns. Check out Chapter 18 to find what you need to do in order to obtain this number.

✔ **Projecting your cash flow:** As you gather information about the estate assets and liabilities (see Chapter 7), make a projection of

- The liquid assets, such as the decedent's cash on hand (literally) at death, bank accounts, and final paycheck

- Anticipated payments to the estate, such as life insurance, CDs coming due, and dividends and interest payments

- Debts of the decedent and anticipated expenses of administration, such as taxes and fees

Your projection will necessarily be just that, a projection, but it will be an important means for you to keep a handle on your cash needs as the estate itself flows along. Don't forget, if the decedent had a funded revocable trust before death, it is now an important source of funds for the estate. The trust most likely contains a provision enabling the trustee to provide funds to the estate for debts of the decedent and administration expenses, such as taxes and fees.

# Eyeing the Surviving Spouse's Rights and Decisions Regarding Property

Surviving spouses may have some important rights to collect on and decisions to make with regard to the will and the decedent's estate. This section highlights a few important rights, allowances, and decisions the surviving husband or wife needs to make when the decedent has died and probate has begun. Your duty as executor is to inform the surviving spouse of these rights as soon as possible after the death of the decedent.

# Exercising rights ahead of the provisions of the will

In just about every state the surviving spouse, (and sometimes the decedent's children) has rights to certain property whether or not there is a will, and no matter what the will says. These rights come ahead of the provisions of the will for disposition of the property. Check with your probate court if your decedent leaves a surviving spouse and/or children. For instance, in Michigan, the surviving spouse is entitled to the following, all indexed for inflation:

- ✔ **Homestead Allowance:** The surviving spouse receives a homestead allowance of $21,000 as of 2012. If there's no surviving spouse, the $21,000 is divided equally among the minor children and each dependent child.

- ✔ **Family Allowance:** A "reasonable amount" can be paid to the surviving spouse for the benefit of the spouse and the minor and dependent children each year the estate is in existence (limited to one year if the estate is inadequate to discharge allowed claims), as a family allowance. While no amount is set in the law, it can be up to $25,000 per year as of 2012.

- ✔ **Exempt Property:** The surviving spouse is entitled to exempt property in the amount of $14,000 as of 2012, including household furniture and furnishings, appliances, personal effects, and automobiles. If there is no surviving spouse, the decedent's children are entitled to this property.

# Electing against the will

The surviving spouse has the right to *elect to take against the will.* In other words, instead of receiving what the decedent left to him or her as a beneficiary under the will, he or she may choose to receive instead what that surviving spouse is entitled to under state law; his or her *statutory share.* The statutory share isn't the same as the *intestate share* (what the surviving spouse would have received had the decedent left no will).

Because you, as executor, represent the estate and not the surviving spouse, you should not advise the spouse on whether to accept the will's bequest or to take the statutory share. However, be sure that the surviving spouse is aware of this right. In some jurisdictions, you are required to provide a form of Notice to Surviving Spouse of Elections and Allowances and file it, along with a proof of service and the spouse's election, with the court.

In some jurisdictions, a spouse electing against the will just has to file a document waiving his or her share under the will and claiming the statutory share within a set period after the allowance of the will. Electing to take against the will is an all-or-nothing proposition; the surviving spouse can't cherry-pick, accepting some provisions, but not all. If the decedent and the surviving spouse prepared their estate plan documents together and were in agreement on their plans, such an election is unlikely.

Electing to take against the will has many consequences, some of which may not be readily apparent. For example, if the decedent exercised a *power of appointment* (which we explain in Chapter 17) in the will over a trust in favor of the surviving spouse and the spouse elects against the will, the spouse also loses the property subject to the power of appointment. The estate tax consequences of a waiver should also be kept in mind (the marital deduction will be affected), as should the fees and expenses involved in dealing with the waiver and its results.

## Claiming dower

*Statutory dower* (governed by legislated law) exists in many states to replace *common law dower* (governed by customary law) and *curtesy. Dower* is the right of a surviving spouse to an estate for life in a portion of the property owned by the decedent at death, subject to any encumbrances on the property. ***Translation:*** The surviving spouse gets the use of, for instance, one-third of the real estate for life. Depending on what the real estate is, that use can be, for instance, to live in one-third, or collect one-third of the rents, or receive one-third of the profits from the crops grown on it. Although dower originally only applied to widows, it now applies to widowers as well, because common law *curtesy* (the right of the widower to the use of all the wife's real estate for life) has generally been abolished.

To claim dower, the surviving spouse files a claim in the probate court within a fixed period after death. If dower is claimed, the surviving spouse must also waive the will (if applicable) and take his or her statutory share. Few spouses actually find it beneficial to claim dower because they've planned their wills together and don't have a reason to take against the will, and dower is a clumsy means of inheritance. Someone may choose this option if his or her deceased spouse didn't include them in his or her estate plan.

# Chapter 7

# Marshalling and Liquidating Assets

## In This Chapter

▶ Figuring out what the decedent owned

▶ Taking stock of the big-ticket possessions and other assets

▶ Keeping tabs on the household items and getting property appraised

▶ Checking for employee benefits, insurance policies, and miscellaneous death benefits

▶ Taking a probate inventory and selling what needs to be sold

*M*arshalling the assets brings to mind wonderful pictures of bank accounts, cars, houses, and the beautiful barometer on the wall all standing in an orderly line, just waiting for you to acknowledge and count them. As the executor of an estate, your first job is to *marshal* the assets — to determine what exactly the *decedent* owned on the day that he or she died. In this chapter, we discuss step by step the best ways to search for each type of asset. Your ease in finding all the assets depends, to some degree, on how well you knew the decedent (for the more obvious assets) and on the decedent's state of mind at the time of death. Someone who suffered from Alzheimer's disease or another form of dementia may well have done unusual things with his or her assets or asset records (including disposing of them).

As you figure out what the decedent owned, you also come across what the decedent owed. Debts of the decedent or claims against the estate come to light in several ways. You may find record of them in the decedent's papers, receive bills in the decedent's mail, or hear from a creditor as a result of notifying creditors as your local probate court requires (typically by publishing such a notice in a local paper). You may even get a knock on the door or hear from a friend or relative from whom the decedent borrowed money. See Chapter 8 for details on paying creditors.

# Understanding Why You Need to Determine What the Decedent Owned

Most decedents won't have had the foresight to leave you an *inventory*, or list, of their assets with a helpful notation of where each asset is located. One of our aunts (who lived to be 101) made a hobby of it, but in our experience, she's the exception. More common are decedents who not only didn't plan but also couldn't possibly have told you everything they owned. Still, in order for you to carry out their wishes and fulfill the requirements of the probate court, your job is to look under the sofa cushions, check under the floorboards, and behind not only Door Number One but also Doors Number Two and Three in order to find everything owned by the decedent on the date of his or her death.

Whether you're handed a helpful list or need to start excavating on your own, your starting point in organizing an estate and planning its administration is to locate and list all the decedent's assets. From this inventory, you're able to determine whether probate of the decedent's estate is necessary (depending on whether or not the decedent owned property in his or her name alone). If the total value of the probate assets is small enough, or if your state allows for informal probate for all estates, you may be able to do a simplified version of the probate process. Otherwise, you'll have to go through full probate. Not to worry though, the probate process itself isn't really so bad. We guide you through the entire process in Chapter 6.

So if you're wondering about what some of the items in this chapter are and why you need to include them in your list of estate assets, don't worry. Although some of these items may be unfamiliar to you, we have you covered. They all appear on **Form 706, United States Estate (and Generation-Skipping Transfer) Tax Return**, which we describe more completely in Chapters 16 and 17. But see Chapter 16 to determine if you even have to file a **Form 706,** as the exemptions from estate tax are sizeable.

As you create your list, be sure to note who actually owns each asset. For instance, an asset may be held in the individual name of the decedent, jointly with one or more other people, in trust, or in partnership. You need to know this to decide whether the asset must be probated (if in decedent's name alone, held as a tenant in common, or jointly for convenience only). See "Preparing and Filing the Probate Inventory" for more info.

# Observing the Obvious: Big-Ticket Items

When you list the assets, the big-ticket items are probably one of the easier places to begin. Some assets, such as the decedent's home, are so obvious that they present themselves to you on a silver platter, so to speak. The following sections identify these bigger items and tell you how to handle them.

## The bricks and mortar: Real estate

When you think of an estate, the first picture that pops into your mind may be a home. However, regardless of whether the decedent owned a big home, a smaller condo, or a vacation home in Bora Bora, you need to locate *all* the real estate.

To find all real estate the decedent owned at death, look to where he or she was living. Look for deeds, tax bills, mortgage statements, and insurance policies that refer to the residence and show who exactly owned it — the decedent alone, jointly (with a spouse, a child, or some other person), or in trust or nominee partnership. In each case, locating the deed is crucial because it shows who owned the real estate.

If the deed is in the decedent's name alone, the property is part of the probate estate (even though in Massachusetts, at least, the title to the property vests in the heirs immediately upon the death of the decedent (subject to the claims of creditors, estate taxes, and the like).

---

### Dealing with a limited liability company (LLC)

One of the most common forms a small business takes is that of a limited liability company, or an LLC. LLCs are recognized in all 50 states, and provide the owner of the business a curtain of liability protection between the owner personally and the business. With an LLC in place, if the business is sued, the plaintiff (the person suing) will have a difficult time shifting the responsibility, and the liability, to the person of the owner.

LLCs coming in several flavors: single entity LLCs, LLCs treated as partnerships, and LLCs treated as S corporations. Remember, the terms *sole proprietorship, partnership*, and *S corporation* are tax entities governed by the Internal Revenue Code; LLCs are legal entities governed by applicable state law.

If you discover that the ownership interest in a business is in the name of an LLC, you'll probably want to keep that designation intact, at least until you decide what you're going to do about the business. Check with a competent small business attorney to be certain that all your corporate and tax filings are kept up-to-date.

---

# *Things that move: Cars, boats, and cycles*

Cars, boats, motorcycles, and other vehicles may be sitting quietly in the decedent's driveway or at the dock, making them easy to locate. In that case, putting your hands on the registration and insurance documents helps you determine whether the decedent owned them in whole or in part. In some states, title to the car passes automatically to any surviving spouse (unless the decedent disposed of the car otherwise in his or her will), thus avoiding the need to probate the vehicle and giving the surviving spouse quick access to a car he or she may need to use.

However, the car still needs to be reregistered in the surviving spouse's name, and the automobile insurance must be changed to reflect the new owner. Check with your state's Department of Motor Vehicles, Registry of Motor Vehicles, or the equivalent agency to determine the procedure in your state.

# *Small (and closely held) businesses*

If the decedent was the owner, in full or part, of a small business, your job as executor is not only to value the business as of the date of death but also to figure out whether to continue the business or sell it now that the owner has died. You need to know how the business is set up before you can decide what to do with it. Businesses may be set up in the following ways:

- ✔ **Sole proprietorship:** The most common form of small business ownership, the *sole proprietorship,* is an unincorporated organization that is accounted for entirely on **Schedule C** of the decedent's **Form 1040.** The company may do business under a name other than the taxpayer's (sometimes referred to as a doing business as [d/b/a]), and it may be organized as a limited liability company (LLC). It may even have its own Employer Identification Number (EIN); see Chapter 18. If the decedent's business is reported on **Schedule C** of the **1040,** you're dealing with a sole proprietorship or an LLC where the decedent owned the entire business, and you need to value it as such.

- ✔ **Partnership:** If the decedent held a partial interest in a business, the business may have been formed as a partnership. Once again, the best way to find exactly how the business was organized, and how it's currently operating, is to locate the decedent's tax returns and look for the partnership entry on **Schedule E.** A decedent's tax return is the road map to determine what businesses the deceased had ownership interest in. After you determine that the deceased had a partnership interest, you can then get a copy of the most recent partnership tax return (**Form 1065**), which tells you not only what percentage of the partnership the decedent owned but also exactly how the decedent held title in that property. If the partners had a formal partnership agreement, it may include a provision for the surviving partner(s) to buy out the decedent's partnership interest, including a formula for setting the buyout price. Or they may have a separate buy-sell agreement. In the case of a sale, your job is to obtain the best price possible, unless the price was set by a previous agreement. This price sets the value for estate tax purposes if it reflects the fair market value of the partnership interest. The partnership may dissolve upon a partner's death if the agreement doesn't contain a provision to the contrary.

✔ **Subchapter S corporation:** These types of businesses are very popular because only the shareholders pay income taxes on profits instead of paying tax first at the corporate level and then again when the profits are paid out as dividends. Your decedent's most recent income tax returns should tell you whether he or she was an S corporation shareholder; you can make certain by reviewing the corporation's income tax return **(Form 1120S)**.

Because you can transfer S corporation shares only to an individual or to a qualifying trust (see Chapter 3 for which trusts qualify), you need to tread carefully when dealing with these shares. Selling or otherwise transferring shares to a nonqualified shareholder can cause the corporation to lose its S status. Because you can't change the terms of any trusts created by the decedent to make them qualifying trusts, be alert for this pitfall. The shares of stock that the decedent owned in the Subchapter S corporation require valuation by an expert unless a buy-sell agreement is in place that fixes the formula or purchase price of the decedent's stock by the remaining stockholders on his or her death. For the estate's purposes, that price or formula is fair market value.

✔ **Closely held C corporation:** If the decedent owned stock in a non-publicly traded company, and it's not an S corporation, you're looking at a closely held (or privately held) C corporation. With a C corporation, you don't have any income tax concerns about who may inherit the stock. As with other privately held businesses, the corporation may have a buy-sell agreement that sets the price at which the other stockholders may buy the C corporation stock. This agreement sets the stock's value for estate tax purposes, if the IRS considers the price fair market value.

# Tracking Down All the Other Assets

You don't need to be a detective to find all the decedent's assets, but an inquisitive mind and a good imagination often help. Family knowledge or lore about what the decedent owned can be handy. For example, in one estate we're familiar with, the family was well aware of the decedent's collection of valuable jewelry. After she died, however, the jewelry was nowhere to be found — that is, until an estate administrator, on the second or third search of the home, touched a loose board in a closet wall and found it. Consider this section your Sherlock Holmes 101, where we provide you some tips on sleuthing and uncovering all the assets.

## *Reading the mail*

Despite everything your mother told you about how rude reading someone else's mail is, this is one time when it's not only permissible, it's also admirable. As you read the decedent's mail, you may find references to many assets, including bank accounts (from bank statements), the safe deposit box (from any rental bills), real estate (from real estate tax and insurance bills), stocks and bonds (from dividend and interest checks, brokerage statements, mutual fund statements, retirement account statements), and correspondence regarding other assets.

Checking the mail isn't just a great way to figure out what the decedent owned; it also works well for eliminating items that may have been on your preliminary list but no longer exist (perhaps the decedent had told you or a family member about something years ago). More than one administrator has been surprised to find that longtime family heirlooms now belong to someone else. The following sections describe two types of mail you especially want to focus on.

### Bank statements

Make no mistake about it: Bank statements contain a wealth of information. Not only do they give you account numbers and at least an idea of how much value the accounts contain, but they also let you know how the decedent held title to the accounts. He or she may have owned it outright (in his or her name alone), with another person, or even through a trust. Although his or her recollections while alive may be a bit sketchy, your task is much easier after you have your hands on at least one statement from each account. Armed with a copy of your appointment by the probate court as executor (see Chapter 6), you have no difficulty in obtaining the most current statements, as well as any prior statements you need.

If you manage to uncover the bank statements for the checking account, you've hit pay dirt! Our experience is that, especially as our clients and family age, their once-pristine check registers become, well, less pristine, and determining what their typical monthly bills look like is often difficult. With the checking account bank statements in hand, figuring out who's been paid, for what period, and who's still waiting (often very patiently!) is easier. As banking has become more and more deregulated, many people are paying their monthly bills by using an account with a mutual fund company or an investment firm; these statements may also be a rich source of information.

Banks issue statements periodically (usually monthly, but sometimes quarterly) and not always on the last day of a month. In your initial search for assets, you want to find the one dated most closely to the date of death to give you a general idea of the value in the account on the date of death. As soon as you know the asset exists, contact the bank directly in order to get an exact balance, including any accrued interest, as of the date of death (you need the balance with interest for both the probate inventory (see "Preparing and Filing the Probate Inventory") and the **Form 706**. And don't forget the online bank accounts and accounts for which the decedent had elected not to receive paper statements! (Check out the "Sleuthing for digital assets and info" section to find out more.)

If you're not sure whether you've found all the bank accounts, write a letter to each local bank (and each bank in any city where the decedent has a vacation home) inquiring whether it houses any accounts (or safe deposit boxes) in which the decedent had an interest. You should get full cooperation if you include a certified copy of your appointment as executor.

### Brokerage statements

As good as finding the bank statements feels, finding the brokerage statements feels even better. In most estates that contain any valuable property outside of real estate, brokerage accounts are where you find most of it. Identifying where those accounts are, and in whose names they're registered, takes you a long way toward compiling a complete list of what the decedent owned. Don't forget the online brokerage accounts and those for which the decedent elected not to receive paper statements, either!

Brokerage statements typically give you the market value of the individual securities on the statement date. Because determining the general size of the entire estate relatively quickly is important (you need this information to figure out whether you have to do a full probate or not), find the statement closest to the date of death to get a general sense of what these assets were worth on that date. Chapter 17 tells you how to determine the actual value (down to the penny) of these assets as of the date of death.

If your decedent had a brokerage account, review as many statements as you can locate (it wouldn't hurt to ask the broker for at least the last two years' statements) for any evidence of churning (placing trades frequently with the sole intention of earning more brokerage commissions). If you find what seems to be inappropriate, unnecessary trading, as was the case with one of our decedents, an elderly widow, seek out an attorney, a CPA, or an EA who is an expert in spotting stockbroker fraud to review the account's investment history for signs of churning.

## Perusing other personal papers

Although you may feel like you're invading the decedent's privacy by rummaging through his or her desk and computer, put those feelings aside. You need to uncover everything about the estate. As you dig, you may find such treasures as safe deposit box keys, jewelry appraisals, insurance policies (sometimes with riders cataloguing personal and household items of unusual value, in the case of homeowners' policies), references to real estate, rented storage facilities, and even stock certificates and registered bonds that the decedent didn't put away for safekeeping. Keep an open mind; as many estates as the two of us have been involved in, we're still constantly amazed at what people stash. What may appear to you as a jumble of worthless paper may contain such gems as bearer bonds, savings bonds, and bags of unset diamonds. You never know until you dig; dig methodically and carefully. Never throw out any piece of paper (or bag of trash) without reviewing it for clues to estate assets.

We'd love to be able to tell you that no one ever tried to take advantage of Uncle Henry's death to weasel out of money owed but, unfortunately, we can't. In your search through the paperwork and records, you may find that Uncle Henry made loans to family members that he always intended to collect on. Any loans, notes, or other debts owed to the decedent are assets of the estate, and your duty as executor is to include them on the inventory, along with interest accrued through the date of death. You must then pursue the collection of the note or debt.

If you find documents for such a loan (a promissory note, perhaps, or even a mortgage), they remain in force even after Uncle Henry's death unless there's specific language in the documents or in his Last Will that forgives them upon death. If the documents exist and this language doesn't, these loans are assets of the estate, and the estate administrator (that's you) must enforce the terms. Not doing so leaves you open to accusations by Uncle Henry's other relatives or heirs that you've failed in your duty as a fiduciary.

## Finding the hiding places

People stash what they perceive as valuable in different ways and places; your job, as the executor, is to insert yourself into the thought processes of the decedent and attempt to find all these hiding places. For example, one of us keeps her personal papers in the bottom drawer of a locked file cabinet, in a locked fireproof safe, and scattered around her desk. Savings (such as they are) are littered on the floor in the form of loose change, and jewelry is spread here and there among no fewer than seven jewelry boxes and old tool chests. The other of us just has the locked file cabinet. As the executor, you have to find everything applicable for the estate, and your search needs to include the following:

- ✔ **House safes:** Many houses have safes drawn into the plans, and some have safes built in later; most of the time, though, the house safe is a locked, fireproof box that's stashed in some out-of-the-way place, with an eye to keeping certain documents and other valuables free from prying eyes and catastrophic acts of nature. Unfortunately, the location of the house safe isn't usually at the forefront of the mind of someone about to die, and so after death, the search is on. Check closets, drawers, under beds and dressers, and in the attic and the basement. Be sure to check the freezer (especially the freezer chest out in the garage that hasn't worked for years). Don't assume that because a place looks too dark and dingy to ever be considered as a hidey-hole that it's not.

After you locate the safe, you need to have the lock professionally attended to if it's locked and you don't have a key or the combination. The locksmith will need a copy of your appointment as executor to open the box. You probably also want an additional witness with you so that you have an extra set of eyes to note what's in the box and, more important, what isn't. Make an inventory of the contents of the box as soon as you open it, sign the inventory, and have the second person sign it as a witness to the contents.

✔ **Other unusual spots:** Don't beat yourself up if you fail to find everything that the decedent stashed. Do, however, make sure that you've at least made a reasonable search for anything that may be either intentionally or unintentionally hidden. We've all heard tales about buried treasure located behind the furnace or under the floorboards or the mattress. Well, the tales are often true, either because the decedent didn't trust banks to keep money safe or through accidental circumstances, such as a piece of jewelry slipping off unnoticed and being found in the backyard or the back of a closet years later. One of us worked on an estate where more than $20,000 in cash was found stashed behind the kitchen stove, behind a loose brick in the fireplace, and literally under the floorboards. Although the decedent also had the requisite number of bank and brokerage accounts, the money discovered in the house represented more than loose change.

One of our grandmothers had a habit of burying silverware she couldn't adequately clean. Although we dug through all her houseplants and the garden before she moved, we never recovered all the missing spoons. We did, however, find a gold chain she'd lost many years earlier, one which, when we had it appraised, was worth more than $5,000.

# Emptying the safe deposit box

Locating and emptying the decedent's safe deposit box (if he or she has one) is a key step in finding the valuables in the estate. The quickest way to find the box is, of course, to ask the question before death; if you forgot to have that conversation before it was too late, not to worry.

Most people choose to rent a safe deposit box in the bank where they do the majority of their business, so check there first. You may find a record of the box, either in a notation somewhere (like **Schedule A** of the decedent's income tax return) or in a paid bill for the box rental, among the decedent's papers. If you don't find any record, you can approach the bank(s) directly and ask, after you receive your appointment as the estate's executor. Provided that the bank can see you have the authority to receive this information, it'll be happy to comply.

After you discover where the box is, you have to open it. If you don't have the key or the combination, you can have the lock drilled for a fee. Again, as long as you're armed with a copy of your appointment by the probate court, you'll find the bank very helpful in accessing the contents.

Don't open the box on your own. Take a witness with you and write down a list of everything inside. Even better, have the witness videotape you opening the box and what you find. Remember, when you're dealing with property that's not yours, especially property that may have significant monetary or sentimental value, you can't be too cautious.

You never know quite what you'll find in the safe deposit box. Often, you come across jewelry, deeds to real estate, stock certificates, bonds, and perhaps even the original Last Will of the decedent. Other times, you find items that have no intrinsic value, and you wonder at their sentimental value as well. Quite frequently, you find that the box is empty. Until you open it, though, you'll never know.

## Sleuthing for digital assets and info

If your decedent owned a computer or other electronic device, it's an important resource for sorting out what the decedent owned; you need to be able to access the information on the decedent's computer, tablet or smartphone. If the decedent and/or his estate planner were really on top of things, they'll have included the digital estate in the estate plan. You can hope for a list of digital devices and their passwords, and a list of online accounts. If no one thought to leave you this information, in most cases, the computer will probably give up its files fairly easily, but if the decedent was technically adept, you may have some difficulties in breaking through passwords and other safeguards. Far be it from us to advocate hiring a hacker, but you may find it helpful to use someone who is computer savvy in order to get to the information you need.

Before you begin digging for files, make a complete backup of the hard drive, and of any loose disks, flash drives, CD-ROMs, or DVD-ROMs you find lying about that contain data. You want to be cautious about losing data, and making backups ensures that you have the information that was most current on the date of death. The best, quickest way to back up any computer is to purchase an external hard drive, plug it in, and then use the software that comes with it to start backing up all the files located on the computer's hard drive. You can also copy the contents of floppy disks, CD or DVD-ROMs, and flash or thumb drives to the external hard drive to give you a complete copy of the decedent's computer files. If you're concerned about the cost of the external hard drive, don't worry — it's a valid expense of the estate (including the cost of a technician if you really don't want to do the backup yourself), and you should pay it from estate funds, not from your own funds.

You may find nothing of value on the computer, or you may find the decedent's entire financial life. As more people computerize their financial records and replace paper statements and bills with virtual equivalents, the computer may contain the only records of those bank and brokerage accounts. On the computer, you can see evidence of sources of income as well as debts owed. You can probably even find copies of tax returns. In fact, you can often find everything on the computer that used to be kept in a well-organized file cabinet if only you take the time to look.

If your decedent left you a list of passwords to his e-mail accounts and social media accounts, you may feel that you've hit the jackpot, but be forewarned — the Terms of Service contracts (and who ever reads these?) on these accounts sometimes say that these accounts terminate on the user's death, and some contracts say that the password may not be shared, and you may violate a state or federal law by using it. The safer way to access these accounts is to provide the e-mail or other account service with certified copies of the decedent's death certificate and your appointment as executor. Case law is still undecided, but you may receive access to the content of the accounts on that basis. Don't forget, we're in a whole new cyberworld here, and the law in this area is still developing.

On occasion, you'll discover that you can't find anything at all in the computer files, but you do have some disks that the computer can't read. You need to judge whether you think you've reasonably uncovered all the assets through traditional methods, or if you have some gaping holes. If you do have holes, and you can see evidence of financial software on the computer, you may want to consider having the corrupted disk restored through a restoration service. The cost can be substantial, but when you compare the cost to the benefit of finding a major asset that you would otherwise have missed, it's reasonable. And remember, it's an estate expense and fully deductible.

## Checking over prior tax returns

When looking for a snapshot of someone's financial affairs, digging through the person's tax returns provides you with a mountain of information — you not only find sources of income and deduction, but you're also able to eliminate many items you thought he or she owned but actually didn't.

If you find paper copies of tax returns, you may be fortunate and find the supporting documents to those returns in the same spot. Those official little slips of paper (**Forms W-2**, **1099**, and **1098**) can direct you to the decedent's employer (if he or she was still employed at the date of death), as well as to all the interest-bearing bank accounts and dividend-paying stocks he or she owned. You can find evidence of retirement income and mortgages owed. In fact, depending on the complexity of the tax return and the amount of underlying info, you can gain a fairly clear picture of the decedent's financial life just from the tax return.

If you're unable to locate prior tax returns, either on paper or buried somewhere on the computer hard drive, all isn't lost. You can obtain copies of prior years' tax returns, including copies of all **W-2s**, **1099s**, and **1098s**, directly from the IRS by filing **Form 4506, Request for Copy of Tax Return** and sending it, together with the fee of $39 for each year requested, to the IRS Service Center indicated on the form instructions. Remember to send a copy of your fiduciary appointment with the **Form 4506**; the IRS won't give you information if you're not authorized to receive it. If you don't need to see an actual copy of the entire return but only want to know the information that's on it, you can save the $39 per year fee by filing **Form 4506-T, Request for Transcript of Tax Return** instead. This form is free, and can be downloaded and faxed to the IRS, or even requested online at www.irs.gov/Individuals/Order-a-Transcript.

# Listing Personal and Household Effects

The preceding section helps you establish at least a preliminary list of the decedent's financial affairs. Now you need to consider all the stuff you find in the decedent's residence(s). Everything the decedent owned outright on his or her date of death is now under your care as executor; you're responsible for making sure that you account for this stuff and that it ends up where it's supposed to. You need to prepare a detailed inventory of all the personal and household items (being sure not to include any that belonged solely to the surviving spouse). This inventory is necessary to put a value on the items for the probate inventory and the **Form 706** (see Chapters 16 and 17).

If the decedent has a surviving spouse, the personal and household items may be staying in place after the decedent's death, except items the decedent specifically *bequeaths* (leaves by will) to others. If the decedent has no surviving spouse and the house needs to be dismantled, you still need to list and document everything and set aside anything of real value for later valuation.

Don't allow relatives and friends to rummage through the house and remove items until you've listed them, and if valuable, valued them. Seriously consider collecting all outstanding house keys immediately after the death or, even better, changing the locks as soon as is humanly possible. And if you don't get to the house until after Cousin Hester has emptied it with a moving van because she knew the decedent wanted her to have "a few special things," you'll need to try your best to either retrieve the items removed, or value what you remember and then charge that against Cousin Hester's eventual share of the estate (if she has one).

Most often, going through the personal and household property is an exercise in clean up and clear out. For most people, these tangible items, though they have great sentimental value, rarely have a correspondingly large cash value. Clothes, for example, are usually given to a local charity, and household furnishings that family and friends don't latch onto either follow the same route or are disposed of in a yard sale or on eBay or Craigslist. Surprisingly, sometimes items you thought you'd have difficulty giving away are extremely popular; one of us had a bidding war for her grandmother's hats from the 1940s and 1950s, but this situation is more the exception than the rule.

Of course, not all the personal and household effects are intrinsically valueless, and your job is to separate out the wheat from the chaff. Just because something may not be your style doesn't mean that it has no value; in fact, we've found that some of the most hideous pieces of furniture are among the most valuable! Regardless of your personal opinion, you need to carefully check the furniture, the knickknacks, the dishes, what's hiding in the attic and the cellar, and the garage. If you're familiar with the contents of the house before inventorying what's there, you may want to obtain a recent valuation guide to gain some idea of what you're looking at and a rough idea of its value. If you know before you go into the house that it contains items of great value, you may also want to consider bringing an antiques dealer or auctioneer with you to help sort out what has value from what doesn't.

Make sure that you have witnesses with you when you inventory and dispose of the contents of the house. If you can, take huge numbers of pictures or videos of each room before you move anything, so that, should someone take it upon themselves to question what was there when you opened the door, you have visual proof as well as third-party confirmation.

# Appraising the Property

After you discover where all the assets are hiding, you need to determine what they're worth. Some are obvious (the unused postage stamps, for example, or bank accounts that only hold cash), although others are more difficult to pin down. You may have to call in experts to help you out.

Some property doesn't vary in price much from day to day or week to week, but the value of most property fluctuates. When appraising an estate, make sure to value the property as of the date of death, even if you're having it appraised months afterwards. Be sure to let your property appraiser know this stipulation in advance — her appraisal needs to explicitly state that the value is as of the date of death. The next sections explain what you may need to have appraised and how to do so.

## Tangibles

*Tangible* property refers to both real estate (which we discuss separately) and other stuff — furnishings, jewelry, fur coats, cars, boats, collectibles, and artwork. If you can hold or touch it, and it's not securities or cash, you're holding tangible property.

You can take several avenues in valuing tangible property, provided that, whichever one you use, it's a reasonable approach. Some of the ways include

- ✔ **Do it yourself.** The Internet has many resources to help you appraise a wide assortment of items. For example, if you want to reasonably appraise a collection of books, you can search for matching volumes in online auction sites and booksellers.

  Obtaining a value for the car is easy! Just plug in the make, model, year, and condition into the Kelley Blue Book site on the Internet at www.kbb.com.

- ✔ **Turn to experts.** If you need experts to assist you in valuing the tangibles, make sure that you hire someone who is truly a specialist in the type of property you need appraised. For example, if you tried to value something online and you can't find an identical copy, say of the book (and identical matters — there's a huge difference between first and second editions), you may choose to take that collection to a rare book dealer, who'll be happy to appraise your collection in writing for a price.

  If you need some antique furniture valued, make sure that you ask an antiques dealer who specializes in the same type of furniture you have. (Asking a dealer who specializes in Louis IV furniture to appraise your aunt's collection of 19th century Japanese prints isn't the best choice.) Finding the experts you need can be as simple as word of mouth; if you're using an attorney for help with probating the estate, he may have a list of appraisers of various types of property that he has used in the past. You can also search the Internet for local appraisers or check in the local phone book under dealers or appraisers for the item in question. Asking that appraiser who specializes in Louis IV furniture for a recommendation of someone who specializes in Japanese prints can't hurt, either. Contacting a museum that contains items or works of art similar to yours can also lead to a recommendation of an appraiser. See Chapter 4 for more discussion of appraisers.

In the world of appraising, documentation is king. Be sure to obtain written appraisals from any experts you use, even if you must pay a fee. Likewise, if you're relying on other sources, such as online auctions, keep copies of your research in a file. That way, should someone question your valuation, you have proof of what the property was worth on the date of death.

# Intangibles

Although valuing tangible property may give you scope for some creative research, calculating the value of an estate's intangible property, those bank and brokerage accounts, and any stocks or bonds that the decedent physically held, should speak to your brain's quest for absolute order. Provided that you have a complete list of the intangible property, figuring out what it was worth on the date of death should be a simple matter of math. So grab your calculator and get ready.

### Bank accounts

Figuring out how much was in each bank account on the date of death isn't too difficult. Just send a letter to the bank explaining what you want, together with a copy of the death certificate and your appointment as executor. Be sure to request the balance at the date of death plus any interest that has accrued between the last payment date and the date of death.

Remember, the decedent may have written checks prior to death that hadn't cleared the bank by the date of death. In this case, adjust for these withdrawals by subtracting them from the balance given to you by the bank. Of course, in the interest of showing all your work (make your former math teacher proud), list the bank's balance and then the offsetting checks.

### Securities

Valuing securities, such as stocks, bonds, and mutual funds, isn't quite as easy. When determining their value, you're required to take an average of the high and low costs for the date of death and then multiply it by the size of the holding. For example, if your decedent held 50 shares of XYZ Corporation, and on the date of death, it traded at a high value of $50 and a low value of $40, the average cost per share would be $45. When multiplied by the 50 shares owned, the total value of that holding on the date of death would be $2,250. If the decedent died on a weekend or holiday, you have to average the average cost on the last trading day before death and the first trading day after death in order to arrive at the date-of-death value.

If the decedent held securities in a brokerage account, you may be able to obtain a valuation from the broker as of the date of death, especially if you ask for it as soon after the death as possible. Be certain that the broker understands that this is a date-of-death valuation, though, because otherwise she will give you the closing price for that day, not an average of the high and low costs. Another source for the date-of-death high and low of a stock or bond is *The Wall Street Journal* issue from your decedent's date of death, which is available at your local library if you don't have a subscription. If you have access to the Internet, we also like Prudential-American Securities Inc. (www.securities-pricing.com), which can give you date-of-death values or alternate valuation for all stocks and bonds, including municipal bonds, for four dollars per issue, with a minimum charge of ten dollars. ***Remember:*** This fee doesn't come out of your pocket; it's paid for with estate funds.

### Intellectual property and copyrights

Intellectual property and copyright issues used to arise only in the estates of artists, authors, inventors, and owners of closely held businesses, and of course, if your decedent is one of those persons, you may have that issue in your estate. But now, if your decedent had any digital music and or video accounts or an e-book reader, you're talking intellectual property too.

- ✔ **Digital music, videos, and e-books:** Whether you as executor can transfer the contents of digital music and video accounts (such as iTunes) and e-book readers to the beneficiaries of the estate is a question that is still being litigated. You'll want to check with an attorney to see the state of the law as cases currently in the courts are decided. You can, however, distribute the decedent's device which contains the contents of the account — but that device, of course, can't be split among beneficiaries or copied, which is a problem where the decedent hasn't left the device to one person specifically.

- ✔ **Other intellectual property and copyright issues:** If your decedent was an artist, author, inventor, and sometimes, the owner of a closely held business, you're going to have intellectual property and copyright issues. When we talk about intellectual property, think designs, inventions and discoveries, published and unpublished written and musical works, artistic works, and more. Intellectual property rights can include copyright, patent, trademark, and industrial design rights. If there is intellectual property, the first thing you must decide as executor is whether the beneficiaries can inherit it — that is, whether it survives the decedent's death. You'll want an intellectual property attorney or an estate attorney experienced in handling intellectual property to help you with this decision and with any other issues that may arise regarding this property, including its valuation for inventory and federal estate tax purposes. If the decedent was a writer, he or she may have appointed you as executor of his or her estate property in general, and appointed a literary executor specifically to deal with posthumous publication of his or her work.

## Real estate

The trickiest asset to value may be real estate because no two pieces of real estate are identical, and real estate is valued by looking at comparable sales. To value real estate, keep the following in mind:

- ✔ Sometimes, you can use the assessment as the value at the date of death (or, in some states, twice the assessment). The *assessed value* is the value your local real estate tax assessor places on the property for real estate tax purposes. Compare the assessed value with similar properties sold around the date of death or for sale at that time in your locale to see whether the assessed value is in the ballpark. If the values are comparable and the estate is small enough that it won't have an estate tax, using the assessed value works because it clearly reflects the market value of the property at the date of death.

> ✔ If the assessed value in your area doesn't reflect the market value of the real estate (if you're unsure based on your market comparison, ask the local real estate tax assessor), have the real estate appraised, or use the following valuation methods to obtain a value for the probate inventory.

If a federal estate tax return (**Form 706**) is required, have the real estate appraised. As with all estate appraisals, hire a reputable appraiser who has experience in preparing estate appraisals. The appraiser typically refers to several *comparable* properties (that is, properties that have sold recently and are as similar to your property and as close in location as possible), in addition to other factors, in determining a value as of the date of death. The appraiser adds or subtracts value based upon the differences between your real estate and the comparable sales (for instance, an additional bathroom in your property increases the value; if your lot is smaller than the comparables, your value decreases) in arriving at a date-of-death value for your property.

Often, you have a buyer for the real estate before you have a chance to obtain an appraisal. Provided you sell it in an *arm's length* transaction (a transaction between the executor and someone who has no relationship to the executor or the estate) soon after death, you use the sale value as the date-of-death market value.

# Contacting the Employer about Employee Benefits

Although the decedent's employer hopefully already knows about the death, in order to collect employee benefits, you need to formally contact the employer. A letter to the employer (and to former employers) inquiring about any death benefits should meet with full cooperation if you include your certified appointment as executor, although where there are named beneficiaries, the employer may choose to deal only with those beneficiaries. Most likely, you'll find beneficiary designations on file with the employer that the decedent signed during his or her lifetime. For benefits where the decedent has named no beneficiary, the fallback provision under the employer's plan or the insurance policy typically designates the surviving spouse or the executor of the estate as beneficiary. The employer will need at least one certified copy of the death certificate. Note that not all employee benefits have a death benefit (for instance, the decedent may have been collecting pension benefits that ended upon death). The following outline some of the benefits that may apply:

> ✔ **Death benefits:** The decedent may have had term life insurance, accidental death insurance, or other death benefits through the employer. Typically, the employer takes care of the paperwork to process those claims, but you often have to provide them with gentle reminders.

✔ **COBRA benefits for surviving spouse and dependent children:** The decedent may have had certain benefits through an employer, such as health, dental, and/or vision insurance that the surviving spouse or dependent children may be eligible to temporarily continue by paying a premium. Check with the employer to see what, if any, benefits qualify for continuation under COBRA (Consolidated Omnibus Budget Reconciliation Act of 1986).

✔ **Flexible spending accounts (FSAs) and health savings accounts (HSAs):** Some employers provide their employees with a way to pay for out-of-pocket healthcare and/or dependent-care expenses with pretax dollars. Deductions from the employee's salary fund these accounts, (sometimes known as flexible spending accounts [FSAs]), so if the account has a balance at the date of death, that balance can be used to pay for either healthcare or dependent-care expenses incurred prior to death. Check with the employer. And don't forget *HSAs*, savings/investment accounts for pretax dollars the decedent put aside to cover healthcare costs. These accounts, which let you save and invest the unspent money in them from year to year (unlike FSAs, which are use-it-or-lose-it), can transfer to a surviving spouse on death, who can make withdrawals at any time, free of income tax, for healthcare costs.

✔ **Retirement accounts:** Check for any employer-sponsored retirement accounts. The 401(k) is probably the most common, but you may also find a Savings Incentive Match Plan for Employees (SIMPLE) [look for this plan if the decedent worked for a small company or was self-employed] a Simplified Employee Pension Plan (SEP), a Defined Contribution Profit Sharing Plan (not too common nowadays), and a Defined Contribution Pension Plan (also quite uncommon nowadays).

Figuring out all the places the decedent worked during his or her lifetime isn't easy, but finding and notifying former employers and employee unions is often worth the effort. Frequently, retirement plans and other benefits are still in place with former employers or with the unions, who won't find out about the death unless someone (usually you) tells them. Although employers often automatically pay out retirement plans valued at less than $5,000 when employees leave, they're under no obligation to do the same with larger sums, so finding plans in place with old employers that hold tens or even hundreds of thousands of dollars isn't uncommon. To locate former employers, look at W-2s on prior tax returns to which you have access, ask family members of the decedent about any prior employers, and even ask the most recent employer, who may have information about prior employers on file on the decedent's resume. You may also find references to prior employers or unions in the decedent's papers. If you're fortunate enough to find a copy of a resume, you've just hit the mother lode!

✔ **Unpaid salary, bonuses, vacation time, and/or comp time:** Don't forget to ask the employer about unpaid salary, bonuses, vacation time, comp time, and sick time. Some of these may be owed and payable upon death, depending upon the employer's practice. And don't forget reimbursable expenses! Ask if the employee or estate is entitled to anything else. *Remember:* just because the decedent wasn't around to collect his or her last paycheck doesn't mean that he or she isn't entitled to that income; make sure that you collect it!

# Locating and Collecting Insurance Proceeds

Many people carry life insurance — your job is to find all the policies and collect the proceeds, or at least advise the beneficiary to file a claim. Your search of the decedent's papers may have turned up some clues to any insurance on the decedent's life. You may have found the policy itself, records of premiums paid or due, dividend information, or other papers pointing toward a policy.

To collect the policy's proceeds, send a certified copy of the death certificate and a copy of your appointment as executor or administrator to the insurance company. If the company wants the policy itself, which it probably will, be sure that you send it certified mail, return receipt requested, or some other form of delivery service where you'll receive proof that someone at the insurance company received it. Be sure to request IRS **Form 712, Life Insurance Statement**, at the same time that you request the proceeds. You'll need it to prepare **Form 706** and any state estate or inheritance tax form, as we show you in Chapter 17. It's much easier to get it now rather than search for it later.

Insurance may come in a couple different forms. Keep an eye open for the following:

✔ **Traditional life insurance:** Traditional life insurance owned by the insured can be whole life, term, or some other product. Regardless of type, if the policy was *in force* on the date of death (the policy hadn't lapsed through nonpayment of premiums, for example), life insurance pays out an amount specified in the insurance contract to the beneficiary designated by the insured, minus the value of any outstanding loans taken against the cash value in the policy. Note that insurance on the decedent's life that is owned by another person or entity isn't included in the decedent's probate estate or taxable estate.

When searching for life insurance policies, you often need to look in less-than-obvious places. Many people have small policies as a courtesy from their banks or credit unions. Because you're writing to request date-of-death balances for all the decedent's bank accounts, inquire at the same time whether the decedent also had a life insurance policy in force.

✔ **Mortgage, credit card, and other loan insurance:** Insurance is available to cover the balance due on a mortgage, credit card, or other loans upon the death of the person. You want to keep your eyes peeled for any reference to such insurance in the decedent's papers, and ask the holders of any mortgages, credit cards, or other loans if any exist.

# Ascertaining Any Other Death Benefits

When mining the decedent's personal papers, note any other death benefits you find and contact the appropriate authorities. Be sure to check with any professional, retirement, and union organizations. Start with the following places to determine whether any other death benefits exist:

✔ **Social Security:** If the decedent has a surviving spouse or minor children who meet certain requirements, the survivors may receive a one-time death benefit of $255 if the decedent worked long enough. To inquire about and collect the benefit, contact your local Social Security office or call their toll-free number at 800-772-1213. Dealing with the local office, which is usually quite helpful, is sometimes easier than going through the maze of the telephone system.

The surviving spouse and any dependents and/or dependent parents may be entitled to monthly survivors' benefits. Apply for these benefits as soon as possible because, in some circumstances, the benefits begin from date of application, not of death.

✔ **Veterans' Administration:** Eligible veterans, their spouses, and their children are entitled to burial in a national cemetery, a flag, and an inscribed grave marker. Other benefits may also be available. If the decedent was a veteran or the spouse or child of a veteran, you can call the Department of Veterans Affairs at 800-827-1000 or go to www. cem.va.gov for help in determining whether any benefits apply. (See Chapter 5 for more details on burial benefits).

✔ **Individual retirement accounts (IRAs):** Even though you probably won't be cashing out any retirement accounts the decedent owned, you need to know what retirement accounts he or she had, their value on the date of death, and who the beneficiaries are. The decedent may have had IRAs, Roth IRAs, or other self-funded retirement arrangements. After you identify the accounts, a letter from you to the account's trustee (the bank, brokerage, or mutual fund company that holds the assets), together with a copy of the death certificate and your appointment as administrator, executor, or personal representative, should be all you need to obtain that date-of-death value.

## Suing from beyond the grave

If the decedent was involved in an ongoing lawsuit at the time of his or her death, or if a reason to sue arises due to the manner of death, it's the duty of the executor or administrator to continue or pursue the lawsuit. One of us had a case where a surviving spouse didn't want a lawsuit pursued against the driver who caused the death of his spouse. However, the executor was required to pursue the suit to protect the interests of the minor children in the lawsuit and in the estate. And unlike criminal actions, which expire when the defendant dies, civil suits can survive the death of the original parties. One of our grandmothers, who was hit by a car and sued the driver five years before she died, didn't finally collect her judgment until she'd been dead for three years.

Rights of action and claims in tort or in contract (lawsuits) are included on the inventory, and you must determine the status of the suit and pursue it if it survives the decedent's death. The estate's attorney can help the executor to determine whether the cause of action survives.

Choosing how to pay out retirement plans such as IRAs can be a minefield, littered with serious tax consequences to the beneficiary. With traditional IRAs, give a great deal of thought to how the benefits will be paid out, because they may be fully taxable to the beneficiary for income tax purposes. If the beneficiary is a *qualifying individual,* payments can be spread out over the life of the beneficiary, thus tempering the income tax hit. So be sure that you don't inadvertently elect a lump-sum distribution! And if the beneficiary is the surviving spouse, he or she can treat the inherited IRA as their own.

Contributions to Roth IRAs were taxed for income tax purposes at the time the decedent made the contributions, so provided that the account was open for at least five years, all withdrawals from it are income tax free. Be sure that you know which kind of IRA you're dealing with, traditional or Roth. This would be a good time to consult with a tax expert with regard to withdrawals because a number of complex issues are at play here.

# Preparing and Filing the Probate Inventory

After you find every asset of the decedent (you hope!) and value it, prepare the inventory required by the probate court. Your local probate court has a form for you to use, and if all your probate assets don't fit on it, just add additional sheets in the same format. Include all the assets subject to probate on the probate inventory, including those assets in the decedent's name alone, held as a tenant in common, joint for convenience only, or payable to the estate. Your court probably has a deadline by which the inventory is to be filed, but check to see whether, in practice, it's a hard and fast deadline. You may need the extra time to collect and value the estate assets.

In some jurisdictions, the inventory deadline is likely to be close to the due date for filing the estate tax return (nine months after date of death). In other states, the inventory must be filed before you're allowed to sell real estate. Be sure to use the sales price on your inventory; if you're selling for less than inventory value, you may have a problem receiving any necessary license from the probate court. The inventory limits your liability as executor to the values shown on the inventory, if you have used market values as of the decedent's date of death. There is usually an inventory filing fee, based on the value of the assets, payable by the estate.

# *Liquidating Assets*

As the executor or personal representative of an estate, one of your primary responsibilities after you take a complete inventory of the assets is to *liquidate,* or distribute or sell, some or all of them. If the decedent specifically bequeaths or *devises* (leaves a piece of real estate by will) an asset, the executor or administrator can't sell it unless it's necessary to pay debts of the decedent and/or expenses of the estate (see Chapter 8). Among the reasons for liquidating assets before distribution of the *residue* (what's left over after paying all debts, expenses, taxes, and specific bequests and devises) are the following:

- The necessity to raise cash for *pecuniary* (or monetary) bequests, and for debts of the decedent, expenses of estate administration, and taxes

- Ease of division and distribution of the residue

- Fairness (you may not be able to distribute the assets unless they're held in an equitable manner)

You as executor or personal representative decide what and when to liquidate.

Don't forget that your duty as the executor or administrator is to preserve the assets, not to grow them. If the estate holds stocks and bonds that go down in value, the executor may be accused of not fulfilling his or her fiduciary duty to preserve the assets. And the executor doesn't receive a bonus if the assets increase in value. It can be wise to have a special, or temporary, executor or administrator appointed before the executor is even appointed, for the express purpose of selling stocks and bonds. After assets are liquidated, they can be held in safe investment vehicles such as a bank account or accounts (so that each account is fully FDIC insured), money market funds, and other stable investment vehicles. The following sections discuss what you need to do to liquidate the securities and real estate.

# Selling stocks, bonds, and other securities

Most people now hold stocks, bonds, and other securities in brokerage accounts, and gaining access to them so that you can sell them requires that you provide the brokerage with a copy of your appointment as executor, personal representative, or administrator. Check out the two scenarios:

- **If the decedent held all securities in a brokerage firm account which you transferred to the estate's name or if you placed them in a brokerage account in the name of the estate:** Call the broker to sell them.

- **If your decedent still liked to hold onto his or her physical stock and bond certificates:** Your job just became a bit tougher. In order to sell securities held in physical form — if they're in the decedent's name alone — you need the original stock certificates, a certified copy of your appointment as executor or administrator, and a stock assignment form, with your signature guaranteed by a commercial bank.

  If you can't locate the original certificates, get ready for a shock to the wallet because the cost can be up to $500 per certificate to replace each one lost. You must replace the certificates before you can transfer the stocks. We know of two estates that are still open because the decedents, husband and wife, each had advanced Alzheimer's disease. Their stock certificates are yet to be found, and at $500 per certificate, their executor isn't rushing to replace them.

# Disposing of real estate

If you need (or want) to sell the real estate, the quickest way to assure a sale at the highest price is typically to have the property listed with a reputable broker. If you're not familiar with the area, ask the decedent's relatives or friends, attorney, accountant, or other professionals for recommendations of real estate brokers and then interview the brokers yourself at the property. You want to get a feel for the broker personally, and for his brokerage company. Don't necessarily use brokers who offer to list the property for the highest price. They may be doing so just to get the listing, at which point they'll find it necessary to drop the price to make a sale. Instead, go with the broker who has the comparable properties to back up the price he proposes and with whom you're most comfortable.

As with any real estate transaction, the executor or administrator must be able to give clear title when selling real estate out of the estate. *Clear title* means there's no question as to the ownership of the real estate and it has no liens upon it.

If the decedent had a will, it may or may not require the executor to obtain the approval of the probate court prior to any sale; if the power to sell isn't specifically stated in the will, you need to get approval of the probate court for the sale if the real estate is held solely in the name of the decedent. Of course, if the decedent had no will, or the powers granted under the will aren't broad enough, the probate court will have to grant a license to sell real estate (or something similar) before the property can be sold and title passed to a new owner. The purchaser or the title insurance company (the company the purchaser pays to guarantee that the title to the property is clear) may also require probate court approval, such as a license to sell, for the sale to proceed. By granting the license to sell or other evidence of court approval (depending on the state the real estate is located in), the probate court is assuring title clear of claims of heirs, and of debts and claims of the estate.

You have a duty to get the highest price for the property; in some states, a license to sell from the court protects the fiduciary by conferring the presumption that the highest sale price was obtained. This step avoids the cumbersome task of putting the real estate at auction or worrying about getting a higher offer after you have agreed on a selling price with a buyer. Thus, as executor, you may want to get a license to sell or its equivalent even if you're not absolutely required to.

# Chapter 8

# Paying the Debts, Expenses, Bequests, and Devises from the Estate

. . . . . . . . . . . . . . . . . . . . . . . . . . . . . . . . . . . . . . . . .

### In This Chapter

▶ Identifying the decedent's debts and administration expenses

▶ Prioritizing and paying debts from estate assets

▶ Letting beneficiaries know about their right to disclaim

▶ Segregating and distributing named personal property

▶ Dividing other personal property equitably and dealing with the rest of the assets

. . . . . . . . . . . . . . . . . . . . . . . . . . . . . . . . . . . . . . . . .

*A*fter you set up the estate and have some idea what all the assets are worth (refer to Chapter 7 if you're not sure), you need to start identifying and paying the decedent's debts, the estate's administration expenses, and any claims against the estate. Only after you're sure that you've discovered and paid them all, can you begin distributing the estate's remaining assets to its heirs.

This chapter points out how to determine and pay the debts of the estate and administration expenses, help a beneficiary to make an effective disclaimer of a bequest or devise, effectively divide personal and household articles among the decedent's heirs (often the trickiest area to negotiate among those heirs), and divide and distribute the rest of the decedent's assets.

## Determining and Paying Debts of the Decedent and Administration Expenses

As executor, you should have all the decedent's bills (or be in the process of collecting them; see Chapter 5 for tips on going about this). One of your first tasks is to pay all administration expenses and legitimate debts of the decedent before you make any distributions to beneficiaries. That is, if you have enough assets to do so. In the following sections, we explain how and when to make these payments.

## Finding out how and when to pay claims

One of your first duties as executor (after the payment of administration expenses; see the "Prioritizing payment" section) is to pay the debts incurred by the decedent during his or her life. Some types of claims that frequently arise include

- ✓ **A lease on the decedent's residence**: Be sure to review the lease, because some may have a provision for termination upon death. In many cases, you can reach an agreement with the landlord for early termination of the lease. In any event, payments under the lease are claims against the estate, but extensions of the lease by the executor while the estate is administered are administration expenses, as are all utility bills for periods of time after the decedent's death.

- ✓ **Child support and alimony:** Agreements or court orders to pay alimony and child support are claims against the estate, and you must hold back sufficient funds for future payments.

Here are a few points to keep in mind when you're paying off the decedent's debts:

- ✓ **A debt is only considered a claim against the estate if the debt was created before the decedent died.** If it wasn't created before death, it may still be enforceable against the estate as an administration expense; administration expenses are dealt with differently than debts of the decedent. Check out the "Prioritizing payment" section, later in this chapter, to see how they're different.

- ✓ **Before you pay any debts, verify the validity of each claim.** Doing so is a simple matter for most debts, such as utility bills, but you may have to investigate others more thoroughly. For instance, if a relative, friend, or nurse provided care to the decedent with an oral understanding that they would be paid from the proceeds of the estate or left all or a portion of the estate, go directly to an attorney who is expert in probate law. Your state's legal precedents can likely help determine whether the claim is valid and can be paid. If actual services were rendered (such as living with and caring for an elderly relative for an extended period of time), the claimant is probably entitled to something from the estate.

✔ **Check to see whether any life insurance related to the debt (such as life insurance relating to a mortgage) is intended to pay it off upon death.** Also make sure that no agreements are in place that make the indebtedness vanish upon the death of the decedent. An uncle of one of us, for example, bought a new car, complete with a new car payment, shortly before he died. Fortunately, he took the additional insurance offered, which paid off the car loan upon his death.

✔ **Consider whether the debt is legally enforceable.** Debts such as charitable pledges may only be considered moral obligations.

✔ **Frequently, your decedent's largest obligations don't need to be paid in full.** Many are secured obligations that stay with the property they're attached to. Mortgages and auto loans, for instance, stay with the property, and whoever inherits the property inherits it with the debt attached.

Keep in mind your state's statutory requirements regarding claims. Unless your estate qualifies to use a small estate procedure, you'll have to give notice to the decedent's creditors of the estate's deadline for filing of claims by publishing a notice in a publication approved by the probate court. You'll receive a publisher's affidavit, which you'll file with the probate court. And, typically, you must also give actual notice to each estate creditor of whom you are aware within a set period of time (you must use "reasonably diligent efforts" to discover creditors). You must also give notice to the trustees of the decedent's revocable trust. If proper notice was given, then a claimant will have a set amount of time in which to file a claim (such as four months after the date of publication). Be aware, however, that each state has exceptions to this statute of limitations, including the following:

✔ Federal claims, including the federal estate tax

✔ State estate or inheritance tax, if any

✔ Creditors' liens on property

✔ Certain governmental and private claims for environmental damage

---

# Settling secured debt

Secured debt, such as a mortgage on the decedent's residence (including a reverse mortgage) or a car loan, can be settled by the lien holder claiming the property or by a beneficiary who wishes to retain the property. He or she may refinance the property and thus assume responsibility for the debt. The decedent could even provide in his or her will or trust that the debt be paid off on his or her death (if funds are available) and the property be retained in trust or distributed outright to a beneficiary.

## Medicaid claims

You might think that your decedent's estate wouldn't be subject to a Medicaid claim. After all, Aunt Martha wasn't indigent. She still had a lovely home, even if she was residing in a nursing home at the time of her death. However, if Medicaid was paying for all or a part of her long-term care, then depending on what state she lived in and how title was held to her home and any other assets which she owned at the time of her death, that state may file a claim against her estate for its portion of the cost of her care. Every state has some kind of Medicaid Estate Recovery Program (MERP), whereby they attempt to recover their Medicaid spending on certain long-term care recipients after their deaths. What assets a particular state will attempt to recover and in what situations varies by state. For instance, some states only attempt to recover from those assets that pass through probate. And states are prohibited by federal law from making Medicaid recoveries during the lifetime of a surviving spouse and in certain other circumstances. If your decedent was receiving services covered by Medicaid, consult with an attorney familiar with the Medicaid recovery process in that state before paying any lower priority claims and continuing with the distribution of the estate property.

State statute may also provide that, after that period for filing a claim (unless you have notice of claims of a large enough amount for you to be concerned that the estate may not have sufficient funds to cover its debts), you may pay those claims that have been presented to you, and you won't be held liable if funds are needed for later claims. Check with the probate court to see what the requirements are in the decedent's state of domicile.

## Prioritizing payment

When the estate doesn't have enough money to pay all the claims against it, don't start paying bills on the basis of the order received or who's screaming loudest for the money. Every state sets its own order of priority; check with a competent attorney or with the probate court to determine in what order you must pay the claims.

The following is a list of the types of claims that typically take priority:

- Reasonable administration expenses, including attorney and other professional fees
- Reasonable funeral expenses and the expenses of last illness
- Homestead allowance
- Family allowance
- Exempt tangible property

> ✔ Debts and taxes with priority under federal law, including medical assistance payments that are subject to recovery (Medicaid liens)

> ✔ Reasonable and necessary medical and hospital expenses of the decedent's last illness, including compensation of persons attending the decedent

> ✔ Debts and taxes with priority under other laws of the state

> ✔ Federal and state taxes

> ✔ Medicaid claims

Generally, you can only pay any other claims after you've paid all these claims in full.

## Declaring the estate insolvent

When you have more claims against the estate than assets to pay them, you must declare the estate *insolvent*. Before taking this step, consult with a probate attorney who has experience with insolvent estates in your jurisdiction. You're going to need her guidance to know the procedure for declaring insolvency in your state and to figure out what you're allowed to pay.

---

## Identifying conditional legacies and devises

The testator and the state can place *conditions* (clauses or laws modifying bequests and devises) on *bequests* (gifts of personal property under a will) or *devises* (gifts of real property under a will). Be on the lookout for the following, and remember, not all conditions created by a testator are recognized as valid, depending upon your state law:

✔ **The testator:** A decedent will sometimes leave a bequest or devise with a condition attached. Depending on your state law, some conditions are recognized as valid, and some aren't. For instance, in many states, the condition that the legatee not oppose the will if he or she wants to receive the bequest (known as an *in terrorem* clause) is valid. Conditions that are against public policy are usually found to be invalid. For instance, a bequest to the testator's son, on the condition that he divorce his wife, would be found to be invalid because it's against public policy, and the son could inherit without divorcing. Check with a competent attorney in the field of probate law if your testator placed conditions on any bequests or devises in the will.

✔ **State law:** Divorce doesn't revoke a will but, in most states, a provision in the will for a spouse from whom the decedent is divorced at the time of his or her death *lapses* (fails to vest in the divorced spouse, and he or she doesn't inherit), unless the decedent has specifically provided in the will that it shall not lapse upon divorce.

If the decedent had a funded revocable living trust, you can usually (depending on what state he or she lived in) use it to satisfy creditor's claims. Hopefully, a decedent who funded a living trust made provisions in it for the payment of debts and expenses of administration by the trustees; that way, an insolvent estate doesn't have to go through the courts to access the trust fund.

# Informing Potential Beneficiaries of Their Right to Consider Disclaimer

Under both transfer tax law, including estate, gift, and generation-skipping (see Chapter 17), and state probate law, a beneficiary may elect to *disclaim*, or refuse, an interest in property he or she doesn't want to accept. Why on earth would anyone choose not to inherit, you ask, unless he or she has taken a vow of poverty? As with many decisions in a person's financial life, the answer is "for tax reasons." When someone effectively disclaims an interest in property, he or she is refusing it before receiving it.

As the estate's executor, it's your responsibility to inform the beneficiaries that they have the option to disclaim any or all of their legacies. In practice, if you have a feel for the beneficiaries' relevant financial situations, you'll know whom to approach with this information — that would be the beneficiaries who already may have taxable estates for federal estate tax purposes (see Chapter 16 for the current taxable estate levels). For purposes of inheritance (including federal and state gift and estate or inheritance tax purposes), a disclaiming beneficiary is treated as though he or she predeceased the decedent. The assets disclaimed then pass to whomever is next in line to receive them. You may know the respective beneficiaries' financial situations (probably because they're descendants of the decedent, who shared their financial situations with you during life); otherwise, you can just present this option to each appropriate beneficiary as a possibility.

Consult your state's law for specifics, but generally speaking, to *make an effective disclaimer* (refuse the inheritance) the disclaimant must

- ✔ Refuse the property, in writing, within a reasonable time after becoming aware of it. Check state statutes, but *reasonable time* is often nine months, which is the same as the deadline to file **Form 706** without extensions.
- ✔ Accept no benefits from the property.
- ✔ Have no control over who receives the disclaimed property.

Disclaimers can be very helpful in correcting overfunding or underfunding of marital deductions, or simply in not growing the disclaimant's taxable estate unnecessarily if he or she is content with the new recipients of the disclaimed property.

## Knowing about pretermitted heirs

A child or issue of a deceased child who isn't provided for in the decedent's will, known as a *pretermitted heir*, is entitled to the share he or she would have received if the decedent had died without a will (*intestate*). However, the pretermitted heir isn't entitled to anything if the decedent has either provided for that child or issue during life *or* made it clear, usually in the will, that the omission was intentional. Check the fine points of your state law if this situation arises.

Testators who really want to disinherit an heir are very canny about crossing their *t*'s and dotting their *i*'s, and will likely have included a specific clause in their Last Will either saying that no provision has been made for that beneficiary under the will because he or she was provided for during lifetime or leaving that beneficiary some token amount, like $1 or $100.

So, for instance, if a beneficiary's descendants stand to inherit the beneficiary's share if he or she predeceases your decedent, an effective disclaimer will pass the assets to that next generation at no estate or inheritance tax cost to the disclaimant. Of course, the estate will have a transfer subject to generation-skipping transfer (GST) tax in that illustration, which you as executor must keep in mind in preparing the **United States Estate (and Generation-Skipping Transfer) Tax Return (Form 706).** See Chapters 16 and 17, and consult a competent estate and GST tax expert.

# Segregating and Distributing Specific Property

As the estate's administrator, you're responsible for securing all assets, including personal and household property. If a decedent *bequeaths* (leaves in his or her will) any specific items to a beneficiary or beneficiaries, you're responsible for separating and segregating those items.

If you don't take the necessary precautions (such as locking them away out of the reach of light-fingered relatives) to protect the assets, you'll be in a pretty pickle if, when the time comes for distribution, you can't come up with Aunt Hattie's engagement ring or Cousin Minerva's pearls. These are exactly the kinds of items that can come up missing when family and friends with a feeling of entitlement have unsupervised access to the residence of the decedent.

The following sections take a closer look at specific scenarios you may encounter when segregating and distributing the different types of property and what you must do to ensure that the beneficiaries receive what's due to them.

## Treading slowly before distributing

When securing the decedent's assets before you actually distribute anything to beneficiaries, you want to ensure that you tread carefully. Take your time and carefully refer to the will and its instructions before making any distributions. Keep the following in mind before you release anything:

- ✔ If the property named in a specific bequest or devise is no longer owned by the decedent at death, that bequest or devise has no effect and is considered *adeemed.* The legatee receives nothing, unless state law provides otherwise. For instance, if the decedent left a particular bank account to a beneficiary under the will and the bank account no longer exists, the beneficiary receives nothing.

- ✔ If a named beneficiary of a specific bequest or devise died before the decedent and the will makes no provision that the beneficiary's heirs or another person inherits, the bequest or devise fails or *lapses*, unless state law provides otherwise. Massachusetts law, for example, provides that if the named beneficiary who predeceased the decedent is a child or other relation of the decedent, that beneficiary's issue, if any, inherit unless the will provides otherwise.

- ✔ If the decedent left a will, check to see whether it contains a clause saying that all debts, expenses, and taxes are to be paid from the *residue* (the amount left after paying out all specific bequests and devises) of the estate. Be sure to also review any revocable living trust for similar language regarding paying expenses of the estate.

- ✔ If the decedent's state of domicile has an inheritance tax, be sure that the tax isn't attributed to the legatee or devisee and payable by them or from what they inherit from the estate. If the beneficiary is liable for the tax, you want to pay it from their share or have proof they've paid it before distributing their bequest or devise, unless the will provides that the estate pay such tax.

- ✔ If a *pecuniary devise* (a devise of a dollar amount) takes place more than a year after your appointment as executor, depending on state law, the estate may be charged interest on the devise, So be sure to note that date on your calendar and make distributions before then, if possible.

## Making the distributions

Although in some states you have the power to make distributions under your general powers as executor, in other jurisdictions, you need to follow specific guidelines, which may include delivering a proposed distribution schedule to the beneficiaries before you make distribution. If a beneficiary doesn't object in writing within a set period of time (for instance 28 days), he or she has waived the right to object.

As you distribute each asset, follow these important general steps:

1. **Have the recipient date and sign a receipt for the property.**

   Have a receipt prepared describing the property you're distributing and, in the document, have the beneficiary acknowledge receipt of it.

2. **If the distribution completely fulfills the bequest or devise to that beneficiary, and you're using supervised administration, or another form of probate that requires notice to the beneficiaries or their consents, obtain the beneficiary's signature on an assent to the allowance of your accounts as executor.**

   That way, if and when it's time for you to have the probate accounts allowed, you don't have to track down the beneficiary. The receipt and assent will be filed with the probate court when you have your estate account(s) allowed (and, of course, remember to keep copies for your estate records). See Chapter 9 for more on account allowance procedures.

Under supervised administration, discussed in Chapter 6, you'll need a court order to make partial or full distributions, and you'll need to give notice of hearing or obtain waivers and consents. The final distribution can be contained in the petition for complete estate settlement discussed in Chapter 9.

The following sections focus on specific types of property and any unique requirements you have to meet when distributing them.

## Considering tangible property

*Tangible property* is property you can touch or feel, such as a chair, a handkerchief, or a piece of land. Tangible property can be divided into two classifications: tangible personal property and tangible real property. Knowing these two classifications is important because, in your role as executor, these terms come up frequently and it's helpful to know what property the court (or whomever) may be referring to. Also, tangible real property (real estate) is always handled differently than other estate assets. How it's handled depends on the law in your decedent's state:

- ✔ **Personal property (*bequests* — gifts under the will of personal property):** If the decedent left specific bequests of personal property, you may distribute those bequests only after you've been appointed as executor, the property has been appraised, the date for filing of claims, if any, has passed, you've made sure that you have adequate funds to pay all estate expenses, and you've checked the estate and income tax consequences described earlier in this chapter.

- ✔ **Real estate (*devises* — gifts under the will of real property):** In some states, title to real estate passes automatically to the heirs upon the decedent's death, subject to any mortgage or lien on the property and to payment of debts of the decedent (including any estate taxes owed). You need take no formal action. In many other states, real estate held in the decedent's name alone appears on the estate inventory and must pass through probate in the same manner as any other probate property. In some states, to distribute specifically devised real property, you must petition the court for approval of distribution of the real property and obtain a court order allowing the distribution and including the property description. The resulting court order is then recorded with the register of deeds in the county where the property is located to show the chain of title passing to the beneficiary. Check with your local probate register to determine the method of transfer in your state.

## Looking at intangible property

*Intangible property* is property that has no value in and of itself but is the evidence of value, such as a stock certificate or bond. You can distribute intangibles at the same time and in the same manner as tangibles, except that, unless they're *bearer bonds* (which aren't held in any name), you may have to go through a process to reregister them in the beneficiary's name.

To have stocks and bonds reregistered in a beneficiary's name, either send or take the following items to the transfer agent directly for each security (the transfer agent will be shown on the face of the security), or send or take all securities to a bank or brokerage firm (each of whom will likely charge for this service):

✔ The bond or stock certificate.

✔ A form entitled "Assignment Separate from Certificate" (commonly referred to as a *stock power*) with your signature guaranteed (you can obtain this form from the bank or brokerage house if necessary, and they can also guarantee your signature). If you have a bank or brokerage firm with which you have a friendly relationship, one of their employees who is qualified to do so may be willing to guarantee your signature at no cost.

✔ A certified copy of your Letters of Authority as Executor (the certification by the court needs to be less than 60 days old). You obtain this document from the court for a small fee.

✔ Depending on the transfer agent and your decedent's state of domicile, you may also need an affidavit of domicile, a waiver of state taxes (from your state taxing authority), and certified copies of the decedent's death certificate and will.

If you're holding the security in an estate brokerage account, you distribute to the beneficiaries by instructing your broker, in writing, of the names in which the securities should now be registered. Of course, in establishing the estate brokerage account, you've gone through similar transfers for each security, although the broker will have handled the paperwork.

If you're actually reregistering physical stock and bond certificates, the new certificates in the beneficiary's name should be returned to you. Make everything as easy as possible for the beneficiary to comply with. Send the new certificates to the beneficiary, certified mail, return receipt requested, along with a receipt for the beneficiary to sign and return in the postage-paid return address envelope that you enclose.

## Fulfilling bequests of specific dollar amounts

To fulfill a bequest of a specific dollar amount, called a *pecuniary bequest,* simply write a check on the estate's checking account (making sure that you have transferred funds to the account for this purpose) at the appropriate time, which is the same as for tangible personal property and, of course, obtain the necessary receipt.

For example, if the decedent left a bequest to her nephew of $10,000, after the period for filing of claims against the estate has passed, and it's clear there's plenty of money to pay all taxes, debts, and expenses, you may write a check to the nephew from the estate's checking account in the amount of $10,000 and mail it to him, certified mail, return receipt requested. Be sure to send along a receipt for the bequest and an assent by him to the executor's accounts, both for his signature to be returned for your files and for the probate court, if necessary.

# Dividing Other Personal Property Equitably

Divvying and dividing the personal and household articles is frequently one of the stickiest parts of estate administration. Whether the estate is large or small, we've both witnessed many times the passion heirs can feel toward the personal property of the decedent (and toward the other heir who gets something they wanted). Unfortunately, sometimes figuring out how to divide up the property isn't so crystal clear. This situation arises under the following conditions:

✔ The decedent leaves all *personalty* (person and household items) to a class of beneficiaries, such as "those of my children who survive me."

✔ The personality falls into the *residue* (the assets left after payment of all debts, administration expenses, and bequests and devises) for lack of a specific bequest, and the residue goes to a class or group of people.

✔ The decedent dies *intestate* (without a will) and a group, such as the decedent's children and the issue of any deceased child, *per stirpes* (by right of representation, that is, the children of such deceased child, and if any of those children is deceased, that deceased child's children, and so on) inherit.

None of these three conditions are completely black and white. In each of them, no plan is available for distributing the personal articles. You can always hope the decedent at least left labels or stickers on the bottom of furniture, but stickers can dry up and fall off (or get switched; perish the thought). In the next sections, we discuss ways to deal with this unfortunate and messy situation.

## Basing division on letter of intent

The best of all possible worlds is when the decedent has left a *letter of intent* written during his or her lifetime, where he or she listed which items of property are to go to whom. This letter may even be referred to in the will. Such a letter takes the burden of division off you as executor and, although the beneficiaries may still harbor hard feelings, they have only the decedent to blame (not each other). Although this letter doesn't have the legal standing of a will and shouldn't be used in place of one, it's very effective at silencing family bickering and beneficiaries' claims that Mother always intended for them to have the family silver.

All you have to do is follow the decedent's clear wishes in the letter of intent and distribute the respective assets to the designated persons. ***Remember:*** Always get receipts listing each item received and assents to the accounts.

## Creating a system for heirs to choose

If you're left no guidance by the decedent, such as a letter of intent, you must create an equitable system for the beneficiaries to choose the items they want to have. So how do you do that, you're wondering? One method is to draw the names from a hat (or whatever vessel you have handy) to establish the order in which they may choose. Each person then takes a turn choosing one item, perhaps applying color-coded stickers as they do so, until all items of interest are accounted for. Don't be surprised if this process goes down to the last pie plate. Again, getting a receipt listing each item received by a particular beneficiary is crucial.

# Disposing of unwanted personal property

As you're distributing the personal property, you may come across some items that no beneficiary really wants. If that's the case, you have several options. If you have enough items to attract an auctioneer, you can hold an auction, with the proceeds divided among the beneficiaries. Or you can donate the unwanted personal property to any charity that takes such property. In fact, many charities make house calls if you have large items or specific items they're interested in. Just be sure to get a receipt if you're thinking of taking that tax deduction, if it's allowed.

If the will directs you to give the personal property to charity, you can deduct the amount of the gift on **Form 1041, Schedule A,** which is located on the back of the form. Do an Internet search of the local area or check the phone book if you aren't familiar with charities that accept donations of personal property.

# Slicing Up the Residue

The *residue* of the estate represents all assets left in the estate after payment of all debts, administration expenses, and taxes and the distribution of all specific bequests and devises. Your job here is pretty clear cut: Either your decedent made provision for the disposition of the estate's residue in his or her will or the state laws of intestacy provide for the manner of distribution. (See Appendix B for brief summaries of individual state laws.) If your decedent left a will that leaves the residue to his or her revocable trust, the residue simply *pours over* into that trust, and you merely bring about the transfer of the assets into the trustee or trustees' names in whatever manner those trustees direct (for instance, into a brokerage account in their names).

To fulfill a bequest of a specific dollar amount, simply write a check on the estate's checking account (after making sure that you've placed sufficient funds there to do so). You may pay the bequest after the period for filing of claims, as we discuss earlier in this chapter.

The following list briefly touches on the main two ways to handle the rest of the pie and distribute the residue:

- **Dividing up the residue by percentage or fractional share:** If the residue is to go to more than one person or entity, the will may provide that the residue be divided by percentage or fractional share of the total assets. Each will have the same effect. For instance, it may say, "25 percent to each of my four children who are then living, per stirpes," or, "¼ to each of my four children who are then living, per stirpes." In each case, one-quarter of each asset is distributed to the then-living children and the issue of each deceased child. (In this example, the will would hopefully make provision for the contingency of a child dying who leaves no issue. Typically, that share would be divided among the other children).

✔ **Dividing by per capita or per stirpes:** If the residue is to be divided *per capita*, each person gets an equal share, no matter what the relationship to the decedent. If the residue is to be divided per stirpes, or by right of representation, you divide it equally at each generational level, with any issue of a deceased person taking his or her share. For instance, the residue may go to all the decedent's children living at the decedent's death, with the issue of any deceased child dividing that child's share equally per stirpes.

# Chapter 9

# Closing the Estate

• • • • • • • • • • • • • • • • • • • • • • • • • • • • • • • • • • • • • • • • • • • • •

## In This Chapter

▶ Getting the necessary documentation to close the estate

▶ Taking care of the last administrative expenses

▶ Doling out the rest of the distributions

▶ Preparing and filing the final paperwork

• • • • • • • • • • • • • • • • • • • • • • • • • • • • • • • • • • • • • • • • • • • • • •

*A*dministering the estate has been a long haul, but the finish line is within easy reach now. If you're ready to close the estate, you just need to make sure that you wrap up all loose ends. Closing the estate may seem like a lot of work, but trust us: Compared to what you've already accomplished, this final step is a cakewalk.

In this chapter, you reach the culmination of your hard work, dedication, and attention to myriad details on behalf of your decedent. Here's where you find everything you need to do as executor to wind up the estate and just how to do it: getting releases of lien for real estate, paying final administration costs, making final distributions to residuary beneficiaries, preparing probate accounts and getting them approved by the court, preparing final income tax returns, obtaining tax closing letters, and filing with the probate court all those receipts you collected from the beneficiaries.

# Obtaining Tax Closing Letters

If you filed a **Form 706 United States Estate (and Generation-Skipping Transfer) Tax Return** (see Chapters 16 and 17), and/or a state estate or inheritance tax return, you need *estate tax closing letters* (letters saying that the IRS and the state have accepted the returns, as filed or with adjustments) before you can close the estate. At this point, you pay any added taxes caused by adjustments; if you're lucky enough to avoid those, you may even get a refund (although that's unlikely).

The two types of tax closing letters you'll receive are

- ✔ **From the IRS:** The IRS issues an estate tax closing letter when it concludes that the return is accepted as filed or that the required adjustments are completed. You can then proceed to close the estate.

- ✔ **From the individual state(s):** After you receive your federal estate tax closing letter, file it with your state tax authority, including any information on adjustments made to the estate tax return as filed. (You may have a deadline on this filing, so be aware.) The state taxing authority then issues its closing letter, making any adjustments based on the federal return.

Don't put the federal estate tax closing letter in the pile of things to get to when you have a chance. File it promptly in any states where you've also filed an estate or inheritance tax return or paid any estate taxes (check out Appendix B for a list of states that currently charge taxes on estates or inheritances). Remember, you can't put this task of estate administration behind you until you finish all these seemingly minor — but actually fairly important — details.

# Acquiring Releases of Lien for Real Estate

Whenever someone dies, the title to any real estate he or she owned (whether alone or with someone else) gains a little cloud, an estate (or inheritance) tax *lien,* that prevents you from selling the property with a clear title until you (the executor) have taken care of it. Liens are how states and the federal government make sure that they receive the taxes they feel are due, and you can only release the lien if you pay those taxes. The lien attaches to the property automatically, and no recorded notice is required. The IRS may decide to file a lien for recording with the Register of Deeds (or its equivalent in your state) to gain protections not afforded by the general estate tax lien.

To obtain a federal estate tax release of lien where the lien has been recorded, use a **Form 4422, Application for Certificate Discharging Property Subject to Estate Tax Lien**, to request that a **Form 792, Certificate of Release of Lien,** be issued when filing your **Form 706** (see Chapter 16). If no estate tax lien was recorded or no **Form 706** is required to be filed for your estate and your purchaser wants proof that there is no lien or that it has been satisfied, provide the purchaser with either

- ✔ A copy of the **Form 706**, the estate tax closing letter, and proof of payment *or*

- ✔ Documentation showing that no **Form 706** was required to be filed

Check with your state's department of taxation to see what steps you need to take to release the state's lien. Liens should be released prior to the sale of the property, but that's not always possible. Don't fear if some taxes are due but you don't have the money to pay them; the state sends someone to the closing to collect the taxes owed in exchange for a release of lien. If there's some question as to whether taxes are due, the state often accepts an escrow payment, which it refunds after a final tax determination has been reached.

If there's no taxable estate for federal estate tax purposes, you can't get a release of lien, but you can sometimes have your real estate or estate attorney prepare a recordable affidavit stating that no estate tax is due and sign it in your capacity as executor, administrator, or trustee, whichever applies.

After you have the release of lien or affidavit in your hot little hands, run, don't walk, to the Registry of Deeds in the county or town where the property is located to record that baby. The release of lien or affidavit becomes part of the title history attached to that property, and every time it's sold or refinanced, that lien and its subsequent release or the affidavit will be noted on the title examiner's report. Check with your local probate court, register of deeds, or a local probate attorney to see which method is used in your state to obtain clear title on the real estate.

# Paying Final Administration Expenses

When you're about to finish administration and close an estate, it may be tempting to make final distributions to residuary beneficiaries before you pay amounts still owed for administration. Be patient, though, and make sure that all administration expenses are paid first; otherwise, you may find yourself begging, usually unsuccessfully, for the residuary beneficiaries to give back some of what they received so you can pay what's still owed. Here are the fees that are typically still owed as you come toward the end of the estate's administration:

- **Attorney's and accountant's fees:** For preparation of **Form 706** and **Form 1041**, and for the probate accounting.

- **Executor's or administrator's fee:** Pay yourself your executor's fee, which must be reasonable. You establish your fee in one of several ways: The decedent's will determines the amount (or at least spells out how to calculate it), state statute fixes the amount based on a fee schedule, or in some jurisdictions, your fee as executor must be what would be considered *reasonably necessary* (or words to the same effect). Some of the factors that may be considered in determining your fee include

  - The size of the estate and the extent of the risks and responsibilities you assumed

  - The complexity of estate matters that you're called upon to handle

  - The amount of time you spent administering the estate (here's where your detailed time records are useful)

- How well you did your job

- Fees received by others for similar work

- The results of your efforts

You're also allowed reimbursement for reasonable expenses you incurred in administering the estate, from appraiser's fees you paid out of pocket to the cost of envelopes and postage.

Be sure to itemize all such expenses in your accounting so the court can see where the money has gone.

✔ **Miscellaneous administration expenses:** Pay any other unpaid expenses of administration, including to other professionals and the court, or set aside funds for their payment. Any funds set aside, which should be minimal at this point, should be kept in a noninterest-bearing account to avoid having to recalculate the estate income tax for very small earnings or file another year's return to satisfy the IRS.

✔ **Estate income taxes:** Although owing any estate income taxes on the final returns is uncommon, make sure that you pay anything you do owe.

Here's where your up-to-date checkbook and accounting records come in handy. Check them to see what fees are outstanding. Also check out Chapter 8 for more info on paying these different expenses.

# Making Final Distributions to Residuary Beneficiaries

Although you can sometimes make partial distributions of *residuary* (what's left after payment of expenses, debts, taxes, and specific bequests and devises) shares after the period for filing claims has passed and you know the amount of the estate and inheritance taxes, such partial distribution is by no means required. However, in order to completely close the estate, you should make final distributions of residuary shares when you've settled all the affairs of the estate, including receiving the estate and inheritance tax closing letters, and prepared the final account (and, in some circumstances and/or jurisdictions, not until after its allowance by the probate court). If you haven't paid all the final expenses, keep a reserve to do so. (Refer to Chapter 8 for the lowdown on how to make distributions to residuary beneficiaries.)

# Preparing and Filing Final Estate Income Tax Returns

After you distribute all the estate assets, you may now prepare the final estate income tax returns, even if you haven't reached the end of your tax year. Because no tax is due, you're not in any danger of paying taxes before you have to; you're only making sure that you don't forget this important step. Write the dates of the tax year you're using at the top of the form, and be sure to mark this return "Final" by not only checking the box but also writing the word *Final* across the top of page one in black or red marker. Trust us, this part feels terrific! Chapter 19 explains just what happens to the estate income and deductions for tax purposes in the final year of the estate.

Check out Chapter 18 for a thorough discussion of how to prepare the estate income tax returns. You've no doubt been preparing and filing these right along on a yearly basis and in a timely fashion, even if you haven't done much other accounting work until now, because Uncle Sam waits for no man, woman, or executor.

# Readying Accounts for Allowance by the Probate Court

You may feel that we overemphasize the importance of keeping good records, but good records really come into play now when you're closing the estate and preparing the estate accountings for *allowance* (approval by the probate court). Those records you've kept will pay off in spades.

The exact procedure and order of events for allowance of accounts and for closing your estate varies by your decedent's state (and even county) of *domicile* (the decedent's legal residence) and by the type of probate you've elected (see Chapter 6). The following sections set out some of the typical options found in a state that has adopted a version of the Uniform Probate Code. Be sure to check with your local probate court for the proper procedure and order of these events; you've come so far, it would be a shame to mess up now.

For all the probate court forms we reference in the next sections, check out your local probate court's online system or your states online system. There's a good chance one or both entities have posted the necessary forms for you to download at your leisure. You can also check in person with your local probate court for these forms.

# Using the appropriate form of accounting

Prepare your probate accountings based on the accounting form used in your local probate court. You may prepare your accountings on an annual basis as you do your estate income tax returns (and, in fact, some courts may require that you do so and file them annually with the probate court). Check to see what forms of accounting apply in your jurisdiction and when they're required to be filed and allowed. Even if they're required to be filed annually, you may not be required to seek their allowance until the final account is filed — and sometimes not even then. The first (which is sometimes also the final) accounting starts with the assets you listed on the estate inventory.

Check with your court to see which one of the following forms of probate accounting you should use.

## Principal and income

Some states require an accounting that differentiates between income and principal, but most don't for estates (but may for trusts under wills):

- ✔ *Income* is interest, dividends, rents, and the like; the earnings on the principal during the period of the accounting.
- ✔ *Principal* is the assets of the estate on which income is earned.

*Principal and income accounting* basically means that the principal and any additions to or subtractions from principal are accounted for on their own schedule (or in a separate column, depending on the form the court is using), and income to the estate is accounted for on its own schedule (or in its own column of the accounting). The income and principal are then reconciled at the end of the accounting or at the bottom of the columns. Check out Chapter 14 for more on the differences between these two terms and a sample account.

## Receipts and expenditures

In some states you have to report assets or income received (*receipts*) on one schedule, including as your first entries those assets on the probate inventory (for example, **Schedule A**), expenditures on another schedule (for example, **Schedule B**), sometimes a schedule of gains and losses on the disposition of assets (for example, **Schedule C**), and property on hand at the end of the accounting period on a third or fourth (for example, **Schedule C or D**). This form of accounting is called *receipts and expenditures accounting*. If your accounting balances (as it should) and this is your final account, your ending balance will be zero because you'll have distributed all the assets of the estate before you file your final accounting.

### Length of accounting period

Some courts may require that an annual accounting be filed, but others permit your accounting to run from the date of death through the closing of the estate, even if that period is several years. If you're preparing an annual account, you may have two choices to bring your account to a full year after your decedent's date of death:

- ✔ Using a calendar year-end (which coincides with those **1099**s you may be receiving)

- ✔ Using a *fiscal year-end* (any month end other than December)

If your court allows a choice, choose whatever works best for you. ***Remember:*** Just because you may have chosen a fiscal year-end for income tax purposes doesn't mean that you're required to choose the same year-end for your probate accounting. (Refer to Chapter 18 for help deciding which choice may be right for you.)

## Following the proper probate procedures

Following are the steps to take to close the estate under each form of probate administration we introduce in Chapter 6.

### Informal unsupervised administration

You may use informal unsupervised administration to close the estate whether you used formal or informal unsupervised administration to commence it.

- ✔ **Final account:** File a final account and serve it on all the interested parties, who at this point will probably be just the residuary beneficiaries, as the specific beneficiaries will have already received their bequests and will no longer have any interest in the estate. File the proof of service with the probate court along with the accounting.

- ✔ **Sworn Statement to Close Informal Administration:** Prepare the Sworn Closing Statement, serve it on the interested parties, and file it and the proof of service with the court. In the Sworn Closing Statement, you're saying that it's been more than a certain period of time (such as five months) since you were appointed executor; the period for filing of claims, if any, has passed; and that you've paid the claims, expenses, and other taxes and distributed the assets to the persons entitled to them. You're also listing the interested persons; saying whether state estate tax was due and paid, and stating that you've sent a copy of the Sworn Closing Statement and the account to the interested persons.

- ✔ **Objections:** All interested persons have a certain period of time (such as 28 days) to file any objections to the Sworn Closing Statement.

- ✔ **Certificate of Completion:** If there are no objections, you're entitled to a certificate of completion. Note that the Certificate doesn't preclude any action against you or the surety on any bond that you have obtained, and your appointment doesn't end until one year after the Sworn Closing Statement is filed. So don't go canceling that bond and surety just yet (if you have one)!

### Formal unsupervised and supervised administration

You may want to close the estate with a formal proceeding even when you have unsupervised administration because then you will be immediately released from liability as executor, unlike with informal unsupervised administration, where you must wait a year. This would also be a good time to use a formal proceeding if you haven't yet done so because this gets the will formally admitted, and there's no statute of limitations on a will that has been informally admitted to probate. And, of course, if you're using supervised administration, you must use formal closing procedures and a Petition for Complete Estate Settlement:

- ✔ **Final account:** File a final account and serve it on all the interested parties. File the proof of service with the probate court along with the accounting. Note that no service is required where an interested party has signed a waiver and consent.

- ✔ **Petition for Complete Estate Settlement:** File a petition for Complete Estate Settlement with the court after the time for filing of claims has elapsed. If testacy wasn't already formally adjudicated (meaning the will was allowed), ask for that now if you want. On the form:

  - List the interested persons and their representatives.

  - If distributions were made to beneficiaries, provide the details.

  - List the final attorney and executor fees.

  - If all distributions haven't been made, list the assets and who they're intended for.

On the petition you'll also state the following:

- The time for presenting claims has passed.

- All claims have been paid, or, if not, a schedule for payment is attached.

- The final account has been served or is served with the petition on all interested persons.

- All assets have been distributed or, if not, a schedule of distribution is attached and served on all interested persons.

- No state estate or inheritance tax was due or it was paid.

- If the will is being adjudicated, the facts regarding the will are set forth.

Service of the petition on interested persons isn't required where they have given their waivers and consents.

✔ **Other required filings:** File any of the following that haven't yet been filed: the inventory, accountings, notice of appointment, attorney fee notice, notice to spouse of elective rights and allowance, any notices of continued administration, and proofs of publication (if any). See Chapters 6, 7, and 8 for further discussion of some of these probate forms.

✔ **Settlement Order:** Use a Settlement Order in a formal unsupervised proceeding when the will hasn't been *proven* (admitted to probate) and you don't want to do so at closing either. Note that no notice to heirs is required because you're not proving the will. Of course, a will contest hasn't been precluded when you go this route.

✔ **Order for Complete Estate Settlement:** You're entitled to (and need to prepare a draft of) an Order for Complete Estate Settlement in a formal unsupervised proceeding where the will has been proved and in all cases of Supervised Administration. This order approves the final account, attorneys and executor's fees, distributions and payments of claims, terminates your appointment as executor and discharges you as executor, cancels your bond, and closes the estate.

✔ **Order of Discharge:** A separate Order of Discharge of you as executor can be entered upon payment of any claims and distributions set out in the Order for Complete Estate Settlement.

## Remembering filing fees

Most, if not all, states have a statutory filing fee, with the amount set by statute that must accompany the filing of the account with the probate court. In order to file the account, you need to make sure that you pay these fees. The amount of the fee may be based on either the size of the estate or the length of account (so much per year, if you have a multiple-year accounting) and is intended to cover the cost of the probate court's review of the account. Check with your local court before filing your accounts because the fees are subject to change.

## Appointing a guardian ad litem, if needed

A *guardian ad litem* (GAL) must be appointed under certain circumstances to represent the interests of persons not yet born or ascertained (such as when the residuary beneficiary is a trust under the will for the decedent's descendants, and the executor is also the trustee), or legally incompetent (such as a minor with no legal guardian). Seek advice from an attorney experienced in probate law if you're uncertain whether you need a guardian ad litem. If a GAL is required and appointed by the court, you give service of notice to the GAL and provide them with a copy of the account and ask that they assent to it. You then file a form from the GAL assenting to the account, along with the proof of service on the military affidavit (see the next section), with the probate court.

## Filing a military affidavit, if necessary

In some states, before you can close the estate, you need to file a military affidavit stating whether any beneficiary is in the military service. You must file it whether or not a beneficiary is in the military. If so, an assent must be obtained from that person or a military attorney appointed to represent them. The same person can act as military attorney and *guardian ad litem*.

## Notifying the surety

One year after you've received the Certificate of Completion in informal unsupervised administration, and immediately upon receiving the Order for Complete Estate Settlement in both formal unsupervised administration and supervised administration, notify the surety on the bond as applicable. The surety will then stop billing the estate for its services. (Recall that the *surety* is the company guaranteeing the bond, to whom the estate has paid a fee, unless the bond was allowed with personal sureties, such as attorneys known to the court.)

# Part III
# Operating a Revocable or Irrevocable Trust

## An Example of Calculating Trust Accounting Income

| Description | Income | Principal |
|---|---|---|
| Income received | | |
| Ordinary dividends | $1,000.00 | |
| Taxable interest | $10,000.00 | |
| Tax-exempt interest | $2,000.00 | |
| Rents and royalties | $600.00 | |
| Long-term capital gain distributions | | $500.00 |
| Short-term capital gains | | $1,000.00 |
| Long-term capital gains | | $1,500.00 |
| **Total Income** | **$13,600.00** | **$3,000.00** |
| Deductions | | |
| Trustee's fee | ($500.00) | ($500.00) |
| Tax preparation fee | ($250.00) | ($125.00) |
| Investment advice | ($1,000.00) | ($1,000.00) |
| Federal income taxes paid | | ($500.00) |
| State income taxes paid | | ($350.00) |
| **Total deductions** | **($1,750.00)** | **($2,475.00)** |
| **Net additions to principal** | | **$525.00** |
| **Trust Accounting Income** | **$11,850.00** | |

If you expect your estate to result in considerable assets, you may want to establish a trust of your own. Find out the benefits of setting up a trust at www.dummies.com/extras/estatetrustadministration.

# In this part . . .

✔ Get a better understanding of the trustee's duties, the terms of the trust agreement, and how you can best protect the trust's assets.

✔ Discover how to fund the trust, both while the creator of the trust is alive and after his or her death, and how to transfer various types of assets.

✔ Receive guidance on investing and diversifying the trust's assets, choosing investment advisors, providing for the needs of the beneficiaries, paying the trust's expenses, and setting up a trust filing system that works.

✔ Determine who the trust beneficiaries are, and how and when you'll make distributions to them.

✔ Find out how to terminate the trust down the road, including preparing the final accountings and income tax returns.

# Chapter 10

# Understanding the Trustee's Duties

. . . . . . . . . . . . . . . . . . . . . . . . . . . . . . . . . . . . . . . . . . . . . .

*In This Chapter*

▶ Making sure that you understand the trust instrument

▶ Using your discretion to fulfill the grantor's wishes

▶ Keeping an eye on the assets and their best uses

▶ Staying on top of the paperwork

. . . . . . . . . . . . . . . . . . . . . . . . . . . . . . . . . . . . . . . . . . . . . .

After you've been named, and agreed to serve, as *trustee* (a person who holds property for the benefit of another) of a *trust* (a right of property that one person holds for the benefit of another; the conditions of the trust are usually spelled out in a *trust instrument*), you need to understand the trustee's duties and powers as soon as possible. Your duties may vary based on the type of trustee you are (independent or family), but regardless, you now have fiduciary duties! Hopefully, the trust creator asked whether you were willing to serve before he or she named you as a trustee.

Whether or not you were asked beforehand, you don't actually become a trustee until you accept the position; you can always decline to serve. Assuming you've agreed to serve, go over that trust instrument with a fine-toothed comb and ask the grantor's attorney (or one of your choosing) for the answers to any questions you have regarding the document itself or your role as trustee. This is no time to be shy, just as with the rest of life, ignorance of the law is no excuse.

This chapter covers the role you've assumed, the duties you'll be expected to carry out, and the expectations others will have of you as a trustee. Read on, and enjoy the confidence the grantor has expressed in you!

# Getting Acquainted with the Trust Instrument

The trust instrument is your new bible, and reading and understanding its intentions is the first step in identifying your duties and powers as trustee. In the trust instrument, the trust's *grantor* (creator) includes all the powers he or she wants you to have and may specify some you can't have! The laws of the state the grantor chooses to govern the trust address any issues you can't find an answer for in the trust instrument; that state's laws also trump the trust instrument if it goes against them. With respect to the validity of a trust, the grantor must choose a state's laws with some connection to the trust. The grantor has the option of choosing either the *domicile* (residence) of the grantor, a trustee, a beneficiary, or even the location of trust assets; whichever state's laws the grantor chooses govern all aspects of the trust. For real property held in the trust, the laws of the state in which the property's located govern that property. After you read the trust instrument, you'll also know what the grantor's plans are for the trust over time and for the people included in it as beneficiaries.

Of course, if you know about the trust before you actually assume any power over the property and are on close enough terms with the grantor, it's always a good idea to talk with the grantor about his or her hopes and dreams for the property and exactly what benefit he or she wants the beneficiary to derive from the trust. Many trust instruments are couched in such nonspecific language as to allow the trustee the widest possible latitude, but the grantor's actual intent may be much more specific. One of us, for example, has been named trustee for a trust set up to look after the grantor's sister and friend. Although the terms are intentionally vague, conversations with the grantor have made it clear what his intent is; now the job of the trustee is to carry that out to the best of her ability.

The following sections help you take the trust instrument and develop a plan to execute it. Furthermore, we explain all the individuals who may play a role in a trust.

## Creating a plan based on the trust's terms

The terms of the trust govern what happens to the trust assets: who takes care of them (the trustee), who benefits from them (the beneficiaries), and how they will be invested. The terms of the trust instrument also dictate whether the property funding the trust remains in a single trust or is divided into multiple trusts governed by the same instrument. If the grantor wants multiple trusts, the instrument also directs when to divide the assets and when and how to make payments to beneficiaries. You, as trustee, make your plan for caring for the trust assets and beneficiaries based on what the trust instrument tells you to do and when to do it.

For example, say you're trustee of the Abigail Jones Trust, which is receiving assets from the Abigail Jones Estate. Under the terms of Abby's trust, you divide the property you receive upon her death equally into three trusts, one for each of her children, with the trusts lasting for their lifetimes. As trustee, you have broad discretion under the trust instrument to pay or accumulate income and principal from each trust. Abby's eldest child is a spendthrift; money runs through his hands like water. You know you'll need to be parsimonious in making distributions to him, so you place a fair amount of the assets in long-term growth investments. Abby's middle child is a young schoolteacher. She'll never make a large salary, but she lives within her means. However, she'll have a hard time accumulating a down payment for a home, which you know was a priority of Abby's. So you place a portion of the assets in her trust in a fairly liquid investment, for the time soon to come when that down payment is needed. Abby's youngest child is still in high school and will be applying to college next year. You place four years' worth of college costs in liquid investments staggered to mature at one-year intervals. You pay out the money if she isn't lucky enough to get a scholarship. The balance you invest in a mixture of assets that will provide income to the beneficiary, as well as increasing the value of the trust assets as you wait to see how this child develops.

## Identifying the players

> "All the world's a stage, / And all the men and women merely players. . . ."
> — Shakespeare, *As You Like It*

The grantor of the trust may not have had Shakespeare's words in mind when creating the trust, but he or she has indeed set the stage for his or her wishes to be played out under the trust instrument. As trustee, identifying the players is one of your important first steps because you need to know who the beneficiaries and remaindermen are (you presumably already know the grantor if he or she appointed you as trustee) and if there are any co-trustees acting with you.

Here is a typical "cast":

- **Grantor:** Sometimes called the *settlor,* this person creates the trust.

- **Trustee:** The person or corporation charged with safeguarding and managing the assets of the trust and making distributions to beneficiaries in accordance with the grantor's stated wishes in the trust instrument. The trustee can be either independent or non-independent (usually a family member), and trusts may have either type of trustee or both.

  - **Independent trustee:** An *independent* (or *professional*) trustee is one the IRS considers independent of the grantor and the beneficiaries for estate tax purposes. That way, the principal of the trust isn't included in the beneficiary's taxable estate upon his or her own death. The independent trustee may be either an individual independent trustee or a corporate independent trustee. The *individual independent trustee* is (ideally) an expert in trust administration, such as an attorney, accountant, or enrolled agent. The *corporate independent trustee* is a bank or trust company whom the grantor appoints as trustee; this entity always qualifies as an independent trustee.

  - **Family or non-independent trustee:** A *family* or *non-independent* trustee is one who is the grantor or a beneficiary (or is related to the grantor or a beneficiary in such a way that he or she wouldn't be considered independent for estate tax purposes). Grantors frequently use family trustees with independent trustees so that a family member or another non-independent source can give input on trust matters that don't affect the trust's tax status. As long as the family trustee doesn't have the power to make unrestricted distributions to himself or herself or to a dependent, he or she may participate in all other issues relating to managing the trust.

- **Beneficiary(ies):** Beneficiaries are those people or entities who/that have an interest in the trust, whether now (a *present interest*) or in the future (a *future interest*). An interest as a beneficiary can also be *contingent* (relying upon an event in the future that may not happen) or *vested* (not subject to any contingencies). For instance, a person who could only become a beneficiary if the current beneficiary dies during the first person's lifetime is a contingent beneficiary.

- **Remaindermen:** *Remaindermen* are those people or entities who will receive the trust property after an interest in it has expired. If, for instance, Uncle George leaves his property in trust for the lifetime of his wife, Aunt Rose, for her benefit, with the property to go outright to his nieces and nephews upon Aunt Rose's death, the nieces and nephews are the remaindermen.

You, as trustee, are balancing the rights of the current and future beneficiaries and the remaindermen when you make your judgments as to distributions of principal and trust investments. If principal distributions are discretionary, assets left in the trust to accumulate benefit later beneficiaries and remaindermen, and your decisions as to what mix of income earning and growth investments to hold in the trust affects both the income beneficiary and the remaindermen (see Chapter 12).

## Reforming the trust

Many jurisdictions allow a trust to be *reformed,* or modified, by a court in order to carry out or conform to the settlor's intent, or if there is an unintentional omission or error in the document. For instance, in a recent Massachusetts case, the decedent settlor intended to set up a charitable trust, but due to poor drafting by the attorney, the trust didn't qualify as income tax exempt, thus leaving less income for charity. The trustee filed an action to reform the trust, and a Massachusetts court allowed the reformation. You should be aware that although trust reformation may be possible in your neck of the woods, you will probably have a high burden of proof and, if any beneficiaries will be adversely affected, you may not succeed. It's our experience that trust reformations are few and far between, so your best hope for smooth administration of your trust is that the attorney who drafted it was highly competent.

# Empowering the Trustee

The powers the grantor gives you in the trust instrument are crucial. Not only can these powers determine what the beneficiary(ies) receive from the trust and when, but the administrative powers also ensure the smooth running of the trust. You have to strike a critical balance here. Hopefully the grantor gives you enough powers to run the trust with ease, economy, and diligence without giving you enough power to hang yourself (metaphorically, we hope!).

## Buying and selling assets

You, as trustee, typically have the power under the trust instrument to buy and sell assets (except for any unusual asset the grantor wants retained in the trust). Aside from any other specific directions in the trust instrument or state law, you must follow the *prudent man rule* — that is, to act as a prudent person would in managing their own affairs. In addition, most states have a *legal list* of investments that are suitable for trusts. (Chapter 12 gives you more detailed info about buying and selling the assets in the trust.)

## Trusts with foreign interests

As people in general begin to invest more widely in foreign businesses and foreign property, the assets being used to fund trusts are becoming more international in scope. Most foreign assets are owned using American Depository (ADR) shares and are traded through U.S. stock exchanges, which don't put any extra compliance requirements on you as the trustee. But if the trust actually owns non-ADR shares, or assets that are physically located outside of the United States, you may want to read carefully and get good advice.

The Foreign Account Tax Compliance Act (FATCA) disclosure rules require U.S. trusts and estates to file forms annually that list the foreign assets owned, whether shares in a publicly or privately held corporation, partnership, limited liability company or any other entity, a bank or brokerage account, an annuity contract or insurance policy, or an interest in a foreign investment fund, a hedge fund, a mutual fund, or any private equity fund. In addition to the infamous **Form TD 90-22.1, Report of Foreign**

**Bank and Financial Accounts** (fondly referred to as the FBAR), which is due on June 30 of each year for the year just passed, you now may also have to file IRS **Form 8938, Statement of Specific Foreign Financial Assets, Form 5471, Information Return of U.S. Persons with Respect to Certain Foreign Corporations,** and/or **Form 3520, Annual Return to Report Transactions With Foreign Trusts and Receipt of Certain Foreign Gifts,** all of which are due on the due date for the trust's income tax return, including extensions.

Don't mess around with your obligation to file the necessary foreign asset and account disclosure forms. The IRS isn't joking about stepping up FATCA enforcement, and the penalties, both financial and personal, are stiff. If you aren't sure whether your trust meets the disclosure thresholds, ask. And if you determine that you need to complete any or all of these forms, get help, at least in the first year. After the initial year, you'll have a template that you can copy for the future, if you so desire.

## Determining distributions to beneficiaries

The grantor can determine the frequency and amount of the distributions to the beneficiaries in the terms of the trust, or he or she can leave it to your discretion as trustee. If the grantor leaves it to your discretion, your job includes observing any guidelines set forth by the grantor in the trust instrument, and adhering to the overall intent of the grantor. The following sections highlight some of the types of distributions you may need to make as a trustee. Chapter 13 provides more in-depth info about paying specific distributions.

### Income distributions

Frequently, trust instruments direct that all income is to be distributed at least quarterly. Alternatively, income distributions may be made at other specified intervals, or at your discretion. Very often, the distribution schedule is based on the age of the beneficiary so that younger beneficiaries often only receive discretionary distributions (great for paying for college while still keeping financial aid options open), and older beneficiaries may become entitled to mandatory income distributions. No two trusts are the same, so you need to be sure to read the instrument upon your appointment and then reread it periodically to be certain that you're still following the guidelines set out.

### Principal distributions

Unscheduled distributions of *principal,* or *corpus,* are often allowed at the discretion of the trustee(s) for a specific purpose (such as buying a house, starting a business, or obtaining an education), or purely for the health and welfare of the beneficiary. The trust could also provide for no principal distributions, especially if the grantor wants to maintain the principal for a later generation of beneficiary.

Many trusts are set up with the intent of distributing the trust principal to the beneficiary over a period of time, usually between five and ten years, and at very specific ages (for example, a distribution of one-third of the trust principal at age 25, one-half at age 30, and the remainder at age 35). Keep an eye out for this language as you make your plans for the administration of the trust and the investment of the assets, and mark those dates down in your calendar.

Trusts contain different standards for when principal distributions, if any, can be made to a beneficiary based on whether the trust has an independent trustee. The following are two reasons for different standards for principal distributions:

- ✔ **With no independent trustee:** If there isn't an independent trustee (and the trust is for the benefit of someone other than the grantor), the IRS has identified certain "magic words" that restrict the distribution of principal and keep the trust from being included in the beneficiary's estate for estate tax purposes. Although this structuring may seem incredibly technical, it's an important point, especially for the beneficiary and his or her heirs. The magic words that keep this trust out of the beneficiary's estate are "health, education, maintenance, and support," which constitute an *ascertainable standard.*

- ✔ **With an independent trustee:** Unfortunately, *comfort* isn't one of the IRS's magic words; using the word *comfort* makes a trust taxable in a surviving spouse's estate. Because many grantors feel the ascertainable standard described previously is too limiting, especially in a trust for the surviving spouse, grantors frequently elect to have an independent trustee so that the grantor can bestow broader powers of principal distribution without causing adverse tax consequences to any party.

## Hiring and firing advisors

The grantor and the person drafting the trust instrument understand that not every trustee will be a wizard at all aspects of trust administration, so trust instruments typically give the trustee the power to hire and fire advisors. Look for this power in your trust instrument. If you do decide to hire an advisor, check out Chapter 4 for more specific advice about finding out what's a good fit.

After all, your grantor wants you to have any advice you need to run the trust and fulfill your fiduciary duty. And, if an advisor isn't working out, including one whom the grantor has chosen, you need the power to let the advisor go — whether for personal incompatibility with the trustee or a question of competence. If you feel that you've given an advisor a fair chance to prove himself to you (and fair is defined by you as trustee, unless your trust instrument provides otherwise), then by all means fire him and hire another of your choice.

# Coloring Inside the Lines: Understanding Fiduciary Duty and Limitations

As a trustee, you have a *fiduciary duty* to the trust; that is, you must always act in accordance with the terms of the trust and in its best interests and the best interests of its beneficiaries and remaindermen. Your fiduciary duty is further spelled out in the governing state law and in court cases in that state over the years. Your attorney can advise you as to the law regarding your duties and limitations as any questions arise. Your failure to fulfill your fiduciary duty or overstepping your powers as trustee can lead to the beneficiaries taking legal action against you. To avoid any potential lawsuits or problems, the next sections provide you with some important points you need to remember when administering a trust.

## Exercising discretion

How much power you have to exercise discretion in your role as trustee depends on the language of the trust instrument, some of which is dictated by tax law if you're a family trustee. The grantor, in choosing you, gave you a framework within which to work, but he or she also trusted you to make the best possible choices when circumstances dictate. In our experience, circumstance almost always dictates at some point or other.

Whether you have a great deal or only a tiny amount, some discretion is necessary as trustee. You must be able to make and change investments in a way you feel benefits the trust; for example, even if you're following the prudent man rule. And you must have some discretion in whether or not to make principal distributions (if principal distributions are allowable).

As trustee, you're often in the position of acting in place of the grantor, and somehow, you're expected to do what he or she would have done in the same situation. Sound impossible? It is, but that doesn't excuse you from trying your best. Obviously, the closer your personal relationship with the grantor, the more likely you'll be to act in a way the grantor would have approved of. So, when you're faced with the question of whether to pay that school tuition bill for one beneficiary, buy a car or a house for a second beneficiary, or bail a third beneficiary out of jail for the third time, applying what you know about the grantor to the question at hand may well provide you with the guidance you need to make these sometimes sticky decisions.

So, when faced with a decision, what do you do? Never make distributions willy-nilly, but document everything that you're asked to distribute by the beneficiary. If you're helping him or her to buy a house, make sure that you have copies of all the house purchase documents. If it's school tuition that's on the line, keep a copy of all the school bills you pay. And if you choose to bail someone out of jail, keep the receipt from the bail bondsman. Of course, if you opt to leave him or her there in timeout to think, write a memo to the file, laying out your reasoning for that decision, too.

## *Obtaining errors and omissions insurance*

At one point in time, no one would have dreamed of suing a trustee. But in these litigious times, no one is immune to lawsuits, and that includes you in your role as trustee. So in order to protect yourself, don't forget to obtain *errors and omissions insurance*. This insurance protects against claims by beneficiaries that you haven't fulfilled your fiduciary duty in managing and administering the trust. Contact your insurance broker about obtaining this insurance, which is a deductible trust expense.

Without errors and admissions insurance, if you make a mistake in administering the trust, no matter how unintentional, a disgruntled beneficiary can go after you and your personal assets. If you have insurance coverage, the insurance company will defend you against a questionable lawsuit because it won't want to pay out a claim unless it feels the claim is justified. Buying this insurance is money well spent.

# Protecting the Trust's Assets

Among the myriad of duties you assume as trustee is a duty to protect the trust assets. In today's financial world, protecting the assets most likely doesn't mean hanging on to those assets with which the trust was funded — unless those assets consist of shares of a closely held business, a family-owned farm, or the like, that the grantor specifically instructed be retained in the trust.

In that case, you fulfill your duty as trustee by retaining the asset and seeing that it's managed as competently as possible. However, barring an instruction in the document to retain specific assets, as trustee you must constantly look at the assets to see whether they're the most appropriate to serve the trust purposes. The following sections give you the lowdown on how to guard the assets.

## Diversifying the assets

"Don't put all your eggs in one basket" doesn't just apply on the farm. One of the cornerstones of today's investment philosophy is to diversify assets into different classes, such as stocks and bonds, and into different industries, such as transportation, healthcare, consumer goods, energy stocks, and so on. That way, you spread the risk among several classes of investments and several industries, and the danger of overall loss lessens. The theory behind this is that not all investments respond in the same way to all market conditions, so you're better prepared for market changes in one class of asset or one industry if you're invested in several. Diversified mutual funds or mutual fund families can be one answer to diversifying assets in a smaller trust.

Unlike investing your own money, where you're allowed to invest in anything that's legal, investing as a trustee requires that you exercise due diligence in researching investments and assume only moderate risk. Speculating, although not specifically prohibited, is strongly discouraged. Your goal shouldn't be to scale great heights but rather to allow modest gains and prevent drastic losses. Chapter 12 gives you more detailed info about investing the trust's assets.

Failure to adequately diversify the assets held inside the trust (except those assets which the grantor specifically requires that you retain) can leave you open to accusations of incompetence (or worse) from the trust beneficiaries or remaindermen. If you choose an investment policy that runs counter to the standard wisdom, document your reasoning and be prepared to defend your choices — in court, if necessary.

## Asking for help

Getting recommendations — by word of mouth, from other professionals, and even from advertisements — is great, but be sure to check them out thoroughly. Call the Better Business Bureau, the state bar association (for attorneys), state board of accountancy (for CPAs), or the IRS (for Enrolled Agents) to see whether any complaints have been filed against them. Here are some professionals you may find useful:

✔ **Investment advisors:** An investment advisor is a person or company who advises the trustee as to what investments to make, given the purpose of the trust, its size, and the needs of the beneficiaries. If you choose to use an investment advisor, always use one that charges a fee for services, not one who receives a percentage of sales!

✔ **Trust companies, banks, and brokerages:** Trust companies and banks that have trust departments can be useful for holding the assets of the trust. They can prepare periodic statements, annual accounts, and income tax returns and also invest the assets (all for a fee, of course). Trust assets may also be placed in a brokerage account or accounts, which provide you with periodic statements and investment advice. Generally, the fees involved in this option are for trades. Some brokerages prepare annual accounts and tax returns for an additional fee; others don't. If you need this service, ask before you open the account.

✔ **Lawyers, accountants, and Enrolled Agents:** Lawyers who specialize in trust law can be useful to you in interpreting the trust document and guiding you as to state law and your role as trustee. Depending on individual state laws, law firms may also have trust departments, where the assets of the trust can be invested and the trust can be administered. Accountants and *Enrolled Agents* (tax professionals licensed by the U.S. Treasury Department) who are familiar with trust administration can prepare accountings and income tax returns.

See Chapter 4 for choosing the appropriate professionals to help you.

# Preparing and Filing Annual Income Tax Returns and Accounts

As trustee, you're responsible for preparing annual accounts and income tax returns or having them prepared by the appropriate professional. Don't forget that, whoever prepares them, you're responsible for their contents, so review them carefully!

If the trust was created under a will rather than under a separate trust instrument, you must file annual accounts with the probate court (or its equivalent in your jurisdiction) and have them allowed by the court. Trusts under wills are a rarity nowadays, precisely because they require court supervision. We don't even attempt to go into detail here on the details of allowance of such accounts.

When you have the annual accounts ready, send copies to all current beneficiaries along with a document by which he or she assents to the account. See Chapter 14 for more specific details regarding preparation of annual accounts and Chapter 18 for how to prepare the income tax returns.

# Chapter 11

# Funding the Trust

● ● ● ● ● ● ● ● ● ● ● ● ● ● ● ● ● ● ● ● ● ● ● ● ● ● ● ● ● ● ● ● ● ● ● ● ● ● ● ● ● ● ● ● ● ● ● ● ● ● ● ● ●

## In This Chapter
▶ Moving assets into the trust while the grantor is alive
▶ Reregistering existing assets
▶ Funding a trust after the grantor's death

● ● ● ● ● ● ● ● ● ● ● ● ● ● ● ● ● ● ● ● ● ● ● ● ● ● ● ● ● ● ● ● ● ● ● ● ● ● ● ● ● ● ● ● ● ● ● ● ● ● ● ● ●

*T*he trust instrument has finally been signed. You've agreed to serve as trustee and have also had a chance to look over the provisions of the trust, so you probably have a good idea what you may and may not do as trustee. Now you have to identify the property that belongs in this trust and figure out how you're going to move it from point *A* (the grantor's possession) to point *B* (the trust).

This chapter explains how to transfer all sorts of property and what special considerations you need to make allowances for. We show you how to make sure that the transfer process is smooth and alert you to possible gift tax consequences for transfers made during the grantor's lifetime.

## Putting Assets in Trust during Life

If you're the trustee of a trust whose grantor is still living, or if you're both trustee and grantor of a trust that's ready to start operations, you're probably ready to start moving *assets* (items of value owned by any entity) into the trust. For example, the grantor may have designed the trust to avoid probating certain assets and/or to make everything accessible for the grantor's benefit if he or she becomes incapacitated. (To verify the trust's purpose, refer to Chapter 3.)

Whatever the reason for establishing a trust, now that it's up and running, you need to give it something to run on: assets. Before you begin to transfer assets into the trust, have the following documents handy:

✔ **Certified copy of the trust instrument:** Usually just a photocopy of the instrument, with the words, "A True Copy. Attested by" typed on the front page, and the trustee's original signature. You may make multiple certified copies, but all must have original signatures on the front page.

✔ **Federal taxpayer identification number:** If you haven't already applied for one, you absolutely need one (unless the trust's a revocable living trust [see Chapter 3] in which case you may use the grantor's Social Security number during the grantor's lifetime) before you can open any accounts or transfer any assets. Check out Chapter 18 to find what you need to do in order to obtain this number.

✔ **Proof of ownership:** You must show documentation that proves the grantor owns the property before you can transfer it to the trust; for example, a deed to real estate, stock and/or bond certificates, or bank or broker account statements.

Depending on the type of property you're transferring, you may also need new registration forms, signature cards, or other documents; the company where you're transferring the property will provide the necessary forms.

# Signing It Over: Giving the Trust Asset Ownership

When funding a trust during the grantor's lifetime, you may be changing ownership of many types of property, from money, securities (stocks and bonds), and real estate to life insurance policies and all sorts of personal property. Basically, when you change the ownership of a piece of property to the trust, you're transferring title from the grantor's name to the name of the trustee. For instance, a bank account held in the name of James E. Jones is transferred to *Martha A. Jones, Trustee of the James E. Jones Trust UTA (under trust agreement) dtd 02/11/13.*

No matter the type of property, you must document all transfers from the grantor to the trust. The following sections highlight the different types of property that can be transferred and how you can address each kind.

## Cash and securities

Although all sorts of assets can be held in trust, cash and securities are two assets commonly used to initially fund a trust. And with the advent of technology, funding the trust with cash and securities is quick and easy.

Changing ownership of cash and securities from an individual to a trust is as old as the hills; what's changed is exactly how it's done. The days of someone handing you a folder filled with stock certificates are largely gone, replaced by securities held in so-called *street* or *nominee* name, where your record of ownership is maintained either by the company who issued the shares or bonds, or by a brokerage firm or bank. And even though cash (and checks) haven't entirely gone by the wayside (one of us once had someone hand her a $10,000 cashier's check to fund a trust), sending large sums over the Federal Reserve wires is far more common.

After the new custodian(s) for the property have assured you that they've received all the assets, double-check to make sure that all the assets have left the first custodian and arrived safe and sound at the second. The transfer often takes more than one try to get right. In fact, one of us was involved in a trust where one $500,000 bond took a three-year long detour into never-never land. Follow up on your transfers (on both ends) with phone calls, but always ask for an account statement or some other written evidence that the property is where it should be and that it's been correctly titled.

You may transfer cash and securities in the following ways, depending on how the assets are held to start with and where you want them to end up.

### Transferring within the same financial institution

If the cash or securities being transferred are already in the hands of a financial institution in street name and you're changing only the ownership registration, all you have to do is set up new accounts (to hold cash, securities, or both) in the name of the trust. The bank or brokerage will provide you with the necessary paperwork, such as account applications, signature cards, and **Form W-9, Request for Taxpayer Identification Number and Certification.** After the paperwork is complete, the grantor can initiate the transfer of the property into the trust's account.

### Transferring from one financial institution to another

If you're moving the cash or securities from one financial institution to another and need to change the ownership registration, you still need to complete the same documentation and account opening forms as with transfers within the same bank or brokerage firm. However, the whole process just takes longer because in our experience the institution losing the property drags its feet; it's never in a big hurry to lose that business and the fee it generates. Make sure that the current institution gets the grantor's letters directing the transfer (certified or registered mail is the way to go here), and then follow up with phone calls and/or e-mails.

You can speed the process along if you obtain cash wire-transfer information from the receiving institution via PDF, fax, or even snail mail, and then pass it along to the sending one. And don't forget to get the new custodian's *delivery instructions,* or the specific routing and account numbers for the new custodian's receiving account, for any stocks and bonds you're having transferred. Be sure that you carefully follow the instructions; even a small deviation from the stated method can delay your transfer.

### Reregistering stock and bond certificates

Although we definitely don't recommend it, sometimes you're faced with no alternative but to hold physical certificates, which you'll recognize by the heavy paper, fancy designs, and colored inks. The simplest way to change the registration on them is to reregister the securities from the grantor's name into the name of the trust. The following are a couple of important points to keep in mind when reregistering certificates:

- The grantor must mail the physical certificates back to the issuing company with his or her written instructions.

- In a separate envelope, the grantor should mail *stock powers* (often titled "Assignment Separate from Certificate"), each of which includes the grantor's name, the company name, the number of shares (or face value of the bond), and the new owner's name. Stock powers must be signed by the grantor and typically also require a *signature guarantee,* or a stamp or seal from a commercial bank or stock brokerage — no savings banks or credit unions here.

The company will cancel the old certificates and issue new ones. If you have a lot of stock powers to prepare, you can get pads of blank powers online or from your local legal stationery store.

Although transferring securities from the grantor into the trust isn't rocket science, it does require that you move carefully and methodically. Here are a few suggestions:

- **Use registered mail when transferring physical securities.** You want a record that you sent them, and an acknowledgment of receipt.

- **Never sign a blank stock power.** Put that together with a stock certificate registered to the power's signer, and you've just put what is essentially cash into an envelope; anyone can walk away with it.

- **Never sign the stock power located on the back of the stock certificate.** Always use a separate document, and make sure that you mail it (registered) in a different envelope than the stock certificate.

- **Keep all stock and bond certificates locked away in a safe deposit box until you need them.** These documents are sometimes extremely valuable (worth far more than the paper they're printed on) and replacing lost, stolen, or destroyed certificates is costly and time consuming. If you need to reference what's on these certificates, photocopy them and place the copies in a file, but keep the originals locked away.

If you've just finished reregistering physical securities, and are in possession of all the replacement certificates, you may want to move them into street name by opening a securities account with a bank or a brokerage. The bank or broker can help you fill out any forms to make that change. After the transfer into street name is complete, your job becomes much simpler because interest and dividends are paid directly into your account, and you needn't deposit a multitude of sometimes-miniscule checks.

## Privately held stocks, promissory notes, and limited partnership interests

Many grantors set up trusts with the intention of funding them with non-publicly traded securities, such as "S" corporation stocks, promissory notes, and limited partnership interests. Grantors do this to avoid probate issues and maintain privacy, in the case of *revocable trusts* (trusts the grantor creates and funds during lifetime to avoid probate, but not intended to remove the items from the grantor's taxable estate; see Chapter 3), or to remove items that have the potential for vast increases in worth over time from their estates and estate tax returns.

Whatever the reason, moving these types of assets from personal ownership into a trust is a reasonably simple matter. What's important is that you carefully document the transfer's completion. That is, make sure that you have something in writing showing the stock certificate in the trustee's name, or the assignment of the promissory note to the trustee, or the limited partnership interest in the trustee's name. The typical way to hold title in trust name is as follows: *X (and Y, if there are two trustees), Trustees of the JJD Trust, UTA dtd XX/XX/XX. UTA* stands for under trust agreement, and *dtd* is the traditional abbreviation for dated in this context. Slight variations on this wording are acceptable.

Check out the following to determine what you need to do to change ownership for these three types of property:

- ✔ **Privately held stock:** With this stock, such as stock in family corporations (including "S" corporations), follow the guidelines in the preceding section for reregistering stock certificates. Complete separate stock powers, which are necessary even though signature guarantees typically aren't. And remember, you can't register privately held stock in street name, so the corporate clerk, secretary, or the corporation's attorney must type up new stock certificates in the name of the trust.

- ✔ **Promissory notes:** A grantor may lend money to a third party and decide to place the promissory note into the trust. He or she may transfer the note to the trust by executing an assignment of the note to the trustees. It's a simple document, but case specific. You can ask whoever drew up the note to draft the assignment. The grantor may transfer it to preserve privacy, to remove the note from the probate estate, or to make a non-cash contribution. After all, the money has already been lent; even though the piece of paper showing the loan represents real value, the cash has already left the building. When the grantor assigns the note to the trust, the grantor must notify the borrower to make future payments of principal and interest directly.

✔ **Non-publicly traded limited partnerships:** These are a popular way of owning real estate with a group of like-minded investors. To transfer a limited partnership interest into a trust, the grantor must notify the *general partner* (the partner who's running the partnership) of his or her intent, in writing. An *assignment of partnership interest* is a more formal way to accomplish the transfer, but a letter signed and dated by the owner of the interest should work. The general partner will then change the records of the partnership. Stay on top of this transaction. Keep after that general partner until he shows you that the records of the partnership have been changed to reflect your transfer to the trustee(s) of the trust; general partners often make snails look speedy by comparison.

## Real estate

Depending on what state real property (real estate) is located in, transferring real estate into trust can be quite simple. The following should happen:

### Step one: The grantor transfers the property's title

The grantor transfers title in the property either directly to the trust, or in some states, to a nominee partnership. A *nominee partnership* is an entity that acts as owner of the property on behalf of the trustee (to avoid the necessity of recording the trust instrument in the registry of deeds and turning it into a public record).

By executing a new deed to the property and filing it with the appropriate government office, the grantor completes the transfer in most cases. This new deed is sometimes referred to as a *grant deed, quitclaim deed,* or *warranty deed,* depending on what level of protections exist within the deed to safeguard the owner's interest and on what state houses the real estate. The new deed usually goes to the local Registry of Deeds or its equivalent; in the case of *registered land*, which exists only in certain states, the deed goes to the local land court to complete the transfer.

In some states that limit property tax increases to an annual percentage, transferring real estate may force the property's reappraisal and trigger large property tax increases. Check the rules in your state prior to making the transfer. After the transfer is complete, you can't change your mind.

### Step two: You draft a new deed

If you have the original deed, drafting a new deed is easy. Simply copy the old one in all respects except for changing the names of the parties (and depending on state law, using a quitclaim deed form rather than a warranty deed, because it's a gift). For example, on the new deed, the name of the grantor replaces the name of the person the grantor originally acquired the property from, and the name(s) of the trust or trustee(s) replaces the name of the grantor on the old deed. Depending on state laws, you may need to specify the trustee capacity of the trustees; for instance, the new deed may name "James Doe, Trustee, and his successors, of the John Smith Irrevocable Trust."

You must also check on what, if any, constitutes the standard *consideration* (money and/or other factors that induce the grantor to *execute,* or sign, the deed) in your state in the case of a gift. On the new deed, the consideration may be worded something like "for $1 and other good and valuable consideration." Even though the transfer is a gift, most states require that some consideration be stated on the deed.

If you don't have the original deed, go to the local registry of deeds office in the town or county where the real estate is located and ask how you can best locate the record of that deed. If you aren't up to going through their dusty old books, or you aren't nearby, you can hire someone to do a title search for you. You can likely get a name at the Registry of Deeds.

If an attorney didn't prepare the deed, have one review the deed before signing; you don't want to mess up the deed. A problem with the deed can affect *clear title* (no legal questions as to ownership) to the property.

### Step three: The grantor signs the new deed

The grantor signs the new deed in the presence of a notary public, who affixes his or her official seal (and, in some states, two witnesses). Requirements regarding additional witnesses vary by state; the original deed that you copied from will show how many witnesses your state requires. Record the new deed with the Registry of Deeds or the land court to complete the transfer.

Some real estate is encumbered by a mortgage, and banks and mortgage companies don't look kindly on you transferring property in which they hold a secured interest. Don't attempt to transfer mortgaged property from the grantor into the trust without first obtaining the mortgage company's approval, in writing. The mortgage company may well be congenial to the transfer, but it will require you, as trustee, to assume the grantor's mortgage. It will undoubtedly have documents that you must complete, sign, have notarized, and record, along with the new deed.

### Step four: You, as trustee, assume all responsibility for the property

After the trust officially becomes the owner of the real estate, you, the trustee, assume all the responsibilities for that property. Don't forget to pay the mortgage, if you have one, or the real estate taxes. And absolutely don't forget to insure it, and be sure that your name as trustee is on the insurance as an insured. If you have a mortgage on the property, the mortgage company will be certain to remind you, but when you own that property free and clear, it's sometimes easy to let certain things slide. Of course, should the property be damaged, or should someone be injured on the trust's property, you as trustee may well be held liable if you've failed to adequately insure it.

# Life insurance policies

Life insurance policies come in many flavors, and they guarantee a reasonably large cash payout down the road for a relatively small investment now. A life insurance policy can fund a trust that eventually creates some available cash for future expenditures, such as anticipated estate taxes. No matter what type, life insurance policies may be acquired by a trust in two ways: The trustee may purchase a policy on the life of the grantor, or the grantor may transfer ownership of an existing policy into the trust.

Because life insurance trusts are generally not funded with large amounts of cash or securities, the grantor typically gifts a large enough sum into the trust each year to pay the annual premium and any fees and expenses the trust may incur. The sole asset in the trust (other than small amounts of cash or money market funds) is the insurance owned by the trust on the grantor's life. When the grantor dies, the face value of the policy pays into the trust, bypassing the grantor's probate estate entirely.

The following sections outline the two ways a trust can acquire a life insurance policy.

## Policies purchased by the trustee

When you, the trustee, purchase life insurance on the life of the grantor, you're responsible for contacting an insurance broker and negotiating the terms of the policy. You'll typically only be doing this if the trust was set up as a vehicle to own life insurance (for instance, a Crummey trust; see Chapter 3). Of course, if you're not an expert on life insurance, you'll want a third party looking over your shoulder. Some attorneys who work with life insurance trusts have become quite expert at analyzing the benefits of various insurance policies. And you'll want a highly recommended insurance broker. In addition to relying on friends' and family's recommendations, check with your state's Secretary of State, who licenses insurance brokers, to make sure that the broker you choose has no black marks on his or her record.

As part of the underwriting process, the grantor may be required to take an insurance-company physical so that the insurance company can determine premiums based on the state of the grantor's health.

## Policies gifted into trust by the grantor

Sometimes, the grantor makes a gift of an existing insurance policy into the trust. It could be a policy on which premiums are still being paid or it could be a *paid-up* policy, where all the premiums have been paid and the policy remains in force until the grantor's death. In either case, an existing policy is an excellent candidate for transfer to the trust because, should the policy remain in the grantor's hands until death, its face value would be included in the gross estate (see Chapters 16 and 17), and a large percentage of the proceeds from the policy would go to pay estate taxes.

To transfer a life insurance policy into the trust, the grantor must complete and sign an assignment or transfer of policy. Be certain to obtain **Form 712, Life Insurance Statement,** from the insurance company at the time the grantor makes the transfer. The value on **Form 712** is the value the grantor declares on his or her **Form 709, United States Gift (and Generation-Skipping Transfer) Tax Return,** if any is required.

## Eyeing the types of life insurance available

All life insurance policies contain an element of *term insurance*, or pure insurance that provides coverage for a set period and builds no cash value. Failure to pay scheduled premiums causes the policy to lapse, usually 30 days after the due date of the missed premium. Besides term insurance, here are some other types of life insurance you may encounter:

✔ **Whole life:** Combining term life coverage with a modest investment motive. Generally, whole life remains the same, year after year, with a portion of the premium paying for term coverage. The remainder is invested by the insurance company, and provides the policy owner (that's the trust) with a stated rate of return. Policies build cash value, so should you decide to terminate the policy prior to the death of the insured, you're entitled to a return of any cash value accumulated within the policy. At the death of the insured, the policy pays the face value, but any cash value existing prior to death is erased. Should you fail to pay a premium, the cash value continues making premium payments until it's exhausted. Only after cash value has been exhausted does the policy lapse.

✔ **Variable universal life:** Similar to whole life, except the cash value in the variable universal life policy may be invested by you in a variety of mutual funds offered by the insurance company. When the stock market does well, the policy's cash value increases; when the stock market performs poorly, so does the policy's cash value. Like the whole life policy, the face value of the policy is paid into the trust when the insured dies. Missed premium payments are made with the existing cash value until it's gone, and then the policy lapses.

✔ **Single premium life:** The one-payment plan, single premium life lives up to its name. The insured purchases a policy with one giant premium payment, which the insurance company calculates based on the insured's health and age. Be cautious of single premium life — although insurance companies market this plan as "one payment covers you forever," they may run through the pool of available cash quicker than planned if they invest poorly, and come back to you years later looking for additional premiums; if you don't pony up, the policy lapses.

By gifting the policy to the trust, the grantor limits the includable value on his or her estate tax return to the value as of the date of the gift, not the policy's face value. And because no policy prior to the insured's death is worth much in comparison to its value after that death, making this transfer now saves tens or even hundreds of thousands of dollars in eventual taxes if the grantor has a taxable estate.

After the transfer, it's up to you, as trustee, to make sure that the endorsements on the policy (that list of information like whose life is being insured, who owns the policy, and who gets the money when the insured dies) are changed. You need to be certain that the trust is not only named as the owner but is also designated as the beneficiary. For instance, the new ownership and beneficiary designation should now read something like this: "John Q. Doe and Thomas H. Doe, Trustees, and their successors, of the John M. Smith Irrevocable Trust under trust agreement dated 02/11/13." And don't forget to pay those annual premiums if the policy isn't paid up. Be sure that you have cash in advance of the payment date every year (from the grantor) to pay the premiums. For a Crummey trust, you'll need to allow enough time to send Crummey notice letters to the beneficiaries (and let the Crummey notice period expire) after you've received the cash and before you pay the premium (see Chapter 3).

Frequently, transfers into irrevocable life insurance trusts (whether cash for premiums or policies with cash value) trigger the need for the grantor to file **Form 709** for each year that he or she makes transfers into the trust in excess of the annual exclusion ($14,000 in 2013).

## Personal and household property in trust

If the grantor has established a revocable trust (see Chapter 3 for more info), he or she can transfer some or all of his or her personal and household items into the trust by means of a one-page declaration, notarized and witnessed. Figure 11-1 shows a sample that's been successful in avoiding probate.

If the grantor has funded an *irrevocable trust* (a trust that can't be changed or revoked by the grantor; check out Chapter 3), he or she definitely doesn't want to include household and personal property (except for, possibly, items that have the possibility of increasing in value greatly during the grantor's lifetime, such as artwork by a well-known living artist who's in poor health). Remember, transfers into an irrevocable trust mean that the grantor is giving up all right, title, and interest in the property. If that property remains in the grantor's house and the grantor continues to use it, the IRS would be well within its rights to question the validity of the transfer and disallow the gift.

DECLARATION OF TRUST OWNERSHIP
AS TO ALL
PERSONAL AND HOUSEHOLD ARTICLES

The undersigned hereby declare that, solely as Trustees of and nominees for the benefit of the JILLIAN J. JONES 2013 TRUST, a revocable inter vivos trust existing under a certain declaration of trust heretofore executed on even date herewith by JILLIAN J. JONES as Settlor with JILLIAN J. JONES and HARRY M. JONES as the initial Trustees, they (i) are acquiring or now hold and (ii) will hold, pursuant to the provisions of subparagraph 9 of Paragraph A of Article XII of said declaration of trust, solely and exclusively for and in behalf of said trust, the following personal and household articles (the beneficial ownership of which JILLIAN J. JONES hereby transfers to said trust):

All of her jewelry, clothing, household furniture and furnishings, personal automobiles, and all other tangible articles of a household or personal nature, or any interest in such tangible personal property, together with all policies of insurance on such property, which she presently owns or hereafter acquires regardless of the means by which acquired.

This declaration of trust ownership is intended to be and shall be binding upon JILLIAN J. JONES heirs, administrators, executors and assigns and shall be revocable and amendable only by written instrument executed by one or more of the then Trustee(s) of said trust (with or without indicating such fiduciary capacity) with all the same formalities as accompanied the execution of this instrument (provided, however, that this declaration may be terminated by JILLIAN J. JONES, individually, by written notice to the then Trustee(s).

This declaration is intended to revoke all prior declarations of ownership, if any, with respect to any and all properties governed by this declaration heretofore executed by JILLIAN J. JONES.

IN WITNESS WHEREOF, JILLIAN J. JONES has executed this instrument this 11$^{th}$ day of February, 2013.

Witnesses:                                 Jillian J. Jones

-----------------------------------        -----------------------------------------------

-----------------------------------        Harry M. Jones


COMMONWEALTH OF MASSACHUSETTS )
                                              )
COUNTY OF MIDDLESEX                            )                February 11, 2013


Then personally appeared the above named JILLIAN J. JONES ad HARRY M. JONES, and acknowledged the foregoing instrument to be their free act and deed, before me.


-----------------------------------------------
Notary Public
My commission expires:

**Figure 11-1:**
Declaration
of Trust
Ownership
as to all per-
sonal and
household
articles.

# Rolling Property into Trust after Death

Often, trusts are created during the grantor's lifetime, but they aren't funded until after the grantor dies. If you're a trustee of a trust where the grantor has died and you need to fund the trust, you have

- ✔ **To assist the executor of the estate in making an orderly transfer of assets into the trust.** Usually, when trusts are funded only after death, the majority of assets flow through the decedent's estate. Probate assets must go through the probate process (see Chapter 6), all debts of the decedent and the estate must be paid (including all estate taxes), and all legacies and bequests must be honored prior to making distribution from the estate into the trust.

- ✔ **To identify any assets that became payable to the trust directly upon the grantor's death, such as insurance policies owned by the grantor with the trust named as beneficiary.** Chapter 8 tells you what you need to know (and what to look for in the decedent's Last Will) to determine whether this trust should be funded with specific assets, a specific dollar amount, or with a percentage of the assets. You may also find guidance as to whether to include or exclude certain property from the funding.

Be careful when funding a trust: Not all available property is eligible. You may not fund a trust with the decedent's 401(k) plan, for example. Very often, the estate is clearly more than large enough to fund the trust even after all other obligations are met. In that case, you (together with the estate's executor) may decide to partially fund the trust earlier than required so that trust beneficiaries who may be relying on trust income for their living expenses may begin receiving distributions. Early funding of the trust must be done with the absolute understanding between the trustee and the executor, in writing, that the trust will honor any financial obligations the estate can't meet.

# Chapter 12

# Investing the Trust's Assets and Paying Its Expenses

*In This Chapter*

▶ Discovering how to differentiate between income and principal

▶ Choosing investment advisors

▶ Understanding diversification and investing in a socially responsible way

▶ Using trust assets to adequately provide for beneficiaries' needs

▶ Knowing which expenses you can and can't pay from the trust

*U*nlike an estate, a trust is an ongoing endeavor and its lifetime may well be longer than yours. Your duty as trustee is to manage the trust's assets to ensure that the trust's beneficiaries will have adequate funds when they need (or are entitled to) money. Your goal is to see that the asset base grows, not to keep it the same or see it shrink.

In order to make your tenure as trustee a successful one, this chapter explains what you need to know about separating principal from income. It also shows some basic investment options, some of which you may decide to use to invest the trust assets and others of which you may think aren't for you, at least not now. The beauty of being trustee, as opposed to executor, is that yours tends to be more of a long-term role, so you have the option of investing one way now and then changing it up later if it's not working the way you want. Whichever you decide, remember that your goal isn't just to preserve the assets but also to put them to work for the benefit of the income beneficiaries, any other present interest beneficiaries (who could also be the income beneficiaries or some other person) and the remaindermen.

# Appreciating the Importance of Income and Principal in Trust Administration

Picture a trust as two boxes. In one box, you keep all the property that's available to produce ordinary income like dividends, interest, or rents. When that income is earned, it goes into the second box. As you make payments, some may come out of either box, depending on what you (the trustee) decide; others, such as beneficiary payments, come only from the income box, assuming it has income in it. Knowing how to differentiate what belongs in the principal box from what should be in the income box is one of the trickiest concepts to grasp in trust administration.

To help you get a firm grasp on principal and income, the following sections give you a clear definition of each and explain why and how distinguishing between the two will help you manage your trust.

The people entitled to receive income (the *income beneficiaries*) may be different than those who will receive the principal (the *remaindermen*) when the trust terminates. One of your many jobs as trustee is to make sure that you don't favor the income interest over the principal interest, or vice versa. You must be fair and equitable to both.

## Defining principal and income

*Principal,* sometimes referred to as the *corpus* or *body,* of the trust, is the property that the trust owns. Principal may include cash, but it may also be stocks, bonds, real estate, business interests, country club memberships, or season tickets to the Met. In fact, anything that the trust can be said to own is principal. Although trust principal starts with the assets that originally fund the trust (see Chapter 11), it may increase or decrease when the sale of trust property creates capital gains or losses; when the grantor makes additional contributions to the trust; when the trust receives a settlement or judgment as a party in a lawsuit; or even when you transfer into principal any accumulated income that's not required to go to an income beneficiary.

Principal in a trust can shape-shift without ceasing to be principal. A common misconception is that when you sell an asset, the cash proceeds that you receive become available to pay the income beneficiary. After all, if you sell something in your personal finances, you can use the cash you receive to pay any of your bills. But that's not the case in a trust, where the cash received from the sale of any asset still remains a principal asset, albeit in a different form. So in the hands of the trust, stock worth $100 is the same as the $100 cash it receives from the sale of that stock, which is the same as the $100 worth of different stock that the trust turned around and purchased with the cash.

Almost everything earned by the principal of the trust is *income.* So stock dividends, interest earned on bank accounts or bonds, rents from real estate owned by the trust, and earnings received from a business the trust owns all constitute income of the trust. In fact, if you receive a payment of any sort and you're not sure where it belongs, you're probably safe in depositing it to the income side of the trust, with a few exceptions we outline in the next section.

## Distinguishing between the two

A great deal of your success as a trustee lies in your ability to determine what's principal and what's income. Your assignment of all receipts to either the income or principal side of the trust dictates how you calculate *trust accounting income,* an amount that determines how much money the income beneficiary is entitled to receive. By understanding the difference between the two sides of the trust and applying your knowledge, you can give the income beneficiary the amount he or she is due (or something close — much of the equation is based on your best judgment as trustee) and hopefully keep everyone happy.

So why does making the distinction between principal and income sometimes seem so difficult? Well, not every type of principal or receipt of income is straightforward, and sometimes figuring out what you have can be perplexing. The largest exception to the income/principal distinction is how you classify capital gains and losses. *Capital gains* occur when you sell a piece of property for more than your acquisition cost (either because the trust purchased the property or because it received the property from the grantor or the grantor's estate as a part of the trust's initial funding). See Chapter 11 for more info on funding trusts. *Capital losses,* on the other hand, are what you get when you sell property for less than your acquisition cost. Whether the trust generates gains (hopefully) or losses (not too often, but sometimes unavoidable), those gains and losses stay on the principal side of the trust.

You also need to be aware of two other tricky types of principal payments you may receive on account of trust assets. Those two types are

> ✔ **Return of capital:** When you receive a *return of capital,* the company that has issued this payment has essentially determined that some part of what you owned no longer exists, and so they issue payments that reduce your acquisition cost. To the extent that you still have an acquisition amount for that particular piece of property, you reduce that amount by the return of capital, record any cash you receive on the principal side of the trust, and don't recognize income of any sort. For example, QZW Corp., which you purchased for $10 per share, later sells off one wicket-manufacturing plant. It sends you a check for $3 per share as the proceeds from the sale of the wicket-manufacturing plant as a return of capital. Your new acquisition cost in QZW Corp. is now $7 per share ($10 original purchase price – $3 return of capital), and you have no capital gain or loss on the transaction.

✔ **Special or extraordinary dividends:** With a *special* or *extraordinary dividend,* on the other hand, the corporation has issued a larger than ordinary slice of the corporate profits. These extraordinary dividends are typically allocated to the principal side of the trust because their payment almost always causes the share price of the stock to drop by at least the amount of the dividend. For example, in November 2004, Microsoft issued a $3.00 per share extraordinary dividend, as opposed to its quarterly $0.08 per share dividend. Not so coincidentally, Microsoft's share price dropped that very day by almost exactly the same amount as the dividend. Unlike the return of capital, an extraordinary dividend is taxable and doesn't reduce the trust's acquisition cost.

If you understand the distinction between income and principal, you should have no difficulty in correctly allocating payments such as returns of capital or extraordinary dividends. However, sometimes the company itself isn't clear on how it should categorize these payments until long after it has actually made the payments. If the correspondence you receive from the company is confusing (and we've read more than our share that boggles the mind), you may want to check in with a tax professional who can help walk you through the correct application of the payment.

Most trust instruments include a provision that states that the final determination of what's principal and what's income rests with the trustee. Trust administration isn't a precise science, and the lines between principal and income sometimes blur. If you're not sure what something is, you may want to seek professional advice from an accountant, Enrolled Agent, or attorney who specializes in trusts.

# Using Investment Advisors Effectively

Investment advisors can make your life as trustee easier. They spend 100 percent of their professional time researching companies and reading balance sheets and annual reports. Their job is to be on top of whatever type of investment they specialize in so that you don't have to be. Check out Chapter 4 for some of the different types of advisors available to you and how to select one or more.

In fact, we would most definitely choose to use investment advisors for trusts we were responsible for. Although we're both extremely competent in lots of areas of trust and estate administration, neither of us wants to have the absolute decision of what to buy and sell (and when) resting on her head.

Your job is to be very specific as to what your expectations are when hiring an investment advisor, so keep the following points in mind:

- ✓ **Set boundaries.** If you don't give an advisor parameters, you're giving too much responsibility to someone whose loyalty to you extends no farther than the size of the fee you're paying. You can reasonably assume that the advisor probably doesn't want to lose your business, but unless you show him otherwise, he'll probably assume that you have no idea what he's doing, won't be able to read his reports, and won't bother to ask questions.

- ✓ **Make sure that you get the right kind of advisor for your trust.** Not all advisors specialize in all types of investments. You can find advisors for every type of investment and combination of types (balanced investments that produce income as well as capital gains, for example). If you're looking for income production but aren't too bothered if you don't see huge capital gains in the account, you want an advisor who specializes in _fixed income securities_ (bonds). Perhaps the trust doesn't yet have an active income beneficiary, and all the income is accumulating in the trust. In that case, you may be more likely to want an advisor who specializes in _growth companies,_ which usually pay a very small dividend (if they pay one at all) and concentrate on increasing the size and value of the company.

- ✓ **Don't limit yourself to one advisor.** You may need only one advisor, or you may want more than one. If the trust is large, you may not want to put all your eggs in one basket with one advisor. And if you sense that you're not getting the service or results you require or want from any particular advisor, don't hesitate to take the trust away from him. Remember, it's not his money, so he has very little at stake (other than loss of fee income). You, on the other hand, have to answer to the income beneficiaries and the _remaindermen_ (the people or organizations who receive whatever's left in the trust after the income beneficiary's interest ends).

- ✓ **Remain in close communication with the advisor.** Any investment advisor worth his salt sends monthly or quarterly reports. Read them carefully. Although he works for you, money often leads people to behave badly, and these advisors have access to lots of it. If something doesn't look quite right to you, such as fees that seem high or huge numbers of purchases and/or sales, often for very small numbers of shares of stock in the same companies, ask questions. If you're not absolutely satisfied with the answers, ask for an opinion from a professional you trust (perhaps an attorney, an accountant, an Enrolled Agent, or even another investment person such as a stockbroker) and have her give the report the hairy eyeball. If anything is fishy there, any of these people should be able to smell it.

# Holding and Diversifying Assets

As trustee, you're responsible for investing the trust property. Although you may have your hands tied by a trust instrument that dictates that you hold onto certain property the grantor has given to the trust, most trusts give the trustee investment control over at least some assets. Your job is to invest it conservatively but broadly, giving that principal a chance to grow. Depending on the powers given to you by the grantor under the terms of the trust instrument, how you go about your task is up to you.

For example, one of us once administered a trust (but, thank goodness, wasn't the trustee) that held a million or so shares of the family business. It just so happened that the family business was a very successful publicly traded corporation, and that those million shares produced a large enough dividend to keep the income beneficiary comfortable for his entire life. That said, though, by not selling those shares and investing in a broader way in the stock and bond markets, the trustee left himself open to all sorts of charges of *malfeasance* (trustee misconduct). Basically, the trustee hadn't done his job, and the result for the trust, the income beneficiary, and the remaindermen could have been disastrous if that family corporation had fallen on hard times, or even gone bankrupt. Think of Enron and its pension plan members, who were only invested in Enron stock.

The following sections explain the different types of assets you may be responsible for as a trustee and, where appropriate, what you must do to ensure they're diversified.

## Stocks

Investing in the stock market is one of the most popular ways to get trust principal working for you and producing income for the trust's income beneficiaries. *Stocks* (sometimes referred to as *equities*) are ownership interests in corporations. As a partial owner in a corporation, the trust is entitled to a share in the corporate profits, which are paid as dividends (usually quarterly but sometimes as often as monthly or as infrequently as annually).

In order to diversify the trust's stocks, the trust needs to invest in a broad range of companies, covering all the major areas of the stock market: from manufacturing to transportation to all forms of medical services and products to commodities, such as oil and gas. And in this increasingly international age, you don't want to focus only on U.S. companies; rather, consider casting your net worldwide. Some experts say that an adequately diverse portfolio should contain stocks in no fewer than 75 corporations; others raise that number to 140 or more. If you're investing a relatively small amount of money, you can circumvent the necessity of buying tiny amounts of stocks in so many companies by investing instead in one or more broad-based mutual funds, which themselves own shares in many, many corporations. Just be sure to read the *prospectuses* (the brochures that every fund has detailing the rules governing the fund and listing a sample investment portfolio in the fund) first, before you invest, so that you understand exactly what it is you're buying. Head to the "Mutual funds" section, later in the chapter, for more information.

You don't necessarily need to buy stock in corporations that pay regular dividends. Some very fine corporations never or only rarely pay any dividend. As trustee, you're on safe ground investing in a non-dividend paying corporation, provided you can see the potential for growth in that company. As a corporation's value grows, the trust (as a partial owner of that entity) is entitled to a share of that growth. As long as the trust continues to own shares, the corporation's increased value translates to an increased market value for the shares you own. When you sell those shares, the money you receive for them should exceed what you paid for them, giving you a capital gain.

## Bonds

*Bonds* are pieces of loans, packaged by a corporation or a government as an investment product. When you purchase a bond, you're purchasing a piece of someone else's debt. In exchange for the money you're indirectly lending, that debtor agrees to pay you interest. Bonds are sometimes referred to as *fixed-income securities* because the income that they generate for the trust is tied to the stated interest rate on the bond. You'll receive no more interest than what's stated, and hopefully, no less.

When investing in bonds, you're typically looking to produce a steady stream of income for the income beneficiary. One of most effective ways to achieve that goal is by *laddering* the maturity dates of the bonds you buy so that bonds mature in sequence, rather than all at once. For example, you may buy one bond that matures in 2013, one in 2014, one in 2015, and so on. By laddering bond maturities, you cushion the income beneficiary from huge drops in his or her income at times when income rates plummet.

Different income beneficiaries have different needs. Some require as much income as you can squeeze out of the trust's principal; others want whatever income they receive to be tax exempt. Still others are best served by a combination of approaches. The most common types of bonds and what they can offer both the trust and the beneficiary are as follows:

- ✔ **Corporate:** Issued by corporations, these bonds generally carry some of the highest interest rates available. The interest earned is taxable at both the federal and state level.

- ✔ **Foreign:** Other countries borrow money, too, and foreign bonds can be very attractive to investors. If you feel so inclined, or your investment advisor thinks that foreign bonds are a good, safe place for some of the trust's principal, you should consider sticking a toe in this water. What can complicate foreign bonds somewhat is that they're typically sold in foreign currencies (and pay interest that way, too). Although your brokerage can handle all the currency exchange issues, your return on investment isn't just dictated by the stated interest rate (which doesn't change) but also by currency exchange rates (which do fluctuate). Interest on foreign bonds is taxable at both the federal and state levels.

✔ **Municipal:** Issued by states, cities, and towns, these bonds carry lower interest rates because they're exempt from federal income tax, and depending on what state(s) the trust and trust beneficiary pay income tax to, they may also be free from state income tax.

✔ **U.S. Government:** Not to be confused with U.S. Treasury obligations, U.S. Government bonds are the debts of U.S. governmental agencies, such as *GNMA* (U.S. Government National Mortgage Association, in case you were wondering). These bonds typically pay a slightly higher interest rate than U.S. Treasury obligations, but interest from them is income taxable at both the federal and state levels.

✔ **U.S. Treasury:** The safest of all safe investments, these bonds are backed by the full faith and credit of the U.S. Treasury. We're talking Fort Knox stuff here — if you can't sleep at night because you're worrying about how secure the trust's principal is, you don't get any safer than U.S. Treasury obligations. In exchange for lending money to the U.S. Treasury, it pays you interest and as an added bonus, the interest is tax exempt in every state (so you pay only federal income tax).

Just as you may not consider loaning money to your shifty Cousin Norman, you may not want to lend the trust's money to some corporations or municipalities with reputations for mishandling money or being perpetually in debt. How can you tell? If it seems too good to be true, it probably is; be very wary of bonds that promise extraordinarily high interest rates. Face it, if the corporation, city, or town could borrow money and pay less interest, wouldn't they do so? These very high interest rate bonds are sometimes referred to as *junk bonds* or *high-yield bonds*. If you're in a position where you need to generate a large amount of income for your income beneficiary, you may want to venture into this arena, but go very carefully. These bonds carry not only a high interest rate but also a high rate of default. ***Remember:*** If the bond issuer defaults on the loan, not only do you not get your interest payments, but you also just lost your principal investment.

If you're not sure about a bond you're considering purchasing, you may want to check that particular bond's *rating,* which is essentially a grade assigned to that bond by the rating agencies. The two major agencies, Standard & Poor's (S&P) and Moody's Investor Services, assign ratings when a bond is first issued and then periodically review their ratings based on how the borrower is doing financially. You can phone Moody's rating desk at 212-553-0377, or you can access Standard & Poor's ratings by going to www.standardand poors.com and then clicking on "Ratings." For both services, you need the bond's identifying number, a nine-digit alphanumeric identifier called its *CUSIP number,* in order to check a specific bond. Every publicly traded security has a CUSIP number; it's listed on the face of the bond. If the broker holds the trust's securities, the CUSIP number appears on the original purchase confirmation or on your monthly or quarterly statement.

As a result of the Great Recession of 2007–2008, the underlying value of S&P and Moody's bond ratings has become suspect, with many corporations and municipalities defaulting on loan obligations graded as investment quality or higher. Turns out, the S&P and Moody's are both supported by fees paid by the companies and municipalities they rate, so what we once thought were unbiased opinions apparently are not. By all means, use the S&P and/or Moody's ratings, but use them with caution and a heavy dollop of good sense. If you're hearing rumblings that a corporation, or even a country, may be in financial trouble, perhaps that's not the safest place to invest your trust's assets.

## Grasping basic bond terminology

Investing in bonds can be one of the safest and easiest ways to invest, yet many people shy away from these investments because they may not understand all the words used in their descriptions. How is it possible to know exactly what you're buying? Here's a short course in Bond Terminology 101.

All bond descriptions carry certain required information that can tell you a great deal about what you're buying. They should all have a *face amount,* which is nothing more than the amount of money the bond issuer promises to repay you when the bond matures. It also gives an *issue date,* or the date the loan was created, and a *maturity date,* or the date the loan will be repaid, plus the interest rate.

Bonds actually come in three varieties, based on how long you hold them. *Bills* are issued for a period of one year or less. *Notes* are issued for periods of less than ten years. *Bonds* are issued for periods of ten years or greater. Both bonds and notes are issued at their face value (you

pay $100 for a $100 note) and they pay interest semiannually based on the date of maturity, not the date of issue. Bills, on the other hand, are purchased at a discount (you pay $95 for a $100 bill), and they only pay interest at maturity, when you receive the full face value of the bill.

Some bonds are *prerefunded.* Even though they're issued with a stated maturity date, the issuing authority has the option of paying off the loan early, at specified dates (the *prerefund dates*). Other bonds are *convertible,* which means that the corporation may exchange them for its common or preferred stock at its own instigation. When corporations convert their bonds, bondholders always have the option to take cash rather than stock. Corporate bonds may also be *subordinate,* causing this particular bond issue to stand behind other debts of the corporation. In other words, if the corporation goes belly up, the subordinated bondholders don't get any of their money back until other corporate debts are paid first.

## Mutual funds

If buying individual stocks and/or bonds isn't your cup of tea because you're unsure about what (and how much of any particular security) to buy, then you may want to consider investing the trust's money in a mutual fund. Diversification is the name of the game with mutual funds. A *mutual fund* is something like a buying club, where a bunch of like-minded investors (like you) pool their money, hire an advisor, and allow the advisor to invest the pooled cash in a way that's been determined by the investors. In exchange for the cash, the individual investors receive shares in the fund, not shares in the individual investments that are purchased and sold by the fund.

In fact, by their very nature, mutual funds are diverse and specialized. You can buy funds made up entirely of stocks or ones that only invest in bonds. You can purchase international funds, municipal bond funds, socially responsible and green funds, and funds that specialize in transportation companies. If you want, you can even buy a fund that only invests in so-called *sin stocks* like tobacco, alcohol, and weapons manufacturers.

When diversifying a trust's assets, mutual funds can be a very savvy trust investment. In exchange for the fees that every shareholder, either directly or indirectly, pays the fund manager, you receive expert advice, as well as the potential for great diversification. In fact, you may become so caught up in picking and choosing mutual funds that you lose sight of your goal of diversifying the trust's principal and investing in all sectors of the economy. Before you invest in any mutual fund, check its prospectus very carefully to make sure that you understand what you're buying. We've both been involved with trusts that relied heavily on mutual fund investing, where the funds overlapped so significantly that the trustees hadn't really diversified the trust's assets at all, although they thought they had.

Just make sure that you're careful about the fund's fees when investing the trust's money in mutual funds. Funds are allowed to charge a variety of fees, including sales charges (sometimes referred to as a *load*), redemption fees, exchange fees, account fees, purchase fees, management fees, and/or distribution (sometimes called *service*) fees. You can reasonably expect to pay a fee for having someone invest your money for you, but you need to figure out up front how much of a fee you're willing to pay. So-called *no-load* funds, which have no up-front or deferred sales charges, sound like a good deal, but make no mistake: Even no-load funds charge fees — you just may not be able to see them.

## Cash needs

As much as you want to maximize the income being earned by the trust's principal, you need to keep some cash on hand at all times to meet not only the trust's expected needs, like scheduled income distributions and quarterly estimated tax payments, but also unexpected expenses, such as unanticipated medical expenses for a beneficiary or larger-than-expected taxes for the trust. For example, you never want to sell an investment right before the April 15 tax deadline in order to pay a tax bill because everyone else who owes taxes is facing the same tax deadline. Sales tend to flood the stock market around April 15 of every year, causing prices to plunge. Instead of selling when everyone else is, keep enough of a cushion of cash on hand in the trust to pay those bills when they roll around. And after you've paid your bills, make sure to replenish your cash stash — you never want to be caught short.

Cash on hand doesn't need to sit in an account earning nothing. Plenty of lower-risk money market accounts pay you something on your deposits, even though it's usually not enough to write home about. The money in the account remains very liquid, and you can pull it out at any time without a penalty when you need it. Every bank offers money market accounts, as do all mutual fund companies and stock brokerage firms. You'll have no difficulty opening one of these accounts wherever you keep your assets, although you may want to shop slightly farther afield. Some of the highest interest rates paid are offered by Internet banks, which have no local branches and very few employees, keeping their costs low.

## Real estate

Real estate may not seem like a typical trust investment, but it's more common than you may think. Often, the grantor's residence ends up in the trust, either during his or her lifetime or after the grantor's death. Or, the grantor may have held interests in either residential or commercial real estate, outright, or through partnerships.

Dealing with real estate inside of a trust is really no different than dealing with it on a personal level, whether the trust owns the property the grantor's family is still living in or you're dealing with a trust version of Donald Trump with hotels, casinos, apartment houses, and shopping malls. The trust must pay the taxes, the insurance bill, and any other costs involved with the maintenance of that property.

The expenses involved with maintaining the grantor's home aren't always clear cut. If the family residence remains in trust while the family is still in residence, part of your job is determining which expenses the trust should and shouldn't pay for. Mortgage payments, taxes, and insurance on the house itself clearly belong to you. You can also make a good case for lawn/garden care and trash and snow removal. If the house's contents are trust property, you need to pick up that insurance tab as well. But be cautious about many of the other costs associated with running a house, such as utility payments and the housecleaner. Discuss with the family precisely what items the trust is responsible for. Take into consideration what you think the grantor's purpose was in placing the house into trust, and act accordingly. Failing to have a stated plan in place may leave you in the unenviable position of rejecting reimbursement for food, medical care, or even bills to have the dog groomed. Believe it or not, one of us had a trust beneficiary who steadfastly maintained that because the trust undertook to pay the cleaners and the dog's hair increased the amount of cleaning to be done, the grooming bills actually should be paid by the trust.

Although the rules for owning real estate, including buying and selling, are the same for trusts as they are for individuals, two exceptions exist. Although individuals are entitled to a $250,000 capital gains exclusion for the sale of a personal residence (provided they've owned the house for at least two years and used it as a personal residence for two out of the last five years), trusts aren't. On the other hand, if that same residence is sold at a loss, the trust is allowed to claim the loss on **Schedule D** of the trust's **Form 1041** because the house isn't the trust's personal residence.

## Small business stocks

Whether a trust receives *small business stock* (stock from a closely held or non-publicly traded corporation) during the grantor's lifetime or as part of the decedent's estate rolled into the trust after death, you may find yourself holding a substantial interest in a small business on behalf of the trust. The trust's grantor has hopefully prepared you for the receipt of this stock. Perhaps the trust's share of the stock is part of the greater plan to transfer ownership to the next generation. Or you may have instructions to sell the stock (presumably, in this case, because the grantor has buyers lined up and waiting).

If you, as trustee, find yourself holding shares in a small business, you're not only allowed to participate in the business, but you're also somewhat required to. Even if you don't want to be involved in the day-to-day running, don't be shy about asking to see financial reports and any other information the other owners may have regarding the company. Remember, one of your duties as trustee is to protect and conserve the assets of the trust. Even if you're not in a position to man the store, be an active player in what goes on behind the scenes. Otherwise, you'll have a difficult time justifying your care of the trust assets to the beneficiaries and/or remaindermen should the company go belly up.

If the company in question is an S corporation, be sure that the trust is eligible to be an S corporation shareholder. Check out Chapter 3 for descriptions of which trusts qualify either as a qualified Subchapter S trust (QSST) or as an Electing Small Business Trust (ESBT). And if you're not sure, seek advice. Making a mistake here may have disastrous consequences not only for the trust but also for the corporation.

# Going Green in a Trust

As trustee, you have the ultimate choice of investments, and you can choose based not only on the basis of a company's balance sheet but also on your philosophy of life. *Socially responsible investing* has been around for a long time, beginning with the Quakers in the 18th century, but it's taking on greater importance and variety as we work our way through the 21st century. If you want to invest only in companies whose stated goals are making the world a better place, you now have plenty of company and an abundance of options. You can elect to invest in companies that guard the environment, practice ethical business, protect human rights, foster consumer protection, stay far from unhealthy lifestyles and behaviors, and so on.

When it's your money, you can invest it as you please; when the money belongs to the trust, you must invest with a profit motive in mind. Even though no one can ever guarantee that an investment will provide *x* amount of income or increase in price by *y*, investing always carries the presumption of making money. Remember, so long as a socially responsible corporation or mutual fund can show that it's acting to produce a profit, you're okay in putting trust money there. But if the company is merely concerned with doing good in the world and not with producing profits for its shareholders, you're required to keep your trustee hands in your trustee pockets no matter how much you want to applaud its good work.

Not only can you invest in individual companies, but also there is an ever-lengthening list of socially responsible mutual funds offered by a variety of mutual fund companies. The following sections highlight ways you can invest the trust's principal in a socially conscious and politically aware way.

## Socially conscious

Investing used to be so straightforward. In order to create a balanced portfolio, you purchased *blue-chip* stocks (stocks in well-regarded, stable companies with good records of earnings and price stability) or all the stocks listed on the Standard and Poor's index. Now, of course, it's not enough to buy what everyone else has been buying for generations. Today, if you want to be socially responsible and conscious, you also need to look closely at each corporation's hiring practices, treatment of their employees, environmental impact (and whether that's improving), and kinds of goods produced. For example, is the company manufacturing more garbage for landfills, or are they using an environmentally sustainable model in production? In fact, in order to be a truly socially conscious investor, you need to study far more than the balance sheet — you need to check out the corporate philosophy and its implementation.

Socially conscious investing isn't an easy matter. No corporation is going to come up trumps in every category you may be concerned with, and if you're interested only in buying ones that do, your potential list of corporations is going to be very short indeed. Instead, in this oh-so-imperfect world you may want to create your own set of criteria, focusing on those areas of social responsibility you are and aren't willing to compromise on. So you may find a company that promotes women at the same rate as men but hasn't reached energy sustainability just yet. Or you may find the (almost) perfect corporation, and then discover buried in its annual report the fact that it invests its excess cash in the stock of a corporation you despise. Remember, no corporation is perfectly conscious — perfect consciousness is a Zen concept that just doesn't translate very well to the corporate boardroom.

## Politically aware

In addition to being socially conscious, many investors are also trying to push one political agenda over another in their choices of investments. There's some proof that this strategy works — who can deny that South Africa is a very different place today because investors deserted South African companies as an attempt to force change in that country? At the same time, Cuba is very much the same place today despite sanctions, so the strategy isn't foolproof.

No laws prohibit buying or boycotting companies based on the countries where they're located or companies whose stated business purpose supports one political point of view. So long as you, as trustee, are sufficiently convinced that a company has a solid business plan and all the tools in place to turn a profit and add to the trust's bottom line, that company represents a valid investment for the trust. The fact that you have the ability to further your own political agenda at the same time is kind of a nice side benefit.

# Looking to the Beneficiaries' Needs

If all that was involved in investing trust principal was choosing the investments and then seeing how well they did, anyone could be a trustee. However, being a trustee requires much more. You've been chosen because the grantor trusted that you'd be able to determine exactly what the income beneficiaries, and any other present interest beneficiaries need at any given time (and how best to make sure that they receive it), while at the same time balancing the desires of the remaindermen to have something at the end of the trust period.

Beneficiaries' needs change over time, and trust investments need to change in relation to them. As the trustee, you have to determine what the trust must do in order to meet those needs. You need to know when to switch investments in order to produce more income and when you should tailor them to produce less income. It's sometimes a balancing act worthy of the Flying Wallendas — only now it's you on the high wire.

Don't worry though. You don't have to do it all on your own. Remember, you may have quite a bit of guidance lurking in the trust instrument itself, with specific instructions as to when you should make certain distributions and other, less specific wording, regarding where your discretionary powers lie. And don't forget your investment advisor (check out the earlier section, "Using Investment Advisors Effectively"), who can help ensure that your investments meet the beneficiaries' needs. You also need to keep the following pieces of information in mind about the beneficiary.

## Age

As trustee, you need to judge when beneficiary payments are useful, and when they're unnecessary. Even if the trust has a mandatory income beneficiary, you can still limit the distributions to that beneficiary by limiting the amount of income earned by the trust. Many trusts are invested primarily in nonincome-bearing investments for that very reason. At the same time, you can select high-income-bearing investments to benefit a beneficiary who really needs the income from the trust to pay for living (or other) expenses. For example, a young child who is a trust beneficiary likely needs little from the trust, especially if his or her parents are still alive and are able to provide life's necessities. As that same child begins college, he or she may look to the trust to pay for some or all higher educational expenses. Or a working adult may require little from the trust now, but those needs may increase after retirement.

Although we don't advocate treating trust beneficiaries like you do your own children, it often feels like that with regard to money issues. The very items that concern you when your children are growing are the ones that factor into your decisions as trustee.

## Purpose of trust

Grantors often establish trusts for very specific reasons — to pay for college, to provide money to make that first home purchase, or to provide a safety net for someone the grantor isn't sure can completely provide for himself or herself. If you're a trustee of such a trust, you need to read the instrument very carefully to make certain that you know why the trust exists in the first place and then create a plan that answers that need. The next sections describe some common reasons grantors create trusts.

### Trusts that distribute income currently

Very often, grantors create trusts to provide a steady stream of income to one or more beneficiaries, year in and year out. The beneficiaries who rely on this income look to you to make sure that they continue to have enough to live on, so you have to make sure that the trust generates not only enough income this year but also next year and ten years down the road. The only way you're going to be able to keep pace with inflation is to make sure that the trust's principal grows.

Adding difficulty to an already complex task is that trust beneficiaries often require more than just the income in order to live, and you may feel you need to make some principal distributions so someone you feel responsible for can pay the rent. All we can say is this: Before you make a principal distribution to the beneficiaries, consider all your options. Making principal distributions can be a slippery slope, and reducing the amount of available principal isn't a smart way to increase the income for future years. However, depending on the terms of the trust instrument, you may have the discretion to do so, and sometimes principal distributions aren't only appropriate but are also what the grantor would have wanted. Also keep in mind that income beneficiaries have a nasty habit of becoming used to higher payments. After they start receiving them, they expect them to continue. Income beneficiaries not only won't understand your explanation of the difference between income and principal, but they also won't want to understand.

### Trusts that are age-based

Many trusts are created to behave one way while the beneficiary is one age and completely differently as that beneficiary gains years and hopefully wisdom. If you're trustee of such a trust, make a calendar of when your beneficiary hits those ages.

An age-based trust is known as an *accumulation trust* during the early stages because it doesn't make distributions while the beneficiary is young and therefore accumulates income. You want to invest an accumulating trust very differently than one where the beneficiary depends on regular income distributions (such as a currently distributing income trust, described in the preceding section). An accumulation trust is typically invested in a way that minimizes the trust's income tax hit. Trusts, like individuals, pay a graduated income tax; however, a trust's run through the various tax brackets happens much more rapidly than an individual's, and a trust can be paying the top tax rate with just a little more than $11,500 of ordinary income. Ouch!

If your trust is still in the accumulation stage, buying stocks that pay small dividends is a popular investment strategy because it limits the amount of taxable income, while still allowing the value of the trust to grow. However, the trade-off you should expect from a stock that pays a small dividend, or even no dividend at all, is that the market price of that stock should grow substantially because the company is plowing its profits back into the business rather than paying them out to shareholders. If you fail to see growth over time, don't hesitate to sell the stock, even if you sell it for less than you purchased it for. Everyone makes mistakes sometimes; better to realize that you've made one and get out than to hang on forever, waiting for the company to turn around. Check out *Stock Investing For Dummies,* 4th Edition, by Paul Mladjenovic (Wiley), for the nuts and bolts of knowing when to get out of a bad investment.

As the beneficiary ages, and the trust begins to make distributions, you're now free to shift the investments to ones that produce as much, or as little, income as you think it wise to give the beneficiary. After the beneficiary is receiving income from the trust, the tax liability for that income is paid by the beneficiary, not by the trust.

### Spendthrift trusts

One of the most popular reasons a grantor creates a trust is because he or she doesn't think the beneficiary of that trust is able to handle large sums of money. A *spendthrift trust* is designed to deal with that situation, giving complete control of the money to the trustee, who then must make the decisions about how much money to distribute and how often.

Authorizing distributions from a spendthrift trust is entirely at the trustee's discretion; as trustee, your only requirement is to keep the best interest of the beneficiary front and center at all times. You may distribute no income, some of the income, or even all the income if, in your best judgment, it benefits the beneficiary, even if the payments aren't made directly to the beneficiary. You may even distribute principal, if the income generated by the trust is not adequate for the beneficiary's needs. For example, if a spendthrift trust beneficiary has medical issues that require care, you may opt to pay the beneficiary's health insurance premiums, doctor and pharmacy bills, or even hospital and nursing home care bills directly to those organizations instead of giving the money to the beneficiary to do so.

# Paying the Trust's Expenses

In addition to making payments to the beneficiaries, as trustee, you're also responsible for paying the expenses you incur in administering the trust. The following sections outline the primary expenses you'll have and what you need to remember when paying them.

## Trustee's fees

If you're not a professional trustee (or acting for an institutional one), chances are good that you agreed to be trustee out of the goodness of your heart, and you'd really do this work for nothing. Still, even if you're a family trustee closely related to the grantor and the beneficiaries, you've probably already figured out that administering a trust can be a time eater. You're not unreasonable to want to get paid for that time. And that's all a *trustee's fee* is: the amount the trust pays to compensate the trustee for his or her time.

There is no set trustee's fee. You can choose to base it on a small percentage of the market value of the assets plus a percentage of the income earned by the trust, or you may opt to calculate the number of hours you spend and bill by the hour. You may even charge a flat fee, which is more like an *honorarium* (basically, a professional thank-you gift). What you may not do is overcharge. How much is too much? Like the Supreme Court standard for pornography, people tend to know it when they see it. We prefer to think of it as the stink test. If either of us sees a fee and her nose starts to twitch, she's going to be looking for an explanation of that fee pretty quickly.

Trustee's fees are an income tax deduction for the trust but taxable income to you. You must declare these fees on your **Form 1040,** where you place them on line 21, Other Income. If you're a professional trustee (an attorney, accountant, Enrolled Agent, or other financial professional), this income is also subject to Self-Employment Tax; otherwise, it's income taxable only.

Trustee fees are typically paid both from principal and income so as not to burden either side unduly. After all, your job is to look after both sides of the trust; it's only fair that both contribute to paying your bill.

## Investment advice

Investment advice is deductible to the trust minus that pesky 2 percent haircut that miscellaneous itemized deductions are subject to. Chapter 18 describes how to calculate the deduction in all its hairy details.

## Accounting fees

Unless you're preparing **Form 1041** by yourself, you also have to pay accounting or tax preparation fees. You may choose to pay these from income or principal, or a combination of the two. We usually pay them from income, but that's just our habit. Accounting fees in a trust are usually charged on an hourly basis or calculated on the complexity of the returns being prepared, and are fully deductible — no haircut here.

## Taxes

State and local income taxes, real estate taxes, personal property taxes — these bills are all deductible if paid by the trust on trust obligations. So, if the trust owns real estate, it gets to deduct those taxes. If, on the other hand, the trust pays the real estate taxes on property owned by the income beneficiary, the trust has actually made a distribution to the beneficiary. Here are some other items to keep in mind regarding taxes:

- ✔ If the trust is only paying a capital gains tax, you pay that from principal. (Remember, capital gains remain in the trust and aren't distributed to the income beneficiary.)

- ✔ If the trust is accumulating income, you pay the entire tax from principal because the accumulated income is transferred to principal at the end of each year and becomes part of the principal.

- ✔ On occasion, when you don't transfer accumulated income to principal, you pay taxes on the ordinary income of the trust from the income side, and the capital gains taxes from the principal side. For example, one of us works with a trust where the accumulated income is payable to the income beneficiary's estate when he dies. In this case, paying the taxes owed on income that would be payable to the beneficiary (if he chose to take it) from the income side, and the taxes on the capital gains (to which the beneficiary isn't entitled) from the principal side isn't only advisable, it's mandatory.

To the extent that income is available in the trust to pass out to a beneficiary (for an expense such as the real estate taxes mentioned earlier), that tax payment becomes an income distribution and the beneficiary will receive a **Schedule K-1** from the trust in due course. Chapter 20 explains all you need to know about the **K-1** and how items from the trust's checkbook can eventually end up on the beneficiary's tax return. It's a pretty nifty trick.

# Chapter 13

# Paying Trust Beneficiaries

. . . . . . . . . . . . . . . . . . . . . . . . . . . . . . . . . . . . . . . . .

## In This Chapter

▶ Establishing who the trust's beneficiaries are (and getting the info you need from them)

▶ Setting up the distribution schedule

▶ Making proper distributions at the proper times

▶ Handling beneficiaries who ask for or need unscheduled distributions

. . . . . . . . . . . . . . . . . . . . . . . . . . . . . . . . . . . . . . . . .

Going through all the song and dance of creating the trust, funding the trust, and then investing the trust assets is basically pointless unless you do it to benefit someone else: the trust beneficiary. The *trust beneficiary* is the person or institution who's named in the trust instrument to receive income and/or principal from the trust.

In this chapter, we explain how, when, and why you make distributions over the lifetime of the trust to the trust beneficiary or beneficiaries. We give you the lowdown on the information you need from and about the beneficiaries before you can write that first check, and how to determine whether you should ever pay more than the absolute minimum the trust instrument directs you to pay. And when it's time to completely discharge your duty as trustee, we tell you what you need to know to make those final distributions.

# Notifying Beneficiaries of the Trust

Even though some trust beneficiaries, such as spouses or children, know well in advance of that first distribution that a trust has been established for their care and feeding, we've noticed that *grantors* (the person who establishes the trust) often fail to tell named beneficiaries that trusts exist for their benefit. Sometimes it's because they want to encourage that person to strive and achieve without the knowledge that there's a safety net securely fastened beneath them; other times, the grantor doesn't want to discuss his or her own mortality with a child or grandchild. Whatever the reason, it often falls to you, the trustee, to inform the beneficiaries of the existence of the trust and the fact that they'll reap some benefit from it.

Notifying a beneficiary doesn't have any formal steps to follow; basically, it's really up to you to figure out how best to impart the news. If you know the person, a telephone call can accomplish the task with very little fuss and bother, and gives the beneficiary an immediate chance to ask questions. If you're not acquainted with the beneficiary, a simple letter suffices, advising him or her of the existence of the trust, and that he or she is a named beneficiary. Include all your contact info (telephone, e-mail, and snail mail), and urge the beneficiary to contact you at his or her earliest convenience. *Remember:* You won't be able to begin making distributions until you set up a reliable form of communication with the beneficiary.

The next sections point out the necessary info you need to retrieve from the beneficiaries after you make contact with them.

## Obtaining addresses and Social Security numbers

After you notify the beneficiary, you need to obtain his or her address and Social Security number. Beneficiary payments may, and probably will, contain elements of taxable income. Because he or she must pay the tax on that income, you shouldn't make any payments without obtaining tax reporting information up front.

Trust beneficiaries often plead poverty or extraordinary circumstances, especially when waiting for that first trust distribution. Resist the temptation to play the nice guy — keep your hands on the cash and don't make any payments until the beneficiary coughs up his or her address and Social Security number. If you pay before you have the information you need, you may still be waiting for it when you sit down to prepare the trust's tax returns many months later.

Of course, you can't force a beneficiary to give you his or her Social Security number, and you can't withhold payments indefinitely. If you find yourself in a position where you made distributions without first receiving that all-important number, you may be forced to file a tax return for the trust (**Form 1041**) that's missing this required piece of information. File the return anyway, making sure that you include as much information, such as the beneficiary's address, as you can on **Schedule K-1** (see Chapter 20). Provided you can show the IRS that you made a concerted attempt to obtain the information, you should be off the hook for filing an incomplete return.

## Verifying dates of birth

Knowing the beneficiary's birth date is important, and not just so you can send a card every year. Many trusts are created with payout schedules based on ages; as trustee, you need to know when the beneficiary has reached a certain age and adjust the mandatory payments accordingly. Obtaining third-party verification of a birth date isn't necessary. Usually, beneficiaries are more than happy to provide you with their correct date of birth.

Knowing the trust beneficiary's age is also relevant because it helps you choose appropriate investments, allowing you to minimize certain types of income at a time when the beneficiary is in a higher tax bracket. If a beneficiary's under the age of 19 (or 24, if a college student), he or she may be subject to the so-called *Kiddie Tax* on investment income, which essentially charges tax on the child's income at his or her parents' highest applicable rate. Unfortunately, investment income is exactly what a trust produces, so all income received from a trust may be subject to this additional tax. After the beneficiary has left college and is earning, you can then change the investment mix to one that produces more income taxed at a lower rate.

# Determining Scheduled Distributions

Although not every trust makes distributions to its beneficiaries on a continuing basis (either monthly, quarterly, or annually), all trusts are required to make distributions at some point in their existence, even if the only distribution made is the one that terminates the trust. As trustee, you have to figure out what that schedule should be and make sure that distribution dates are noted on a calendar somewhere. It doesn't matter whether you write them on a chalkboard on the wall, enter them into your computer database, or arrange to have reminders sent telepathically on the appropriate dates. What does matter is that you have a plan in place to be certain that distributions required by the trust instrument are made when they're due to be made. If you're not sure where to begin when making distributions, the following sections can help ensure you know how much to pay and when.

## Figuring out how much to pay

When trying to determine how much to pay beneficiaries, you first want to look at the trust instrument for direction:

- ✔ **Fixed amount distributions:** Sometimes, the trust instrument instructs you to pay a set dollar amount on a certain date. One of us, for example, prepares the tax returns for a family of trusts a grandmother set up for her grandchildren. Although Grandma is long gone, each of her grandchildren still receives $1,000 each and every year as a birthday gift.

- ✔ **5/5 provision:** Often, a trust for the benefit of a surviving spouse contains a so-called *5/5 provision*, where the surviving spouse may request a distribution of either 5 percent of the assets or $5,000 annually, whichever is greater.

✔ **Trust accounting income:** Far more usual than the fixed amount distribution, though, is a distribution that's based on the net income of the trust, or *trust accounting income*. The trust may require all income to be distributed annually, quarterly, or even monthly. If the instrument contains this requirement, you need to be sure that the payments are made within a reasonable amount of time after the due date. You're allowed to be a bit late — sometimes you can't possibly calculate the actual income until after the supposed date you should have sent out a check. But you really should try to make that distribution as soon as you possibly can. Remember, in accepting the role of trustee, you've agreed to abide by the terms of the trust; failure to do so may give the beneficiary grounds to try to have you removed.

✔ **Discretionary distributions:** Although it's by far more frequent for a beneficiary to come to you, hat in hand, to ask for more money (see the section "When Beneficiaries Request More Money: Paying Out Extra Distributions," later in this chapter), sometimes you may see a need that the beneficiary doesn't. He or she may be struggling financially but is too proud to ask for help. Or the beneficiary may have some medical problems that an injection of cash can help alleviate. Most trusts provide you, the trustee, with the discretion to make additional, unscheduled distributions. Often, the terms of the trust limit these distributions to issues of health or education. Sometimes, though, the trustee's discretionary powers are extremely broad, and the trust instrument contains language to the effect that the trustee may act as he sees fit. Read your instrument closely to see how much discretion you're allowed. In the case of discretionary distributions, you're not limited to distributing only income, but may also make principal distributions if you, in your estimation, feel that they're warranted.

### Calculating trust accounting income

*Trust accounting income*, or *TAI* for short, is the formula that determines how much income is available to be distributed to the income beneficiary. You calculate it by adding together all items of income and then subtracting all expenses attributable to income. Here's an example. The Albatross Trust owns principal assets that include both taxable and tax-exempt bonds, dividend-paying stocks, and an interest in a shopping mall. In addition to the trustee fees the trustee pays herself, she also pays an investment advisor to assist her in investing in the stock and bond markets and an Enrolled Agent to prepare the trust's income tax returns.

To arrive at TAI, the trustee of the Albatross Trust adds up all the interest, dividends, and rental income earned, even if some of that income may be tax exempt on the trust's income tax return. Then she subtracts whatever share of trustee, investment advice, and accounting fees she actually pays from the income earned (she may, and probably does, pay a portion of all these fees from the principal side of the account). In addition, she also subtracts any income taxes paid from the income side of the trust and any miscellaneous expenses (even if they're not tax deductible).

In Table 13-1, you see how the Albatross Trust's trustee assigns items of income between the income and principal sides of the trust, and also how she allocates the fees charged to the trust. Although the rules for allocating income are fairly rigid, the trustee may be much more flexible and use her judgment in allocating fees and expenses. However, that allocation must be a reasonable one that doesn't unduly favor either the income beneficiaries or the *principal remaindermen* (the people who get the assets in the trust when the trust terminates).

| Table 13-1 | Calculating TAI | |
|---|---|---|
| *Description* | *Income* | *Principal* |
| Income received | | |
| Ordinary dividends | $1,000.00 | |
| Taxable interest | $10,000.00 | |
| Tax-exempt interest | $2,000.00 | |
| Rents and royalties | $600.00 | |
| Long-term capital gain distributions | | $500.00 |
| Short-term capital gains | | $1,000.00 |
| Long-term capital gains | | $1,500.00 |
| **Total Income** | **$13,600.00** | **$3,000.00** |
| Deductions | | |
| Trustee's fee | ($500.00) | ($500.00) |
| Tax preparation fee | ($250.00) | ($125.00) |
| Investment advice | ($1,000.00) | ($1,000.00) |
| Federal income taxes paid | | ($500.00) |
| State income taxes paid | | ($350.00) |
| **Total deductions** | **($1,750.00)** | **($2,475.00)** |
| **Net additions to principal** | | **$525.00** |
| **Trust Accounting Income** | **$11,850.00** | |

If you're required to pass out all the income in the trust, calculating TAI gives you the exact number you need to pay to the beneficiary. If, on the other hand, you're directed to make no payments, set payments, or purely discretionary payments, calculating TAI is something you need only do when preparing your annual **Form 1041, U.S. Income Tax Return for Estates and Trusts;** it doesn't have any impact on the distributions you do make. Chapter 18 tells you how to complete this tax return.

We're noticing that a lot more trusts are investing in foreign securities, and income earned from foreign securities often means paying foreign taxes. Although the U.S. has tax treaties with most of these countries that entitle you to claim a refund for these foreign taxes you're paying, in most cases the amounts you're chasing after don't warrant the additional work required to collect the refunds. Instead, you may choose to claim a **Foreign Tax Credit** on **Form 1116**, which you then attach to your **Form 1041**. Foreign taxes paid are not income taxes chargeable to the trust. If you're distributing the income from the trust, you're probably also distributing the foreign tax credit to the trust's beneficiary. If this is your situation, don't subtract foreign taxes paid when calculating TAI. In fact, by passing the credit through to your beneficiary, you're actually making a distribution to him or her that should be included in TAI.

### Making distributions after the end of the year (Section 663(b))

What's left after adding together income and subtracting all the income-related expenses is the trust's TAI. If you're administering a trust that requires all, or a percentage of, income to be paid out currently, you need to calculate TAI before you can make distributions. If you want to make distributions more frequently than annually, you can make an educated guess for the first three quarters of every year. Then in the fourth quarter, you have to calculate TAI for the entire year and adjust the fourth-quarter distribution accordingly.

Of course, because the fourth quarter doesn't end until December 31, it's basically impossible to have all the information you need before the end of the calendar year. The IRS understands (some of those agents have trusts, too), and accordingly gives you 65 days after the end of the calendar year to make your calculation and pay that final distribution. If you use this extra time to make a year-end distribution, be sure to tick the box on question 6 at the bottom of page 2 of **Form 1041**. You've just made a Section 663(b) election for the trust.

## Creating a payment schedule

How can you be certain that you'll have cash in the account when you're required to make a payment, whether to the beneficiary, to pay fees, or to pay taxes? Simple. Just develop a payment schedule. Remember, with the exception of emergency discretionary distributions that no one knows about and no one can predict, the cash needs of the trust should be fairly easy to anticipate. Keeping the following pointers in mind will help you:

✔ **Project what your income and expenses will be throughout the year, and when you expect to be making payments for fees and expenses in the trust.** If the income generated by the trust is uneven, so that you receive large amounts in one or two months but very little the rest of the year, be sure to schedule your fee and expense payments after you receive the bulk of the trust's income. Only after those payments have been made should you make payments to the income beneficiary. So, if you receive large payments in May and November but not much else for the rest of the year, for example, you should schedule your fee and expense payments for early June and December, and then you can safely pay whatever income is remaining to the beneficiary toward the end of June and December. You can create this schedule for your trust on a slip of paper or in a computer spreadsheet program.

✔ **Make sure that you pay all other obligations before you ever write a check to the beneficiary.** Income from interest and dividends posts most heavily into accounts around the 1st of each month, and most tax payments are due on the 15th. Service providers almost always bill you on or about the first of the month. After the trust pays these obligations, then you can arrange to make beneficiary payments, usually toward the very end of the month or quarter.

✔ **Most important, don't ever leave yourself short at tax time.** Although accountants and attorneys may not be happy about having to wait for payment, and income beneficiaries may plead poverty endlessly in your ear, no one has the same ability to turn your life into a miserable wasteland as the IRS and the state tax authorities. In addition to tacking on penalties and interest for late payment or late filing, the IRS can also *levy,* or reach in and grab the taxes due directly from the trust's bank or brokerage account. And good luck pleading hardship — this is a trust, after all, and as far as the IRS is concerned, anyone with the wherewithal to form a trust can't be suffering that much financially!

# Distributing When the Beneficiary Reaches a Specific Age

Trusts are often designed to keep large sums of money out of the hands of people who may not be able to handle them. Of course, people change over time, and most of us become more responsible the older we get. In recognition of this fact, many trusts contain provisions to distribute income and/or principal of the trust to the trust's beneficiary at certain ages. The following are two of the most common scenarios:

✔ **Income required:** Trusts often don't begin mandating distributions of income to the beneficiary until he or she reaches a certain age. On occasion, distributions may begin as young as age 18. More frequently, they start at age 21 or even age 25. Rarely (although it does happen), the grantor may delay the start of mandatory income distributions as late as age 30.

✔ **Principal distributions:** Because (in most states) trusts aren't allowed to exist forever, a termination scenario is usually spelled out in the trust instrument. In many cases, the trust terminates when the income beneficiary dies. In other cases, where money is held in trust for a beneficiary who the grantor may not feel is mature enough to handle large sums at the time the trust is created, the principal distributes to that beneficiary as he or she attains certain ages. Depending on the grantor's wishes, distribution ages may start as early as age 21; however, age 25 or even age 30 is far more common as a starting point. Principal is commonly distributed in shares at five-year intervals, so that a beneficiary receives, for example, one-third of the principal value at age 25, one-half of the remaining value at age 30, and the balance of the trust principal at age 35. These distributions come in two varieties:

   • **Cash:** A cash distribution is by far the easiest type of distribution to make because all you need do is calculate the amount of the distribution required and then write a check. If you know when the distribution is due to be made (and you should know because you placed the date on your calendar when you began administering the trust), you may accumulate a war chest of cash and money-market-type investments if you're not making a total distribution of the trust's assets.

   • **Division of assets:** If the trust has more than one beneficiary who is entitled to a share of the principal assets, you may have to distribute assets rather than cash, especially when the trust terminates. In this case, be certain that each beneficiary entitled to a share gets a share of the fair market value on the date of termination. In the case of *marketable securities*, or those assets that can be bought and sold on the major stock, bond, or commodities exchanges, obtaining market values on that date is easy (check out Chapter 7 for a quick refresher on how to value assets) and divvy up the assets accordingly. With privately held assets, such as a business or real estate, you need to obtain independent appraisals before making distributions. Be sure that each beneficiary receives an equally valued share, even though each may receive substantially different assets.

# When Beneficiaries Request More Money: Paying Out Extra Distributions

The trust is now up and running. The principal is invested and generating income, you've figured out how to pay everyone who needs to be paid and still have money at the end of the month or quarter to give something to the income beneficiary, and all seems well in your world.

But wait! The phone rings — the beneficiary has just decided to return to school, buy a house, start a business, have that little medical procedure done that isn't covered by insurance, or invest in a foolproof way to turn straw into gold. As long as we've been in this business, you'd think we'd heard all the excuses for wanting more money. We've posted bail for clients and even paid for them to sue us, the trustees.

In fact, the only certainty in administering a trust is that, as much money as you manage to pay out to the income beneficiaries that's mandated by the terms of the trust, they'll always want more. How much more varies, as does the worthiness of the requests. If you do receive requests for extra distributions from the beneficiaries, your job as trustee is to shovel through the rationalizations before handing out any money. You must determine

- ✔ **Does the request have merit?** You're not required to give in to each and every demand from the beneficiary, nor should you. Not every request deserves a positive response.

- ✔ **Would the grantor have given the money for this purpose?** You need to put yourself in the grantor's shoes and make that determination. If, for example, the grantor wanted to encourage home ownership, and the beneficiary is asking for help with a down payment, your answer is clear. If, on the other hand, the beneficiary is asking for money to attend bartending school and the donor was a fervent teetotaler, you may want to think twice.

- ✔ **If you make this extra distribution, how will it affect the ongoing purpose of the trust?** If the purpose of the trust is to provide a safety cushion for an income beneficiary who is relying on that income to live, and depleting the principal of the trust in order to make this discretionary distribution would severely impact the trust's ability to provide that ongoing financial cushion, you may want to think twice, or even three times, before writing that check. Be willing to ask for more information regarding how the beneficiary plans to use this distribution. For example, if the distribution would enable the beneficiary to reduce living expenses (perhaps by purchasing a house for cash rather than requiring a mortgage), the loss of future income may be more than offset by the long-term reduction in the beneficiary's expenses.

- ✔ **Are you being asked to make a distribution to a spendthrift beneficiary?** In our experience, a fair number of trust beneficiaries are only trust beneficiaries because money runs through their fingers like water. When parents and grandparents place inheritances in trust for such heirs, it's usually for the sole purpose of preventing them from frittering away the money. Unfortunately, because trusts for spendthrifts tend to restrict access to any of the money except at the trustee's discretion, a beneficiary of one of these trusts can almost be guaranteed to live in your pocket, constantly asking for money for this, that, or the other.

Weigh these requests carefully; some have merit, but many don't. As we show in the section "Making the Decision to Distribute Discretionally: Eyeing the Trust's Terms," you have to place yourself in the grantor's shoes to make that determination. And, should you choose to make a distribution, be certain to obtain proof that the money is being used for the purpose intended. Depending on the beneficiary, you may want to pay the beneficiary's bills directly instead of giving the money to the beneficiary and relying on him or her to make those payments.

If you're the trustee of a spendthrift trust, you want to carefully document all your dealings with the beneficiary. If possible, all requests that come directly from the beneficiary should come in writing so that you can see, on paper, the scope of the request. And, if the beneficiary is requesting money to pay a specific bill or fund a project, don't rely only on the beneficiary's say-so, but request a copy of any third-party documentation, such as the bill that needs to be paid. Don't hesitate to contact that third party directly for verification.

And, if you choose not to make the distribution, be sure to notify the beneficiary, in writing, of your decision, referencing the part of the trust instrument that gives you the discretion to say no. In our experience, although many beneficiaries of spendthrift trusts are absolutely wonderful individuals who are merely challenged by money, some are merely looking for an excuse to make your life miserable. By keeping a well-documented paper trail, you protect yourself from having your past decisions rebound on you.

# Making the Decision to Distribute Discretionally: Eyeing the Trust's Terms

Very often, trust instruments give you, the trustee, a great deal of guidance as to what sorts of discretionary distributions the grantor thought you may be asked to make. Some of these so-called discretionary powers are quite narrow, but others leave you with almost completely unfettered range, both with regard to requests you receive from the beneficiary, as well as those needs of the beneficiary that you, yourself, identify. The following sections provide some guidance to help you make these decisions.

## Ensuring health and well-being

Among the most popular of discretionary power standards is one that allows the trustee to make payments to ensure the health and well-being of the trust's beneficiaries. Usually, this power extends the class of beneficiaries well beyond the stated income beneficiary: that person's spouse, children, grandchildren, or other issue. And, unless explicitly stated in the trust instrument, it's not just to cover medical expenses. Instead, the health and well-being standard can be used, if the trustee chooses to interpret it as such, to provide a wide variety of extras to the beneficiaries. In addition to paying doctors' bills and providing health insurance for those who don't have any, the trustee may also determine that vacations, ballet lessons, summer camps, and other such items add to the beneficiaries' general health and well-being.

Of course, although the standard is broad, it's not unlimited. Although most trustees would probably agree that replacing an aging, mold-infested residence with something that provided a cleaner environment meets the health and well-being standard, they probably would also agree that replacing one adequate residence with another, larger one doesn't.

## Paying for education

Saving money for education in a trust can be a very effective way to pay for college, and many people use trusts for this purpose. Saving for education inside a trust allows much greater flexibility when the time comes to pay for that education — and, should the child or grandchild named as beneficiary receive merit scholarships or choose not to go to college, the money can easily be used for other purposes at other times.

If the trust you're administering allows you discretion to make distributions for education, you should be aware that education isn't limited only to post-secondary schools. You may also use trust monies to pay for private primary and secondary education, for supplemental educational programs, for summer camps that have some sort of educational focus (we know of several trust beneficiaries who've attended summer music camps, thanks to discretionary trust distributions), for tutoring, or even to buy a computer. In fact, if you think the request is reasonable, and you can rationalize that it furthers the beneficiary's education in some way, you're most likely on safe ground in making that distribution.

## Buying a home

Although not all trust instruments include specific language allowing you to make a distribution to a beneficiary so that he or she can purchase a house, very few trust instruments explicitly prohibit you from making distributions either for down payments or for the total purchase price of a house. This is one of those gray areas that you have to deal with and one of the places where you need to look not only at the trust's resources but also at the beneficiary's decision making.

When deciding whether or not to use trust assets to buy a home, be certain that the beneficiary will actually be able to afford to live there. He or she will now be responsible for the house's ongoing expenses, maintenance (both major and minor repairs), and real estate taxes. If you've gone to the trouble of purchasing the house and distributing it outright to the beneficiary, you want to be certain that the beneficiary won't turn around and try to drain it of cash. One of us worked on a trust that used almost all its assets to buy the beneficiary a house outright. A month after the closing, the beneficiary was already trying to raise a mortgage on the house; two years after the purchase, the city where the beneficiary lived foreclosed on his home for nonpayment of taxes.

If you think the beneficiary would be better off living in stable housing rather than going from rental to rental, but you're not sure that he or she is likely to be able to afford the upkeep and taxes on a house, you always have the option of having the trust purchase, and own, the property. This way, you know that the necessary bills are being paid, and you can arrange regular inspections to determine what, if any, maintenance must be done. Although doing so is more work for you, at least you'll rest assured that, whatever shortcomings the beneficiary may have in his or her life and financial dealings, at least he or she will have a stable and comfortable place to sleep each night.

## Starting a business

In most cases, stifling the earning capacity of the trust's beneficiary isn't the grantor's goal; still, you, the trustee, face a tough decision when the beneficiary comes looking to you for money with which to start a business or to additionally capitalize a business that may require a cash infusion in order to stay afloat.

Your decision to distribute trust funds for this purpose depends largely on your confidence in the abilities of the beneficiary and his or her business plan. Your job isn't to be a nice guy; it's to request and study a business plan and to make your judgment based on sound business principles, not pie-in-the-sky projections.

You may determine that you don't want to deplete the trust's assets in order to support the beneficiary's business, but that the business plan has merit. If you feel that the beneficiary would be able to obtain a loan from a bank or other lender on the strength of the business plan, you may loan the money to the beneficiary, making sure to have the beneficiary sign a promissory note that requires repayment of the principal and payment of interest at market rates. If you're not sure what interest rate to charge, the IRS issues *Applicable*

*Federal Rates* every month, which tells you the minimum interest rate you can charge on a loan in order for it to be considered a fair market rate. You can find these rates at www.irs.gov under the Index of Applicable Federal Rate (AFR) Rulings.

## Using trustee discretion

The grantor, in creating the trust, may have thought he or she'd covered every possibility, but life has a funny way of presenting situations you thought were impossible. Welcome to the world of the trustee's discretion, where truth is often stranger than fiction. If a beneficiary asks for a distribution and the trust instrument isn't clear about that request, you, Mr. or Ms. Trustee, need to decide. Remember that the grantor trusted you with making these types of decisions.

Keep your wits about you. Ask the beneficiary lots of questions and review third-party documentation, when available. Most of all, take your time and deliberate carefully. Put yourself in the grantor's shoes as you weigh your decision, taking what you know about the beneficiary into consideration. Even though many of the requests you receive from beneficiaries will be valid, others may be creative attempts to separate the trust's assets from the trust. On the small end, we've received requests to pay veterinary bills and buy new cars. On the larger side, we've helped buy major-league sports teams and financed blockbuster movies. Sometimes the distributions have been made and other times they haven't. Remember, you're not required to dispense money just because a beneficiary requests it.

# Chapter 14

# Creating and Keeping Trust Records

*In This Chapter*

▶ Putting together a filing system

▶ Creating an Inventory

▶ Preparing annual accounts

*Y*ou probably know at least one person who never balances his checkbook, who keeps track of his money by rounding to the nearest dollar or ten, who thinks that he must have money in the account because he still has checks in the checkbook, and who shows up at his accountant's office on April 14 with a shoe box of receipts. We'd love to be able to tell you that you can administer a trust this way — that the trust elves come in each night to do all the work of the trust — but we'd be lying. A competently managed trust is one where you keep, maintain, and update records on a regular basis. You have no room in trust management for approximation or procrastination; every penny counts and must be counted. In this chapter, we explain the nuts and bolts of what records you should keep, the information you need to create them, and how long to retain them.

## Creating a Filing System

Organization is the key, and no more so than when you're a trustee. The grantor has relied on you to handle the trust's assets competently. When you're organized, you know where the trust's important documents and records are, which helps you to properly and efficiently administer the trust.

Organizational lapses can mean extra time spent searching for a crucial piece of correspondence or, more important, failure to make a required distribution or file and pay the trust's taxes. Start off your administration in as organized a fashion as you possibly can, and as with most things in life, you'll find that almost everything you do will be easier and take less time. The following sections help you set up the initial structure.

# *Getting started: Organizing the right way*

Beginning on the right foot when administering a trust is important. So where do you start? The day you discover you're a trustee is the day you should begin organizing the trust's administration. What do you do to begin? Even though much administration is done online these days, you may still want to head to your local office supply or stationery store for the following items:

- ✔ **Paper supplies:** Pick up manila files, file folders, labels, special accounting pads (if you're not comfortable working with a computer spreadsheet), legal pads (or whatever you prefer to make notes on), and anything else you think may be useful to you.

- ✔ **Various ink stamps (and ink if necessary):** If you're going to be collecting dividend and/or interest checks, you may want to purchase a "For Deposit Only" stamp for the back of your checks, or a date stamp to put on all trust correspondence you receive.

- ✔ **A file cabinet:** You really want one that locks and is reasonably fire resistant.

- ✔ **A computer, printer, and Internet connection (if you don't already have them available to you):** If the trust is large enough, complex enough, and will continue long enough to warrant the cost, these investments will be invaluable.

Most of the work you need to do for any trust can be done on a computer, and having one can save you a great deal of time and money over the course of the trust's administration, but it's important to maintain current backups of everything (and we do mean everything), preferably both on paper and on computer media. That means photocopying documents and putting them in multiple places, having offsite Internet-based backup, and even backing up onto an external drive that you then lock in a fireproof safety deposit box. Don't assume that, just because everyone else says they're keeping backups, you can re-create your records if they're lost.

With your supplies in hand, create some file folders. Here are some you positively, definitely want to have, whether you have a manual or electronic filing system. Keep in mind that some of these files can be destroyed at a later date; others you may want to have bronzed. The following list shows you which files you want to keep permanently:

- ✔ Trust instrument
- ✔ Beginning inventory
- ✔ Annual accounts

You can destroy these files after you're done with them. Remember, though, that the concept of temporary is relative. In many cases, you're not going to want to toss these files onto the bonfire for many years:

- **Bank statements and canceled checks, filed by date:** You can destroy them after you've prepared the annual accounts and after beneficiaries have assented to those accounts. If this is a probate trust, hang onto them until the probate account has been allowed.

- **Brokerage statements and stock trade confirmations, filed by date:** Hang onto them as long as you keep the bank statements and canceled checks.

- **Income tax returns, either filed sequentially by date in one folder or in separate folders for each year's returns:** Keep copies of all income tax returns for at least seven years after you file them.

- **Correspondence, filed by date:** Depending on the content of the letters, you may want to hold onto old correspondence until the trust terminates and all accounts have been assented to. You can place the really old correspondence into storage, though.

- **E-mails, plus memos and notes regarding phone conversations and meetings, filed by date:** Hold onto them as long as you keep your correspondence files. You'd be surprised how often you need to reference historical information.

- **Billing:** Yes, as trustee you bill the trust for your fees, unless you choose to forgo a trustee fee because the trust is for a family member or for some other reason. You want to keep a record of what you bill and what you base your fee on. You can destroy them together with the bank and brokerage statements.

- **Miscellaneous:** This file is where you put anything that you think is important but doesn't really fit into any of the other categories. If you're placing old correspondence, e-mails, and memos into storage, you probably should put these old miscellaneous files there as well. After the trust terminates (see Chapter 15), you can destroy them.

Of course, every trust is different, and you may find that your miscellaneous file is the biggest one in the drawer. If that's the case, see whether you can group that information into some additional file categories and shrink that miscellaneous file down to a manageable size. The more finely you're able to slice and dice the information you're keeping, the more easily you can find exactly what you're looking for when you need it. If you're administering multiple trusts, or if you just want to make your file folders more portable, file them in an expandable manila file and then in the locking file cabinet.

## Keeping the trust instrument handy

You may have already read the trust instrument and are fairly certain you know what's contained in it. But believe us when we tell you that reading a trust instrument isn't like reading a novel; you can't read, and comprehend, everything in it sequentially. We can guarantee that before you hit the bottom of page 2, your eyes will be glazed over, and you'll wonder what you did to deserve this. By the time you actually reach the signature pages at the end, you won't even remember the name of the trust, let alone recall what Article VII or Paragraph 3(B)(ii)(c) says.

Because a trust instrument can be quite confusing, you want to be able to refer to it whenever possible to clarify any questions you may have. That's why you want to keep a copy of it close by so you can easily access it. You may want to scan a copy into your computer, where you can open it at will whenever necessary. Or you may prefer to maintain a hard copy in a three-ring binder or a manila folder. Whatever you do, and wherever you keep it, make sure that it's fastened in and that all the pages are fully legible. If you choose to use any sort of binder, make sure to reinforce the punched holes. We can guarantee that you'll read and reread this document so many times over the years that the paper will begin to shred over time. Make sure that the instrument is always fully legible; as pages begin to fade, you should recopy and replace them as necessary.

## Compiling correspondence

A trust is an ongoing organism, and what happens today most certainly impacts tomorrow and next year. That's why keeping careful records of all correspondence that you receive and send is essential. You may want to compile these records in a folder in a manila file, as we discuss earlier in the chapter, or in a three-ring binder. As your correspondence grows, you may want to separate it out by subject or type, such as correspondence from the grantor, or correspondence with the IRS.

Sometimes the most important aspect of a particular piece of correspondence is that you sent it. When you mail anything that you're required to mail, such as tax returns or certain correspondence to beneficiaries or courts, make sure to send it certified mail. When you need to know that something you mail has been received, send it certified mail, return receipt requested. And because you're paying extra to prove that you mailed something or that someone's actually received it, staple those receipts to the copies of the letters you sent so that you have the evidence handy should anyone need to see it.

The key to organizing nonpostal communication is keeping a paper (and/or electronic) trail. Remember to keep copies of all e-mails that you send and receive, and keep notes on all phone conversations, listing the date and time of the call, to whom you spoke, the subject matter, and whatever course of action or resolutions were decided. By keeping a pad of paper and a pencil next to the phone where you conduct trust business, you'll always be sure to have the tools necessary to keep accurate records. If you have meetings with the beneficiary, an investment advisor, or for any other trust-related purpose, take and keep dated notes of all pertinent information from the meeting.

It's also a great idea to exchange meeting or phone conversation notes with the other party or parties. That way, if one of you heard the discussion one way, and the other heard it differently, your miscommunications can be corrected as close to the time they happened as is possible.

## Filing financial records

As trustee, you also want to keep accurate records of the trust's financial records you receive from banks, brokerages, or other sources. Keep all those brokerage and bank statements year by year in individual files. For a trust that maintains two bank accounts and a brokerage account, for example, you should have three files for each year, one for each of the bank accounts and one for the brokerage account. In each file, keep the monthly statements, as well as any canceled checks, deposit slips, or purchase and sale confirmations. Files should be kept in date order so that when you need to find a particular transaction, you can put your hands on it easily.

## Preserving annual accounts

If you compare organizing financial information to making a big pot of soup, the financial records you receive from all sources are the ingredients, and the soup they create is the annual account. *Annual accounts* are those compilations of all the trust's activity for any 12-month period that you distill from all the information you receive. Check out "Assembling the desired information," later in the chapter, for info on how to prepare one.

Not every trust instrument requires that you have annual accounts, but preparing them on a regular and timely basis is a really good idea whether they're required or not. Your trust instrument should indicate clearly whether you're required to prepare these accounts annually or only if a beneficiary asks to see one. Either way, pulling together all your financial data into one place allows you to see how the trust has done over the past year. You can see what investment mistakes you've made and how to avoid them in the future. And, should a beneficiary or court demand to see one, you won't have to scurry around, trying to create one under pressure.

After you begin accumulating annual accounts, make sure that you have a file ready to hold the finished product. Like with financial statements, file them in date order so you can access them easily. It's not at all uncommon to have to go back through years of annual accounts in order to mine certain types of information, such as unequal distributions to beneficiaries. By having these accounts prepared, in order, and easily found, culling the information you need is a simple task.

## Referencing tax returns

Maintaining copies of the trust's income tax returns for seven years seems fairly obvious; after all, that's what you do with your individual returns, right? As trustee, you need to keep copies so you can easily reference past tax returns as needed. Depending on the size of the tax return, and the amount of underlying information that's needed to prepare the returns, you can either choose to file all tax returns by date in one file, or open a new file for each tax year.

Very often, the initial assets inside a trust arrive via a decedent's estate. When this happens, make sure to obtain a copy of the **Form 706, United States Estate (and Generation-Skipping Transfer) Tax Return.** In it, you'll find the estate tax values (which will be the trust's cost basis, as we discuss in Chapter 18) of all the assets that have now rolled into the trust. Hang onto a copy of **Form 706** for as long as the trust is in existence; although you'll refer to it less and less as time goes on, you may need to find an estate tax value on some quirky little asset that landed in your trust many, many years after the grantor's death.

If the trust owns business or partnership interests, consider hanging onto the trust's income tax returns (including all supporting documentation) for the trust's lifetime because the year-to-year activity in the partnership or business may impact the trust's cost in that business or partnership. When the entity dissolves, or the trust sells its share, having that information handy may be crucial in determining what tax, if any, is owed.

You may be able to obtain copies of your tax returns, or transcripts of what was on them, from the IRS, but don't rely on this as your sole backup method. The IRS permits access to copies of the actual returns for just seven years (at a cost), and transcripts for the current year and three prior years. If there's information on returns that predates that and the IRS was your backup plan, you'll be plain out of luck.

# Preparing an Initial Inventory and Valuing the Assets

The starting point for any trust is the property funding it. This property is listed on the trust's *initial inventory* (that is, a list you create of all the initial assets of the trust), where you show each asset's *cost basis* (the acquisition cost it carries as it enters the trust, which may be the grantor's purchase price, or the date-of-death value for assets that flow into the trust from a decedent's estate).

Although preparing the initial inventory may seem like a daunting task, it's really not. You already should have all the necessary information; it's just scattered. The next sections show you how to collect and sort the data into a nice, neat package. Remember, the beginning inventory is the starting point of the trust's history, which you'll eventually trace from inception to termination by creating accounts, which we explain later in this chapter, in the section "Producing Annual Trust Accounts."

## Arriving directly from the donor

When putting together the list of assets, you need to value the decedent's assets to ensure that your records are complete. Property placed in trust during the donor's lifetime carries with it the donor's adjusted basis and acquisition date. How can you calculate that basis? It's usually as simple as the amount the donor paid to obtain the property. Thus, 50 shares of XYZ Corp that the donor purchased on April 15, 2000, for a total of $5,000, and then donated into his revocable trust on April 15, 2013, has a basis inside the trust of $5,000 and an acquisition date of April 15, 2000. If the trustee then sells these shares on April 16, 2013, for $10,000, the holding period is 13 years, not 1 day, and the capital gain is long term.

The donor's basis may be adjusted if, for example, he or she reinvests dividends or if improvements are made to property (or a portion of the property is damaged due to a casualty loss). Also, if the trust is revocable before the donor's death (refer to Chapter 3), the basis of assets the donor has placed inside the trust prior to death will change to the value on the donor's date of death, or to the value six months after death, if the estate chooses to use alternate valuation. Check out Chapter 16 for more on how basis changes at death.

If a donor funds an *irrevocable inter vivos trust* prior to death (see Chapter 3), the assets in the trust retain the donor's adjusted basis and acquisition date. There is no change in basis or acquisition date when the donor dies.

## Coming from the donor's estate

Property that funds a trust via the donor's estate carries with it the donor's date-of-death value (or alternate valuation, if the executor has elected to use that method of valuation in order to reduce estate taxes). Whether valued as of the date of death or an alternate valuation date, it'll be considered as acquired on the date of death. Any sales within the first year of acquisition are long term for the purpose of calculating capital gains and losses.

# Compiling Records of All Transactions

After you create an initial inventory, you can begin tracking the activity in the trust account. Just like maintaining a running balance in your own check-book, tracking this basic information helps in any number of ways. With it, you can determine how much is available to distribute to the income benefi-ciaries (Chapter 13), while at the same time keeping track of the trust's ongo-ing tax situation (Chapter 18). By recording all the transactions, you'll gain some insight into how much you should charge for your trustee's fee. So, every time you buy or sell a security, receive interest or dividend payments, or make any payments (taxes, fees, or beneficiary payments), you need to record that transaction. If there's activity in the trust accounts, you need to capture it. If you miss something along the way, watch out! When it comes time to create your annual account, missing transactions will mean that your account won't balance.

## Knowing the difference between income and principal

As you keep track of these transactions, you need to understand the differ-ence between income and principal. Unlike your personal accounts, where you probably lump all your funds together and then pay your bills from the pot of cash, trusts differentiate between *principal,* or the assets of the trust, and *income,* or the money earned by the assets. Distinguishing between income and principal can sometimes be confusing because certain types of income are actually considered principal (such as capital gains), and others remain segregated on the income side of the account. Chapter 12 discusses more fully how to make the distinction.

However, just keeping track of the approximate records isn't enough when administering a trust. Precision is the key to success, both for administration and for tax compliance, and no more so than when keeping track of basis information. (*Basis* is your carrying cost in any piece of property of whatever type. It may be the price you paid for the property, the price the donor paid for it, the estate tax value if you received the property from an estate, or any combination.) You have to know what the trust's cost is in an asset before you can make an informed decision as to what to do with it; should you decide to sell it, you need to know the basis, down to the last dollar, in order to correctly calculate the capital gain or loss.

Even though brokerages were required to begin reporting cost basis information to the IRS in 2011, that only relates to publicly traded securities acquired after December 31, 2010; for mutual funds, that date is December 31, 2011. Don't rely on brokerages or mutual fund companies to keep track of your cost basis in securities you owned prior to those dates. Our experience is that they're satisfied with approximate costs for the non-covered securities (ones acquired before the magic dates of December 31, 2010 or 2011), so they do things like merge tax lots or fail to allocate basis to new companies spun off from a parent corporation. Why does it matter? Each time you buy a security, you create one tax lot; each time you sell, you may choose which lot or lots you're selling. By designating which shares are sold, you can generate either a larger or smaller capital gain or loss, depending on what's most advantageous to the trust. Keeping track of each specific tax lot allows you to keep all your options open.

Even if your broker supplies you with an informational schedule for your sales of non-covered securities with its version of gains and losses, you're not obligated to use it — provided you have the supporting documentation necessary to back up yours. For covered securities, though, you may want to pay closer attention over the course of the year to make sure that the records are correct. Now that the IRS is going to be matching up acquisition costs as well as sales proceeds, you're far more likely to receive a notice from them if you report numbers different than your broker's.

## *Filing income tax returns annually*

A trust is a taxable entity, and any income it earns must be reported annually, either on the grantor's **Form 1040**, in the case of a revocable trust, or on **Form 1041, U.S. Income Tax Return for Estates and Trusts.** Almost all trusts are required to file, using a calendar year (ending December 31), and the tax return is due on April 15 of the following year. If you're unable to complete and file the return by the filing deadline, you may file **Form 7004, Application for Automatic 6-Month Extension of Time to File Certain Business Income Tax, Information, and Other Returns** instead. Remember, any taxes owed for the prior year must be paid by April 15; the extension of time to file isn't an extension of time to pay. Chapter 18 tells you what you need to know in order to prepare **Form 1041.**

# Producing Annual Trust Accounts

Trust administration is fairly similar to organizing your own finances. You have bank and brokerage accounts to manage, taxes to file, bills to pay. However, you do have to tangle with one major difference: Although your own finances probably toddle along quite nicely without you ever compiling the activity into one place, you need to create a trust account for every year of the trust's existence. This account traces all the activity in the trust from the ending balances of last year's account (or from the initial inventory, if this is the trust's first year of operation) to the closing balances at this year's end.

How do you know what to include and how to create a trust account? Don't feel too overwhelmed. The following sections show you what you need to do.

## Assembling the desired information

Trusts, unlike estates, account for their activity with a strict separation between principal and income. Although you can format them in a variety of ways, Figure 14-1 shows a sample account in a form commonly used by most trust accountants. Remember that the mathematical concepts here are very simple: Schedule A minus Schedule B must equal Schedule C, and Schedule D minus Schedule E must equal Schedule F.

If all your assets are in one basket, so to speak, held either by a bank, a brokerage, or a law firm *fiduciary* (trust and estate) department, they should send you annual trust accounts. If you've scattered the trust's assets among a variety of financial institutions, the responsibility of compiling all the information into one easy-to-read account becomes yours.

Although annual account preparation may seem like a lot of work for little benefit, we strongly urge you to go through the steps to do it each and every year. Not only do you pick up any inconsistencies in your recordkeeping this way, but you also create a permanent record of set points in the trust's timeline. Down the road, should anyone question your handling of the trust, you'll have these accounts to support your arguments that the trust actually blossomed under your management.

### PRINCIPAL

| Item # | Date | Description | Principal Cash | Schedule A: Gains and Additions | Schedule B: Charges, Losses, Distributions |
|---|---|---|---|---|---|
| 1 | | Balance as per last prior account | 0.00 | 100,000.00 | |
| 2 | 03/15/13 | ZYX Corporation Sold 50 shares @ $25 | 1,250.00 | 250.00 | |
| 3 | 05/14/13 | QRS Corp Sold 40 shares @ $50 | 2,000.00 | | 400.00 |
| 4 | 06/18/13 | MNO Inc Purchased 100 shares @ $32.50 | (3,250.00) | | |
| 5 | 10/15/13 | Trustee's fee paid – principal portion | (1,000.00) | | 1,000.00 |
| 6 | 12/31/13 | Cash balance as per Schedule C | 0.00 | | |
| | | | | 100,250.00 | 1,400.00 |

#### Schedule C: Principal Balance

| Item # | Par Value or # of Shares | Description | Book Value | Market Value (unit price) at 12/31/13 | Total Market Value at 12/31/13 |
|---|---|---|---|---|---|
| 1 | 450.000 | ZYX Corporation | 9,000.00 | 45.00 | 20,250.00 |
| 2 | 100.000 | MNO Inc | 3,250.00 | 30.00 | 3,000.00 |
| 3 | 86,600.000 | ABC Money Market Fund | 86,600.00 | 1.00 | 86,600.00 |
| 4 | | Principal Cash | 0.00 | | 0.00 |
| | | Balance Schedule C | 98,850.00 | | 109,850.00 |

### INCOME

| Item # | Date | Description | Schedule D: Receipts | Schedule E: Payments |
|---|---|---|---|---|
| 1 | | Balance as per last prior account | 0.00 | |
| 2 | 01/31/13 | ABC Money Market: interest | 252.00 | |
| 3 | 02/28/13 | ABC Money Market: interest | 254.00 | |
| 4 | 03/31/13 | ZYX Corporation: dividend | 500.00 | |
| 5 | 04/30/13 | QRS Corporation: dividend | 250.00 | |
| 6 | 10/15/13 | Trustee's fee: income portion | | 400.00 |
| 7 | 12/31/13 | John Smith: income distribution | | 856.00 |
| | | | 1,256.00 | 1,256.00 |

#### Schedule F: Income Balance

| Description | Book Value | Market Value (unit price) at 12/31/13 | Total Market Value at 12/31/13 |
|---|---|---|---|
| Income Cash | 0.00 | | 0.00 |

**Figure 14-1:** Sample annual account for the XYZ Trust.

## Obtaining assents of beneficiaries

You've gone to the trouble of generating an annual account. Now you should sign it and then provide copies to all the beneficiaries for their *assent*, or agreement to what's contained in the account. The best, and easiest, way to do this is by preparing a summary cover sheet (which then becomes part of the account) for the account you've prepared, signing it as trustee, attaching it to the six schedules you previously prepared, and providing a copy of the complete packet to the beneficiary, together with a photocopy of that cover sheet, which the beneficiaries then sign and return to you. These photocopies, after they have the beneficiary's original signature on them, become the beneficiary's assent to the account.

After obtaining assents from all the beneficiaries (and we do mean *all* the beneficiaries, including those people who aren't currently receiving any distributions but may in the future), attach these signed documents to the front of your account, and keep the whole kit and caboodle together in a permanent file (which you're hopefully keeping in a fireproof safe). Figure 14-2 shows a sample cover page, with the assent line included, for the annual account shown in Figure 14-1.

## Filing with the probate court

If your trust is governed by an instrument contained within the Last Will of the creator of the trust, you may file annual accounts with the probate court. In most cases, the annual account format shown in Figure 14-1 should be adequate, although you want to obtain the court's specific guidelines prior to finalizing your account. Instead of using the cover sheet shown in Figure 14-2, you have to use the court's cover, which you can obtain from the court by just showing up (one of the court officers will help you), by requesting that they mail you a cover, or even online (yes, even probate courts are moving into the digital age).

Despite the fact that the probate court is, in fact, a court, and despite the fact that annual accounts may be required for testamentary trusts, all the courts we've been involved with haven't been exactly on top of us to get these accounts done and filed. Not getting pressure to file doesn't waive the requirement to file, and much like teachers and late homework, when the court goes looking for an account that's not there, they tend to get testy. If you must file accounts, prepare and file them in a timely fashion; finding all the financial records you need years after the fact is often difficult, and your memory of events may be spotty at best.

**The Fifth Account of Jane Smith, Trustee of the XYZ Trust**

This Account is for the period beginning with the 1$^{st}$ day of January, 2013 and ending with the 31$^{st}$ day of December, 2013

**Principal**

Schedule A   Opening balance plus additions and gains $100,250.00

Schedule B   Payments, charges, and losses          $1,400.00

Schedule C   Balance at end of period               $98,850.00

Market Value                                         $109,850.00

**Income**

Schedule D   Opening balance plus receipts          $1,256.00

Schedule E   Payments and charges                   $1,256.00

Schedule F   Balance at end of period               $0.00

_____

Jane Smith, Trustee

Within account is hereby approved by: _____

John Smith, beneficiary

Dated: _____

**Figure 14-2:**
Sample
cover page
for XYZ
Trust annual
account.

# Chapter 15

# Terminating the Trust

*In This Chapter*

▶ Making final income and principal distributions

▶ Planning for, and preparing, the final tax return

▶ Gazing into your crystal ball for future expenses

▶ Wrapping up the final account

*A*ll good things must come to an end, and that includes trusts. A day will come when you've fulfilled all the terms of the trust and the need for it just goes away. This may happen when the income beneficiary dies or reaches a certain age, or when all the principal has been spent. Whatever the reason, when the time comes for you to terminate the trust, you don't just get to wash your hands and say, "I'm done." Although the end scenario isn't difficult, you do need to follow a few rules and perform a few rituals before you can walk away from your duties as trustee.

In this chapter, we tell you what needs doing and when you need to do it. We explain how to make those final distributions, prepare that last tax return, set aside something for those contingent expenses that always seem to crop up, and finally wrap a nice bow around the whole package with your final account, which should show zero balances in both income and principal on the last day.

## Distributing All Assets According to the Trust Instrument

No matter what event triggers the termination of a trust, you need to find new homes for the remaining assets before you can wrap up its affairs. Of course, none of this division is left to your discretion; the trust instrument has the disposition of the remaining assets spelled out in neon. All you need to do is go back to the instrument and find those provisions.

The trust instrument spells out clearly who gets the principal when the income interest in that trust terminates. It may be the income beneficiary, who's reached a certain age and becomes entitled to the principal. Or it may be some other person — perhaps the income beneficiary's child, or some other descendant of the donor. The trust may even terminate in favor of one or more charities. These individuals are referred to as *remaindermen*. In fact, you may have any combination of events, with portions going in several directions. Your job, as trustee, is to determine how to slice the remaining asset pie. This section spells out who receives the distributions.

Just because a trust is terminating as of a particular date doesn't mean that you need to make all the final distributions on that date. Trusts can be complicated, and doing the final wrap-up may take some time. Be patient, and move carefully. As long as you complete the business of the trust within a reasonable length of time (and no one, as far as we know, has ever truly defined *reasonable*), you're on safe ground here.

## Calculating final income distributions

Before you can distribute the principal to the remaindermen, you must be certain that all the required income has been distributed to the income beneficiary. Making this determination is easy if the income beneficiary and the remainderman are one and the same person because that individual will receive everything, no matter how it's categorized. But if the principal is going to someone or someplace other than where you've been making income distributions, you have to pay out all the income that's required to be distributed before you can distribute the principal.

How do you make the determination of how much you owe, if anything, to the income beneficiary? You do it all by dates. The income interest may end on the date the income beneficiary dies or turns a specific age, or after the trust has been in existence for a certain number of years. Read the instrument and be sure that you've identified the correct date. After you know the date the trust officially terminates, you can then calculate the final payout. For example, if the income interest terminates on February 2, you need to pay to the income beneficiary all the income still in the trust on that date plus all the income that the trust was entitled to receive by that date but that hadn't yet been paid to the trust. So, if the trust owned QPWR Corporation stock, which said it would pay a dividend to its shareholders of record on February 1, but which wasn't actually paying the dividend until February 10, you need to include that dividend in your final income calculations, even though it wasn't received by February 2. Any income that's accumulated in the trust prior to the termination date belongs to the income beneficiary, unless the trust document provides differently. In addition, though, you're going to make adjustments for the following items when terminating a trust:

- ✔ Accrued interest earned on any bonds held by the trust, or earned to the termination date in any bank accounts. Interest is earned on a daily basis, even though it's paid only periodically.

- ✔ Stock dividends that are owed to the trust but haven't yet been paid.

- ✔ Rents owed but not yet paid for the period from the end of the last rental period to the termination date.

- ✔ Partnership and business income from the date earned but not yet paid, through the termination date.

- ✔ State tax refunds attributable to income earned prior to the termination that are due but haven't been received.

- ✔ Any other miscellaneous income earned but not yet received prior to the termination.

Although doing the research and making all these calculations yourself is possible if you're only dealing with a few securities, save yourself the hassle and call your broker or a valuation service if the trust owns tens or even hundreds of securities. The amount you pay for the service is probably a pittance in comparison to the amount of time you'll spend doing the work yourself.

## Holding back funds for final taxes and fees

Prior to fully terminating a trust, you need to ensure that you've put money aside to pay Uncle Sam and any other fees. Income needs to be reduced by any expenses accrued as of the termination date, such as trustee's and investment advisor's fees; state, local, and foreign taxes on income received and accrued; miscellaneous expenses; probate court costs (for filing annual accounts); and any other such fees attributable to the income earned in the trust as of that date. (Check out the later section, "Submitting the Final Income Tax Returns," for more on submitting the final tax return.)

If you've collected all the income but haven't yet paid all the expenses, you really don't need to continue to keep all that income in the trust. Instead, determine how much you think you'll need to pay the expenses and then pay out what remains to the income beneficiary. Be sure to estimate the expenses on the generous side; nothing is worse than having to ask the income beneficiaries to repay money they've already spent. You can either hold the money you set aside for future expenses in a separate, non-interest-bearing, non-trust account (a popular choice of law firms) or you may keep one of the trust accounts open. Remember, though, that after you make this move, you don't want to earn any additional income, especially after you've filed the final tax return. After you finish paying the expenses, the rest of that money should be promptly sent to the income beneficiary to close out the income side of the account.

# *Paying the remaindermen*

After you've paid all the fees and expenses, and you've sent whatever is owed to the income beneficiary, you need to pay the *remaindermen* (the individual(s) or organization(s) named by the trust instrument to receive the remaining property after the trust's income interest has ended) if there are still any assets left (securities, cash, real estate, or that all-important country club membership). To identify these individuals or entities, carefully study the trust instrument to determine who gets what and how much.

As trustee, you have to be certain that your allocation of trust assets among the remaindermen is equitable, but you're not required to give each remainderman a proportionate piece of every asset. Typically, if trust principal is being divvied up into two or more pieces, the starting point for the division is the value of the assets on the trust's termination date, or the date that the income beneficiary no longer is entitled to any more income. Thus, certain assets that are difficult to divide, such as real estate, or businesses, or even some stocks and bonds, don't have to be sold in order to make sure that everyone is getting his or her exact proportionate share of every type of property. All that's required is that the allocation of the total value of all the assets is exactly proportionate to the shares called for in the trust instrument (which may be unequal shares). So if Alvin is scheduled to receive 60 percent of the remainder, and his brother Calvin the remaining 40 percent, of a trust that's worth $100,000 after the income interest ends, Alvin's share is worth $60,000 and Calvin's $40,000. It doesn't matter what property you, as trustee, put into each of their shares to arrive at those final values. All that matters is that each receives property equal to his proportionate share.

Knowing how to make the calculations necessary to divide up the property is one thing; actually transferring those assets to the remaindermen is another. Although cash can be disposed of by writing a check, transferring many of the other assets held by the trust is slightly more complicated. Property may be transferred to the remaindermen in the following ways:

- ✔ **Stocks and bonds (publicly traded):** Notify the broker holding the securities of the transfer by signing stock assignments to transfer ownership to the remaindermen. If you're holding stock certificates in the name of the trust (and we sincerely hope you're not), you have to deliver the certificates, either in person or by using registered mail together with stock assignments, to each of the companies, who then reregister the stock in the name of the remainderman.

- ✔ **Stocks and bonds (privately held):** Contact the companies directly. They're most likely already aware of the transfer, and they'll provide you with the necessary documents to effect the change.

- **Real estate:** Draft a new deed, transferring title from you (as trustee) to the remainderman receiving the property and then record the new deed with the county, city, or town where the property is located. You may want to consult an attorney to draft and record the new deed, to be certain that all the formalities of the real estate transfer are observed.

- **Partnership interests:** Contact the general partner of the partnership with the name and federal tax identification number or Social Security Number of the new partner. Be aware that many partnerships are run by professionals (in which case the transfer will likely happen almost seamlessly), but others are operated by scratching notes on the backs of envelopes. If you don't receive confirmation that the transfer has happened, and you receive a **Schedule K-1** from the partnership still in the name of the trust for a year following the transfer, make a nuisance of yourself. Sometimes the surest way to get results is to be the squeaky wheel.

- **Royalty interests:** If the trust has interests in natural resource leases, notify the manager of the change in ownership. Like with partnership interests, give them a reasonable amount of time to change their records and then feel free to become insistent. If the royalties in question derive from intellectual property, such as music or books, provide the publisher with the information she requires to change the ownership interest.

- **Promissory notes or mortgages held by the trust:** Often, the trust will have lent money to a beneficiary or remainderman and evidenced that loan with either a promissory note or a mortgage. If the promissory note in question has the trust as the lender and the remainder interest as the borrower, no transfer is required. Just subtract the outstanding loan amount from the total amount payable to that remainderman, and you're in the clear. If, on the other hand, the loan was made to a third party, draft a new note and change the name of the lender, referencing the old note, and restating the terms. As with the real estate transfer, you may want to have an attorney assist you in making this change. And, if you're dealing with a mortgage that's been recorded, be sure that the attorney records the new mortgage and completes and files a mortgage discharge for the old.

We've said it before, but it's worth saying again: Don't guess at the worth of hard-to-value assets, such as real estate or business interests — obtain a professional appraisal as of the termination date. Or, if all the remaindermen agree, you can give that asset proportionally to them without having a formal appraisal first. For example, assume a trust owns an apartment building and has three remaindermen (children of the grantor). The remaindermen can agree to each take a one-third interest in the apartment building and no appraisal is necessary. The remaindermen have been waiting a long time for their fair share of the trust's principal; any inkling that one or more of them has been shortchanged, and things may get ugly for you in a hurry.

# Submitting the Final Income Tax Returns

You can't walk away from your duties as trustee until and unless you've filed a final **Form 1041, U.S. Income Tax Return for Estates and Trusts.** Fortunately, you're passing out all the tax liability to some or all of the income beneficiaries and remaindermen because you're passing out all the income and assets to them. The final tax return for the trust is, typically, nothing more than an information return.

When preparing the final return, keep the following important points in mind:

✔ **Make sure that you tick the *Final Return* box on the face of the return.** And, in case you think the IRS may miss that little box, feel free to also write "Final Return" across the top of the first page in big red or black letters. We can't begin to tell you the number of times we've received notices from the IRS looking for returns years after we filed the final one. Of course, just because it's looking doesn't mean you have to prepare and file one, but who wants to keep writing letters explaining why you're no longer required to?

✔ **Make sure that the return shows that the trust has reached zero taxable income and zero tax liability.** No matter how you slice it, every final year return should reach the same conclusion: zero taxable income and zero tax liability. The zero taxable income is achieved in two ways — by passing out all items of income and deduction (including capital loss carryovers and net operating losses) to the beneficiaries and remaindermen on **Schedule K-1**, and by disallowing the exemption amount that would ordinarily be allowed on a non-final return. Zero tax liability then naturally results. So, if the return you're preparing doesn't meet those two criteria, you need to sit down and take another look.

Chapter 18 explains how to complete **Form 1041** in glorious detail. Remember to include all your deductions, even if you don't have enough income to offset them; excess deductions on termination of a trust are apportioned and distributed to all the recipients of **Schedule K-1**, who may deduct them on **Form 1040, Schedule A** as a miscellaneous itemized deduction subject to the 2 percent adjusted gross income limitation. We explain how to prepare **Schedule K-1 (Form 1041)** in Chapter 20.

This section points out the final steps you may be required to take to ensure that the trust has met all its tax obligations. Not to worry, though — because you've been handling the trust's taxes for a while already, all the information you need should be easy to access.

## Determining any final tax liability

Just because the final **Form 1041** shouldn't have any income tax liability doesn't mean that you may not still have some outstanding tax obligations, either from a prior year's return or from a state or local government. You need to double-check and determine whether the trust has any final tax liability, perhaps due to tax returns for prior years that haven't yet been filed, an income tax audit that hasn't been resolved, amended returns for prior year(s) that are still awaiting your attention, or even unpaid real estate taxes.

In order to make the determination, be sure that you have completed returns for each year of administration and that you have no knowledge of any open issues regarding any of them. Remember, if you're receiving correspondence from the IRS or any state tax department, that's a sure sign that there's a tax problem that needs resolution. Rough out any tax returns still to be completed or filed at the time the trust terminates its income interest so that you don't receive any unpleasant surprises. Be sure to segregate any taxes you think you owe before making any payments to income beneficiaries or remaindermen. Remember, many trusts terminate in the first few months of a year, before you've finished the prior year's tax returns. Even if the trust won't owe any taxes on the final year return, the same can't be said for the prior year's return that may well be sitting, unfinished, on your desk.

Pay the taxes you think the trust owes before you begin making distributions to the remaindermen, even if you're not absolutely certain of the final tax bill. If you only have a rough idea, generously estimate the payment, and send it in. If you know exactly how much the trust is on the line for, write that check and get it out of the way. Dealing with a tax refund is far easier than getting the remaindermen to cough up money to settle the trust's tax liability.

## Filing a short-year return

Trusts rarely terminate on December 31. Accordingly, the last year of the trust's existence will most likely be a *short year* (less than 12 months), and you may want to file a short-year return. Using a short-year return allows you to conclude the trust's business in a timely fashion instead of allowing preparation of that final return to hang over your head for months after you complete all your other trust-related tasks. Short-year returns are prepared just like any other return, with two exceptions:

- ✔ You're allowed to use the prior year's tax form if the current year's form isn't yet available. If current year forms aren't yet available, you may want to superimpose the correct year over the printed prior year.
- ✔ You must fill in the dates of the short year at the top of the return.

If you opt to use a short year for the final return, don't forget that the return is still due three and one-half months after the end of the year you've chosen. So, if you elect to end the year on November 30, your short-year return is now due on March 15, not April 15.

# Preparing Final Accounting and Obtaining Assents of All Remaindermen

You've distributed the final income amounts, paid all the last expenses, and filed the final tax returns. You're almost done — but not quite. You're not allowed to mark this job complete until you do one last thing: Prepare a final account and obtain assents from all the remaindermen.

## Finally finishing a non-probate trust

Prepare this final account just like all the others you've prepared up until now. You'll know that this is the final account because you'll mark it *Final* on the cover page, and **Schedules C** and **F** will show zero balances. As you prepare this account and then obtain the signatures of the beneficiaries, keep the following in mind:

1. **Don't discontinue preparing your annual accounts just because the income interest in the trust has ended.**

   It may take years after the income interest has terminated before you actually get to prepare the final account. Sometimes, even though the trust is terminating, the assets remaining don't transfer to the remaindermen for a very long time. So long as you're responsible for any assets, you need to account for them. The good news (you knew it was coming) is that trusts that are in the process of terminating aren't usually very active, so the annual accounts are much less involved than they were when you still had income beneficiaries to worry about.

2. **After you prepare the final account and sign the cover page, give it to all the remaindermen to sign off on.**

   You don't need to have the income beneficiaries sign off on your accounts after the income interest has expired.

   You may want to have an attorney draft the final assent letter, one that the remaindermen sign, that releases your liability with acceptance of the distribution. Nothing is worse than when a trustee releases all the assets and fails to obtain assents, only to be sued later when the trust no longer has any assets.

   After you obtain the necessary assents in the manner described in Chapter 14, you're finally finished. Congratulations!

Be sure to provide copies of accounts to beneficiaries and remaindermen when you ask for their assent. And keep the originals of all the accounts, including this final one, and all the signed assents permanently. In a case of better-safe-than-sorry, you can never be certain when someone will raise a question regarding your period of trusteeship; with the accounts and signed assents in hand, you have proof not only that the income beneficiaries or remaindermen have prior knowledge of your acts as trustee but also that they assented to them at the time.

## Polishing off a probate trust

Prepare the final probate account in the same manner as you would a non-probate account, and attach the official probate court cover to it. Here are a few things to keep in mind:

- Be sure to mark the account not only by its number but also as *Final (The Fifteenth and Final Account of Jane Smith, Trustee)*. Sign the cover page as trustee.

- Like the non-probate trust account, you need assents from all the remaindermen before you can officially close the trust. Usually, the probate court provides you with its official assent form to use for this purpose.

- Be sure, when mailing assents out to the remaindermen, that you send them either registered or certified mail, and that you request return receipts. Doing so ensures that if one or more remaindermen is balky in providing the requested signature, you have proof for the probate court that you sent the form and that the obstinate remainderman did receive it.

After you receive all the assents, you may choose to have your accounts allowed by the probate court. If you opt for allowance, the probate judge will review your administration from the filing of the probate inventory through all the annual accounts and ending with the final account. She will check the size of the fees that you took for your administration, will make sure that income was distributed as required, and that the trust principal was distributed in accordance with the instrument. Allowance isn't absolutely required, but if you choose to go that route, it never hurts to know that the probate court, under whose auspices you administered this particular trust, approved your administration.

If, when you petition the probate court to have your accounts allowed, any of the income beneficiaries or remaindermen are minors or are otherwise incompetent to legally act for themselves, the court may require that you have a *guardian ad litem* (literally, a guardian for this matter only) appointed to protect his or her interest. In theory, having someone who's otherwise unconnected to the trust and the family protecting the minor's interest isn't a bad thing; in practice, the court typically appoints a lawyer as guardian — someone who asks lawyerly questions and charges lawyerly fees. Although you can't always avoid the appointment of a *guardian ad litem,* try to steer clear of this step whenever you can by filing your accounts when they're due but waiting until all the income beneficiaries and remainderman are of legal age and capacity before you ask the court for allowance.

# Dealing with Outliers after the Trust Terminates

We'd love to tell you that, when you've completed the final tax returns, the final accounts, crossed your t's and dotted your i's, that you're done, finished, complete. We'd be lying. No matter how careful you are, matters beyond your control may mean small amounts of additional money, or assets you never knew about, whether belonging to principal or income, will find their way into your hands after the fact.

Whether they're dividend payments that arrive well after the fact, securities litigation proceeds that are distributed years after the trust terminates, or tax refunds you didn't know were in the pipeline, you'll most likely receive checks after you close all the accounts. Far less common are assets that are discovered years and years in the future that belonged to the grantor and should have been in the trust.

Good news: The trust is still closed and, in most cases, you don't have to reopen it. Bad news: You have to do something with this money and these assets, and keeping them is not an option. If you were working with an attorney, give any checks to the attorney with instructions as to who these funds belong to (income beneficiary or remainderman). The attorney can deposit the money into his clients' funds account, and then cut a check to the appropriate person. If you're dealing with after-discovered assets, you can contact the transfer agent and ask for the appropriate forms you need to reregister this asset in the name of the remainderman.

The one exception to this general rule is if the asset is still registered in the decedent's name and rightly belonged in the probate estate. In that case, you may want to throw yourself on the mercy of the probate court staff and let them help you to reopen probate. Some, but not all, the steps you danced back in Chapter 6 will have to be repeated. Sorry!

# Part IV
# Paying the Taxes

## *Calculating Cost Basis and Dates*

| Tax Form | Acquisition Method | Basis Cost | Acquisition Date | Holding Period |
|---|---|---|---|---|
| 1040 | From decedent's estate | Date of death value (or alternate valuation) | Date of decedent's death | Long-term |
| | Purchased | Purchase cost | Trade date of purchase | Long-term, if held for more than one year |
| 1041 (estate) | From decedent's estate | Date of death value (or alternate valuation) | Date of decedent's death | Long-term |
| | Purchased | Purchase cost | Trade date of purchase | Long-term, if held for more than one year |
| 1041- Revocable trust funded during grantor's lifetime | From grantor | Grantor's acquisition cost | Grantor's acquisition date | Long-term, if held for more than one year after grantor's acquisition |
| | Purchased | Purchase cost | Trade date of purchase | Long-term, if held for more than one year |
| 1041 Irrevocable Trust | From grantor during lifetime | Grantor's acquisition cost | Grantor's acquisition date | Long-term, if held for more than one year after grantor's acquisition |
| | From grantor after death | Date of death value (or alternate valuation) | Date of grantor's death | Long-term |
| | Purchased | Purchase cost | Trade date of purchase | Long-term, if held for more than one year |

Visit www.dummies.com/extras/estatetrustadministration to find out about the specific tax returns you may have to prepare as part of administering the decedent's estate or trust.

# In this part . . .

✔ Discover how to tell whether your estate needs to file **Form 706**, the estate tax return, and if so, how to prepare it.

✔ Get help preparing the most common **Form 706** schedules and familiarize yourself with the more obscure schedules just in case you have to deal with them.

✔ Prepare and file income tax returns for the decedent, the estate, and any trusts.

✔ Assign types of income to **Schedule K-1** of **Form 1041** and report the same.

✔ Plan the best, and smartest, way to report income and deductions after death.

# Chapter 16

# Preparing the Estate Tax Return, Part 1

## In This Chapter

▶ Determining whether your estate needs to file

▶ Filling out pages 1–4 of the estate tax return

▶ Deciding which elections to take

▶ Taking the final steps after you've filed the return

"**N**othing's certain in life apart from death and taxes." Ben Franklin said it, and it's generally true. Although death is unfortunately inevitable, the federal estate tax isn't if the decedent's *estate* (the property owned by the deceased person on his or her date of death) is small enough. For decedents passing away in 2013, the amount exempt from federal estate tax is $5.25 million ($5 million indexed annually for inflation).

The federal estate tax, sometimes mistakenly referred to as the *death tax,* is a tax on the value of all the decedent's property at the date of death, minus any amounts owed by the decedent but unpaid at that time, funeral costs, and the costs of administering the estate. It's not a tax on a share received by any particular beneficiary, and no beneficiary pays any gift or estate tax on what he or she receives. The executor or administrator pays any estate tax owed from estate assets nine months after the decedent's date of death.

In this chapter, you find out how to decide whether you must file a **Form 706, United States Estate (and Generation-Skipping Transfer) Tax Return** for the estate, as well as whether any tax is due. With the information located here, you can prepare the opening pages of the **706**, make the appropriate elections for the estate, compute the tax, and file the return.

# Figuring Out Which Estates Must File

The good news is that making the decision about which estates must file is easy. Uncle Sam already made the decision; most estates need not file an estate tax return at all. Read on to see whether you can dodge this particular bullet or need to start filling out the forms.

## Who must file

The IRS estimates that only a small number of estates are required to file. So how do you figure out whether the estate you're administering falls into that category? The answer depends on the size of the *gross estate,* or the total value of everything the decedent owned as of his or her date of death, and the year in which he or she died. If, for example, you're administering an estate for a decedent who died in 2013, you don't need to worry unless the gross estate is worth more than $5.25 million. That exclusion amount is adjusted annually for inflation.

Of course, figuring out whether you must file is never quite that simple. In order to accurately determine whether you have to file **Form 706** for the estate, you need to also consider

## Who may want to file: People who qualify for the Deceased Spousal Unused Exclusion (DSUE)

As of January 1, 2011, one spouse can elect to transfer any unused exclusion amount to the surviving spouse. So, if your decedent doesn't have a taxable estate but the surviving spouse has or may have a taxable estate, you'll want to file a **706** for your decedent. The amount transferred to the surviving spouse is called the *deceased spousal unused exclusion* (DSUE).

As executor, you can elect transfer, or *portability,* of the unused exclusion to the decedent's surviving spouse, but you must do so on a "completely and properly prepared" and timely filed estate tax return. The surviving spouse can later apply the DUSE amount received from his or her last deceased spouse against his or her own subsequent lifetime gifts and transfers at death. The IRS recognizes that preparing and filing a **706** when you wouldn't otherwise have to is a burden and has said that, in valuing the property for inclusion on a return which is being filed solely to elect the transfer of the DSUE, the executor may estimate the total value of the gross estate based on a determination made "in good faith" and with "due diligence" regarding the value of all the assets includible in the gross estate.

✔ **What the decedent gave away over his or her lifetime as gifts:** The decedent's most recent gift tax return **(Form 709),** if any, lists all gifts he or she made during lifetime that need to be added back. If you can't locate the decedent's most recent **709,** you can request a copy from the IRS by using **Form 4506.** (Check out Chapter 7 for how to do so).

✔ **Whether the decedent's estate looks like it could be anywhere close to the exempt amount for the year in question:** If so, you need to do all the valuation calculations we explain in this chapter and Chapter 17 to be sure that you don't need to file, including getting appraisals where necessary. Filling out drafts of the schedules is a helpful way to accomplish this.

Check carefully before you begin preparing a **Form 706** to make sure that the form is actually required. The easiest place to check is the IRS itself at www.irs.gov. Look for **Publication 950, Introduction to Estate and Gift Taxes,** for the exclusion amount applicable to the year in which your decedent died.

## Who actually files Form 706 and when

As the executor, administrator, or personal representative (fiduciary) of the decedent's estate, you're responsible for filing **Form 706** nine months after date of death if the gross estate is larger than the applicable exclusion amount for the year in question. If the estate has no fiduciary, and you're a trustee in actual or *constructive* (meaning you have control over the property even if it's not held in the trustee's name) possession of any of the decedent's property, you're responsible for any required **Form 706.** Any executor or other court-appointed representative who's filing the return must provide documentation, such as a certified copy of the appointment, proving his status.

You may file a six-month extension of time to file, using **Form 4768** (discussed in the later "Extensions of time to file and pay tax" section), by the due date for filing the return.

The estate and generation-skipping transfer (GST) taxes are due in full nine months after the decedent's date of death unless you request and are granted an election under Internal Revenue Code (IRC) Section 6166 to pay in installments, or under IRC Section 6163 to pay the part of the tax attributable to a reversionary or remainder interest at a later time. (See the later sections, "Electing to pay the tax in installments" and "Electing to postpone taxes," for more info on IRC Sections 6166 and 6163, respectively.)

If the tax you're paying with the return differs from the balance due shown on the return, attach a statement explaining the difference. If you've already made payments to the IRS, staple a statement to that effect onto the return.

## Reaching the applicable exclusion amount

The *applicable exclusion amount* (the amount of the decedent's assets you can actually exclude from estate tax) is a rather difficult concept. Lucky for you, you never have to make this computation. It's all done for you on page one (the cover page) of **Form 706** by means of a credit subtracted from the gross estate tax calculated. So for example, in 2012, the applicable credit subtracts $1,772,800 from the gross estate tax, which shelters the first $5.12 million of the taxable estate. (Fun fact: Every time the baseline amount for a taxable estate rises due to inflation, so does the applicable exclusion amount.)

# Obtaining a Release from Personal Liability

Whether you filed the decedent's **706** as executor or trustee, you always want to obtain a release from personal liability under IRC Section 2204 (do the same for the decedent's income and gift tax returns). Why? Because even if the estate or trust is later found to be liable for additional tax (perhaps due to assets discovered years later, for instance), if you've obtained the release from personal liability, you aren't personally liable for the tax. Send a letter to the IRS in your capacity as executor or trustee and as the person charged with filing the **Form 706**, requesting that the IRS set the estate tax and discharge you from personal liability.

After the IRS receives your request, it has nine months to act on it. As soon as you pay the tax the IRS assesses, you're released from personal liability for any tax deficiency later discovered. You're then free to pay other debts and expenses of the decedent — which come after the federal estate tax in priority of payment — and distribute the assets. Even if an asset appears later, you're off the hook; if additional tax is later assessed after you've distributed the assets, the estate or the beneficiaries will be liable, not you.

# Understanding Some of the Nitty-Gritty Rules for Filing Form 706

You need to know some basic rules for how and where to file **Form 706,** how to pay the tax, how to get an extension of time to file or pay tax, and what documents to file with the return. The next sections cover these delightful topics and more.

# *Where and how to file*

The IRS generally loves the concept of electronic filing for just about everything, but the estate tax return is one return you can't submit online. You must file **Form 706** nine months after the decedent's date of death, on paper, by snail mail. Send the completed tax form to Department of the Treasury, Internal Revenue Service Center, Cincinnati, OH 45999. Use either certified mail or a private delivery service that can provide you with documentation. The IRS accepts the following delivery services:

- **DHL Express (DHL):** DHL Same Day Service

- **Federal Express (FedEx):** Fed Ex Priority Overnight, FedEx Standard Overnight, FedEx 2Day, Fed Ex International Priority, FedEx International First

- **United Parcel Service (UPS):** UPS Next Day Air, UPS Next Day Air Saver, UPS 2nd Day Air, UPS 2nd Day Air A.M., UPS Worldwide Express Plus, and UPS Worldwide Express

Be sure to get written proof of the mailing date from the delivery service because that day is considered the date of filing and of payment of the tax.

# *How to pay the tax*

You have three options for paying the estate tax:

- **Check, bank draft, or money order:** Make it payable to "United States Treasury." Be sure to include on the check the decedent's name, Social Security number, and the words "**Form 706**" to indicate to the IRS what tax you're paying and for whom.

- **Electronic submission:** Pay electronically though the Electronic Federal Tax Payment System (EFTPS), a free service of the Department of Treasury. Payments must be completed by 8 p.m. EST the day before they're due and must be scheduled in advance of the due date. Go to www.eftps.gov or call 1-800-555-4477 for more information about EFTPS.

   Paying through EFTPS is relatively painless, but it does take some time to set up the account with the IRS. If you're planning on paying the estate tax on the due date, plan at least two full weeks prior to initiate opening your account. The IRS will send you the security information to complete your account by U.S. mail.

- **Credit card or debit card:** Go to www.irs.gov and enter "pay taxes by credit card" in the search box. Clicking on the first search result gives you a list of all the service providers you may use, their fees, and their websites and telephone numbers.

Be aware that the IRS convenience fees for credit card payments can be substantial (between 1.89 and 2.35 percent of the tax payment at the time of this writing). You may find it much more prudent to make sure that you have the funds available to write a check or pay electronically than to explain to the heirs or a judge reviewing your estate accounting why you incurred the convenience fee.

## Penalties for late filing, late payment, and understatement of valuation

Do all you can to file your **706** by the due date (as extended) and pay the tax on time, because you incur penalties for late filing and late payment unless you can show reasonable cause for the delay. If you're filing the **706** after the due date and any extensions, be sure to attach an explanation to the return to try to show reasonable cause. In addition, you pay interest on the amount of tax due from the due date for filing until the tax is paid, unless you've applied for and received an extension of time to pay the tax as explained in the later "Extensions of time to file and pay tax" section.

Absolutely nothing is worse than getting slammed with penalties because the IRS catches you undervaluing assets. Not only do you have to pay the additional tax, but valuation understatements that result in tax increases of more than $5,000 also cost you a whopping 20 percent penalty. The IRS defines a *valuation understatement* as reporting the property's value as 65 percent or less of its actual value on the **Form 706.** The penalty jumps to 40 percent for property valued at 40 percent or less of actual market value. And if you think you like your chances of avoiding an audit, think again. In 2006, although audit rates on individual income tax returns hovered around 1 percent, the IRS examined almost 10 percent of all **Forms 706.** For estates reporting values of 5 million dollars or more, that rate rose to more than 23 percent, and as the exemption from estate tax increases and the number of estate tax returns required to be filed dwindles, the number of returns audited is expected to increase. Valuations aren't places to cut corners or hope to get lucky, although you certainly want to use the lowest valuation supportable, in most cases.

When might a higher valuation be beneficial to the estate? When the estate doesn't owe any estate tax anyway, the value at which the property is included on the **706** is its new "stepped-up" cost basis for income tax purposes. See Chapter 18 for a discussion of the step-up in basis of a decedent's property to the date-of-death value for purposes of computing capital gains.

## Signature and verification

List all executors or administrators on the return if you're dealing with more than one because you're all responsible for the return's contents. You're also all liable for any penalties for erroneous or false returns. However, only one of you, as coexecutor, is required to sign the return regardless of how many of you are on the team. We strongly recommend that all coexecutors sign the return if at all possible so that it's clear to each of you that you're all liable for the return as it's filed. Relying on one coexecutor who is knowledgeable in **706** preparation to prepare the return is fine, as long as everyone else thoroughly reviews the return, asking any and all questions they may have. Feel free to ask to see the supporting information!

The executor who prepares the return must sign the declaration on page 1 under penalty of perjury. If you rely on a paid preparer, such as an attorney, accountant, or Enrolled Agent, to prepare the return, that person must also sign and complete the preparer info on page 1 of the return.

# Extensions of time to file and pay tax

Sometimes you may need a few extra months to get everything squared away with the estate before you can file the **706**. If you need an extension, send your extension request to the Department of the Treasury, Internal Revenue Service Center, Cincinnati, OH 45999, no later than the original due date for the return (nine months after the decedent's date of death). File **Form 4768, Extension of Time to File a Return and/or Pay U. S. Estate (and Generation-Skipping Transfer) Taxes** to apply for extensions of both time to file and time to pay.

## Extension of time to file

You receive a six-month automatic extension of time to file with regard to **Forms 706, 706-A, 706-D, 706-NA,** and **706-QDT,** as long as you file the extension request by the due date and include payment of the estimated amount of the estate tax (or generation-skipping transfer tax). Just check the applicable box in Part II of the form.

If you have multiple executors or administrators, only one of you needs to file. Or you can have your authorized attorney, certified public accountant, Enrolled Agent, or agent holding power of attorney file for you.

You may apply for a discretionary additional extension of time to file the **706** only if you are an executor and are out of the country. Attach a statement explaining why it's impossible or impractical to file the **706** by the due date.

If you don't file for an automatic extension of time to file by the due date of the return, all is not lost. You can still file for an extension of time to file if you can show *good and sufficient cause*. Although there's no definition given for this phrase in the **706** instructions, be sure to attach a statement explaining why you weren't able to apply for an automatic extension, why it was impossible or impractical to file by the due date, and why the extension should be granted. Note, however, that the extension, if granted, is for no more than six months after the due date of the return.

## Amending Form 706

You often discover additional assets or expenses that you should have included on the **Form 706** long after you file it. If you come across assets or deductions after filing the **Form 706** and within the *assessment period* (three years from the date of filing the **706**, or six years if the additional assets represent more than a 25 percent increase over the gross estate as it was originally reported, except in two instances; if there is fraud committed in the filing of the **706** or no **706** is filed, there is no statute of limitations), or if you need to make any other allowable change to the return, you can amend it as follows:

1. **Prepare and file another** 706, **typing "Supplemental Information" across the top of page 1 of the form.**

2. **Attach copies of pages 1–4 of the** 706 **as originally filed.**

If the return is being audited, send the information directly to the IRS office conducting the audit.

### Extension of time to pay

You may also use the **Form 4768** to apply for an extension of time to pay the estate tax under IRC Section 6161 (a discretionary extension of time to pay for reasonable cause), for an IRC Section 6163 election (reversionary or remainder interest), or for an IRC Section 6166 election (closely held business). We cover IRC Sections 6163 and 6166 later in this chapter.

## Supplemental documents

Completing the **706** may seem bad enough to you, but you probably have a pile of supporting documentation that you need to send with it. If you do, attach whichever of the following documents are applicable in your decedent's estate to the return when you file it.

Consider preparing an index, or list, of exhibits. Attach the index directly behind the **706** and label each of the documents on its face as Exhibit A, Exhibit B, and so on. Using index tabs for each exhibit is also a terrific idea. Also, when referring to each of the attached documents in the **706**, give them specific names (such as Exhibit A, Exhibit B, and so on) for clarity. The clearer you make things for the IRS, the happier it'll be as it reviews your tax return (and the more comfortable it'll be that you're disclosing everything).

Among the documents to attach to the return are

 A certified copy of the decedent's death certificate (required in all cases). Chapter 5 explains how to obtain copies of the death certificate.

✔ A certified copy of the will, if the decedent died with a will. You obtain certified copies of the will from the court where the will was filed for probate. If you're unable to get a certified copy, attach an uncertified copy and explain why it's not certified.

✔ A certified copy of your appointment as executor or *letters testamentary*.

✔ An IRS Power of Attorney (**Form 2848**). See the nearby sidebar, "Filing the IRS Power of Attorney and Declaration of Representative (**Form 2848**)," for more info.

✔ Receipt for payment of state inheritance or estate tax. See Chapter 2 and Appendix B regarding state estate and inheritance taxes.

✔ Appraisals of property. See Chapters 7 and 17 for more info.

✔ Life insurance statements (**Form 712**). See the discussion of **Schedule D** in Chapter 17.

✔ Gift tax returns (**Form 709**).

✔ **Certificates of Payment of Foreign Death Tax (Form 706-CE).** See Chapter 17.

✔ Copies of trust documents.

✔ For closely held businesses (see Chapter 7), earnings statements and balance sheets.

## Filing the IRS Power of Attorney and Declaration of Representative (Form 2848)

You may find it valuable to file a **Form 2848, Power of Attorney and Declaration of Representative,** with the IRS as executor or administrator, appointing an attorney, certified public accountant, Enrolled Agent, family member, or someone else who prepared the tax return in question to act on your behalf with regard to some or all of the decedent's tax matters. **Form 2848** may be filed at any time after your appointment as executor or administrator. If you file a **Form 2848,** be sure to attach a copy to **Form 706** as an exhibit.

You may find it convenient to have someone available who can deal with the IRS on your behalf, and you can add powers not already listed on the **Form 2848** or delete any you don't want to bestow. You can also rescind the power of attorney at any time. If you have different tax

preparers for different types of returns, you may want to have a separate **Form 2848** for each.

Keep in mind that the **Form 706** contains its own version of a power of attorney, specific to that return, in Part 4 under General Information. However, you can name only one person (who must be an attorney, certified public accountant, or Enrolled Agent), and that person can't enter into agreements with the IRS on your behalf regarding the **Form 706,** unlike a person appointed under the **Form 2848,** making the **Form 2848** more useful to you in obtaining a **706** closing letter.

*Remember:* Always be sure you're using the most current version of **Form 2848,** which you can find at www.irs.gov under the "Forms and Publications" category.

Chapter 17 discusses when you need to attach these documents while using the individual schedules of the **706**.

If the decedent was a U.S. citizen but not a resident, you need to attach the following additional documentation:

- ✔ A copy of the property inventory and schedule of liabilities, claims against the estate, and administration expenses as filed with the foreign court, certified by the appropriate official of the foreign court
- ✔ If the estate is subject to a foreign tax, a copy of the tax return filed under the foreign death tax act, whether estate, inheritance, succession, legacy, or otherwise

# Completing the Form 706, Pages 1–4

If the estate you're administering requires a **706** for any reason, you must complete the first four pages, together with all the other schedules needed to report your decedent's assets, deductions, exclusions, and credits. The following sections help you determine which schedules apply to your decedent's situation.

If a schedule doesn't give you enough space (and it often doesn't), attach a continuation schedule directly behind it. A *continuation schedule* is simply a blank schedule that you can use as an additional page for any other schedule in the return. One of us prepared a **Form 706** with 17 pages filled with $50 U.S. Savings Bonds. A blank continuation schedule is contained as part of the **706.** Make as many copies as you need.

## Part 1: Decedent and Executor

On the face of the **Form 706,** fill in the decedent's name, address, Social Security number, year *domicile* (residence) was established in the decedent's state of residence, date of birth, and date of death. On line 6a, list the executor you want to have contacted by the IRS; list any additional executors on an attached sheet as an exhibit and refer to it here. The rest of Part 1 is fairly self-explanatory.

## Part 2: Tax Computation

Now you get to start with some numbers, or so you may think. But wait — although this section is on the first page of the return, you really can't do anything with it until you've completed everything else. So if you're just beginning, skip ahead to Part 3 (the next section). If you've completed all the other schedules and parts and are now ready to put this baby to bed, read on.

On lines 1–20, enter the figures indicated to arrive at the total transfer taxes due, if any. We highlight here anything we feel isn't self-explanatory or included in the **Instructions for Form 706 (Rev. August, 2012)** ("the Instructions").

✔ **Line 3:** The state death tax deduction referred to on line 3b is available if estate, inheritance, succession, or legacy taxes are paid to any state or the District of Columbia as a result of the decedent's death.

✔ **Line 4**: Enter *adjusted taxable gifts* (total taxable gifts made by the decedent after December 31, 1976, other than gifts includible in the decedent's estate). If the gifts are includible in the decedent's estate, you've included them in the number in line 1. Use the Line 4 Worksheet TG — Taxable Gifts Reconciliation on page 6 of the Instructions. You need the decedent's **709s** to complete the worksheet. Keep in mind that, besides any gifts reported on **709s**, you must include any taxable gifts from prior years that you're aware of that weren't reported on **709s** but should have been. To the extent that you come across gifts from earlier years in the decedent's papers that weren't reported, keep a tally year by year to see whether they're taxable. The annual exclusion amount (the amount that can be gifted without incurring any gift tax) has changed over the years, so you need to look on the instructions for that particular year's **709;** you can download it at www.irs.gov or call the IRS forms line at 800-829-3676.

✔ **Line 7:** Enter the total gift tax paid or payable by the decedent on gifts he or she made after December 31, 1976. Include gift taxes paid by the decedent's spouse for that spouse's share of *split gifts* (gifts made by one spouse that are divided 50/50 between both spouses on their gift tax returns) only if the decedent was the donor of the gifts and they are includible in the decedent's gross estate. Use the Line 7 Worksheet — Gift Tax on Gifts Made After 1976 on page 7 of the Instructions. Page 8 of the Instructions discusses split gifts further.

✔ **Line 9b:** If the decedent had a spouse who died on or after January 1, 2011, enter the deceased spousal unused exclusion (DSUE), if any, from Section D, Part 6-Portability of Deceased Spousal Unused Exclusion. See "Part 6: Portability of Deceased Spousal Unused Exclusion (DSUE)."

✔ **Line 10:** Enter adjustments, if any, to the applicable credit amount. You have adjustments only if the decedent (or the decedent's spouse, in the case of split gifts) made gifts after September 8, 1976, and before January 1, 1977, for which he or she claimed a specific exemption. If so, the unified credit (applicable credit amount) on the estate tax return is reduced. Compute the reduction by entering 20 percent of the specific exemption that was claimed for these gifts.

✔ **Line 13:** Enter any credit for foreign death taxes from **Schedule P** and attach **Form(s) 706-CE.**

✔ **Line 15:** Add lines 13 and 14 to arrive at the total credits. In addition to using line 15 to report the totals of line 13, credit for foreign death taxes, and line 14, credit for tax on prior transfers, you may also use it to take a credit for pre-1977 federal gift taxes under a formula laid out on page 9 of the Instructions. If you do so, be sure to identify the credit and make a note on the dotted line to the left of the entry, noting it as an "IRC Section 2012 credit." (You may refer to the regulations under IRC Section 2012 for more information, but you may also want to see your tax advisor at this juncture!) Also complete and attach **Form 4808, Computation of Credit for Gift Tax.**

You may also use line 15 to claim the Canadian marital credit under the 1995 Canadian Protocol. When doing so, enter the credit on line 15 and make a note on the dotted line to the left of the entry, noting it as a "Canadian marital credit." Also attach a statement as an exhibit to the return referring to the treaty, waiving *qualified domestic trust* (QDOT) rights, and showing the computation of the credit. You can see the Canadian income tax treaty protocol for details on computing the credit, and by this point, you're probably also visiting your tax advisor.

Assuming you've done all the math to arrive at line 20, you've now completed the **706**, which is no small accomplishment. Congratulations!

## Signature of executor(s)

We recommend that all executor(s) or administrator(s) sign and date the return at the bottom of page 1, although only one signature is required. If none exist, the person(s) holding assets who is/are filing the return, such as the trustee(s) of a trust, sign.

## Signature of preparer other than the executor

If you paid someone else to prepare **Form 706,** she signs the return here and completes it in accordance with the Instructions.

## Part 3: Elections by the executor

In Part 3, you must decide whether to make four important elections, if they apply to your decedent and would be of benefit to your estate. Each carries with it an Internal Revenue Code section reference. Consider each one thoroughly to see whether the facts fit your decedent's estate.

### Alternate valuation

*Alternate valuation,* which you elect on line 1, Part 3 of **Form 706,** is probably the most commonly used election. This election allows you to value the property of the estate, in general, as of six months after the date of death rather than as of the date of death. Using it protects the estate from paying tax on the date-of-death value of the assets if the estate's total value has dropped steeply six months after death, before the estate tax is even due. If elected, it applies to all assets; you can't pick and choose which ones to apply it to. And you can elect it only on the return as originally filed — and only if it decreases both the gross estate and the total of the estate and GST taxes. After you make the election, you can't revoke it. Finally, if you elect alternate valuation, you must still show every asset's date-of-death value as follows:

- **Property distributed, sold, exchanged, or disposed of in any other way within six months after the date of death:** Value it as of the date of distribution, sale, or other disposition.

- **Property still in the decedent's estate as of six months after the date of death:** Value it as of that six-month date. If no date in that sixth month corresponds to the decedent's date of death, use the last day of the sixth month.

- **Property that changes value due to the mere lapse of time:** Value it as of the date of death *or* as of the date it's distributed, sold, exchanged, or otherwise disposed of.

If you elect alternate valuation, don't include increases or decreases from either the date-of-death value or the alternate value that are due entirely to the lapse of time. For example, at the date of death, a bond is worth not only the market value of the bond but also the value of *accrued* (accumulated but not yet paid) interest owed to the bondholder (the decedent) at that date. In the case of alternate valuation, only the market value of the bond changes to the value six months after death; the accrued interest on the bond remains the same as it was on the date of death. Similarly, rent accrued to the date of death on leased real or personal property of the estate goes in the gross estate, but rent accrued after the date of death does not. You include dividends that were declared to shareholders of record on or before the date of death in your alternate valuation calculations, but you don't include dividends declared after the date of death.

The exception to this last example: When dividends declared after the date of death affect the number of shares of stock so that they no longer reflect the same property as they did at the date of death, include their value at the alternate valuation date for alternate valuation purposes (unless these dividends are paid from earnings of the corporation after the date of death).

Although this scenario may seem fairly arcane, it happens more frequently than you may think because corporations often dilute the number of shares with stock splits, and somewhat less frequently, spin off baby companies from the parent company or issue stock dividends.

### Special use valuation

The *special use valuation* election allows you to value real estate at its actual use rather than its highest and best use under certain circumstances (think family farm versus land for a new subdivision of mansions). You may elect to value real property the decedent owned that the decedent or a family member used in the operation of a family farm or closely held business for a certain number of years prior to the decedent's death at its farm or business use value rather than at its presumably higher fair market value, under IRC Section 2032A. There is a ceiling on special use valuation, indexed for inflation. For 2012, the ceiling is $1,040,000.

You actually have the option of electing both alternate valuation and special use valuation with regard to the property. Because you must meet a number of conditions in order for the real property to qualify for special use valuation, you most likely want to discuss this election with a qualified tax preparer instead of tackling it on your own, both to see whether your real estate qualifies and because not meeting any one condition can invalidate the election.

### Electing to pay the tax in installments

If you elect installment payments, consult with a qualified tax preparer to ensure that you meet all the conditions.

In one of the quirks of the tax code, if the estate qualifies for installment payments under IRC Section 6166, the interest payments are deductible on **Form 1041,** despite the prohibition against deducting personal interest on income tax returns. A major difference between income tax for estates and trusts and for individuals is that you're allowed deductions on fiduciary income tax returns for expenses that you've paid solely because it's an estate or trust, even if that same expense isn't deductible on an individual return. So even though IRC Section 6166 interest is personal interest, similar to credit card interest, you're paying it because you elected an option available only to estates; therefore, it's deductible for income tax purposes.

### Electing to postpone taxes

On line 4, Part 3 of **Form 706,** you may elect, under IRC Section 6163, to postpone the tax on any future interests (reversionary or remainder) until six months after the termination of the *precedent interest* (interest which comes before the reversionary or remainder interest) in the property. And you can request a further extension of a reasonable period up to three years after the original extension for reasonable cause.

Reversionary and remainder interests are each a right to the future enjoyment of property which is being used by another at present. (See Chapter 17 for more info on these two interests on **Schedule F.**)

We advise you to consider making this election if the estate will otherwise be left short of cash by paying the tax currently, and if the reversionary or remainder interest makes up a sizeable portion of the taxable estate. Note, though, that if you make the election, you must post a bond to the IRS for twice the amount of the tax and estimated interest.

# Part 4: General Information

You only began telling the IRS about the decedent in Part 1. Now you really have a chance to fill out the picture in Part 4.

The first item under Part 4: General Information on Page 2 of the return is the authorization to receive confidential tax information, act as the estate's representative before the IRS, and make written or oral presentations on behalf of the estate. If the return was prepared by an attorney, accountant, or Enrolled Agent, he or she signs it and fills out all the necessary information. Remember, only one such person can be appointed here. If you want to appoint more than one, or if you want to appoint someone with the power to enter into closing agreements with the IRS regarding the estate and the **706,** use **Form 2848, Power of Attorney and Declaration of Representative,** instead. (See the earlier related sidebar for more information on filing this form.)

- **Line 4:** You must complete line 4 regardless of whether the decedent has a surviving spouse. For no spouse, simply enter "none" in line 4a and leave lines 4b and 4c blank. Otherwise, in line 4c, "Amount received," enter the amount the surviving spouse actually receives. If exact amounts aren't available, as with future interests, a *reasonable estimate* (for instance, from actuarial tables) can be used.

- **Line 5:** Include all individuals (other than the surviving spouse), trusts, and estates that receive more than $5,000 in benefits from the estate either directly (as an heir, devisee, or legatee) or indirectly (for instance, as beneficiary of an insurance policy). Don't include charities listed on **Schedule O** here (see Chapter 17 for more info). Include the following information about each entity:

  - Name.

  - Social Security or (for an estate or trust) taxpayer identification number (TIN) in the column headed "Identifying number."

  - Relationship to the decedent in the column by that name (for example, "daughter" or "decedent's revocable trust").

- Amount received in the column entitled "Amount." Enter the amount each person or entity actually receives; if exact amounts aren't available, use a reasonable estimate.

✔ If the space provided isn't large enough to include all the beneficiaries, create your own schedule based on the one in line 5 and include it as Page 5a to the return, referencing it in the schedule on the return itself.

Underneath the individual beneficiaries, include a total for everyone who received less than $5,000 apiece and for all *unascertainable beneficiaries.* The total of all these distributions should approximately equal the gross estate less funeral and administrative expenses, debts and mortgages, charitable bequests, and federal estate and GST taxes.

✔ **Line 6:** Check the appropriate "yes" or "no" box to indicate whether or not the estate is filing a protective claim for refund. If you will be filing a claim, complete and attach two copies of **Schedule PC** to the return for each claim. By filing **Schedule PC,** discussed further in Chapter 17, you preserve the estate's right to a refund of estate taxes paid if a claim or expense which is the subject of controversy at the time you file the return later becomes deductible under IRC Section 2053.

✔ **Line 7:** Check the appropriate "yes" or "no" box to indicate whether the estate includes any qualified terminable interest property (QTIP) from a prior gift or estate under IRC Section 2044. If it does, show the assets on Schedule F. If the decedent was a surviving spouse, he or she may have received QTIP property for which the marital deduction was taken on either a **706** or a **709** from the predeceased spouse. If the decedent still retained an interest in the QTIP property as of death, it's included in his or her estate even though the interest terminated at his or her death. Chapter 17 explains how to show this info on the return.

✔ **Line 8:** On line 8a, indicate whether the decedent ever filed gift tax returns, and if so, attach copies as exhibits. On line 8b, list the periods covered by the returns, and on line 8c, list the IRS offices where the gift tax returns were filed.

Lines 9–17 are to remind you of other property that may be includible in the decedent's estate. If you aren't including it, the IRS wants an explanation.

✔ **Line 9**: If any insurance on the decedent's life isn't included on the return (because the insurance wasn't owned by the decedent), answer "yes" on line 9a, complete **Schedule D,** and attach as an exhibit **Form 712, Life Insurance Statement** (we tell you how to obtain a completed **Form 712** from the insurance company in Chapter 17), together with an explanation of why the policy isn't includible in the estate. On line 9b, follow the line 9a process for any policy that the decedent owned on the life of another but isn't being included in the estate.

✔ **Line 10:** If the decedent held property as a joint tenant with right of survivorship, one of the joint tenants was someone other than the surviving spouse, and you're including less than the full value of the property on the return, tick "yes" on line 10 and report it on **Schedule E.**

✔ **Line 11:** Line 11a asks whether the decedent owned an interest in a partnership or unincorporated business or stock in an inactive or closely held corporation. On line 11b, you need to disclose whether you discounted the value of any of these interests for any reason. If you did take market discounts, check out the instructions for **Schedule F.**

✔ Although you're certainly entitled to take a market discount, have all your backup information organized and your ducks in a row, and be prepared for an audit. The IRS loves to audit these discounted valuations of closely held corporations.

✔ **Line 12:** Complete **Schedule G** if the decedent made any transfers during life under IRC Sections 2035 (adjustments for certain gifts made within three years of death), 2036 (transfers with a retained life estate), 2037 (transfers taking effect at death), and 2038 (revocable transfers).

This line is a good place to check with your tax advisor.

✔ **Line 13:** On line 13a, answer "yes" if any decedent-created trusts existed at the decedent's death. Attach a copy of the trust as an exhibit. For line 13b, answer "yes" if the decedent possessed any power (such as a power to appoint a beneficiary of the trust), *beneficial interest* (interest whereby the decedent derived any benefit from the trust, such as, as a beneficiary), or *trusteeship* (decedent was a trustee of a trust) under any trusts not created by him or her. Line 13c is trying to determine whether a GST taxable termination occurred on the death of the decedent. If so (and you can find out by asking the current trustees of any such trust), obtain a copy of the trust and attach it as an exhibit along with the name, address, TIN, and phone number of the trustees of that trust. See Chapter 17 to determine whether there was a taxable termination.

Here's another good place to check with your tax advisor. On line 13e, if the decedent transferred or sold an interest in a partnership, limited liability company, or closely held corporation to a trust described in lines 13a or 13b at any time during his or her lifetime, provide the Employer Identification Number (EIN) of that entity here.

✔ **Line 14:** If the decedent possessed, exercised, or released a general power of appointment, complete **Schedule H.** A *general power of appointment* is a power to appoint the assets of a trust in favor of anyone, including the holder of the power. Look for it if your decedent is a surviving spouse; many folks use it in marital trusts for the surviving spouse because it qualifies the trust for the marital deduction. Be careful not to confuse a general power of appointment with a *limited power of appointment,* where you may only appoint in favor of certain specified people or entities, usually limited to your children, grandchildren, other lineal heirs, and charitable organizations.

- **Line 15:** If the decedent owned, or had any interest in, a foreign bank or brokerage account, answer "yes" to this question.

  Don't be confused by foreign stock ownership — those shares of European and/or Asian companies routinely showing up in stock portfolios aren't what the IRS is asking about here.

- **Line 16:** If the decedent was receiving either an annuity described in the instructions for **Schedule I** or a private annuity, complete and attach **Schedule I.** An *annuity* is income paid in a series of payments.

- **Line 17:** If the decedent was ever the beneficiary of a trust created by a predeceased spouse for which the marital deduction was claimed and the trust isn't reported on this **706,** answer "yes" here and attach an explanation as an exhibit. (For instance, the funds in the trust may have all been spent for the spouse's benefit.)

## Part 5: Recapitulation

*Recapitulation* is where you summarize the gross estate by carrying forward the asset totals from **Schedules A** through **I** and the deductions from **Schedules J** through **U,** all of which we cover in detail in Chapter 17.

On line 18, enter the amount of allowable deductions, which is most likely the same amount as line 17. One exception: instances where the line 17 amount is greater than the value of the property subject to claims. In this case, enter whichever is greater: the value of the property subject to claims or the amount actually paid at the time you file the return. Unfortunately, you're not allowed to take a deduction for amounts you're not required to pay (because you don't have enough property to pay it) unless you actually do pay that amount before filing the return. Remember this rule when planning your payments of claims. Also, be sure to pay all deductible amounts that you aren't paying from property subject to claims before you file the return so you can deduct them.

## Part 6: Portability of Deceased Spousal Unused Exclusion (DSUE)

Part 6 of **Form 706** is where you elect Portability of Deceased Spousal Unused Exclusion (DSUE), which we define earlier in this chapter. This list details what do for each section of Part 6:

- **Section A, Opting Out of Portability:** Check the box to elect out of portability. Don't complete B and C. If no estate tax return was filed for a decedent, he or she is assumed to have opted out of portability.

✔ **Section B, QDOT:** If any assets of the estate are being transferred to a qualified domestic trust (QDOT), which would be because the surviving spouse isn't a citizen of the United States, then check yes. Otherwise, check no. If you answer yes, the DSUE amount is deemed preliminary, until there's a taxable event.

✔ **Section C, DSUE Amount Portable to Surviving Spouse:** Complete this section only if electing portability. The amount portable to the surviving spouse will be the lesser of the basic exclusion amount in effect on the date of death of the decedent whose DSUE is being computed or the decedent's applicable exclusion amount less the amount on line 5 of Part 2 – Tax Computation on Page 1 of the **706.** Exclude amounts on which gift taxes were paid in doing this computation.

✔ **Section D, DSUE Amount Received from Predeceased Spouse(s):** Report any DSUE amount received from the decedent's last deceased spouse and any previously deceased spouses. Unused amounts from previously deceased spouses can't be used on this return, but amounts used previously in making gifts must be reported here. The remaining DSUE amount from the last deceased spouse is carried forward to Line 9B of Part 2 – Tax Computation on Page 1 of the **706.**

# Being Ready for and Handling an Audit

Given that only estates with a relatively high asset threshold have to file **Form 706,** you can understand that the IRS audits a higher percentage of these returns than any other type. Assume that yours will be one of the ones chosen and prepare the return and all its exhibits with that in mind. This way you save yourself a lot of headache instead of trying to re-create what you did six months or a year after you filed the forms.

Keep the following pointers in mind in case the IRS comes knocking:

✔ **Get all the appraisals from reputable appraisers so the results will stand up under audit.** Each appraiser should know what the IRS expects in an appraisal and should attach his or her credentials to the appraisal for the IRS to see. An appraisal from an unqualified appraiser won't stand up to scrutiny on audit.

✔ **If you take a valuation discount for closely held stock, have the calculations done by an expert in the field.** Be sure to attach these calculations to the **706.**

✔ **Keep a copy of every piece of paper that you use to determine an asset existed, whose name it was in, and its value.** Store these papers in an organized file (a file broken down by schedule is one good way to do it) so you can lay your hands on any given piece of paper that the IRS may require at audit. Doing so goes a long way toward making the IRS agent conducting the audit feel that you've done a thorough job and have nothing to hide.

If your return is selected for audit, you receive a letter (and sometimes a phone call) from the IRS requesting further information, such as the decedent's income tax returns for the past few years. If that's the case, supply the information requested. Usually, the IRS accepts the additional documentation and concludes the audit. After all questions are satisfied, the IRS will issue its closing letter.

If the IRS conducts a larger audit and any issues arise, we recommend you turn to your tax expert for assistance.

# Getting an Estate Tax Closing Letter

If the IRS accepts your estate tax return as filed, or if you and the IRS reach agreement as to any changes after a **706** audit, the IRS will issue Letter 627, Estate Tax Closing Letter. The closing letter, although not a formal agreement, shows the IRS's final determination of estate tax. The IRS isn't likely to reopen the case, but it retains the option if evidence of fraud, malfeasance, collusion, concealment, or misrepresentation of a material fact surfaces. The IRS may also reopen a case if it discovers a clearly defined substantial error based on an established IRS position existing at the time of the previous examination (basically, if it realizes it missed something it clearly should have caught), or if other circumstances exist that indicate failure to reopen would be a serious administrative omission.

An executor may reopen a case if the *period for assessment* (three years from the filing of the **706,** and six years from filing if unreported assets constitute 25 percent or more of the gross estate stated in the return as filed) hasn't expired. You want to do this if you subsequently discover assets of the decedent; we've certainly both had assets turn up after a closing letter was issued. You may also file a claim for refund.

---

## Dealing with state estate and inheritance tax

As convoluted as the information in this chapter may seem, we only cover federal rules. But wait, everyone who dies lived in a state, too, and many states have either an estate or inheritance tax as well. Check with your state taxing authority to see whether your state has either. Then refer to Appendix B to determine whether your decedent's state of residence has an estate tax (based on the decedent's assets), an inheritance tax (based on what each beneficiary receives), or a legacy or succession tax. Appendix B also contains addresses, telephone numbers, and websites for your use in contacting state authorities to obtain forms and information about any state tax.

# Chapter 17

# Preparing the Estate Tax Return, Part 2

*In This Chapter*
- Filling out the most common **Form 706** schedules
- Seeking help for all the rest

*F*or many, preparing the **Form 706, United States Estate (and Generation-Skipping Transfer) Tax Return,** is the sterling achievement in the quest to competently administer an estate. After all, in most instances, the return is a fairly straightforward accounting of what the decedent owned and owed when he or she died. (Chapter 16 helps you with filling out the basics of **Form 706.**) However, if you're not completely confident after we walk through the schedules in this chapter, and if you find yourself faced with some of the more complex schedules, which we don't deal with at length here, we suggest that you consult with either an attorney or an accountant who's knowledgeable about estate tax matters for assistance.

In this chapter, we give you an in-depth look at the schedules you're likely to take a crack at completing yourself and a heads-up on the schedules that address more complex areas of tax law.

## Tackling the Most Common Schedules

**Form 706** has a schedule for every occasion, but only rare estates have property and/or expenses diverse enough to require you to prepare every schedule. Basically, *schedules* are the places you list the individual assets, broken down by type of asset, such as **Schedule A, Real Estate,** and the different types of deductions, such as **Schedule K, Debts of the Decedent.** Still, every estate that's required to file a **Form 706** must complete at least some schedules. In the following sections, we guide you through the most commonly prepared schedules: the ones that show the types of property and the sorts of expenses you regularly find in even the smallest estates which are required to file.

# Focusing on real estate: Schedule A

If the probate estate contains any real estate or interest in real estate, complete and file **Schedule A: Real Estate.** Include all real estate the decedent owned in his or her individual name or as a *tenant in common.* When title is held as tenants in common, each tenant's interest in the property is separate from the interests of the other tenants in common and passes to his or her heirs upon death, as opposed to a *joint tenancy with right of survivorship* or a *tenancy by the entirety,* where title passes automatically to the surviving joint tenants.

For each piece of real estate, include the following information about the property on **Schedule A:**

- ✔ Land area.
- ✔ Any improvements such as house and landscaping.
- ✔ Street address.
- ✔ The legal description (the description on the deed).
- ✔ Any *accrued* rent (rent earned prior to the decedent's death but not paid until after the date of death).
- ✔ The appraisal or other basis for valuing the property. Describe the appraisal on **Schedule A** and attach a copy as an exhibit at the end of the return. If the assessed value reflects the market value in the area, the IRS may accept the assessed value in lieu of an appraisal. Attach a copy of the tax assessment closest to the decedent's date of death as an exhibit. If the property is sold shortly after the decedent's death, the selling price may be used. The IRS doesn't have to accept a sale price as the fair market value price, especially if the property was purchased by a related party or pursuant to an option to purchase. Attach copies of the sales contract and closing statement as exhibits.

If the decedent owned a fractional interest in real estate that you or your appraiser are discounting, attach as an exhibit a statement explaining the discount taken on the interest (due, for instance, to lack of control or lack of marketability), and be sure that the appraiser can defend the discount if the return is audited.

If the decedent was liable for a mortgage on the property (that is, if the mortgage wasn't solely chargeable against this property), report the mortgage in the property description but include the full value of the property on this schedule and deduct the mortgage on **Schedule K.** If a mortgage is solely chargeable against the property, so that the decedent's estate isn't liable for it, deduct the mortgage from the amount reportable on this schedule.

## Going with special valuation: Schedule A-1

If you elect special use valuation under section 2032A, valuing real estate used in the operation of a farm or closely held business at its farm or business use rather than its fair market value, you get to complete **Schedule A-1: Section** **2032A Valuation** in addition to **Schedule A.** Because this concept is so complicated, please consult a qualified professional to complete this schedule. (And for more information on special use valuation, see Chapter 16.)

Don't forget to also include all such real estate the decedent had contracted to sell. If the contract is a purchase and sale agreement, you'll hopefully have cancelled it and re-executed it as executor because of the decedent's death (as we discuss in Chapter 21) so you can report the real estate at its full value on this schedule and thus receive a step-up in cost basis before the sale. If you haven't canceled the contract entered into before the decedent's death, don't include the property on **Schedule A.** Instead, report the contract to sell on **Schedule C.** If the decedent was selling property under a land contract, report the property on **Schedule A** and refer to the land contract. List all jointly held real estate on **Schedule E** (not on **Schedule A**). Real estate held as part of a sole proprietorship belongs on **Schedule F** (not **Schedule A**).

# *Identifying stocks and bonds: Schedule B*

If the decedent owned any stocks, bonds, mutual funds, or other securities in his or her name alone at the time of his or her death, report them on **Schedule B: Stocks and Bonds,** along with any accrued but unpaid dividends or interest.

If the decedent owned any securities subject to foreign death taxes and you paid any estate, inheritance, legacy, or succession tax to a foreign country on those securities, report them on this schedule, grouped together under a heading you add titled "Subjected to Foreign Death Taxes." The following outlines what to include on this schedule.

## Description

The description of each stock should include

- The number of shares.
- Whether it's common or preferred stock.

✔ Par value, where that's necessary for identification. You can find the par value on the face of the certificate; it's typically only necessary for preferred stock.

✔ The price per share. We show you how to arrive at the correct value in the next section.

✔ Corporation name.

✔ Principal exchange on which the stock is sold, if any.

✔ Nine-digit CUSIP number. Every publicly traded security has this alphanumeric identifier. If you can't find it on the face of the certificate, get it from the stock's transfer agent. If the stock is in an investment account, the investment advisor can supply you with the CUSIP number.

The description of each bond should include

✔ Quantity and denomination.

✔ Name of the obligor.

✔ Date of maturity.

✔ Interest rate and interest due date.

✔ Principal exchange on which the bond is sold, if any. If you have a stock or bond that's not listed on an exchange, show the company's principal business office.

✔ Nine-digit CUSIP number.

### Valuation procedure

You report stocks and bonds on the **706** at their fair market value (FMV) as of the date of the decedent's death. If you're using alternate valuation, you report their value as of the alternate valuation date, exactly six months after the date of death. (We explain more about alternate valuation in Chapter 16.) The FMV of a stock or bond, whether it's listed or unlisted, is the *mean,* or average, between the high and low selling prices on the decedent's date of death.

If only closing prices are available (net asset values for mutual funds, for example), use the mean of the closing price on the date of death and the closing price on the day before the date of death. Find the mean by adding the two valuation numbers together and dividing them by two. For example, the opening price of X Company's stock is $20 per share, and the closing price is $22 per share. The computation is ($20 + $22) ÷ 2 = $21.

## Using the Employer Identification Number rather than a CUSIP number

Whenever the gross estate includes an interest in a trust, partnership, or closely held business, you need to include the Employer Identification Number (EIN) of that entity in the column titled "CUSIP number or EIN, where applicable." That's because these entities don't have CUSIP numbers (nine-digit alphanumeric indicators) to identify them. This switch applies to whichever of the following schedules you're completing at the time: **Schedule B, E, F, G, M,** or **O.** Also include the EIN of an estate, if it has one, on these schedules where applicable.

If the decedent died on a weekend, use the mean of the value on the Friday before and the mean of the value on the Monday after, and prorate the difference between the mean prices to the actual date of death, the Saturday or the Sunday. For example, assume the decedent died on Saturday. Y Company's common stock was selling for a mean of $10 per share on Friday and a mean of $13 per share on Monday. The FMV of a share of Y Company stock on Saturday is therefore $11, computed as follows: (2 days × $10) + (1 day × $13) ÷ 3 days total = $11.

You can apply the same principle when valuing stocks or bonds with no sales on the date of death. Find the trading dates closest in time prior to the decedent's date of death and after the decedent's date of death and apply the same computation, substituting the appropriate number of days and mean value per share. *Note:* The trading days must be reasonably close to the date of death. If you can't find sales reasonably close to the valuation date, use the mean between the *bona fide bid* (what a buyer says she'll pay for a stock) and *ask* (the seller's price to sell) prices, if available. Stocks listed on the NASDAQ Stock Exchange are listed, and sold, by bid and asked prices rather than highs and lows for any given day, unlike those listed on the New York Stock Exchange, which lists highs and lows.

If you can obtain sales prices or bid and asked prices for before the date of death but not after, or vice versa, use the mean between high and low sale prices or the mean between the bid and asked prices on the date they're available. And be sure to indicate the date used.

### Finding values for publicly traded stocks and bonds

To find the FMV of publicly traded stocks and bonds on the decedent's date of death, check out the following resources:

✔ ***The Wall Street Journal:*** You can find it at your local library if you don't have a subscription or didn't happen to save your copy from that date.

✔ **Broker:** If the securities were in a brokerage account at the date of death, the broker may be able to give you a valuation as of that date. Be sure that the broker understands that this value is for estate tax purposes; otherwise, he or she will give you the closing price rather than the mean of the high and low selling prices for the date of death. If you use such a broker's letter in valuing your securities, refer to it on **Schedule B** and attach it to your **706** as an exhibit.

✔ **Online pricing service:** If you don't have easy access to a broker and don't want to go digging into old issues of *The Wall Street Journal,* you can, for a fee, access the information you need by using an online pricing service. Plug something like "estate valuation pricing service" into your search engine and check out the services of several online pricing companies.

### *Finding values for unmarketable stocks and bonds*

Figuring out the value of *unmarketable securities* (securities not traded on any public exchange), including inactive stocks and stocks held in non-publicly traded corporations, is governed by rules contained in the Internal Revenue Code (IRC), as explained in section 2031 of the regulations. That statement, by itself, should be enough to send you to a qualified professional for expert assistance in preparing this valuation. Attach all information used to determine the value to the return as exhibits, including balance sheets and statements of net earnings for each of the five years before the date of death.

### *Handling securities of no value*

You may very well have a decedent who owned some securities that have lost most or all of their value. If you have one or more of these obsolete securities or securities of nominal or no value, report these last on **Schedule B.** Include the state and date of incorporation and the address of the company, if any, and attach as exhibits copies of correspondence or s tatements used to determine that the security is of no value.

### *Including dividends and interest*

Don't forget to include dividends and interest accrued on **Schedule B.** Here's a breakdown of what to also note:

✔ **Cash dividends:** Keep three dates in mind when determining whether a dividend is due (or accrued) on a particular stock as of the decedent's date of death:

  • The *declaration date* (date the dividend is declared)

  • The *record date* (date used by the corporation to determine which shareholders receive the dividend)

- The *payment date* (date the dividend is paid to shareholders of record)

Include the dividend on the return if the decedent died after the record date and before the payment date. You can get this information from either *Standard and Poor's Weekly Dividend Record* or the decedent's broker.

✔ **Stock selling ex dividend:** Stock sells *ex dividend* (when you purchase the stock, you also get the dividend that has already been declared, so the stock price is slightly depressed) for a few days before the record date for a dividend. If an *x* appears in *The Wall Street Journal* before the number of shares of a stock traded, you know that stock is selling ex dividend. When a stock is selling ex dividend, its price is reduced by approximately the amount of the dividend. If you have a stock selling ex dividend in your decedent's estate, add the value of the dividend to the value of the stock (the mean of the high and the low) instead of reporting the dividend separately.

✔ **Accrued stock dividends:** Sometimes a *stock dividend* (a dividend of shares of stock)rather than a cash dividend is declared. Report this dividend in the same manner you do a cash dividend. Commerce Clearing House's *Capital Changes Reporter* is one place to find information on stock dividends. You can also check with a broker.

✔ **Accrued interest:** In calculating accrued interest on a bond through the date of death, divide the number of days since interest was last paid (from the date of death) by 365. Multiply that result by the annual interest paid on the bond. The result is your accrued interest through the date of death; include this number on the **706.** If a bond is selling *flat* (with no accrued interest) on the date of death, it will have an *f* after its name in the bond listings, and you don't include any interest on the **706.**

## *Addressing mortgages, notes, and cash: Schedule C*

You report mortgages, notes, and cash on **Schedule C: Mortgages, Notes, and Cash.** Bear in mind that you're listing *assets* of the estate here, not debts, so any mortgages or notes listed here are amounts *owed* to the decedent, not amounts owed by him or her. Report the following items in this exact order:

✔ **Mortgages and notes payable to the decedent, not by the decedent.** In describing the mortgage, include the face value, unpaid balance, date of mortgage, name of maker, property mortgaged, date of maturity, interest rate, and interest date.

✔ **Promissory notes.** Report and describe them in the same manner as mortgages.

✔ **Contracts by the decedent to sell land.** Make sure that you include the following information:

- • Name of the purchaser

- • Contract date

- • Property description

- • Sales price

- • Initial payment

- • Amounts of the installment payments

- • Unpaid balance of the principal

- • Interest rate

✔ **In reporting cash in the decedent's possession, list it separately from cash in bank accounts.** You can aggregate all the actual cash you find; it's not necessary to list separately the cash in the bureau, the cash under the bed, and the cash hidden behind the fireplace.

✔ **List cash in banks, savings and loan associations, credit unions, and all other financial organizations as follows for each account:**

- • Name and address of the financial organization

- • Amount in the account, including accrued interest

- • Serial or account number

- • Kind of account (checking, savings, certificate of deposit)

For checking accounts, be sure to report the amount in the account *after* you account for all those checks outstanding at the date of death. To obtain the date-of-death balances, including accrued interest, send a letter to each financial institution requesting that information (you can make up a form letter and send a variation of it to each institution). Retain the response from each institution in your files.

## Considering life insurance: Schedule D

On **Schedule D: Insurance on the Decedent's Life,** list all policies on the life of the decedent, whether or not any policies are includible in the gross estate for estate tax purposes. (Insurance that the decedent owned on someone else's life is includible on **Schedule F.**)

Include the following insurance on **Schedule D:**

✔ **The full amount of the proceeds of insurance on the decedent's life receivable by the estate or usable for the benefit of the estate:** If any legally enforceable obligation on the beneficiary to pay taxes, debts, or other charges of the estate stands, regardless of who the owner and beneficiary of the policy are and who paid the premiums, it's includible.

✔ **Insurance on the decedent's life not payable to the estate and not usable for its benefit:** If the decedent held any *incidents of ownership* in the insurance, it goes in the taxable estate. Some examples of incidents of ownership are the following:

- The right to name and change the beneficiary

- The right to assign the policy to another or to revoke an assignment

- The right to surrender or cancel the policy

- The right to pledge the policy as collateral for a loan or to obtain a loan against the surrender value from the insurance company

✔ **A reversionary interest in the policy if the reversionary interest was more than 5 percent just before the death of the decedent.** An interest is *reversionary* if the decedent gains or regains any of these listed rights (such as the right to name the beneficiary) if the beneficiary predeceases the decedent or some other stated contingency occurs.

All the information you need to complete **Schedule D** is included on the **IRS Form 712, Life Insurance Statement,** which you must request from each life insurance company. Ask for **Form 712** when you request the proceeds of the policy from the insurance company, as described in Chapter 7. In the description column of **Schedule D,** refer to the **712** as an exhibit and attach it to the return as such. If a policy on the decedent's life isn't includible, list it on this schedule, including the same information as for any other policy, but don't include a value in the value column. Do, however, include in your description of the policy your reasons why the policy isn't includible.

## *Eyeing jointly owned property: Schedule E*

Schedules A through D all deal with property the decedent held in his or her name alone. All of this changes in **Schedule E: Jointly Owned Property.** If the decedent held any property of any kind (including real estate, personal property, and bank accounts) jointly at the time of his or her death, you must file **Schedule E,** whether or not any of the jointly held property is includible in the decedent's taxable estate.

Describe the property on **Schedule E** in the same manner you do on its respective schedule. For instance, describe real estate as set forth in the discussion of **Schedule A,** bank accounts as set forth in the discussion of **Schedule C,** and so on. (Refer to the earlier sections in this chapter for details on handling the individual schedules.) The amount of the property includible in the taxable estate depends on the decedent's interest in the property, as we explain in the following sections.

### Part 1 of Schedule E

Part 1 of Schedule E deals with qualified joint interests held by the decedent and his or her spouse as the only joint tenants (IRC Section 2040 (b)(2)). Here you want to list all the property the decedent held with his or her surviving spouse, either as joint tenants with right of survivorship (if they're the only joint tenants) or as tenants by the entirety. In either case, include the full value of the property at the date of death (and alternate valuation date, if applicable). These properties are qualified joint interests under IRC Section 2040(b)(2), which provides that, if property is held by the decedent and his or her spouse as joint tenants with right of survivorship (with no other joint tenants), or as tenants by the entireties, only one-half of the property is includible in the gross estate. (*Note:* Legally, only husband and wife can hold property as tenants by the entirety.)

You may only claim the special treatment under IRC Section 2042(b)(2) and list the property on Part 1 of **Schedule E** if the surviving spouse is a U.S. citizen. Otherwise, include the property on Part 2 of **Schedule E.**

Total the values of the properties on line 1a and include one-half of the value of the properties on line 1b. The amount on line 1b is the amount includible in the gross estate.

### Part 2 of Schedule E

Part 2 focuses on all other joint interests. Under 2a, list the names and addresses of all other surviving joint tenants. If you have more than three joint tenants, create a continuation sheet.

In completing Part 2, enter the letter corresponding to the surviving joint tenant's name and address in the second column. In the third column enter the property description, and in the column entitled "Percentage includible," enter 100 percent unless you can show that

- Part of the property originally belonged to the surviving tenant or tenants and wasn't acquired by gift from the decedent.
- Part of the property was acquired with funds that came from the surviving joint tenant or tenants.
- The decedent and the other joint tenant(s) acquired the property by gift, bequest, devise, or inheritance.

If you can prove any of the above, you may exclude an amount proportionate to what the surviving joint tenant(s) contributed to the property from the gross estate.

Giving up the right to dower, curtesy, or other marital rights (see Chapter 2) in the decedent's estate doesn't count as contributing toward the joint property in this instance.

If you aren't including the full value of the joint property in the gross estate in Part 2 (which, of course, you're usually trying not to do so as not to increase the decedent's gross estate), be sure to attach as an exhibit proof of the extent, nature, and origin of the interests of the decedent and the other joint tenants for each such property.

## Considering other property: Schedule F

If the decedent owned it and it doesn't go on any of the earlier schedules, you place it on **Schedule F: Other Miscellaneous Property Not Reportable Under Any Other Schedule. Schedule F** is always required to be filed with the return. (The IRS figures you're always going to have something to report on this schedule, and, if not, they'll want to know why.) Examples of items that are reported on **Schedule F** include

✔ **Personal and household articles, including clothing and jewelry:** If the decedent owned any works of art or collectible items worth more than $3,000 or any collections whose combined value exceeds $10,000, attach an appraisal by an expert in the field as an exhibit to the return. (Note that your appraiser will need to attach a statement of his or her qualifications.)

You may ask, "How will I know whether the value of the decedent's collection of frog figurines is worth over $10,000, or if one of them is worth over $3,000?" If you have any suspicion that an item may have some value, have it appraised. We had a client whose frog collection was worth far more than $10,000. And one of us had a client whose highly touted stamp collection just didn't get the stamp of approval from the appraiser. So even we don't always know what we have until we get an expert's opinion. (We share how to find an appraiser in Chapter 4.)

If the decedent transferred ownership of an item to his or her revocable living trust during life as part of his or her estate plan, you don't need to include it on **Schedule F.** Instead, report the item on **Schedule G.**

✔ **Automobiles and all other motor vehicles:** Book value or a letter from an auto dealer (or whatever other type vehicle) is usually sufficient. If your decedent had a collectible car, get an expert appraisal.

- ✔ **Debts (other than notes and mortgages reported on Schedule C), judgments, claims, and refunds due the decedent:** When the decedent and a surviving spouse receive a tax refund on a jointly filed return, the amount you include on the **706** as the decedent's portion of the refund is the excess of the amount the decedent paid of the total tax paid over his or her actual tax liability (unless local law says the contrary, in which case you want to consult a local attorney or tax preparer who's an expert in these matters).

- ✔ **Checks payable to the decedent, whether received before or after death:** These include final paychecks, dividend checks, and any other checks.

- ✔ **Rights, royalties, and leaseholds:** If the decedent held copyrights or other rights, received royalties, or had a *leasehold* (an extended right to lease property), obtain expert valuations and include them here.

- ✔ **Farm products, growing crops, livestock, and farm machinery:** If the decedent owned a farm, you'll likely have some or all of these items to report. Fortunately, you can get them valued by a competent farm appraiser.

- ✔ **Insurance on another person's life:** Be sure to obtain **Form 712** for each policy from the insurance company and attach it as an exhibit to the return. **Form 712** gives you the value of the policy as of the decedent's date of death. (For more on **Form 712,** turn to the earlier "Considering life insurance: **Schedule D**" section.)

- ✔ **Interests in partnerships, sole proprietorships, joint ventures, and other unincorporated businesses:** Value these interests as described in the Instructions to **Form 706** (Rev August 2012) (the Instructions). If you have a sole proprietorship that holds real estate, report the real estate here, as part of the sole proprietorship, rather than on **Schedule A.**

- ✔ **Reversionary and remainder interests:** You report both reversionary and remainder interests on **Schedule F.** As we note in Chapter 16, as the executor of the estate, you may elect to postpone the tax on these future interests under IRC Section 6163 until six months after the prior interest terminates, with a further extension of up to three years for reasonable cause.

  - A *reversionary interest* is any future interest that can come back to the decedent where he or she was the original transferor of the interest. For instance, the decedent has retained a reversionary interest in the trust property if during his or her lifetime the decedent transferred property to a trust for the benefit of his or her mother for her lifetime under the condition that it revert back to the decedent upon the death of the mother.

- A *remainder interest* is any future interest that can come to the decedent after a prior interest terminates where the decedent wasn't the original transferor of the interest. For instance, if the decedent's father created a trust with the decedent's mother as the beneficiary during her lifetime, and the decedent or his or her estate is to receive the property upon the death of the mother, the decedent has a remainder interest in the trust.

✔ **Qualified terminable interest property (QTIP):** If your decedent was a surviving spouse, he or she may have qualified terminable interest property (QTIP) received from a predeceased spouse. The predeceased spouse received a marital deduction for the trust, either on his or her estate tax return or a gift tax return. If such an election was made, and the surviving spouse (your decedent) still retains an interest in the property at his or her death, the full date-of-death (or alternate) value of the property shows up in his or her estate even though his or her interest terminates at death. If the QTIP property meets the other requirements for the marital or charitable deduction on the surviving spouse's death, it qualifies for that deduction because it's treated as having passed from the surviving spouse (your decedent). For further clarification on QTIP trusts, check out Chapter 3.

Report the fact that the decedent had a safe-deposit box on **Schedule F,** Question 3. If any property in the safe deposit box isn't includible in the decedent's estate because the decedent didn't own it, you must explain fully why that's the case. So, for example, jewelry or stock certificates owned by the other spouse would be excluded.

## Touching on funeral and administration expenses: Schedule J

All the **Form 706** schedules up to **Schedule J** deal with the decedent's assets. With **Schedule J: Funeral Expenses and Expenses Incurred in Administering Property Subject to Claims,** you're finally beginning the portion of the tax return where you take every last deduction you can on behalf of the decedent (except those you may elect to take on the estate's income tax return; check out the sidebar "Surveying the options for where to take your deductions for more info).

If you're using **Schedule PC** for expenses that aren't currently deductible under IRC Section 2053, report the expense on **Schedule J** with no value in the last column. For the full scoop on **Schedule PC,** head to the later section, "Filing a protective claim for refund: Schedule PC."

On **Schedule J,** you include funeral expenses and expenses incurred in administering property subject to claims. The phrase *property subject to claims* refers to property available to pay the decedent's creditors. The decedent's local (state) law will determine which property is subject to claims. Include on **Schedule J** each separate expense, itemizing each with the name and address of the person or entity to whom or to which the expense is payable, as well as the nature of the expense.

Generally speaking, administrative expenses must be deductible under state law and be considered "reasonable and necessary" by the IRS for them to be deductible on the **706.** What's reasonable and necessary? There's no set standard; rather, it's more a sense of knowing it when you see it. If the **706** you prepared is audited, though, be prepared to substantiate your expenses with receipts and, where necessary, with a scope of the work that's been performed. The IRS loves nothing more than slicing off a portion of the executor's fee as being excessive.

Although the deduction is limited to the amount allowable under local law, it also can't exceed the total of the value of property subject to claims in the gross estate and the amount of expenses paid out of property included in the gross estate but not subject to claims.

Don't deduct expenses of property *not* subject to claims on **Schedule J!** Those expenses are properly deducted on **Schedule K.** If you can't determine the exact amount of certain expenses by the time the **Form 706** is due, estimate as accurately as you can.

### Funeral expenses

Itemize all funeral expenses on line A, **Schedule J.** These expenses include all miscellaneous items billed by the funeral home (such as death certificates); flowers; a newspaper funeral announcement; a tombstone, monument, mausoleum, or burial plot for the decedent and his or her family (including perpetual care costs); and travel expenses for one person to accompany the body to the place of burial if traveling a distance. *Note:* If your decedent was a veteran and the VA provides a burial marker, you don't have that expense to deduct.

Although deducting the cost of the funeral luncheon (also referred to as the *collation*) has been common practice, a tax court case recently disallowed such a deduction in Michigan. They questioned the reasonableness of the expense, the lack of detail on the **706** regarding the expense, and the fact that the luncheon seemed to be to thank people in the decedent's life, rather than to eulogize the decedent, as would be typical at a funeral service. It was also held at a different location than the funeral service. Whether this ruling will apply beyond the specific facts of that case remains to be seen, so tread carefully when deducting that post-funeral feast until the tax court issues further rulings.

# Surveying the options for where to take your deductions

Although many expenses of the estate are only deductible on **Form 706,** you actually have three options for taking some deductions. If you have the option of deducting an expense on different tax returns, think about which deduction benefits the estate the most. Remember, with a couple of notable exceptions listed here, you can't *double dip* — that is, take a deduction for the expense on both the **706** and an income tax return (see Chapter 18). The three options are as follows with some important relevant info about each one:

✔ **Form 706**

✔ The estate's **Form 1041**

✔ The decedent's final **Form 1040**

If you have to file a **706** due to the size of the estate and will owe no tax (perhaps due to an unlimited marital deduction), you want to capture that otherwise-unused deduction on a **1041.**

So how do you decide where to deduct the expenses? Here are some of your options:

✔ **Expenses deductible only on Form 706:** Funeral expenses and debts of the decedent that wouldn't have been deductible on a **1040** of the decedent if paid before death.

✔ **Expenses deductible on both Form 706 and either final 1040 of the decedent or the estate's 1041:** Real estate taxes assessed before death but not paid, other taxes deductible for income tax purposes, interest, and business expenses accrued at the date of death (these are known as "deductions in respect of the decedent") can be taken both on **Schedule K** and on the estate's **Form 1041** or the decedent's final **Form 1040.** In other words, this is a double dip that's allowed!

✔ **Expenses deductible on only one or the other of the decedent's final 1040 or the 706:** Medical expenses incurred at date of death but not yet paid may be deducted on either **Form 706, Schedule K,** or **Form 1040, Schedule A,** but not on both. Recall that medical expenses are only useful as an income tax itemized deduction when they exceed 7.5 percent of the decedent's adjusted gross income (AGI), increasing to 10 percent in 2013 and beyond. If the decedent is filing jointly with his or her surviving spouse, the AGI limitation calculation is based on their combined income, not just the decedent's.

✔ **Expenses deductible only on whichever of the 706 or the estate's or trust's 1041 paid the expense:** Administration expenses and losses (including expenses of sale that will offset the sale price of property). Note that selling expenses are only deductible on the **706** if the sale is necessary to pay debts of the decedent, administration expenses, or taxes; preserve the estate; or carry out distribution.

**WARNING!** Unless the Social Security death benefit is paid to the surviving spouse, reduce the funeral expense deduction by any amounts you receive from the Social Security Administration (currently, and for many years past, $255). If the decedent received any death benefit from the Veterans' Administration, treat it the same way. Remember the fifth grade? Show your math right on **Schedule J!**

### Administration expenses

On line B of **Schedule J,** list the administration expenses for your executor commissions, attorney fees, and accountant fees, indicating whether they're amounts estimated, agreed upon, or paid. If you don't have a probate estate, enter the amount of the trustees' fees of the revocable (now irrevocable) living trust on line B1. If both executors' and trustees' fees are being charged, enter the trustees' fees as a miscellaneous expense under item B4. *Note:* If the decedent arranged to pay the executor through a bequest or devise, you can't deduct the payment.

We strongly recommend that you fill in, sign, and date **Form 4421, Declaration of Executor's Commissions and Attorney's Fees** (available online at www. irs.gov), reference it on line B1, and attach it to the **706** as an exhibit. This action expedites the audit process. **Form 4421** contains a statement as to how much of the attorney fees and executor fees are being taken as a deduction on an income tax return.

Other expenses you may deduct on **Schedule J** include

- ✔ Appraisers' fees
- ✔ Probate court filing fees
- ✔ Certified copy charges and the like
- ✔ *Guardian ad litem* fees (see Appendix A for a definition of this unusual species)
- ✔ Brokers' and auctioneers' fees (but only if the sale was necessary to pay taxes, debts, or expenses of administration, to preserve the estate, or to effect distribution of the property)
- ✔ Maintenance expenses of estate property (including insurance)
- ✔ Investment advisors' fees
- ✔ Other miscellaneous expenses related to the estate such as telephone bills, mileage, and postage

Even interest expenses you incur as executor after the decedent's death are deductible if they're reasonable, necessary to the administration of the estate, and deductible under local law. But if you elect to pay the estate tax in installments under IRC Section 6166, you can't deduct any interest expenses incurred on the installments on the **706.** Don't forget about them, though — you can deduct them on the estate's **Form 1041.**

## Recording debts, mortgages, and liens: Schedule K

List your **Schedule K** items under the following two categories:

### The decedent's debts

Report all unsecured debts of the decedent that existed at the time of the decedent's death, whether or not *mature* (currently due), and that relate to property not subject to claims of the decedent's creditors. As we discuss for **Schedule J** in the previous section, the decedent's state law determines which items of property are subject to claims and therefore whether you deduct these expenses on **Schedule J or K.**

For each item, include the name of the creditor, the nature of the claim, and the amount. If the claim is for services for a certain period of time, state that period of time. Examples of some deductible debts are

- ✓ Household expenses, such as utility bills, accrued before death

- ✓ Property taxes accrued before the decedent's death

- ✓ Federal taxes on income received before the decedent's death (or the decedent's portion — the amount for which the estate would be liable under local law — if it's a joint liability with a surviving spouse)

- ✓ Unpaid gift taxes on gifts the decedent made

- ✓ Certain claims of a former spouse against the estate if they meet the requirements set out in the instructions to **Form 706, Schedule K**

- ✓ Professional fees, such as attorneys' fees, accountants' fees, and so on, for services rendered during life

- ✓ Amounts due on notes, judgments, and accrued interest through date of death

### Mortgages and liens

On the bottom half of **Schedule K,** report only obligations

- ✓ Secured by mortgages or other liens for which the decedent was personally liable (and for which the estate is liable)

- ✓ On property you included in the gross estate at its full value, unreduced by the mortgage or lien

If the decedent and his or her estate aren't liable for the mortgage or lien, include in the gross estate only the value of the property net of the debt. You don't deduct any portion of such debt on this schedule.

## Listing net losses and such: Schedule L

Although you certainly try to avoid shipwrecks or other disasters during your term as executor, you may find comfort in the fact that you can at least deduct them if they occur during the settlement of the estate. Also deductible are losses from theft, fire, storm, and other casualties, except to the extent they're reimbursed by insurance or in some other manner and the loss isn't reflected in the alternate valuation of the property. You may not take the loss on the **706** if you elect to take it on the applicable income tax return, so take a look at your relative tax rates and make your best choice.

Deduct the expenses you incur in administering property included in the gross estate but not subject to claims on the bottom half of **Schedule L: Net losses during administration and expenses incurred in administering property not subject to claims.** Here's where you report the expenses relating to administering a decedent's revocable trust (funded with assets before death, and, of course, irrevocable after death). You may only deduct those expenses paid within the period of limitations, typically three years after the **706** is filed. The expenses must relate to settling the decedent's interest in the property or vesting good title in the beneficiaries. Any expenses deducted on an income tax return may not be deducted here. Report the expenses in the same fashion as those on **Schedule J.**

If you're using **Schedule PC** for expenses that aren't currently deductible under IRC Section 2053, report the expense on **Schedule L** with no value in the last column. Turn to the later "Filing a protective claim for refund: Schedule PC" section for more information on this particular schedule.

# Covering bequests to a surviving spouse: Schedule M

If your decedent left a surviving spouse, you may have a whopper of a deduction available to you, which you report on **Schedule M: Bequests, etc. to surviving spouse.** All property that passes to the surviving spouse as a result of the decedent's death qualifies for the unlimited marital deduction, provided that the surviving spouse is a U.S. citizen. Using the unlimited marital deduction causes no tax to be due on the death of the first spouse to die; when the second spouse dies, his or her estate pays whatever tax is due on the remaining assets of both spouses. Therefore, if your decedent left a surviving spouse, that spouse's estate (not your decedent's) will be responsible for the tax burden, and you can breathe a sigh of relief. The following sections highlight which property does and doesn't qualify for the marital deduction.

### Property qualifying for the marital deduction

Property qualifying for the marital deduction includes assets held either solely in the decedent's name or jointly with the surviving spouse. The following items also qualify:

✔ **Trusts qualifying for marital deduction:** Property left in trust for a surviving spouse qualifies for the marital deduction if, under the trust agreement, the surviving spouse at a minimum is the sole beneficiary, is entitled to receive all the income for his or her life, can withdraw any or all of the principal at any time, and has a general power of appointment exercisable by will.

✔ **Life insurance, endowments, and annuity contracts:** Proceeds from these assets qualify, if payable to the surviving spouse, provided that they meet all the conditions laid out in the **Form 706** instructions.

✔ **Qualified terminable interest property (QTIPs):** Check the will and any trusts carefully for a QTIP trust. If one exists, you may either

- Elect to claim a marital deduction for qualified terminable interest property by listing the property on Schedule M and deducting it (that's all it takes to elect it)

- Elect out of the QTIP, and thus not get a marital deduction

In either case, list the property on Schedule M. If you're choosing not to use the QTIP election (to elect out), be sure to specifically identify the trust as being excluded from the election. Remember, any property for which the election is made will be included in the decedent's spouse's estate when he or she dies.

When would you choose to elect out? When the surviving spouse's estate is much larger than the decedent's and you don't want to increase it further and take it to a higher tax bracket. Of course, when you elect out, even though the property is listed on Schedule M, you may not include it in the total and take it as a marital deduction.

Consult your tax advisor to be sure that you meet all the requirements for making a valid QTIP election.

✔ **Joint and survivor annuities:** If your decedent has a joint and survivor annuity with his or her surviving spouse, that spouse doesn't have to specifically elect to take the marital deduction for that property. If the surviving spouse has the right to receive payments during his or her lifetime after the decedent's death, that constitutes a QTIP election unless you, as executor, affirmatively opt out of the election on the **706**, for the reasons described earlier.

✔ **Charitable remainder trusts:** If you have a surviving spouse who receives an interest in a *charitable reminder trust,* it isn't treated as a nondeductible terminable interest if the interest passes from your decedent to his or her surviving spouse and that surviving spouse is the only beneficiary of the trust (other than charitable organizations). A charitable remainder trust is either a *charitable remainder annuity trust* or a *charitable remainder unitrust* — Chapter 3 tells you what you need to know about these trusts.

✔ **Qualified domestic trusts (QDOTs):** A surviving spouse who isn't a U.S. citizen doesn't automatically qualify for the unlimited marital deduction unless the property is put into a qualified domestic trust (QDOT) for the benefit of that spouse.

The terms of the QDOT are quite specific, and you want to consult with a qualified tax advisor if you need to follow this route. If the decedent left a marital trust that doesn't meet the requirements of a QDOT, you can ask the probate court to reform the trust so that it qualifies for the election. If your decedent left assets not in a trust to the surviving spouse, the spouse or you (as executor) may establish a QDOT trust. The surviving spouse can then transfer assets left outright to him or her into this trust.

As an alternative to attempting to meet the QDOT requirements, the surviving spouse may elect to become a U.S. citizen, although chances are the spouse would have done so by now if he or she wanted to.

### Property not qualifying for the marital deduction

A *terminable interest* is an interest that terminates or fails after the passage of time or upon the (non)occurrence of some contingency. In general, terminable interest property received by a surviving spouse is normally nondeductible. It makes sense because the IRS isn't able to collect estate tax on property when the surviving spouse dies if the interest terminates beforehand. But as usual, a couple exceptions exist:

✔ **The six-month survival period:** If your decedent left a bequest, whether outright or in trust, to the surviving spouse on the condition that the spouse survives for a period not exceeding six months, it's not considered a terminable interest, and so will qualify for the marital deduction. Many estate plans contain this condition.

✔ **Deductions against the marital deduction:** If you claim a deduction as executor on **Schedules J** through **L** against any property you take as a marital deduction, you must reduce the amount of the marital deduction by that **J** through **L** deduction amount. If the marital deduction property has a mortgage or other encumbrance, you may take only the net value of the property after you deduct that mortgage or encumbrance.

# Recording charitable, public, and similar gifts and bequests: Schedule O

Use **Schedule O** to claim a charitable deduction if your decedent left a bequest, legacy, devise, or transfer for a qualified charitable purpose to any qualified charitable organization. See the Instructions for **Form 706** regarding **Schedule O** for the five general categories of qualified charitable organizations.

## Presuming survival with simultaneous death

If both your decedent and his or her spouse die in a common disaster (an occurrence we sincerely hope doesn't arise) and the order of their deaths can't be determined, review each spouse's estate planning documents to see if they assume that the spouse with the smaller estate survived the other spouse. In both the husband's and wife's documents, the presumption would be that the spouse with the smaller estate survived. Thus, the spouse with the smaller estate would inherit marital deduction property from the wealthier spouse, which the spouse with the smaller estate could then use his or her exclusion amount against, making full use of both spouses' exclusion amounts.

If no such presumption is made in the estate plan documents, or if you can't find any such documents, state law governs. In at least some states, each decedent is presumed to have survived the other, thus leaving no marital deduction and perhaps no or less than full use of the exclusion amount by the spouse with the smaller assets. (Refer to the discussion of exclusion amounts at the beginning of Chapter 16.)

You may take an estate tax charitable deduction for amounts transferred to charitable organizations as a result of a qualified disclaimer. A *qualified disclaimer* is a refusal to accept an interest in property under certain, very specific circumstances (see Chapter 8). Consult your tax expert to be sure that you've crossed all your t's and dotted all your i's to qualify for this disclaimer. In addition to disclaimers, the instructions for **Schedule O** list other types of property that qualify for the charitable deduction.

If you have any questions about a charitable gift made by your decedent, or about how to report the gift, consult that estate tax expert we keep mentioning.

# Knowing When to Ask for Help

Although a reasonably competent person can prepare most of **Form 706** without professional help, some of its schedules involve complex areas of tax law. In the following sections, we tell you what you need to know in order to identify whether any of this property or these expenses are in your estate.

However, we strongly discourage you from relying on your own common sense to work your way through reporting these items. Many technicalities here can turn these schedules into a minefield for the unwary, which is why seeking advice from an estate tax professional is wise.

## Listing transfers during life: Schedule G

Welcome to **Schedule G: Transfers during Life,** the land of the look-back, the second glance, the "if only," the "oops, I really wish the decedent hadn't retained that power," and, quite probably, the "I think I'd better check with my tax expert about this schedule. . . ."

If the decedent transferred property during his or her life for less than full payment, sometimes it can be included in his or her taxable estate. Sometimes the decedent knew the property would be included in the estate (when, for instance, he or she funded a revocable trust during life — revocable trusts and the property held in them are always included in the decedent's estate and are reported on **Schedule G**). Occasionally a power over a transfer the decedent made during life is retained unintentionally, causing the property transferred to be includible in the decedent's estate. In either case, or any other that may arise, **Schedule G** is here, courtesy of the IRS, for your convenience in reporting certain transfers made within three years of death, including gift taxes on gifts made within three years of death (even though the gifts may not be includible in the estate) and transfers with certain retained interests.

## Exercising powers of appointment: Schedule H

A *power of appointment* over property, which can be either general or limited, is the power to decide who will be the ultimate owner (or have the enjoyment) of the property and when. It's usually created by someone other than the decedent under that person's will or trust, giving the decedent the authority to direct the use and dispersal of any property controlled by the power. For example, Abe X leaves a trust under his will to his wife, Ida X, and gives her a general power of appointment over all the property contained in the trust. When Ida X dies, her executor must include this power on **Schedule H** of Ida's **Form 706,** listing all the property that was in Abe's trust on the date of Ida's death.

Only property controlled by a *general power of appointment* is included on **Schedule H: Powers of Appointment.** A *general power* can be exercised in favor of anyone, including the decedent, his or her estate, his or her creditors, or the creditors of the estate. A *limited power of appointment* can only be exercised in favor of a limited class of people designated by the grantor (for instance, the grantor's children and their lineal descendants), never including the power holder, his or her estate, his or her creditors, or the creditors of his or her estate.

# *Considering annuities: Schedule I*

The term *annuity,* for estate tax purposes, is an agreement to make periodic cash payments to one or more persons over a specific period of time. An annuity is subject to estate tax if payments (or a lump sum payment) continue after the decedent's death. If the annuity ends with the decedent's death, it's not includible in the decedent's estate. On **Schedule I: Annuities,** report the value of any annuity that meets the requirements set out in the Instructions.

# *Claiming a credit for foreign death taxes: Schedule P*

You may claim a credit for foreign death taxes paid to a foreign country or any of its political subdivisions on **Schedule P: Credit for Foreign Death Taxes** if the decedent is a U.S. citizen or a resident alien, on property situated in the foreign country, and subject to estate tax on the **706.** To obtain the credit, the foreign tax must be a tax on the transfer of the foreign property at death. You may also claim a credit for foreign death taxes under death tax treaties or conventions with many countries. Check the Instructions for **Form 706-NA, United States Estate (and Generation-Skipping Transfer) Tax Return (Estate of nonresident not a citizen of the United States),** for a current list of treaties in effect.

# *Getting a credit for tax on prior transfers: Schedule Q*

Whoever said the IRS didn't have a heart was wrong. In **Schedule Q: Credit for Tax on Prior Transfers,** you're allowed a credit for estate taxes paid by a prior estate on property included in this estate, provided the transfer from the first estate to your decedent happened no more than ten years prior to or two years after your decedent's date of death. The property needn't exist on your decedent's date of death. Property qualifies for the credit if it was subject to estate tax on the prior decedent's (the transferor's) date of death. You may take the credit so long as your decedent was considered the beneficial owner of the property, even if that ownership ended with your decedent's death, such as a general power of appointment (which we describe in the earlier "Exercising powers of appointment: Schedule H" section), annuity, life estate, term for years, or *remainder interest* (whether vested or contingent).

## Generation-Skipping Transfer tax: Schedule R

The generation-skipping transfer (GST) tax assesses a tax on property at each generational level as if it had been owned by someone of that generation, even though ownership of the property skipped over one or more of those generations. Its purpose is to prevent grandparents from leaving property to grandchildren, bypassing the children in between to bypass taxation in the children's estates.

As executor, you want to know enough about the GST tax to recognize whether your decedent's estate may be subject to it. If you've already made that determination, or if you're fence sitting because you're not sure, it's time to call in the experts — be they estate attorneys, accountants, or Enrolled Agents — to prepare **Schedules R and R-1** and to help you determine who are the skip beneficiaries, and what property, exactly, those beneficiaries are receiving. Remember, only assets that skip generations (even if the property lands in a trust for the benefit of a skip person) are subject to the GST tax.

## Electing a qualified conservation easement exclusion: Schedule U

If your decedent's gross estate includes land subject to a *qualified conservation easement,* you may make an election to exclude a portion of the land that's subject to the easement from the estate. For the purpose of **Form 706,** a *qualified conservation easement* is defined as an easement of a qualified real property interest to a qualified organization exclusively for conservation purposes. (Note that an *easement* allows others to use your land for a specific purpose.) After it's made, the election can't be revoked. An easement can also be granted after the decedent's death.

## Filing a protective claim for refund: Schedule PC

A *protective claim for refund* preserves the estate's right to a refund of tax paid on any amount included in the gross estate that would be deductible under IRC Section 2053 (funeral and administration expenses, claims against the estate, charitable pledges, taxes and unpaid mortgages; see **Schedules J** and **K** above), which hasn't been paid or otherwise won't meet the requirements of IRC Section 2053 for deductibility on the **706** until after the limitations period for filing the claim has passed. **Schedule PC** is also used to inform the IRS when the contingency leading to the protective claim for refund is resolved and the refund due to the estate is finalized.

# Chapter 18

# Filing Income Tax Returns for a Decedent, Estate, or Trust

. . . . . . . . . . . . . . . . . . . . . . . . . . . . . . . . . . . . . . . . . . . . . . . . . . . . . . . . . . . . .

## In This Chapter

▶ Applying for a Taxpayer Identification Number

▶ Deciding when the decedent's tax year ends

▶ Determining the decedent's (and the estate's) income

▶ Calculating deductions

▶ Tackling Page 2 of **Form 1041**

. . . . . . . . . . . . . . . . . . . . . . . . . . . . . . . . . . . . . . . . . . . . . . . . . . . . . . . . . . . . .

*F*or the most part, all income tax returns are alike. Of course, there are differences between preparing (and filing) your own **Form 1040** and the decedent's, which you still must file in order to report income and deductions, up to and including the date of death. And those differences become even more pronounced after you move into income taxation of estates and trusts, where some concepts remain the same but others change.

In this chapter, you discover what's similar and what's different with both the decedent's final **Form 1040** and the trust or estate's **Form 1041.** We tell you how to stay in the clear with the IRS as you prepare the final year (or maybe two) of the decedent's personal income tax returns (**Form 1040**), or you complete and file income tax returns for estates and trusts (**Form 1041**).

# Before You Begin: What You Need to Do

Thinking about income taxes may not be high on your list of priorities as you begin administering an estate or trust, but it will soon become a main focus of your administration, whether you're thrilled by the idea or not. Planning for those first income tax returns should begin right away, not at year-end when the first deadline for filing is fast approaching.

The following sections help keep your tax reporting running as smoothly as possible. We explain how to obtain a federal tax ID number and how to choose an appropriate tax year-end.

## Obtain a federal tax ID number

Before you get started on any tax return, you need to know the federal Taxpayer Identification Number (or TIN), which will be either an Employer Identification Number (EIN) for estate and trust returns or the decedent's Social Security number (SSN) for his or her final **Form 1040.**

Finding the decedent's SSN is easy; it's scattered all over his or her financial documents. The EIN, however, doesn't exist until you apply for it. We advise applying for one as soon as you know you're (a) going to have to open an estate bank account or investment account or (b) you're going to have to file any sort of tax return for the estate (either income or estate). Apply for the estate or trust's TIN by using **Form SS-4, Application for Employer Identification Number,** which you can get by visiting any IRS office, phoning 800-829-4933, or going to www.irs.gov (just click on "I need to apply for an EIN" to go directly to the form). When applying by phone or online, you receive your number immediately; you'll receive a response to an application to the IRS service center for your state within four business days. If you file a physical application by mail, it takes up to ten days to receive the form from the IRS, and up to an additional four weeks to receive the number itself.

Every taxpayer needs a TIN, and you're not allowed to file any tax returns without one that has been specifically assigned to that person, trust or estate. You can't use the decedent's SSN to file an estate return, nor can you use the estate's EIN to file a return for a trust that inherits the estate's property. Still, obtaining a TIN only costs you a little time and no money, so don't feel like you're being wasteful because you're not able to recycle ones that are no longer useful, like the decedent's SSN. Be careful, though, and only apply for a TIN once for each taxpayer. Nothing is worse than trying to sort out the confusion with the IRS and your banks, brokerages, and anyone else to whom you've given the information, when an estate or trust has more than one EIN.

If you need to open even one bank or brokerage account for an estate, you have to apply for a TIN to do so. Applying alerts the IRS that a new trust or estate exists; it's going to expect tax returns from that entity, even if there's no obligation to file one. Not to worry — if you receive a notice asking for a tax return, send the IRS a letter explaining that the estate didn't have enough income to file. Or, to avoid the notice altogether, you can prepare and file a return showing no income.

If you need multiple EINs because you have multiple entities, take note: The days of applying for the estate's EIN on the same day as you apply for the follow-up trust's EIN are officially over. A new administrative rule limits the number of EINs you may apply for to one per day, no matter what method you use to apply (e-mail, fax, phone, or snail mail).

## Choose a tax year-end

Although Congress created a general rule in 1986 that all individuals, businesses, and most trusts had to use December 31 as their tax year-end, every rule has exceptions. An estate may choose the last day of any month as its tax year-end, provided the first year doesn't include more than 12 months.

Why choose a date other than December 31 as a tax year-end? Depending on how much income the estate stands to receive (and when), using a different year-end can substantially reduce the total income tax bite, especially if the estate's administration will take more than 12 months from start to finish. If you haven't already, create a schedule of when and how much income you expect the estate to receive.

Because estates and trusts reach the highest tax bracket very quickly, we recommend you split the initial flow of income into two years, if possible. Whether the estate is paying the tax, or distributions to the beneficiaries mean that they'll be responsible for the income tax bill, splitting income into two years can ease the overall income tax burden for both the estate and the heirs.

You'll be asked to declare a year-end when applying for the trust or estate's EIN, but your decision isn't absolutely final until you file that first income tax return and put the year-end on the top of page 1. For example, the decedent died on April 15, and you initially chose a December 31 year-end because you didn't know that you could choose differently. The estate paid large, tax-deductible expenses before December 31, but ended up receiving the majority of its income in January and March of the following year. If the tax year-end remains December 31, the first tax return has no tax due and misses out on large deductions (because it has no income to offset them), while the second year's return will show lots of income, few deductions, and a large tax bill. By changing the year-end to January 31 (which is still less than twelve months after the decedent died), you can move some income back into the estate's first tax year — hopefully enough to offset the deductions — and drastically reduce the amount of taxable income in the second tax year. You've reduced not only the income tax due on that return but also the total amount of income taxes paid by the estate over the course of administration.

If you choose a year-end other than December 31, you're responsible for correctly accounting for all income received because the **1099**s you receive from banks, brokerages, and others may not accurately reflect income for the tax year. Only your good recordkeeping will produce an accurate tax return.

# Calculating the Income

Whether you're filing a **Form 1040** or a **Form 1041,** your first task is to determine how much income the taxpayer (whether trust, estate, or decedent) earned. In the case of an individual (filing **Form 1040**), you're likely already familiar with the types of income you'll see, such as wages, retirement income, interest, dividends, capital gains, rental income, and so on. Not surprisingly, types of income on **Form 1041** are the same (although you rarely see wages, pensions and Social Security, railroad retirement, or veteran's benefits, because these payments tend to stop at death). All you need to do is identify the income, put it on the correct line, and add the total. The next sections walk you through the different types of income you need to know about.

## Interest

*Interest* is income you receive because you've lent money. No matter where or to whom you lend money — to banks, the U.S. Treasury, state and local governments (municipal bonds), corporations, foreign governments, or your nephew Fred — the income earned from that investment is interest.

With the exception of interest you earn when making personal loans, **Form 1099-INT** should tell you how much interest you're dealing with. Just add up all the **Form 1099-INT**s to get this year's total. For non-calendar-year filers, remember that using **1099** information may cause you to either over- or under-report income. Make sure that you keep excellent records to make up for this discrepancy. You report total taxable interest on line 1 of **Form 1041,** or line 8a of **Form 1040.** You show *exempt interest* (interest not subject to federal income tax, like interest from municipal bonds) on the back of **Form 1041,** on Question 1 of "Other Information"; if you're preparing the decedent's final **1040,** place his or her exempt interest on line 8b.

## Dividends

Unlike interest, *dividends* represent profits from a company in which you own shares. You can earn dividends from publicly traded or closely held corporations and from U.S. or foreign companies. You may receive them from specific corporations or from shares owned in a *mutual fund,* which buys and sells the shares of many corporations, giving you tiny pieces of each individual dividend. Regardless of the source, every January you receive a **Form 1099-DIV,** showing how much you earned from dividends.

The most common types of dividend payments shown on **Form 1099-DIV** are the following:

- ✔ **Total dividends:** *Total dividends* are the total amount of ordinary dividends you received. Add these numbers up from all your **Forms 1099-DIV**s and place the total on line 2a of **Form 1041** or line 9a of **Form 1040.**

- ✔ **Qualified dividends:** As a portion of the total dividend, *qualified dividends* reported in box 1b of **Form 1099-DIV** are subject to lower income tax rates. If you received more than one **Form 1099-DIV** and each has an amount listed in box 1b, add all amounts shown in box 1b and either place the total on line 9b of **Form 1040** or split the total between lines 2b(1) and 2b(2) of **Form 1041.** Chapter 20 tells you how to make the allocation between the two lines.

- ✔ **Capital gain dividends:** *Capital gain dividends* are payments you received, primarily from mutual funds, that derive from the sale of assets within the fund and that are subject to a lower income tax rate. You typically place the amounts shown in box 2 of **Form 1099-DIV** on **Schedule D** (for either a **Form 1040** or a **Form 1041**). However, if you're preparing the decedent's **Form 1040** and he or she had no other capital gains or losses, check the box next to line 13 of **Form 1040** and then fill in the amount.

## Business income

*Business income* is income received from operating a business, one that the taxpayer owns either wholly or only in part, like a shareholder in a Subchapter S corporation. If the decedent operated a business as a *sole proprietor* (meaning that he or she was the owner of the company and declared his or her business income on **Schedule C** of **Form 1040;** check out Chapter 7 for more info), you probably have to prepare a **Schedule C** to file with both the final **Form 1040** and with the estate's **Form 1041,** at least while you're wrapping up the affairs of the business. After you complete **Schedule C,** place the total on line 3 of **Form 1041** or line 12 of **Form 1040.** If income is received from a Subchapter S corporation or a partnership, you receive a **Schedule K-1** from that entity's income tax return, reporting all the types of income you need to include on either the decedent's **Form 1040** or the trust or estate's **Form 1041;** only include on the business income lines of these tax returns amounts labeled as *ordinary income* on **Schedule K-1.**

Although paying self-employment tax after a person dies may sound strange, income earned from a sole proprietorship declared on **Form 1040** is still subject to that additional tax. Don't forget to prepare and include **Schedule SE** with the decedent's final **Form 1040.** After the business is operating under the estate's ownership, self-employment tax disappears. Evidently, someone got the memo that the estate would never collect Social Security or Medicare.

## Capital gains and losses

We know you love definitions, so here are a few useful ones to help you calculate the capital gains and losses. *Capital property* is anything that is owned by an entity that is used to generate income, income that may be earned either during the course of ownership or when the property is sold. A *capital gain* is the profit earned when a piece of capital property is sold for more than its acquisition cost (otherwise known as *basis*), whereas a *capital loss* recognizes the difference between a low sales price and its higher basis. Although there's a difference between property held for personal use and capital property in an individual's life (which is why you don't need to report the gains and losses you receive from your annual yard sale), trusts and estates don't use hairdryers and tableware, so all property owned by a trust or estate is capital property, and all gains and losses realized on their sale must be accounted for on **Form 8949, Sales and Other Dispositions of Capital Assets,** with the totals carrying forward to **Schedule D** of **Form 1041.**

Whenever you sell property, the difference between your basis in the property and the sale price determines the capital gain or loss. In order to figure out what number to use on line 4 of **Form 1041** or line 13 of **Form 1040,** you need to know not only these numbers but also the acquisition dates and sale dates of all property sold. Don't worry, though. Proceeds from sales and sale dates are easy to sort out because you receive **Form 1099-B** for the sale of all securities and **Form 1099-S** for the sale of a house.

However, figuring out what acquisition costs and dates and numbers to use can sometimes be confusing. And if that's not bad enough, you also have to calculate the *holding period* — the length of time the entity's owned the property. Here, you have a choice among the following:

✔ **Long-term gain or loss** (property owned for more than one year)

✔ **Short-term gain or loss** (property owned for one year or less)

✔ **Inherited property,** which automatically is treated as long-term, even if the estate or trust has only owned it for a day or less

Table 18-1 shows which acquisition costs to use. *Note:* Alternate valuation is determined six months after date of death and must be elected on the decedent's **Form 706;** see Chapter 16 for further details.

| Table 18-1 | Determining Acquisition Costs and Dates | | | |
|---|---|---|---|---|
| *Tax Form* | *Acquisition Method* | *Basis Cost* | *Acquisition Date* | *Holding Period* |
| 1040 | From decedent's estate | Date of death value (or alternate valuation*) | Date of decedent's death | Long-term |
| | Purchased | Purchase cost | Trade date of purchase | Long-term, if held for more than one year |
| 1041 (estate) | From decedent's estate | Date of death value (or alternate valuation) | Date of decedent's death | Long-term |
| | Purchased | Purchase cost | Trade date of purchase | Long-term, if held for more than one year |
| 1041-Revocable trust funded during grantor's lifetime | From grantor | Grantor's acquisition cost | Grantor's acquisition date | Long-term, if held for more than one year after grantor's acquisition |
| | Purchased | Purchase cost | Trade date of purchase | Long-term, if held for more than one year |

*(continued)*

### Table 18-1 *(continued)*

| Tax Form | Acquisition Method | Basis Cost | Acquisition Date | Holding Period |
|---|---|---|---|---|
| 1041-Irrevocable Trust | From grantor during lifetime | Grantor's acquisition cost | Grantor's acquisition date | Long-term, if held for more than one year after grantor's acquisition |
| | From grantor after death | Date of death value (or alternate valuation) | Date of grantor's death | Long-term |
| | Purchased | Purchase cost | Trade date of purchase | Long-term, if held for more than one year |

Just because the decedent's estate isn't large enough to warrant filing a **Form 706** doesn't mean that the value of his or her property doesn't benefit from the so-called *step-up* or increase in basis. Unless the decedent died in 2010, the basis of the property the decedent owned at death changes to the date of death value, and the new acquisition date is the decedent's date of death. For example, John Smith owns XYZ Corp stock he purchased for $50 per share in 2003. At his death in 2013, the stock was worth $100 per share. Even though Mr. Smith doesn't have a taxable estate, the acquisition cost for his XYZ Corp shares is now $100 per share. When his executor sells the shares for $100 each, no gain or loss is recognized because the sales price equals the stepped-up acquisition cost, so no capital gains tax is due on the sale.

As part of the provisions of the Emergency Economic Stabilization Act of 2008, the decedent's broker is now required to report acquisition costs for stocks and bonds purchased or otherwise acquired after January 1, 2011, and for mutual fund shares purchased or otherwise acquired after January 1, 2012. Beware: Just because the broker gives you the cost doesn't mean it's accurate. He or she may not have revalued all the assets as of the decedent's date of death prior to issuing **Form 1099-B, Proceeds from broker and barter exchange transactions.** If you know the basis information is incorrect, you may make the necessary adjustments on **Form 8949, Sales and Other Dispositions of Capital Assets,** in boxes (f) and (g).

# Income from rents, royalties, partnerships, and other estates and trusts

If the decedent, estate, or trust owned rental property, had an interest in any mining activities, published any works (or had an interest in published works), was a member of a partnership, or was a beneficiary of another estate or trust, you're going to have to fill out **Schedule E, Supplemental Income and Loss.** The good news: Whether you're preparing **Form 1040** or **Form 1041, Schedule E** is the same.

> ✔ Part I of **Schedule E** covers the income and/or loss from rental and royalty income.
>
> ✔ Part II gives you space to show the same information from Partnerships and S corporations.
>
> ✔ Part III wants to know about any income from other estates or trusts that you may have to report on this return.

In addition to being the collection point for information on all these types of income, **Schedule E** is also the spot where you need to decide whether the income you received is active or passive. Basically, you need to determine whether the participant actively participated in the business or was merely an investor (someone not involved in the day-to-day activities of that business). If you're preparing a **Form 1041,** the answer to this question is fairly simple — trusts and estates are rarely active participants in partnerships and S corporations, and rental and royalty income is, by definition, passive, so the income and/or losses from these activities are almost always passive. If you're filing a **1040** return for the decedent, the distinction isn't always so clear-cut and rests on the level of decision-making and management control exercised by the decedent.

Whether you're filing a **Form 1040** or **Form 1041,** if you have passive losses you may deduct them only against passive income; passive losses that exceed passive income are suspended. Calculate your passive loss limitations on **Form 8582, Passive Activity Loss Limitations.**

# Farm income or loss

If the decedent owned a farm, the land doesn't just disappear because he or she has died. The farm will continue operations, at least until you can find someone to buy or lease the property, and you'll need to report any income or loss from it. Before you can fill in a number on line 6 of **Form 1041** or line 18 of **Form 1040,** you're going to have to wend your way through **Schedule F.**

Fortunately, **Form 1041** doesn't have a separate **Schedule F,** so after you figure out how to prepare one, you can easily transfer those skills from the decedent's **Form 1040** to the estate or trust's **Form 1041.**

## Ordinary gain or loss

If your decedent owned any sort of business property (from real estate owned as part of a business to office equipment, cars, or any other property that had a business use), when you sell it you're going to report that sale on **Form 4797, Sale of Business Property.** Use Part I to report sales of property held long term by the decedent, trust, or estate and Part II for short-term sales. *Note:* Property that an estate or trust acquires due to the decedent's death constitutes an inheritance, uses the date-of-death value for its acquisition cost and date of death for its acquisition date, and qualifies as a long-term holding, even if the sale occurs the day after the decedent died.

Like **Form 8949, Form 4797** needs a description of the property sold, acquisition and sale dates, and the taxpayer's cost of acquisition. (Refer to Table 18-1 for help determining the acquisition date and basis cost for property.) In addition to this information, if the property *depreciated* over time (where the property's value is recovered over its useful economic life), you must add the total amount of depreciation to the sale price in order to calculate the gain or loss. Look at the decedent's prior years' income tax return to see what property he or she was depreciating. If there's no sole proprietorship (**Schedule C**), rental property (**Schedule E**), or farm (**Schedule F**), you're off the hook in regard to depreciable property. If any of those schedules are attached to a prior return, you may want to consult a tax expert for assistance in determining how much, if any, of the depreciation taken must be recaptured. If that sounds something like caging a wild animal, well, you're not too far off the mark.

After you complete **Form 4797,** carry the short-term gains or losses from line 17 of **Form 4797** to **Form 1041,** line 7. If you're filing the decedent's **Form 1040,** follow the instructions for lines 18a and b. Some of your losses may end up on **Schedule A, Itemized Deductions;** gains and other losses not reported on Schedule A end up on **Form 1040,** line 14. Long-term gains or losses take a detour through **Schedule D** (**1041,** line 10 or **1040,** line 11) so that you can factor these long-term sales into your tax calculations.

On **Form 4797,** you also report *casualty losses* (which are losses from a theft, or a disaster, such as a fire, flood, or earthquake), and the gain or loss received on *installment sales* (where you receive the proceeds from the sale over a period of years, not all at once) and on *like-kind exchanges* (where you exchange one piece of property for another, similar piece of property). Casualty losses, installment sales, and like-kind exchanges are very technical transactions, and you may want to consult an attorney, an accountant, or an Enrolled Agent before either entering into one or attempting to report the one you've already participated in to the IRS.

## Other income

You've already figured out that you need to declare all income whether it falls into any of the categories described in the previous seven sections or not, and you need to pay any income taxes owed on it. Line 8 of **Form 1041** (or line 21 of **Form 1041**) is where you put those items that defy description, the ones that you can't possibly squeeze into any of the categories already listed. Although on **Form 1040,** popular "other income" items include fees and honoraria and jury duty pay, on **Form 1041,** the most common item will be taxable state income tax refunds. If the trust or estate is a party to a lawsuit (either its own, or as a successor to the decedent), place any taxable awards received here.

# Deducing Deductions

Although the rules governing deductions are generally the same whether you're filing a tax return for the decedent or for an estate or trust, some differences do apply. After all, how interesting would the world be if all rules were absolute? The following sections give you the lowdown on taking deductions on the two different tax forms.

***Note:*** For some inexplicable reason, itemized deductions for **Form 1041** are included on the front of the form; for **Form 1040,** you have to go to **Schedule A, Itemized Deductions.**

# Avoiding double-dipping on deductions

Chapter 17 tells you that many of the deductions available on the **Form 706** are the same as ones listed in this chapter, and you may be wondering if you can have it both ways, deducting them the first time on the **706** and then again on the **1041.** Well, you can't. In fact, the IRS refers to this practice as *double-dipping* and seriously frowns upon it.

So choose. When you have an estate that owes estate tax, compare the tax rates for the estate tax and the income tax (the estate tax is almost always higher) and take the deductions on the return that's paying a higher rate of tax. On the other hand, if you must file a **706** but won't owe any estate taxes (perhaps because of a surviving spouse and an unlimited marital deduction), deduct only things such as funeral expenses and debts of the decedent (which aren't deductible on the **1041**) on the **706.** Include all estate administration costs on the **1041.**

As with every rule, the double-dipping rules have a couple of exceptions. Real estate taxes that have been assessed but not paid as of the date of death are a valid debt of the decedent

on **Form 706,** but as the estate pays them, they also become an income tax deduction available to the estate. And medical expenses billed after death are a debt of the estate on the **706,** but you can include them on the decedent's final **Form 1040** as a medical deduction. Just to let the IRS know that you haven't double-dipped, you must attach a signed statement that any deductions taken on the estate's **Form 1041** haven't been taken on the estate's **Form 706.**

*Tip:* As the highest bracket for federal income tax (39.6 percent) and for estate tax (40%) are now essentially the same, if you have an estate that's subject to both income and estate tax, it may make sense to figure the estate's **Form 1041** and **Form 706** both with and without the deductions that could qualify for either return and then use the deductions on the tax return that gives the estate, and its beneficiaries, the best result. Don't forget to take state income and estate/inheritance tax into consideration when you play with these numbers; remember, you're trying to minimize the *total* taxes, not just the tax paid to either the federal or state government.

# *Interest*

Whether you're responsible for filing a **Form 1040** or a **Form 1041,** the following types of interest are deductible:

- ✔ Interest paid on a mortgage that's secured by real estate (including interest on home equity lines of credit)
- ✔ Interest that you pay for a stock margin account

Personal interest paid on such things as credit card debts, unsecured loans, or unpaid tax bills is never deductible.

But wait! This rule has an exception, too. If you elect to pay the estate tax under Section 6166 (that's an election to spread out the payment of the estate taxes owed over a ten-year period), you get to deduct that interest on **Form 1041,** even though it's interest on an unpaid tax bill. Why? Even though it's so-called *personal interest,* it's also an interest payment that arises only because you're dealing with an estate (or a *successor-in-interest trust,* which receives the assets of the estate after estate administration is complete). You can deduct expenses the estate or trust incurs for being an estate or trust; the fact that only an estate or trust can pay Section 6166 interest overrides the rule that personal interest is nondeductible.

## Taxes

Generally speaking, taxes in a trust or estate refer to real estate taxes and state and local income taxes. Although individuals also have the option of deducting state and local sales taxes rather than income taxes, that option doesn't exist in the estate/trust environment. We think the IRS has figured out that estates and trusts aren't out there buying consumer goods, but that's only a guess on our part.

Just as you get to do on **Schedule A,** you can deduct the actual amounts you paid as taxes during the estate or trust's tax year on line 11 of **Form 1041.** *Remember:* You get the deduction only for amounts you actually paid, so don't include estimated taxes you paid in the first month of the following tax year. However, pick up your fourth quarter estimated tax payment from the prior tax year if you paid it in the current year. Also, if you applied an overpayment from last year's return to this year's, pick up the overpayment not only as income (if you deducted it in the prior year) on line 8 of **Form 1041** but also as a deduction on line 11.

## Fiduciary fees

If you're doing all this work out of the goodness of your heart, you can skip right over line 12 of **Form 1041.** But if you've figured out that the amount of work involved in administering this trust or estate is so much that you really need to be paid, line 12 is where you deduct your fiduciary fees.

*Fiduciary fees* (the amounts executors, administrators, or trustees charge for their services) are generally fully deductible. But if some portion of the income for the estate or trust comes from municipal bonds or other tax-exempt vehicles (tax-exempt money market funds, for example), you're required to allocate fiduciary fees between taxable and tax-exempt income, and you get to deduct only the amount allocable to taxable income. To calculate the allocation, subtotal the income shown on lines 1 through 8 of **Form 1041** and add the tax-exempt income from line 1 in "Other Information" on the back of the return to arrive at total income. Divide the total income by the total taxable income and multiply the results by the total fiduciary fees. You take the deductible fees on line 12 and subtract the balance from the total tax-exempt income to arrive at the *adjusted tax-exempt income.* Place that number on **Schedule B,** line 2.

For estates, you probably want to base the executor's fee you charge on the number of hours you actually work on estate matters. Set a rate that you feel your time is worth, and keep careful track of your time. (See Chapter 9 for a further discussion of how to arrive at an executor's fee.) For trusts, if you're making the investment decisions, you may want to obtain a fee schedule from a trust company, which charges its trust clients a percentage of the market value of the assets it holds, plus a percentage of income collected, as its fee. Your fee shouldn't exceed that of a bank or trust company, and it probably will be less because your overhead is much less. If you're paying an outside advisor for investment advice, you'll most likely want to subtract his fee from the one the bank or trust company charges; after all, investment advice is already included in the fee he charges.

## *Charitable deductions*

The rule concerning charitable deductions is fairly straightforward. You can't give away money from an estate or trust to charity, no matter how good the cause, unless the decedent's will (or the trust instrument) tells you to. Because this rule is absolute, you don't often see charitable deductions on an estate or trust income tax return. You're not even allowed to take a deduction for the contents of the house or the decedent's clothes that you gave away to Goodwill unless the decedent directed you to do that under his or her will.

If the terms of the decedent's will direct that you give a percentage of the estate (or, for particularly generous decedents, the whole shebang) to charity, you calculate the charitable deduction on **Schedule A,** located on the back of **Form 1041.** Other times, charitable deductions can occur when the trust or estate owns a partnership or S corporation interest and that entity gave to charity. Because the decision to give wasn't yours, you may take the deduction.

Frequently, donors establish trusts with either whole or partial charitable interests and fund them either by gifts made before death or from their estates after death. These trusts may either be set up as private foundations, or as *charitable lead* (or *remainder*) *annuity trusts,* or *unitrusts.* In most cases, these trusts don't file a **Form 1041,** and the returns they do file (**Forms 5227** or **990-PF**) aren't for the faint of heart. If you're named as trustee for one of these types of trusts, get an attorney, accountant, or Enrolled Agent experienced with these returns who can assist you in tax preparation. Strangely enough, most tax professionals don't prepare these sorts of returns, so make sure that you find someone who has the expertise you need. Check out Chapter 3 for a description of each of these types of trusts.

## Attorney, accountant, and preparer fees

Although **Schedule A** of **Form 1040** limits deductibility for attorney, accountant, and return-preparer fees, **Form 1041** allows you to fully deduct these fees (which are miscellaneous itemized deductions limited to amounts more than 2 percent of adjusted gross income). If you have tax exempt income on question 1 of the "Other Information" section on the back of the **1041,** you have to split the fees between taxable and tax-exempt income, and are only allowed to deduct the portion attributable to the taxable income. For details on how to allocate between taxable and tax-exempt income, check out the earlier "Fiduciary fees" section. After you add your fees and allocate when necessary, place your deduction on line 14 of **Form 1041.**

## Miscellaneous itemized deductions

If you've run out of specific categories but still have some things you suspect you can deduct, lines 15a and 15b of **Form 1041** are where you need to be. Just like **Schedule A** of **Form 1040,** some of these miscellaneous itemized deductions (which include fees for investment advice, security fees that your broker may charge you, or safe deposit box fees) are subject to the so-called *2 percent haircut* (you can only deduct amounts that are greater than 2 percent of adjusted gross income); others aren't, such as the amount you spend on postage and making photocopies.

 The general rule is that expenses that are incurred only because this is an estate or trust are fully deductible, whereas fees that anyone in the position of looking after investments would pay are subject to the 2 percent exclusion. The following sections outline the miscellaneous itemized deductions you can make.

### Deductions not subject to the 2 percent floor

More likely than not, many of the miscellaneous itemized deductions are subject to the 2 percent floor. So which ones aren't? Because the estate isn't likely to have gambling losses (at least it better not have — otherwise, you may be in trouble with more people than just your corner bookie), impairment-related work expenses of a disabled person, or unrecovered investment in a pension, you may be wondering what, if anything, you can deduct on line 15a of **Form 1041.** The answer is simple.

Any expense the trust or estate has incurred only because of its trust or estate status is deductible here. So if you're dealing with a law firm that charges for every copy and stamp it uses on your behalf, the deduction for miscellaneous costs goes here. So do filing fees for the probate court, publication costs for the newspaper ads ordered by the probate court, and the premium for *surety bonds* (a type of insurance policy indicating that you don't intend to abscond with the funds).

### Deductions subject to the 2 percent floor

Line 15b of **Form 1041** is the place for all other miscellaneous deductions: investment advice, safe deposit box rentals, service charges on dividend reinvestment plans (DRIPs), and travel expenses. Payments to obtain duplicate stock certificates go here. So do costs to purchase your own supplies (stationery, stamps, and the like).

Unless the trust or estate didn't make any distributions to beneficiaries during the year, determining the 2 percent you have to exclude is a tricky, circular calculation. Because you can't find a computer tax-help program for **Form 1041** preparation, you probably want to hire a tax professional to assist you if you have lots of deductions subject to the 2 percent floor.

As a practical matter, if you have only minor deductions here and you feel otherwise equal to the task of preparing the **Form 1041,** leaving those deductions off may be easier. The tax benefit to the trust, estate, or income beneficiaries will be far less than the cost to have the return professionally prepared.

## The Income Distribution Deduction (Schedule B)

Unique to the world of trusts and estates is the concept of the Income Distribution Deduction **(Schedule B).** When trusts and estates pass out payments of income to beneficiaries (as opposed to payments of specific property called for under the will or the trust instrument), those payments carry income tax consequences for the trust or estate *and* for the beneficiaries. The trust or estate receives a deduction, and the beneficiaries must include the amount deducted from the **Form 1041** on their individual **Form 1040. Form 1041, Schedule B,** synthesizes all the info you've compiled to this point into the all-important *income distribution deduction*.

Although **Schedule B** may look intimidating, it's really not so bad. Just follow these steps (unless the trust or estate is in its final year):

1. **Take the total from line 17 on the front of** Form 1041 **(line 1).**

2. **Add that total to the adjusted tax-exempt interest, which is nothing more than total tax-exempt interest less fiduciary and other fees allocated to it (also known as the contents of line 2).**

3. **Enter the net capital gain (flip your tax return to its front, and place the number you see on line 4 onto** Schedule B, **line 6, on the back).**

4. **Subtract that number from your total of** Schedule B, **lines 1 and 2, to arrive at the distributable net income (DNI).**

   DNI is the total amount that could possibly be taxed to the beneficiary if the world were perfectly round and all the planets were aligned.

If you're preparing the return for an estate or simple trust, you can ignore **Schedule B,** line 8. If yours is a complex trust, though, and you're either not required to distribute all income or you distributed more than just income, you need to calculate *trust accounting income* (TAI). To calculate TAI, add lines 1 through 8 from the front of **Form 1041** and the tax-exempt income from line 1 of "Other Information" on the back of **Form 1041.** Subtract capital gains or losses (line 4, **Form 1041**) and all fees and expenses that you charged against the income earned in the trust. Exclude fees and expenses charged against principal (including whatever fees you paid from the capital gains) when calculating TAI, and don't allocate any of the income fees you paid between taxable and tax-exempt income.

On **Schedule B,** line 11, put down the total amount of distributions made from the estate or trust to beneficiaries during the tax year. These amounts may be mandatory, such as in the case of a simple trust, where all income must be distributed in the tax year that you're preparing the return for. In this case, one of three scenarios may apply:

- ✔ If you're required to distribute all, or any part, of the trust's income with no exceptions, place the amount you're required to pay to the beneficiary (even if you didn't actually pay it) on line 9.

- ✔ Any amounts of income you paid to the beneficiary at your discretion, but that weren't mandated by the trust instrument, belong on line 10.

- ✔ Add lines 9 and 10 and place the total on line 11.

On line 12, calculate what portion of that total distribution came from tax-exempt income. If you distributed 100 percent of the income, place the number you have on **Schedule B,** line 2. If you distributed less than 100 percent, calculate the percentage of income you did distribute and then multiply that percentage by the amount on **Schedule B,** line 2. Subtract line 12 from line 11 to arrive at line 13.

The income distribution deduction is an either/or calculation, and now that you've calculated *either* (line 13), you need to also arrive at *or* (line 14). This part is much easier — just subtract line 2 of **Schedule B** from line 7 and place your answer on line 14. Compare lines 13 and 14. The smaller of the two is the income distribution deduction. Place your answer on line 15 of **Schedule B** and then carry the result to line 18 on page 1 of **Form 1041.**

## The estate tax deduction

Very often, an estate has, as an asset, the right to receive items of income on which income tax has yet to be paid. If the estate is large enough to pay an estate tax, those income items (called *Income in Respect of Decedent* or IRD) are taxed twice — once on the transfer of property (estate tax) and again on the receipt of income (income tax). Of course, this double taxation on the part of Congress is grossly unfair and expensive and completely uncalled for. Congress, to its credit, has recognized this problem and instituted the estate tax deduction.

The types of IRD that most commonly trigger the estate tax deduction are pensions and IRAs, final wages, and the sale of property (either due to an ongoing installment sale or because the decedent dies after the purchase and sale agreement is signed, but prior to the actual property transfer).

If you're administering a large estate and have paid an estate tax, you may be entitled to a deduction on the estate or trust's income tax return (on **Form 1041,** line 19) for the portion of estate taxes paid on these IRD items. You determine this deduction by calculating the estate tax based on the value of the total estate, including IRD, and then calculating it a second time on the value without IRD. The difference in the two calculations is the amount of estate tax paid on that piece of income; this is the amount of your deduction. Chapter 16 walks you through the estate tax calculation. After you've done it twice (once with IRD, and once without), you'll be a pro at it.

## Taxes owed

No matter which tax return you're preparing (the decedent's personal return or one for an estate or trust), you have to calculate the tax after you figure out the income and the deductions. If you're working on the decedent's return, you arrive at your tax liability exactly the same way as you would your own. If you're finishing up a **Form 1041** and need to figure out **Schedule G** (on the back), read on. The following is a list of the different types of tax computations you may need to perform before you can put the finishing touches on the tax return you're preparing.

# Paying estimated taxes

The income tax system is a pay-as-you-go endeavor. That's why the government withholds income taxes from some people, and others make quarterly estimated payments. But you'll find exceptions in the world of trusts and estates:

✔ After someone dies, he is no longer responsible for making estimated tax payments on individual federal returns. If the decedent's final individual return is joint with his spouse, only pay estimated taxes on the spouse's income, not on the decedent's.

✔ Because of all the early confusion associated with a new estate (and because you can scarcely determine what the income will be in an estate that's just beginning), the federal government doesn't require you to file federal estimates for the first two years of an estate's existence. If you're dealing with a trust that's essentially operating as the estate, the same two-year exemption applies.

For all other trusts, the pay-as-you-go plan is in place. If you fail to make your estimated tax payments, you'll be charged a penalty for underpayment of estimated taxes. Although the sun still rises when this slip-up happens (and these things often fall through the cracks, especially at first), you never want to cough up extra dollars to the government when you don't have to.

Finally, keep in mind that these are federal rules; beware the state rules, which are often different. Check with the tax authority in the state where the estate or trust is resident to determine when that state begins to require estimated income tax payments.

## Ordinary tax computation

You can find tax rate tables for estates and trusts, which change every year, in the **Form 1041** instructions for that year, which you can locate at www.irs.gov under "Forms and Instructions."

One reason why many executors, administrators, and trustees choose to make distributions to beneficiaries is that the government taxes estates and trusts very heavily on ordinary income. For example, in 2013, ordinary income for estates and trusts of more than $11,950 is taxed at 39.6 percent (the top rate), while an individual's **Form 1040** would have to show $400,000 of ordinary taxable income before paying tax at the 39.6 percent rate in that same year. By making distributions, you pass that taxable income to the beneficiaries, who are, most likely, in a lower tax bracket, reducing the total amount of tax paid.

## Capital gains and qualified dividends computation

No matter whether you're filing a tax return for an individual, a trust, or an estate, capital gains and qualified dividends are taxed at special, fixed rates; you calculate these taxes on the worksheets attached to **Schedule D.** Even though the worksheet looks intimidating, all it does is strip out the various types of capital gains property and apply the correct tax rate to those gains.

If you have any entries on **Schedule D,** or if you have qualified dividends, taking a few minutes with this worksheet can save you big bucks because you pay far lower rates on most capital gains and qualified dividends than you do on other types of income. For example, a trust with $22,000 total taxable income, of which $12,000 is ordinary income and $10,000 is a long-term capital gain, would pay $7,070 in tax if there were no preferential capital gains tax rate, but will actually pay only $5,110 ($3,110 tax on ordinary income, and $2,000 tax on long-term capital gains), a $1,960 tax savings.

Whether you calculate your tax by using the worksheet on the back of **Schedule D** or the tax rate table, place the total tax on taxable income on line 1a of **Schedule G, Form 1041.**

### Tax on lump-sum distributions

Sometimes, through no fault of your own, the estate you're administering is saddled with the payout of the entire balance of an employer's qualified retirement account (see Chapter 7), which shoots the estate's income tax liability through the roof. If the decedent was born prior to January 2, 1936, his or her estate may be eligible to use ten-year averaging and/or 20 percent capital gains rules when calculating the taxes owed, which may result in substantially lower taxes than if you calculated the taxes in the ordinary way.

Prepare these special calculations on **Form 4972, Tax on Lump-Sum Distributions.** Instructions for this form are included with the form, which is available from www.irs.gov. Just look for it under "Forms and Instructions." After you finish **Form 4972,** you place the taxes on lump-sum distributions on line 1b of **Schedule G, Form 1041.**

### Alternative minimum tax

Since 1986, every trust and estate has been required to do the alternative minimum tax (AMT) calculation, even if the trust or estate isn't subject to the AMT. (The *AMT* is a flat tax designed to prevent certain high-income individuals, estates, and trusts from not paying any, or enough, income tax.) And, like the AMT calculations found on **Form 6251** for individuals, the fiduciary calculation is also a bear.

You can find the AMT schedule (all 4 parts and 75 lines) for trusts and estates on pages 3 and 4 of **Form 1041,** under **Schedule I.** Using the following list, which gives you the basics about each part, you should be able to prepare the AMT schedule by using a little patience. You can find the line-by-line directions in the **Form 1041** instructions, available at www.irs.gov under "Forms and Instructions."

### Part 1: Estate or Trust's Share of Alternative Minimum Taxable Income

1. **Take your adjusted total income from page 1, line 17, and add back any interest, taxes, or miscellaneous itemized deductions subject to the 2 percent** (Form 1041, **line 15a) you've previously deducted; subtract any income tax refunds included as income on line 8.**

   Among other frequent AMT add-back items are interest from private activity bonds, net operating losses, and AMT adjustments from other estates or trusts. Check the line-by-line instructions for a complete list.

2. **Add the beginning adjusted total income to your adjustments. Put the total on line 25, adjusted alternative minimum taxable income.**

3. **Subtract the income distribution deduction from** Schedule I, **Part II, line 44, and the estate tax deduction** (Form 1041, **line 19).**

   If your total comes to less than the exemption amount (which you find on line 29 of **Schedule I**), you're finished! This estate isn't subject to the AMT this year. If your total is more than the exemption, move on to Part II.

### Part II: Income Distribution Deduction on a Minimum Tax Basis

If you made distributions to income beneficiaries during the year, you need to complete this part, whether or not the trust or estate is subject to the AMT.

1. **Refer to the section "The Income Distribution Deduction (Schedule B)," earlier in this chapter, to review this calculation.**

2. **Redo the calculation, taking into consideration that your starting point is different and that you may have less tax-exempt interest, in which case your adjusted tax-exempt interest may be different.**

   Private activity bond interest is taxable for AMT purposes.

### Part III: Alternative Minimum Tax

Lines 45 through 56 are where you actually calculate the additional tax, if any, that the trust or estate has to pay due to the AMT. Go carefully through these lines; although the instructions for the calculation are clearly printed on **Schedule I** itself, you can easily make a mistake, especially if you're preparing the form manually.

### Part IV: Line 52 Computation Using Maximum Capital Gains Rates

Lines 57 through 75 mirror the calculations you already made on the back of Schedule D so that capital gains continue to receive preferential tax treatment. Once again, the instructions are on the face of the return. Be careful not to mix up line numbers because this is one form you don't want to prepare twice.

If you're unfortunate enough to have a number on line 56 of **Schedule I,** the trust or estate owes this additional tax. Copy the amount on line 56 onto line 1c of **Schedule G, Form 1041.**

# Credits

After you put the sum of lines 1a through 1c on **Schedule G,** line d, you're ready to see whether you can reduce your tax with tax credits. *Tax credits* are dollar-for-dollar amounts that you subtract from your tax liability; they're much better than deductions. Estates and trusts aren't eligible for most of the tax credits individuals can take, and no credit on **Form 1041** can reduce the tax liability below zero.

However, on lines 2a through 2d of **Schedule G,** you have the opportunity to reduce the trust or estate's tax liability with the following credits:

- ✔ **Foreign tax credit:** You're entitled to take a credit for taxes you've paid to a foreign country with whom the United States has a tax treaty (which is almost everywhere, with a few exceptions such as Iraq, Iran, and North Korea). If the amount of foreign taxes paid is $300 or less, you can just fill in the amount actually paid on line 2a. However, if the amount is greater than $300, you have to become acquainted with **Form 1116, Foreign Tax Credit.** The IRS understands that this form is evil (which is why they allow you to skip it for relatively small amounts), and it estimates that it should take you about seven hours to complete. If you made income distributions to beneficiaries during the year, you should allocate the applicable portion of the foreign tax credit to the beneficiary as his or her percentage share of the total income.

    **Form 1116** has been known to bring even the most brilliant accountants to their knees. If you need to attach one of these forms to your return, especially if you have large amounts of qualified dividends or long-term capital gains, you may want to consult a professional here.

- ✔ **General business credits:** Enter the total of all the general business credits the trust or estate is entitled to on **Form 3800, General Business Credit,** on line 2c of **Schedule G.** If you made income distributions during the year, be careful not to include any credits on **Form 1041** that are allocable to the income beneficiary.

- ✔ **Credit for prior year minimum tax:** If the trust or estate paid AMT in a prior year, it may be eligible to reclaim some part of that tax on **Schedule G,** line 2d. Complete **Form 8801, Credit for Prior Year Minimum Tax – Individuals, Estates and Trusts** to see whether this return qualifies.

- ✔ **Credit to holders of tax credit bonds:** Certain types of loans for items such as clean, renewable energy; Midwestern tax credits; forestry conservation bonds; energy conservation bonds; school construction bonds; and the always-popular Build America Bond allow the taxpayer to take a credit instead of receiving all, or a portion, of the interest that would be earned on that loan. Not all bonds qualify, but your broker will know and should label these securities as such. You should receive **Form 1099-BTC, Bond Tax Credit,** reporting these credits to you. Complete **Form 8912, Credit to Holders of Tax Credit Bonds,** and enter the amount on line 12 on **Form 1041, Schedule G,** line 2d.

## Additional taxes

Even if you manage to reduce the estate, trust, or decedent's income tax liability to zero with a combination of deductions and credits, you may still have taxes to pay. Lines 5 and 6 of **Schedule G, Form 1041,** are where you find these additional taxes. They're not really income taxes, but they're here on an income tax form for lack of any better place to put them.

- ✔ **Recapture taxes:** Sometimes you receive a credit in a prior year, and then in the current year, you find you're no longer eligible for it. For example, say you received a small business credit last year, and then discovered this year that the payments you made to qualify for that tax were later refunded. Welcome to the world of *recapture taxes,* which recapture tax benefits that the IRS doesn't want to let slip away. Complete **Form 4255, Recapture of Investment Credit** or **Form 8611, Recapture of Low-Income Housing Credit,** and then fill in the total on line 5, **Schedule G.**

  Recapture taxes are a fairly technical area. If you suspect you may be subject to them, you may want to check in with a qualified tax advisor for assistance.

- ✔ **Household employee taxes:** When a trust pays for household help for a beneficiary, or an estate pays the final wages of the decedent's household help, you may have to complete and file **Schedule H (Form 1040), Household Employment Taxes.** Put the total household taxes calculated on **Form 1041, Schedule G,** line 6.

# Answering the Questions on the Back of Page 2 (Form 1041)

If you're preparing **Form 1041,** you're almost done. All that's left is to answer some questions at the bottom of page 2. Some of these questions are easy and obvious, but questions 3 and 4 concerning foreign accounts and trusts are more complex; you may want to ask for professional advice if you think the decedent, the estate, or the trust qualifies.

- ✔ Place the total tax-exempt income we talk about in the "Interest" section on the line underneath **Question 1,** and make sure that you check the "Yes" box.

- ✔ When the trust or estate reports earnings of any type that were earned by an individual, check the "Yes" box for **Question 2.**

- ✔ **Question 3** wants to know about cash and securities held in foreign accounts. Refer to the list of assets you compiled in Chapter 7 and see whether this estate or trust has any foreign accounts. If your trust or estate falls into this category, check the "Yes" box and enter the name of the foreign country below question 3. If you answer "yes" and the combined total of all foreign accounts is greater than $10,000, you may have to file **Form TD F 90-22.1, Report of Foreign Bank and Financial Accounts**. You can find this form online at www.irs.gov/pub/irs-pdf/f90221. pdf. If the trust or estate has no foreign accounts but owns foreign securities in a U.S.-based account, the answer to this question is "no."

✔ Along the same lines, **Question 4** needs to know about distributions from foreign sources, or whether or not your estate or trust funded a foreign trust. Be careful here — you may have to also complete and file **Form 3520, Annual Return to Report Transactions with Foreign Trusts and Receipt of Certain Foreign Gifts.**

✔ **Question 5** asks whether the estate or trust is the holder of a residential mortgage and receives interest payments on that loan. Look back over your list of assets and make sure that there's no promissory note or mortgage still generating payments buried at the bottom of the list.

✔ If the trust or the estate elects, it may choose to pay the beneficiaries' income earned in the tax year in question as late as 65 days into the next tax year. If you want to make this election, perhaps because you don't know until after December 31 how much income you should pass out to the beneficiaries, check the box next to **Question 6.**

✔ If you're distributing property in kind (you actually passed the shares of stock out to the beneficiary, instead of selling them and giving him or her a check), you can elect to recognize the gain on that transaction at the trust or estate level. When you include this transaction on **Schedule D** to report the gain, and pay the tax, the beneficiary then receives the property with the higher, date-of-distribution basis. Check the box next to **Question 7** to make this election (under Code Section 643(e)(3)).

✔ **Question 8** assumes that most estates run their course within the first two years of the decedent's date of death. If the estate you're administering stretches out longer than that, the IRS wants a brief explanation. Check the box and attach a brief statement.

✔ **Question 9** is looking for information about skip beneficiaries so that the IRS can attempt to collect even more tax under the generation-skipping transfer tax rules. Generally, a *skip beneficiary* is someone who's more than one generation below that of the transferor of the property. So, grandchildren may be skip beneficiaries of their grandparents' estates. In the case of unrelated parties, a skip beneficiary is anyone who's more than 37½ years younger than the transferor.

# Chapter 19

# Weighing Income Tax Implications

## In This Chapter

▶ Planning for taxes before, and after, death

▶ Equalizing taxable income between the decedent, the estate (or trust), and the beneficiaries

▶ Getting acquainted with the Unearned Income Medicare Contribution tax

*H*ow simple would life be if there were one set of hard-and-fast rules about how to split the income among the decedent, the estate (or trust), and the income beneficiaries? Unfortunately, no such set of rules exists. There is, however, a whole subspecialty called *post-mortem tax planning,* which is merely a way to legally allocate all items of income and expense to the taxpayer who can most effectively use it, whether by keeping everyone's marginal tax brackets lower or by making sure that all deductions are usable against taxable income. All it takes is a little advance planning.

In this chapter, we show you how to keep the income taxes owed by the decedent, the estate, and/or the trust to the bare minimum. After all, no one should pay more than they're legally obligated to pay while they're alive, and that's even truer after death. And there's nothing worse than the realization that, with a little planning, you could have turned a large tax bill for the estate into a minimal or even nonexistent one.

 Estates allow the greatest scope for post-mortem tax planning because they're short-lived and the amounts coming in and going out are often large and one-time only. But you can also apply this sort of planning to minimize the income tax consequences to trusts and their beneficiaries on a more limited scale. Just bear in mind that there's no one-size-fits-all solution; what suits your estate, trust, and/or beneficiaries will be a combination of some, but probably not all, of the techniques we present in this chapter.

# Timing Payments In and Out of an Estate

After death, the rules governing receipt of income in an estate and the payment of its expenses loosen up somewhat. It's not as though the electric company can threaten the decedent with shutting off the power. Because the standard sanction of "you don't pay, we don't provide" doesn't carry any weight with an estate, you have an opportunity to place at least some of your income, deductions, and expenses in years, and on tax returns, where they'll save the greatest amount of income tax across all affected returns (namely the decedent's final **1040,** the estate's income tax return, and the beneficiary's individual return).

You can use the strategies we provide in the following sections by themselves or in any combination to minimize the total income tax bill generated by the estate or trust.

## Benefitting from the estate's fiscal year

In general, taxpayers must use a calendar year as their tax year, with a few exceptions. The biggest of these exceptions exists for estates, which may choose any tax year-end so long as the estate's first tax year is no longer than 12 months.

If you choose a fiscal year-end that isn't December 31, the information on any **K-1** that results from that tax return isn't picked up and reported by the recipient until the end of the recipient's tax year. So, if your decedent dies in February of one year, you can opt to end the estate's tax year in any month from the end of February (just days after the decedent's death) all the way through to January of the following year.

If you suspect that the estate will take more than 1 tax year to complete, or if you think that the income from the estate would be better split between 2 years, you may choose to have a short first year (less than 11+ months), make sure that you receive only as much in income as you plan to pay out in deductible expenses, and have that first tax return show little or no income being taxed. On the other hand, if there's nothing much at all to the estate and you just want to prepare one income tax return for it, do your best to make sure that all items of income have been received and all the deductible expenses have been paid in that one year.

Here's an interesting tidbit: If you chose a fiscal year for the return and taxable income is being passed out to the estate beneficiaries, that income won't be reportable by the beneficiaries until the calendar year that coincides with the estate's fiscal year-end. So, in the example of a decedent who dies in February, 2013, if you elect the estate's first year-end to be January, 2014, income that's earned in February and March of 2013 isn't reported to the beneficiaries until 2014, and they won't have to declare it on their income tax returns until their 2014 returns are due on April 15, 2015. In other words, the estate has received money, but no taxes will be paid by anyone until more than two years later.

## Balancing the estate's taxable income against the beneficiary's

Inevitably, money will leave an estate and move down to the beneficiary. The only question is when that move occurs. An estate, by definition, is a short-lived entity, existing only to effect the transfer of property from the decedent to his or her heirs. The timing of those property transfers can carry significant tax benefits for both the estate and the beneficiary.

Both the estate and the beneficiary are taxed at the lowest rates on the first dollars of income they receive. As they pay on more dollars of income, the rate of tax gradually increases, finally arriving at the top marginal bracket, which is 39.6 percent in 2013.

But, unlike an individual, who has merely one opportunity to go through the brackets from low to high (known as the *bracket run*), when you're administering an estate, you have not only the estate's bracket run but also the beneficiary's. Although an estate's tax brackets escalate much more quickly than an individual's (you hit the top rate of 39.6 percent at a measly $11,950 of income in 2013, adjusted annually for inflation), take advantage of that bracket run if you can. If there's taxable income in the estate, make sure that you pay some of it out to the beneficiary before the end of the estate's tax year-end, if at all possible. This way the beneficiary will pay any income taxes due on the money he or she receives, and the estate will only pay taxes on the income that's left in the estate.

Make sure that you check with the estate's beneficiaries before you make distributions out to them; they won't thank you if they're pushed into a higher tax bracket because of it. Work *with* them to determine when would be the most advantageous tax year for them to receive this income; then make that date your target date for distribution.

## Timing the receipt of income

There may be absolutely no way in the world for you to hold off receiving money that represents income to the estate. For example, that last paycheck will be paid on schedule, and the life insurance proceeds, which include some taxable interest, may show up when you least expect them. But you can arrange for certain types of income to arrive in an advantageous tax year.

# Dividing income and deductions between the decedent and the estate

Just because an employer, bank, brokerage firm, or other payer continues making payments to the decedent doesn't necessarily mean that's whose tax return they should go. As the administrator of the estate, you make the final determination of where these items rightfully belong — and you have the responsibility of reporting them correctly.

Because most taxpayers are cash basis (you report only items that you've actually received or paid out, not items that you owe or that others owe to you), you should be able to determine pretty easily which tax return an item belongs on. If a check is dated after the date of death, it belongs to the estate, even if it's payable to the decedent; checks dated through the date of death belong to the decedent, even if they weren't yet cashed. The same is true for amounts owed by the decedent. If the decedent wrote and mailed the check, he or she gets the deduction; if you pay the bill after death, the deduction belongs to the estate, even if you paid the check from the decedent's checking account (which is a major no-no, as we explain in Chapter 8).

As with any rules, exceptions exist. Property owned jointly with rights of survivorship (a form of joint ownership in which title passes automatically to the surviving joint owner(s)), and property owned as tenants by the entireties (ownership available only to spouses in which title passes automatically to the surviving spouse upon the first spouse's death) transfer at the time of death to the surviving owner(s). So income received after death belongs 100 percent to the surviving joint owner(s) or surviving tenant by the entirety. Likewise, mortgage payments owed on property held jointly with rights of survivorship and as tenants by the entireties become the sole liability of the survivor(s). If property is owned jointly as tenants in common, the scenario changes. At death, the deceased joint owner's heirs become additional joint owners of the property and now automatically receive the decedent's share of the income together with the decedent's share of any debts owed on that property.

The estate often receives income for months — sometimes years — after the decedent's death, with checks still payable to the decedent personally. Don't hesitate to deposit these checks into the estate's accounts — that's where they belong, after all. You have to notify the IRS, however, that the estate is going to declare this income. You can do this by completing a nominee **Form 1099** and filing it with the IRS. Just show the decedent (with his or her Social Security number) as the Payer, and the estate (with its TIN) as the Recipient. (To obtain a **1099**, just call the IRS at 800-829-3676.) If you failed to file nominee **1099**s, you can still let the IRS know where the income you're reporting was originally reported to them. Merely place a notation on the estate's tax return showing that the estate received the income in the name and Social Security number of the decedent.

Finally, although most itemized deductions are equally deductible on a **Form 1040** or **Form 1041**, you may deduct medical expenses only on **Form 1040**, not on **Form 1041**. If, in the course of administering the estate, you pay final medical bills for the decedent, you don't need to lose those deductions. The IRS allows even cash-basis taxpayers to deduct medical expenses paid within a year after death on the decedent's final **Form 1040**.

For example, if a retirement account must be paid out, and you know approximately the amount that will be coming to the estate, make some calculations to see whether the receipt of that income makes sense in a short first year for the estate or whether it can better be used to pay ongoing estate expenses in the full tax year after that initial short year. Because you actually have to request that the money be paid out to the estate, you can decide to receive that income when it has the least effect on your taxable bottom line. It may even be possible to split the income between two or more years, requesting partial distributions in succeeding years.

## Paying the ongoing expenses of the estate

Just like timing income receipts, often you can also time when you pay the estate's expenses. Obviously, some expenses are paid only once, such as filing fees for probate, funeral expenses, and even final medical bills (which you can only take on the decedent's final **Form 1040**). Then there are the expenses that arise month after month, such as the costs of keeping the decedent's home heated and the lawn mowed. These are necessary expenses of the estate insofar as they're required to keep a major asset in saleable condition and are therefore deductible on the estate tax return. But keep your eye on those quarterly and/or annual fees, such as accounting fees and trustee fees, which can be slightly anticipated or delayed in order to coincide with the receipt of large chunks of income into the estate, reducing the estate's taxable income to little or nothing.

If you aren't using the estate's deductions on its **Form 706,** and those payments will be deductible on **Form 1041,** make sure that you have taxable income in the estate before you decide to pay your executor's fee or your accounting professional's fee. It's a terrible shame to pay a large income tax in the estate's first year only because you didn't pay the larger administration bills until the following tax year. The only one who ends up smiling in that situation is the IRS, unless of course you like knowing you've done your little bit to reduce the federal deficit.

# Investing to Minimize Income Taxes

Not all investments are created equal, and certainly not in their treatment by Congress and the Internal Revenue Code (IRC). There are many types of investments, such as wages, rental income, deferred retirement income, royalties, interest, and short-term capital gains that are taxed at the highest applicable rate of the taxpayer (in 2013, that could be as high as 39.6 percent). And then there are other types of income, including qualified dividends and long-term capital gains that may only be taxed at 0, 15, and 20 percent. Still other sorts of income, namely tax-exempt interest, remain untaxable in the hands of the estate or trust and the beneficiary.

If you're dealing with an estate or trust that has substantial assets, you may want to consider crafting an investment portfolio for it that takes into consideration not only the tax consequences of these investments to the estate or trust but also to the beneficiaries. For example, if your beneficiary will be paying his or her living expenses from the distributions from the estate or trust, you want to be certain to invest in income-producing stocks and bonds. On the other hand, if a different beneficiary is already in a high tax bracket because of income from other sources, the trust or estate may want to invest in tax-exempt bonds or low-dividend paying stocks. Your beneficiary doesn't need more income to add to his or her return, and the trust or estate only requires enough to pay the ongoing administration expenses without dipping into the assets.

Be aware and careful of state tax consequences. State tax laws don't always align with federal tax laws, and the results can be startling for you, as executor or trustee, and for your beneficiary. The best result is one that works for everyone's federal and state returns, so take your state laws into consideration when making investment decisions.

---

## Determining where to pay state income taxes

Although this book is primarily concerned with federal tax issues, we wouldn't be doing our job if we didn't alert you to the fact that there are state-specific rules regarding where you pay income tax on the income in an estate or trust. The obvious one is that you file, and pay taxes, in the state where the estate or trust is resident, meaning that

✔ The decedent was a resident of that state when he or she died, or the grantor was resident of that state when he or she funded the trust.

✔ In some states, the fiduciary must also be a resident of the same state.

Of course, depending on the rules in place in the state of administration, sometimes a trust doesn't reside anywhere, and no state returns are required. In this case, there will be no state taxes on income that accumulates in the trust and on the capital gains.

In other instances, you may have an estate or trust that must file tax returns in multiple states because it owns a business or real estate interest in a state other than its state of residence. For example, a trust that's resident in Massachusetts may own New York real estate and have to file a New York income tax return showing only the New York sourced income, that is, the rental income. All the income (including the rental income from New York) will be included on the Massachusetts return, but Massachusetts will give a credit for any state taxes paid to New York.

And, if you have a resident trust or estate, but non-resident beneficiaries to whom you've made distributions, they pay income taxes in their state of residence, not in the trust or estate's state. Are you having fun yet?

The moral of the story is that if you're going to have a state income tax obligation for your estate or trust, estimated tax rules will apply. These are typically similar to federal estimated tax rules, but the penalty thresholds are usually lower.

## Limiting the fiduciary's income taxes

Every new year begins with a little uncertainty as to what the year will bring financially. You could lose a job, obtain a higher-paying job, or even win the lottery. Fortunately, the financial future of estates and trusts is more predictable because the pool of assets in an estate or trust is usually known, which means fewer variables are at play. Of course, there will always be outliers, like a stock market that either rises high or falls precipitously, or a retirement account that's discovered hiding behind the sofa cushions. But for the most part, after you marshal the assets, you should have a pretty good idea of what you have to work with.

From there, it's a reasonably easy matter to decide how to invest it. If you know that distributions equaling at least the total taxable income will be made to the beneficiaries, the only income you have to be concerned with paying tax on is capital gains, which are taxed at lower rates than ordinary income. If you know that you're accumulating the income and making no distributions, you may want to look at ways to invest that will produce less current income.

A trust or estate hits the highest tax bracket at a very low level of income ($11,950 in 2013, adjusted annually for inflation). After it reaches that mark, every dollar earned above that mark (other than capital gains, tax-exempt income, and qualified dividends) gets taxed at the highest rate.

Then again, you may not have much of a choice about how you invest the estate or trust's income. Many trusts and estates hold ownership interest in closely held businesses or real estate that have been in the family for years and which can't be easily sold. In these cases, your opportunities for planning rest solely on any other assets held in the trust or estate, which may be invested so as to produce little or no additional income.

## Protecting the beneficiary

The two of us can't begin to think of all the times one of us has prepared a beneficiary's income tax return, only to have that person wail, "How could I possibly owe that much money?" The answer is usually only too easy to see: He or she received a distribution from a trust or estate and failed to take into consideration that taxes might be owed on that distribution.

The fact is that trusts and estates often don't make distributions regularly, but rather shift large sums infrequently to the beneficiaries. The beneficiary, who may be working a regular job, is used to having taxes withheld at work and has always received an annual tax refund. But along comes the money from the estate or trust and the income that it carries out on the estate's or trust's **Schedule K-1** (see Chapter 20), and not only is there now a large additional amount of taxable income, but that income has pushed the beneficiary into a higher tax bracket. Instead of receiving a refund, the beneficiary now has a large tax bill and no cash because the distribution he or she received is long gone, spent on a new car, a home, or to pay off credit card bills.

Be sure to plan ahead with your beneficiary to make clear that any distributions made to him or her may be partially taxable and that he or she will be responsible for the tax. It's often helpful for you to prepare a quick calculation to see how large an amount of income the beneficiary will have to declare, and then let the beneficiary know. Sometimes, it's possible for you, as executor, trustee, or administrator, to pay estimated taxes on behalf of the beneficiary; that way, the worst of the taxes should be paid before the beneficiary's tax return is ever prepared, and any balance due will be small.

But, even if you can't, or don't, pay the estimated taxes on the beneficiary's behalf, there are investment strategies you can use to lessen the tax impact. If your beneficiary is a resident of one state and you're investing in tax-exempt bonds, make sure that they're the obligations of that state and no other. Doing so makes the income tax exempt, both for federal and state purposes, to the beneficiary. Or if you're at a point of terminating an estate or trust and passing the actual assets out to the beneficiary, you can elect to pay the capital gains tax at the fiduciary level; the property then passes to the beneficiary or remainderman with the new and improved, taxes already paid, basis. Check out Chapter 18 to see how to make this election.

# Introducing the Unearned Income Medicare Contribution (UIMC) Tax

Clearly we don't have enough taxes already, because Congress has just added one more. Effective January 1, 2013, there is an additional 3.8 percent tax on investment income in estates and trusts, thanks to provisions in the Health Care and Education Reconciliation Act of 2010. Now, to be honest, it's not an additional tax on every dollar, but only on the lesser of undistributed net investment income or any amount of adjusted gross income in excess of the highest tax bracket in any year.

What sorts of investment income are included? Here's a list:

- ✔ Annuities
- ✔ Capital gains (including the taxable portion of the gain on the sale of a personal residence)
- ✔ Dividends
- ✔ Interest

> ✔ Passive activity income from partnerships and Subchapter S corporations
>
> ✔ Rents and royalties

You may have noticed that excluded from the list are tax-exempt interest, wages, and distributions from qualified pension, profit-sharing, and stock bonus plans — although you may still be tagged with this tax (or a portion of it) if the trust or estate's overall income is too high.

In addition, it's important to note that the tax is on *net investment income,* not *gross investment income.* As a result, you'll be able to allocate portions of all your deductible expenses against the total income, and only pay the tax on the portion that remains that's over the limit.

All irrevocable trusts that are required to file **Form 1041** are subject to this new tax (check out Chapter 3 to see if your trust applies). However, the following trusts are apparently excluded:

> ✔ Grantor trusts (all income is reported by the grantor on his/her individual income tax return)
>
> ✔ Charitable foundations
>
> ✔ Charitable remainder trusts

The proposed rules surrounding how investment versus non-investment income will be treated in Electing Small Business Trusts (ESBTs) are quite complex. If you're the trustee of an ESBT, you really should check with a competent tax advisor for assistance in this calculation.

As of this writing, the law is in place, but there are no draft forms, no final regulations, and the proposed regulations point to rather large gray areas, especially with regard to estates and trusts. Although it's clear that this surtax will be added, we may not know for a while all the mechanics of how it will be imposed.

The following sections break down what's currently known about calculating the tax and how to lessen the tax's impact on a trust or estate's income taxes.

## Calculating the tax

The UIMC tax was only ever intended to apply to high-income individuals, but the basic inequity in the size of the tax brackets for trusts and estates versus individuals has created an unfriendly environment for estates and trusts, one where only quite small entities will be exempt from paying it. It's clear, though, that the tax will be imposed as an additional tax, after all other income taxes at whatever rates (ordinary income, capital gain/qualified dividend, or even alternative minimum) are levied.

## Lessening the tax's impact

The UIMC tax is only imposed on taxable income in the trust or the estate over certain limits; if the income doesn't reach those limits, there's no additional tax. So, your job as executor, administrator, or trustee will be to try to reduce the taxable income in the trust, while still behaving in a responsible way. You could, for example,

- ✔ **Keep track of your capital gains and plan to offset gains with some losses, if necessary.** As executor or trustee, you should be aware of the aggregate size of the trust or estate's capital gains for the year before the end of the year. If your gains are large but you own something that's a less-than-sterling performer, then if you sell it before the end of the tax year, the loss from that sale will reduce the total gains year-to-date.

- ✔ **Invest in tax-exempt bonds and funds.** Remember, tax-exempt income isn't included in the threshold calculation, so it isn't subject to the tax.

- ✔ **Increase distributions to beneficiaries, but only if the trust instrument allows, and the distribution otherwise makes sense.** You still have to follow the terms of the trust instrument and pay attention to the intentions of the settlor. But if you manage to pass out income to beneficiaries, that income will be included in their threshold calculation for this additional tax, not the trust or estate's. And the threshold for individuals is much, much higher than for a trust.

- ✔ **Plan deductions to fall into years when income is higher and pay fewer deductible expenses in years the trust doesn't perform as well or when more is distributed to the beneficiary.** That's assuming you can predict these things, which you may not be able to precisely. But if you normally pay a trustee fee in January, and your income for the prior year is high enough to trigger this tax, you may want to take the January fee in December of the prior year.

There is no perfect solution here because the techniques that might enable the trust or estate to pay taxes at a lower rate may not be consistent with either the intent of the donor or what's in the best interest of the beneficiary. It's up to you to weigh all these possibilities and arrive at the most equitable solution. Whatever you do, be sure to jot down your reasoning and put it in the file. That way, should anyone ever question your decision, you'll be able to remind yourself why; and next year, when faced with the same questions and the same dilemmas, you'll be able to see what you did in the past and judge for yourself how well it worked.

# Chapter 20

# Reporting Tax Info on Schedule K-1

## In This Chapter

▶ Exploring Form 1041, Schedule K-1

▶ Assigning types of income to Schedule K-1

▶ Adding additional information to help estate and trust beneficiaries

▶ Figuring out nominee **Form 1099**

*L*ooking for hard-and-fast rules for almost anything is human nature. You stop at red lights and go when they turn green, but yellow lights seem to confuse people. Figuring out who gets to pay the income tax on income earned in a trust or estate is something like a yellow light: Sometimes the trust or estate pays it, and other times the beneficiary does.

In this chapter, we focus on **Schedule K-1, Beneficiary's Share of Income, Deductions, Credits, etc.** You see what's included on it and what's not. You also discover the formula necessary to calculate each of the numbers. Finally, you find out how to report income to a beneficiary when you don't have to file **Form 1041.**

## Understanding Schedule K-1

A trust or estate that makes distributions to beneficiaries receives an income tax deduction for the exact amount of taxable income that's been distributed (and income always comes out of the trust or estate first, before the first penny of principal is distributed). This is the so-called *income distribution deduction,* or *IDD,* which is calculated on **Form 1041, Schedule B,** on page 2 of **Form 1041** (see Chapter 18). Although the IDD as determined by **Schedule B** is a lump-sum calculation, it may comprise many pieces: dividends, interest, capital gains, rents, state income tax refunds. In fact, a trust or estate may be passing out pieces of any number of types of income. And when trusts and estates pass out income, that income *retains its character.*

So dividends earned by a trust and then paid to a beneficiary remain taxable as dividends, capital gains stay capital gains, tax-exempt income remains tax-exempt income, and so on. Thus, for example, interest and dividends originally earned by the ABC Trust appear on the beneficiary's **Form 1040** on **Schedule B,** rental income lands on **Schedule E,** and the foreign income earned and taxes paid by the trust but allocated to the beneficiary land on **Form 1116, Foreign Tax Credit.**

Because the income (and deductions, if any) received by the beneficiaries retains its character, you have to tell the beneficiaries what that character consists of. Do this by completing **Schedule K-1 (Form 1041).** The **Schedule K-1** gives the beneficiary the specific allocation between all items of income (and sometimes deductions and credits, too), allowing easy transfer of the information from the **K-1** to the beneficiary's **Form 1040.**

Your job is relatively simple when you're dealing with only one income beneficiary who receives all the income. The total amount of the IDD (**Form 1041, Schedule B,** line 15) is shown on a single **Schedule K-1,** with allocations made only between the different types of income. When there are multiple beneficiaries, though, you're required to prepare a separate **K-1** for each, with the total IDD divided among the beneficiaries on their **K-1**s in the same proportion as the distributions were made. So if the calculated IDD is $10,000, and one beneficiary received half of the total distributed, his or her **Schedule K-1** will show a total of $5,000 of income. The following sections walk you through the **Schedule K-1.**

## General information

If you want, you can compare **Schedule K-1 (Form 1041)** to a giant, combined **Form 1099** and **Form 1098.** And, like **Forms 1099** and **1098,** it contains much of the same identifying information. **Schedule K-1** allows your beneficiary to separate his or her income distribution into all the sorts of income received by the trust or estate; Figure 20-1 shows how much you can cram onto it.

**Schedule K-1 (Form 1041)** is an attachment to **Form 1041,** and you must distribute a copy of it to the income beneficiaries no later than the due date for **Form 1041,** as extended. Don't delay in sending these out. Remember, the beneficiaries can't prepare their **1040**s until they receive their **K-1**s from you.

661112

☐ Final K-1 ☐ Amended K-1 OMB No. 1545-0092

**Schedule K-1 (Form 1041)** **2012**
Department of the Treasury
Internal Revenue Service

For calendar year 2012, or tax year beginning ________, 2012, and ending ________, 20 ____

**Beneficiary's Share of Income, Deductions, Credits, etc.** ▶ See back of form and instructions.

**Part I Information About the Estate or Trust**

A Estate's or trust's employer identification number

B Estate's or trust's name

C Fiduciary's name, address, city, state, and ZIP code

D ☐ Check if Form 1041-T was filed and enter the date it was filed ________

E ☐ Check if this is the final Form 1041 for the estate or trust

**Part II Information About the Beneficiary**

F Beneficiary's identifying number

G Beneficiary's name, address, city, state, and ZIP code

H ☐ Domestic beneficiary ☐ Foreign beneficiary

**Part III Beneficiary's Share of Current Year Income, Deductions, Credits, and Other Items**

| | | | |
|---|---|---|---|
| 1 | Interest income | 11 | Final year deductions |
| 2a | Ordinary dividends | | |
| 2b | Qualified dividends | | |
| 3 | Net short-term capital gain | | |
| 4a | Net long-term capital gain | | |
| 4b | 28% rate gain | 12 | Alternative minimum tax adjustment |
| 4c | Unrecaptured section 1250 gain | | |
| 5 | Other portfolio and nonbusiness income | | |
| 6 | Ordinary business income | | |
| 7 | Net rental real estate income | 13 | Credits and credit recapture |
| 8 | Other rental income | | |
| 9 | Directly apportioned deductions | | |
| | | 14 | Other information |
| 10 | Estate tax deduction | | |

*See attached statement for additional information.

**Note.** A statement must be attached showing the beneficiary's share of income and directly apportioned deductions from each business, rental real estate, and other rental activity.

For IRS Use Only

**For Paperwork Reduction Act Notice, see the Instructions for Form 1041.** IRS.gov/form1041 Cat. No. 11380D **Schedule K-1 (Form 1041) 2012**

**Figure 20-1:** Schedule K-1.

## *Part 1: Information about the estate or trust*

In Part I, fill out the tax identification number (*TIN*), the name of the estate or trust, and the *fiduciary's* (trustee's or executor's) name and address. In Part I, you also have the opportunity to check a box to indicate whether and when you filed **Form 1041-T, Allocation of Estimated Tax Payments to Beneficiaries (Under Code Section 643(g))**.

By checking Part I, Box D of **Schedule K-1,** you tell the beneficiary that he or she now has credit for additional tax payments, even though the trustee originally paid them on behalf of the trust.

Code Section 643(g) is the section of the Internal Revenue Code that allows you to assign estimated taxes paid by the trust or estate to individual beneficiaries in the final year of the trust or estate. For example, Trust XYZ pays estimated taxes of $1,000 during the year, only to find out toward the end of the year that the trust is terminating at the end of the year. Because the trust never owes any tax in its final year, it doesn't need the estimated tax payments. Rather than have the IRS refund the $1,000 to the now-defunct trust after it files its final 1041, the trustee may elect to assign that estimated tax to the trust's beneficiaries by filing **Form 1041-T.**

In theory, **Form 1041-T** is a practical solution to reducing or eliminating underpayment penalties for beneficiaries who had no way to plan for the additional income they're receiving from the trust. In practice, it's not so straightforward. The IRS doesn't see too many **Form 1041-Ts** in the course of a year, and isn't quite sure what it's supposed to do with them when it does. It often applies the tax allocations incorrectly, if at all, leaving you to sort out a mess you didn't make. Use your judgment before filing **Form 1041-T;** if the amounts involved are small, it may not be worth your while.

**Form 1041-T** may only be filed in the final year of the trust or estate, is irrevocable, and must be made on or before the 65th day of the year following the end of the trust or estate's tax year (for calendar year filers, that's March 6, or March 5 during leap years). So, if you made a Code Section 643(g) election and allocated the estimated taxes, you have to check Box E to indicate that it's the final year of the trust or estate.

## Part II: Information about the beneficiary

**Schedule K-1,** Part II is about as simple as it gets. On line F, put in the beneficiary's TIN, and on line G, fill in the beneficiary's name and address.

In box H, choose between a domestic or foreign beneficiary, whichever applies. If the beneficiary lives in the United States (and that includes *resident aliens* who have legally established residence in the United States), no further information is necessary. If the beneficiary resides in a foreign country, you may want to consult with a competent tax advisor who can check the foreign tax treaties involved and make sure that you're not required to withhold U.S. income taxes on distributions to this beneficiary.

# Income items

The best **Schedule K-1** is the one that completely breaks down the information into its component parts. Don't assume that just because the trust or estate's tax returns don't require certain information, the beneficiaries don't either. As fiduciary, you want to make their lives as easy as possible.

Among the different types of income that may appear are

- ✔ **Interest:** Although the total taxable interest figure, including U.S. Treasury interest, belongs on line 1, show allocations of U.S. Treasury interest (included on line 1, but not taxable in any state) and tax-exempt interest (not included on line 1) separately on line 14.

- ✔ **Dividends:** Place the total of all dividends, from whatever source (including foreign) on line 2a. On line 2b, show the *qualified dividends* — those dividends subject to a lower income tax rate. If the trust or estate has income from foreign sources, include that allocation somewhere on **Schedule K-1**, either on line 14 or on a supplemental statement attached to the back of the form.

- ✔ **Capital gains:** As a general rule, trusts and estates pass out capital gain income to beneficiaries in the final year of the trust or estate only. In the final year, place *short-term* (from the sale of capital assets held one year or less) capital gains or losses on line 3, and long-term capital gains or losses on line 4a. If you sold any artwork, collectible items, precious metals, or precious metal certificates (your aunt's baseball cards, for example, or silver or gold certificates), place that amount on line 4b. Depreciation you add back under Code Section 1250 when you sell previously depreciated business property belongs on line 4c. Section 1250 gains can be tricky; if the **Form 1041** you're preparing has this type of income, have a professional help you calculate it.

- ✔ **Other portfolio and nonbusiness income:** What ends up on line 5 is typically the portion of a taxable state income tax refund.

- ✔ **Ordinary business income:** On line 6, place any business income that the trust or estate may have distributed to the beneficiary.

- ✔ **Net rental real estate income:** If the trust or estate owns any rental real estate, or owns interests in rental real estate partnerships, the rental income component of any beneficiary distribution belongs on line 7.

Most of the time, determining what types of income the trust or estate's received won't be difficult; however, on some occasions you may not be sure what you're supposed to do with a particular piece of income. Don't hesitate to contact a competent tax professional to advise you.

## Deductions and credits

In addition to allowing you to split each income distribution into all its component parts, **Schedule K-1** also gives the income beneficiary all the other tax attributes that can pass through the trust or estate to the beneficiary.

### Deductions

Except for in the last year of an estate or trust, a **Schedule K-1** rarely shows any deductions that the beneficiary can use on his or her tax return. *Deductions* are the payments the trust or estate makes that reduce its taxable income. Still, it can happen, so here are a few you may see:

- ✔ **Directly apportioned deductions:** If the trust or estate is passing out any of the following deductions, place these numbers on line 9:

  - **Depreciation:** Deducting a portion of an asset's acquisition cost annually over the period of its useful life.

  - **Depletion:** Deducting the reduction in value of an asset as that asset is used up.

  - **Amortization:** Reducing the cost of an intangible asset over its projected life.

  These calculations can be tricky, and you may want to seek a pro's help here.

- ✔ **Estate tax deduction:** If estate tax has already been paid on a portion of the income earned by the trust or estate, you're entitled to an income tax deduction equal to the estate taxes paid on that income. Place each beneficiary's share of an estate tax deduction on **Schedule K-1**, line 10.

  For example, say the Whipple Estate, which paid an estate tax at the top tax rate of 40 percent, included a retirement account on which no income taxes had ever been paid. Every year, it receives $10,000 from that retirement account that is subject to income tax. The estate tax on each distribution is $4,000 ($10,000 × 40 percent). Assuming that the eventual recipient of the annual distributions is also taxed in a high bracket, the potential income tax on each distribution could be an additional $3,960, making $7,960 in total tax, or 79.6 percent. However, the estate receives an estate tax deduction of $4,000, which may be passed out to an income beneficiary. Even if the beneficiary is in a high bracket, the amount of that distribution subject to income tax reduces to $6,000 ($10,000 distribution − $4,000 estate tax deduction). A 39.6-percent-bracket taxpayer then only pays $2,376 in income tax on that distribution, or $6,376 in total tax, reducing the tax rate to a nominal 63.76 percent. So as you can see, the estate tax deduction doesn't provide a huge benefit, but it's better than nothing.

✔ **Final-year deductions:** Often (and despite your best efforts), you wrap up an estate or trust in a flurry of activity accompanied by an avalanche of final fees without much in the way of income to offset them. If you have more fees (legal, accounting, state taxes, or anything else that's a legitimate income tax deduction for the trust or estate) than income in the final year of a trust or estate, you may give them to the beneficiaries on line 11 of **Schedule K-1.** Short- or long-term capital loss carryovers also belong here, as well as net operating loss carryovers, calculated both for regular tax computations and for the alternative minimum tax.

## Credits

*Credits,* those dollar-for-dollar offsets against tax that are so valuable to taxpayers, don't appear frequently on **Schedule K-1.** But that doesn't mean they're not available. The back of **Schedule K-1** has a list of credits a trust or estate may pass through to its income beneficiaries — you may marvel at the number, even as you wonder how a trust could ever generate an orphan drug credit. Here are the two most common:

✔ **Credit for estimated taxes:** In "Part I: Information about the estate or trust," we introduce you to **Form 1041-T,** and the election that a trust or estate may make to pass estimated taxes it's paid out to its income beneficiaries. If you made the election (you know because you already checked Part I, Box D), place this beneficiary's share of estimated taxes on line 13.

✔ **Credit for backup withholding:** A beneficiary sometimes gets into trouble with the IRS for failing to pay his or her taxes. If that happens, you'll receive a letter from the IRS instructing you to withhold income taxes on any distributions to that beneficiary. If the trust or estate must withhold on distributions, place the amount that you withheld and sent to the IRS on line 13.

# Alternative minimum tax information

Pass through all the tax preference items to the income beneficiaries on **Schedule K-1,** line 12, along with their income distribution. Some of these preference items may carry through from other sources, such as accelerated depreciation on rental property owned by the trust or estate. Others derive solely from the trust or estate itself because of deductions not allowed in the alternative minimum tax (AMT) calculation, such as state taxes or miscellaneous itemized deductions.

Calculate the most common AMT adjustment, the *adjustment for minimum tax purposes,* by subtracting the IDD (**Form 1041, Schedule B,** line 15) from the

IDD on a minimum tax basis (**Form 1041, Schedule I, Part II,** line 44). With a single income beneficiary, the entire result goes on **Schedule K-1**, line 12, Code A; allocate the total adjustment between multiple beneficiaries based on the relative size of their distributions.

The days are gone when messing up AMT adjustments didn't matter much because very few individual taxpayers were actually in the AMT. Although everyone prayed it would be repealed, as of 2013, the AMT is a permanent feature of the Internal Revenue Code.

# Allocating Types of Income on the K-1

Income earned by a trust or estate that's paid out to a beneficiary in the same year as it's earned must be reported to that beneficiary on **Schedule K-1**, and that income maintains its character when it's distributed. But how do you know what type of income you're paying out, and do you, as the trustee or executor, have any discretion in what forms of income you distribute?

The simple answer is, you have almost no discretion. Income passes to the beneficiary in the same ratio as it's earned by the trust or estate. So, if a trust earns 40 percent of its income as interest, 30 percent as dividends, and 30 percent as rental, the numbers shown on **Schedule K-1** will reflect those percentages: 40 percent interest, 30 percent dividends, and 30 percent rental.

The one exception to this rule concerns capital gains. Except in the last year of the trust or estate, capital gains remain trapped at the trust or estate level, which pays all the income taxes due on them. Of course, there's also an exception to the exception. If you, as the fiduciary, determine to distribute to a beneficiary the value of certain property (which must be identified prior to the distribution, and prior to any sale), you may elect to have the beneficiary pay the tax on the capital gain generated by the sale of that property. So if Abe, the trustee of Moe's trust, decides to distribute the value of 50 shares of IBM stock to Sam, the beneficiary, he can sell those identified shares and allocate any capital gain to Sam even though it's not the last year of the trust.

Exceptions aside, you arrive at each individual number by dividing the total for each type of income into the total for all types of income includable on **Schedule K-1** and then multiplying the result by the amount of the IDD (**Form 1041, Schedule B,** line 15). Allocations are made across all classes of income, whether taxable (dividends, taxable interest, and rents, for example) or nontaxable (think interest from municipal bonds and tax-free mutual funds). Table 20-1 shows a sample, using $10,000 of income, with $7,500 of allowable deductions for professional fees and state income taxes.

| Table 20-1 | | Allocating Classes of Income to Schedule K-1 | | |
|---|---|---|---|---|
| *Form 1041* | | *Schedule K-1 Allocation* | | |
| Income Amount | Amount | Income Type | Allocation Calculation | K-1 Amount |
| Interest income | $4,000 | Interest | $4,000 ÷ $10,000 × $2,500 | $1,000 |
| Dividend income | $3,500 | Dividend | $3,500 ÷ $10,000 × $2,500 | $875 |
| Rental income | $2,500 | Rental | $2,500 ÷ $10,000 × $2,500 | $625 |
| **Total Income** | $10,000 | | | |
| **Less Deductions** | ($7,500) | | | |
| **Income Distribution Deduction (IDD)** | $2,500 | **Total K-1 Income** | | $2,500 |

Income shown on all the **K-1**s equals the trust or estate's IDD, not the amount of the distributions actually paid. So even when a beneficiary receives more than $2,500, as in this example, he or she only pays tax on $2,500.

# Preparing Supplements to Schedule K-1

**Schedule K-1** allows you to put a vast amount of information on the face of the form, but you often want to give your beneficiaries even more details. Don't let the lack of specifically labeled spaces stop you. The more information you manage to cram onto **Schedule K-1,** the better off the beneficiaries are.

Trustees and executors often pay personal expenses on behalf of a beneficiary (just to be certain those expenses are being paid). If you paid medical expenses, taxes, or some other form of deductible expenses on a beneficiary's behalf, include that information (listing it by category, not by individual payments) somewhere on either the **K-1** itself or on a separate sheet attached to it so the beneficiary will be sure to take the deductions to which he or she is entitled. The next sections explain other information **Schedule K-1** can include.

## Showing foreign tax allocations

Foreign stocks and bonds are increasingly common in trust and estate accounts; so, too, are foreign taxes paid on foreign income. Be sure to pass out not only foreign income to beneficiaries but also the corresponding amount of foreign taxes paid. Show the foreign tax amount on **Schedule K-1,** line 14, using Code B. Label the foreign income, using Code H on the same line. Alternatively, attach a separate page to the back of the **K-1,** outlining both the foreign income earned and the foreign taxes paid.

## Providing state tax information

Because most states have their own income tax, beneficiaries use their **K-1** information to calculate their state income tax. Be sure to provide them with any differences that may impact their state returns, including the amount of U.S. Treasury interest (don't forget U.S. Treasury dividends earned by mutual funds that only invest in U.S. Treasury obligations) and in-state versus out-of-state tax-exempt interest they received in their distribution.

The beneficiary's residence, not the trust's, is what determines what's in-state versus what's out-of-state for that beneficiary. So, an Ohio trust with a Utah resident beneficiary will want to show the Utah tax-exempt interest on that beneficiary's **Schedule K-1,** not the Ohio tax-exempt interest.

# Creating Nominee Form 1099s

Sometimes, even when the trust or estate doesn't have to file **Form 1041,** you still receive tax information from other sources. When you won't be preparing a **1041** (perhaps the trust or estate has terminated), there won't be a **Schedule K-1** either. Instead, pass along any tax information you receive via a **Form 1099** for income earned by property formerly owned by the trust or estate to the property's new owners by issuing them a *nominee Form 1099.*

To prepare this form, copy the **1099** you received, replacing the payer's name and TIN with the trust or estate's name (adding the words *as nominee* next to the name) and TIN. Place the new owner's name and TIN in the spaces reserved for the recipient. Nominee **1099**s can be typed or handwritten on forms available through stationery stores (available in large quantities only), or directly from the IRS at www.irs.gov/Businesses/Online-Ordering-for-Information-Returns-and-Employer-Returns. Be sure to give a copy to the new recipient and file the top copy (it's preprinted in red) with the IRS together with **Form 1096,** which is just a transmittal sheet; the filing address appears on **Form 1096.**

Don't use the **Forms 1099** that are available on the IRS website (www.irs. gov). These are provided for informational purposes only, and the IRS won't accept them if you try to file them. The preprinted forms are designed to be optically scanned; the forms you print from the website aren't.

Most **1099**s are required to be mailed to their recipients no later than January 31 of the year following the tax year in question, but not so for nominee **1099**s. In fact, you may not receive the relevant **1099** with the information that needs to be split until well after the January 31 deadline. Still, recognize that this is a deadline that exists to enable other people to file their tax returns on time; when you see that a nominee **1099** is required, do it as quickly as possible so you don't hold up the wheels of progress for someone else (or even worse, force them to file an amended tax return.)

# Part V
# The Part of Tens

**web extras**

Head to www.dummies.com/extras/estatetrustadministration for the scoop on how the American Taxpayer Relief Act of 2012 affects the laws regarding estates and trusts.

# In this part . . .

- ✔ Avoid careless mistakes and administrative quagmires by using good fiduciary judgment.

- ✔ Differentiate between transfer taxes and income taxes.

# Chapter 21

# Ten Pitfalls for the Unwary

*In This Chapter*

▶ Avoiding careless mistakes and sidestepping administration dangers

▶ Using good judgment

So much of administering a trust or estate is similar to handling your personal finances. However, you can easily forget that you're actually working in a fiduciary capacity, not an individual one, and that there are some major differences. In fact, one of the biggest issues we've run up against when assisting clients, family, and friends in their adventures in administration is in articulating where the differences lie. This chapter covers many of the lessons we've discovered regarding what you definitely should — and shouldn't — do when administering an estate or trust.

## Failing to Terminate an Existing Real Estate Purchase and Sale Agreement

As far as costly mistakes go, not ending an existing real estate purchase and sale agreement when the decedent is the seller is huge! Keeping the original agreement in place may substantially increase the taxes you'll owe on the sale, costing the estate, and the eventual heirs, big-time.

Real estate rarely changes hands on the day the buyer and seller agree to the purchase and sale; in fact, it often takes many weeks, if not months, between the handshake and the deed. In that period between the agreement and its final execution, the property's in limbo. You've established a price for it that the courts will almost always accept as its fair market value. But you've also created an expectation of money being received, which it hasn't yet been. So, in essence, because the agreement was reached before the decedent's death, you now have two assets:

> ✔ The property itself (reportable on **Form 706**)
>
> ✔ The cash that's been promised (with any gains reportable on **Form 1041**)

You, as executor, are caught in a never-never land; you've lost the all-valuable step-up in *basis* described in Chapter 18, and the estate's also not eligible for the $250,000 per person exclusion of capital gain because the exclusion is per person, not per entity.

When a seller dies in mid-property transfer, canceling the old purchase and sale agreement and rewriting a new one, with the estate as the seller, allows you to take full advantage of the all-valuable step-up-in-basis. It also avoids any income tax on the sale. Remember, the only difference between the old agreement and the new is that the decedent's estate, not the decedent, is now the seller.

# Taking a Lump Sum Distribution from a Pension Plan, IRA, or Deferred Compensation Plan

When you're trying to figure out exactly how much the estate owns, you may be tempted to liquidate everything into cash. Although this thinking may work on some assets, don't do it with any sort of pension plan, IRA, or deferred compensation plan if you can avoid it. As soon as you cash out that plan of whatever flavor, the estate now owes income taxes on every penny that the decedent hadn't already paid tax on. In addition to the income tax bite, if you're dealing with a large enough estate, you may also owe federal and/or state estate taxes on the value of the account as of the date of death (or alternate valuation date, if you make the election; see Chapter 16). Talk about double taxation. One of us had an estate that held a large IRA; between the income and estate taxes paid, the effective tax rate was almost 97 percent.

Rolling the income-tax-deferred account to the heirs, if you can, is far better than taking a lump sum distribution in the estate. If the decedent left a surviving spouse or children, and the decedent (or the plan itself) designated them as beneficiaries, you have no problem. Using the rollover technique, no one owes any income taxes until the new beneficiaries begin to take distributions; additionally, you can spread those distributions out over a number of years, lessening the tax bracket each distribution is taxed at. Of course, if you have a taxable estate, the value of the account at the date of death is still included for estate tax purposes.

Seek competent tax advice as soon as you discover a large IRA because there are time limits imposed on retitling it. If the asset in question is a pension, check the plan documents to determine what options are available to the beneficiary. And if your decedent was deferring a portion of his or her income into a non-qualified deferred compensation plan, oh well. The full plan balance is due and payable upon the decedent's death, and will be included in both income and estate tax calculations.

# Creating a Feeding Frenzy When Splitting Personal Property

Nothing alienates family members like weddings and funerals, and nowhere is this more apparent than when you're dividing up the decedent's personal property among his or her heirs. If the decedent failed to leave instructions regarding who was to receive what property (such instructions are usually kept with the Last Will but are typically not part of it; see Chapter 8), your job as executor is to keep the situation under control.

Keep the following dos and don'ts in mind:

> ✓ **Don't allow anyone into the decedent's residence unsupervised.** After carpets, trinkets, and furniture are loaded into the back of someone's van, they're almost impossible to recover.

> ✓ **Do change the locks.** Do this whether or not you suspect someone may make a casual visit in the middle of the night. It's just a good idea.

We've found that the most equitable way to distribute personal property among the heirs is to use multicolored flea market stickers, easily purchased at any discount or stationery store. Give each heir a different color and have him or her take turns (oldest to youngest, youngest to oldest, or in an order determined by choosing random numbers) tagging one item at a time. By the time you finish, you'll discover that you're either surrounded by a rainbow of tags or that people mostly just want one or two remembrances; you can sell the rest or give it to charity.

# Missing Court Deadlines

Courts hate to be ignored. Make sure that you place all the probate court's deadlines on your calendar, circled, underlined, and in neon (if necessary). Even if you haven't been able to complete the task set by the court (preparing the probate inventory, for example), showing up to explain why you're unable to comply usually buys you additional time. Fail to appear, and the courts often demand immediate compliance.

Don't make the mistake of thinking that the probate court isn't a real court or that the judge isn't a real judge just because proceedings have been fairly low key to this point. These judges have full judicial authority, which includes removing you as executor or trustee, fining you, throwing you in the pokey for contempt of court, or any other such sanctions they deem necessary to make you comply.

# Forgetting Tax Filing Deadlines

You wouldn't fail to file your own tax returns; don't forget to file the trust's or estate's, either. Income tax returns (**Form 1041**) are due three and one half months after the estate or trust's year end, and estate tax returns (**Form 706**) are due nine months after the date of death. Place these dates on your calendar and begin preparation far in advance of the due date so you know about any problems or lack of information far in advance of the filing deadline. Don't forget, extensions are available if you're unable to file returns when due, and you may amend returns that turn out to be incorrect.

What do you do if you know you can't possibly get all the information prior to the return's due date, even if you extend that due date by the maximum five months allowed? If you know it's just a matter of a few months, or a year, you're probably safe in just amending the return after you have all the pertinent data. If what's missing may take longer to acquire (such as litigation begun during the decedent's lifetime, to which you've now become a party), you want to suspend the statute of limitations indefinitely until you resolve whatever's outstanding. To file a protective claim, write "Protective Claim under Reg. Sec. 301.6402-2(2)" across your return in big black letters, and make sure that you otherwise pay all taxes due. *Remember:* Be sure to file your return on time (as extended); protective claims work only if every other aspect of the return you filed has its *t*'s crossed and its *i*'s dotted.

# Failing to Communicate with the Heirs and Legatees

Being a trustee or executor isn't cloak-and-dagger stuff, and the heirs, *legatees* (individuals left specific property under the will), and beneficiaries on whose behalf you're working aren't enemy agents — at least not as their day jobs. Keep them in the loop as much as you can. By letting them know on a regular basis where you are in the process and when they can realistically expect a payment from the estate, you're stopping most, if not all, of their complaints before they have a chance to even think of them.

You can't please all the heirs all the time, especially those who are upset that they weren't named executor. But do be especially responsive to their concerns. The estate process is under the probate court's supervision, so an heir who complains to the judge only creates more work for you because you now have to respond to the judge's questions as well.

# Exercising Poor Fiduciary Judgment

The days are long gone when executors and trustees were only rarely called on the carpet for exercising poor fiduciary judgment. As more people have started investing personally, whether through their retirement accounts or through online brokerages, they think they've become much more sophisticated and knowledgeable about the entire investment process. And they've also become much more likely to comment unfavorably on your handling of the trust or estate's assets. As the executor and trustee, you must act prudently and deliberately, seeking advice when you need it, investing the assets wisely, and paying the bills and the beneficiaries when they're due to be paid.

Remember that the decedent or the donor chose you to look after his or her property because of your good judgment, and part of that judgment is knowing when to ask for help. Don't hesitate to employ a professional to help you in choosing investments for the estate or trust. If you do turn to professional help, make sure that you check references and determine how much experience that person has in the investment of trust and estate assets (which should be fairly conservatively, but broadly, invested across all industries). If a trust is ongoing, for example, a general rule is that the trust should own pieces of between 140 and 175 different companies, in addition to whatever bonds or other savings accounts it owns. If yours is a smaller trust, and buying stock in all these companies would result in purchases of only a few shares, you can easily meet this standard by investing in a few well-chosen mutual funds.

# Underestimating the Devotion Required

People rarely understand the magnitude of the task in front of them when someone asks them to act as executor or trustee. Even if they did, the date when the job ceases to be theoretical and the action really begins is often so far in the future that they can't even imagine such a time.

If you've accepted an appointment as an executor, administrator, or trustee, you've agreed to act reasonably and responsibly. This job isn't a small favor you can discharge in an hour or two, or even in a day or two. It's a major commitment on your part to carry out the stated wishes of the testator or grantor. Treat this commitment with all the care that you would lavish on a beloved relative or friend.

# Taking Nonsanctioned Shortcuts

As you wend your way through the seemingly endless administration of an estate or trust, you may be tempted to look for ways to reduce your workload. After all, most people take shortcuts on their personal finances, and everything usually works out fine. Resist the temptation to find an easier route through the administration process.

No one will ever disagree that many of the steps you're supposed to take seem pointless and laborious, but you must take them nonetheless. So if you're supposed to publish a notice in a certain paper, make sure to do so. If you should have a piece of property appraised, don't assign it a value, and move on; hire an appropriate appraiser, pay the fee, and get the appraisal in writing. Taking shortcuts through an estate or trust may save you some time up front, but the cleanup costs on the other end, when the IRS wants to see the proof that you've valued something correctly or your accounts don't balance, can be huge.

Whether you're administering an estate or trust under the eagle-eye supervision of the probate court or you're merely answerable to the beneficiaries, you're responsible. Failure to follow through on those responsibilities may open you up to removal as fiduciary, as well as potential lawsuits from any person having an interest.

# *Paying from the Wrong Pocket*

Money may always seem like money to you, but within a trust, it belongs to either principal or income. And although making a distinction between the two may seem silly when paying trust bills, you really must. Because different people may be entitled to receive money and property from either income or principal, making payments (whether expenses or distributions) from the correct side of the account is crucial. More than one trustee has been sued because they paid all trustee fees from principal (or income), for example.

When you make all payments from one side, you favor the eventual owners of the property on the other side (because their share will grow faster). To avoid any hint of favoritism, allocate fees and expenses against the type of income that generated that cost. When you're not sure (like with your trustee's fee), create an equitable formula so that a certain portion of your fee is always paid from principal, and the rest from income.

# Chapter 22

# Ten Types of Taxes You May Have to Pay

*In This Chapter*

▶ Making sense of the transfer-tax trio

▶ Figuring out the difference between taxes on income and taxes on owned items

*W*e'd love to be able to be able to tell you that negotiating your way through the tax implications of estates and trusts is an easy matter. Unfortunately, it can get pretty complicated because one event can often lead to multiple taxes being owed. Don't ask us why. We don't make the rules, but we're stuck with 'em the same as you.

In this chapter, we give you the top-ten list of the taxes you may come across in the process of administering an estate or trust. Chances are good you won't be responsible for paying all of them, but the odds are also good that you won't avoid paying taxes altogether.

With the exception of federal income taxes and federal and state estate, gift, and inheritance taxes, all taxes you pay on behalf of the trust or estate are deductible on that entity's income tax returns. Of course, you actually have to have paid the taxes in order to deduct. If the check is written but still sitting in the envelope waiting to be mailed on the last business day of any tax year, you can't use that deduction until the next year.

## Federal Gift Tax

Large transfers made during one's lifetime (what a way to say "a gift") may be subject to the gift tax, one of the group of transfer taxes that also features the estate tax and the generation-skipping transfer tax (which we describe in the next two sections). If transfers are made into a trust during the grantor's lifetime, those transfers may be subject to the gift tax. If, for example, those gifts are over $13,000 in 2012, they would be reported on the donor's 2012

**Form 709, United States Gift (and Generation-Skipping Transfer) Tax Return**, but these gifts would also qualify for the grantor's lifetime exclusion from estate and gift taxes of $5.12 million in 2012. Unfortunately, transfer taxes are notoriously fickle, and the amount of the lifetime annual exclusion is constantly being tinkered with, so the amount of the total lifetime gifts, as well as the amount that can be gifted to each beneficiary, is always on the move and will depend on the lifetime exclusion in effect on the date of the gift.

# Federal Estate Tax

The federal estate tax is the granddaddy of the transfer-tax system. Estates valued in excess of $5.12 million for people who died in 2012 must fill out **Form 706, United States Estate (and Generation-Skipping Transfer) Tax Return** and pay whatever tax is due. If you're lucky enough to be administering a qualifying estate, you're entitled to all the fun of preparing **Form 706**. Don't worry, we explain how to do just that in Chapter 17.

# Generation-Skipping Transfer Tax

The last, and least understood, of the transfer-tax trio, the *generation-skipping transfer tax* (or GST tax) is assessed when property moves from one generation to another, skipping intermediate generations along the way. So property that goes from a grandparent (or grandparent's estate) to a grandchild (or in trust for the benefit of a grandchild) is subject to this tax, provided that the grandchild's parent is still alive at the time the transfer is made. Property transferred between unrelated people who are more than 37½ years apart in age is also subject to this tax.

Unlike the estate tax, which is only assessed after the decedent's death, and the gift tax, which only comes into play while the donor is still alive, the generation-skipping transfer tax may be assessed either during the donor's lifetime or after his or her death. This tax is assessed in addition to, not rather than, the estate or gift tax; it generally equals the amount of transfer tax that would've been generated had the property passed through all the generations instead of bypassing one or more.

Depending on whether this tax is being assessed for a gift made during the donor's lifetime or for a bequest or devise made after death, the GST tax is calculated either on **Form 709, United States Gift (and Generation-Skipping Transfer) Tax Return** or **Form 706, United States Estate (and Generation-Skipping Transfer) Tax Return**.

If you suspect that you may be in the middle of a situation that involves a skip generation, look at Chapter 3 to find out what you need to know.

# State Inheritance or Estate Tax

Just as many states impose an income tax, many also impose estate or inheritance taxes. Most states used to calculate these taxes based on a credit on the federal **Form 706.** In other words, if the federal government was going to allow a credit for state estate or inheritance taxes, most states said, "Hey, just give us that money instead." You didn't end up paying any less tax, but the total tax you paid was split between the IRS and the state. However, as the credit for state estate taxes paid was whittled away and then changed to a deduction on **Form 706,** some states stepped up to the plate and pegged their portion of the tax to what it would've been based on a prior year's calculation. For example, Vermont calculates its estate tax based on federal estate tax rules, but in 2012, taxes lifetime and after-death transfers in excess of $2,750,000. Other states have raised the amount exempt from estate tax or are choosing not to impose a tax so as not to give their residents a reason to choose another domicile. See Appendix B for a complete list of what each state is doing with regard to inheritance or estate tax as of the date of publication of this book.

You need to check with your state's tax department to get the rules in effect at the time of your decedent's death. And if you're faced with an estate that owns property in more than one state, you may want to consult a competent tax professional because the estate may owe estate or inheritances taxes in each of those states.

# Estate and Trust Income Taxes (Federal and State)

Like individuals, partnerships, and corporations, estates and trusts have the ability to earn income — which means that income is subject to income tax. If you have more than $600 of income for an estate, $300 for a simple trust (all income must be distributed currently), or $100 for a complex trust (every other type of trust), you need to complete and file **Form 1041, U.S. Income Tax Return for Estates and Trusts.**

If the trust or estate has a tax home in a state with a state income tax, guess what? You get to file a state income tax return there. How do you know where the estate or trust's tax home is? In the case of an estate, the tax home is the state where the decedent was domiciled at the time of his or her death. For a trust, the rules are slightly more complex. Basically, if the grantor resided in the same state as at least one of the trustees when he or she either set up the trust or died, the trust is deemed a resident of that state. If there's no match between the grantor's and the trustee's domiciles, then the trust is considered without a *situs,* or location, and no state income tax return is required.

# Decedent's Final Federal and State Income Taxes

Just because someone has died doesn't mean he or she gets out of filing income tax returns for the year of his or her death. Well, the decedent doesn't have to, but you do. So in addition to preparing the returns for the estate and/or trust, you also have to prepare **Form 1040, U.S. Individual Income Tax Return** for the decedent. When preparing the form, make sure that you write "Deceased" and the date of death next to the decedent's name. You may also want to write "Deceased" and the date of death across the top of the return in bold letters or red pen. No one ever accused the IRS of reading everything that's sent to it — sometimes you need to surround important information in neon lights to make sure that you're getting your point across.

Surviving spouses need not file a separate return in the year their husbands or wives died. Instead, a surviving spouse may file one last joint return. Both personal exemptions are available, as is the full joint standard deduction, and the slightly lower *married filing jointly* tax rates, even if the deceased spouse died early in the year. Check out Chapter 18 for more information on filing the decedent's final **Form 1040**.

# Local Income Taxes

In the grand scheme of things, few cities, towns, or counties impose an income tax, but enough do so as to affect lots of people. If your estate or trust is resident in one of these locales, you must calculate not only the state income tax but also the local one. Fortunately, these local calculations are usually done right on the state income tax return (we know you're delighted that you probably don't have to fill out yet another tax return), and they piggyback right onto the state calculation. Consequently, figuring out how much you owe isn't tough, provided you've already successfully tackled the state income tax calculation.

# Local Real Estate Taxes

If the trust or estate you're administering owns real estate, you must pay the real estate taxes every year, either by paying the city or town directly or by making sure that you're paying into an escrow account maintained by the bank that holds the mortgage on the property, if any. Real estate taxes, also called *property taxes,* are calculated based on a property's assessed value. This value is subject to reassessment at various times, including whenever the property changes hands or when the city or town in which the property is located decides to update all of its property assessments.

Don't accept your new assessment if you feel it's unjust. You're entitled to question it. If the new assessed value seems unfair, submit your grievance, in writing and within a very short period after you're notified of the change, to either the city assessor or town clerk. (Whom you send your grievance to depends on the rules of your city or town, which should be clearly spelled out and sent with the new assessment.) One of us recently underwent a citywide reassessment that was, at a later date, completely thrown out as unusable because the valuations for similar properties varied so widely and the assessor couldn't provide adequate documentation for her valuations. But the overall assessment was only questioned *after* the flood of grievances was received at city hall. In this case, it was possible to fight city hall and win.

# State Intangibles Taxes

Some states have intangibles taxes rather than income taxes. *Intangibles* are those items of property that you can't readily hold in your hand, such as stocks and bonds. With an intangibles tax, the market value of these items is tallied up once each year. Then the tax is calculated by using a percentage of the market value.

# Excise Taxes

Planes, boats, automobiles, and any other objects that move are often assessed an annual *excise tax.* If the trust or estate you're administering owns property subject to excise taxes, you need to be certain they're paid. Unpaid excise tax bills may lead to tickets and, in extreme cases, seizure by the taxing authority. Trust us, leaving your office for lunch to find a boot nailed to the axle of the estate's car is pretty awful.

Excise taxes, although owed to the state, are usually paid to the city or town where the property is garaged.

# Appendix A

# Glossary

**administrator:** A person appointed by the probate court to administer the estate of a decedent when the decedent left no valid will.

**amortization:** Reducing the cost of an intangible asset over its projected life.

**ancillary administration:** Separate probate of real property in the jurisdiction in which it's located.

**annual account:** All of a trust or estate's activity for a 12-month period.

**annuity:** Income paid in a series of payments.

**applicable exclusion amount:** The total amount exempted from gift and/or estate tax.

**applicable federal rate (AFR):** The minimum interest rate you must charge on a loan in order for it to be considered fair market rate.

**assets:** Items of value owned by any entity, whether an individual, corporation, partnership, trust, or estate.

**basis:** The acquisition cost of any asset.

**beneficial interest:** The right to receive some benefit, profit, or distribution from a trust.

**beneficiary:** The person or entity receiving a benefit from an estate or trust.

**bequest:** A legacy or gift of personal property by will.

**bill:** Any short-term loan packaged as an investment product and issued with a maturity of one year or less.

**bond (fixed-income securities):** Any long-term loan packaged as an investment product and issued with a maturity of more than ten years.

**by right of representation:** See *per stirpes*

**Charitable Lead Annuity Trust (CLAT):** A trust that makes a fixed number of annual payments, calculated as a percentage of the asset value as of the date of the grantor's gift into the trust, to charity. At the end of the lead period, the remaining assets are distributed to noncharitable remaindermen.

**Charitable Lead Unitrust (CLUT):** A trust that makes a fixed number of annual payments to charity, calculated on a percentage of the assets valued on the second business day of each year. At the end of the lead period, the remaining assets are distributed to noncharitable remaindermen.

**Charitable Remainder Annuity Trust (CRAT):** A trust where the grantor receives fixed payments for life, calculated as a percentage of the asset value as of the date of grantor's gift into the trust. At grantor's death, the remaining assets are distributed to charity.

**Charitable Remainder Unitrust (CRUT):** A trust where the grantor receives payments for life, calculated annually based on a percentage of assets valued, usually on the second business day of each year. At grantor's death, the assets remaining are distributed to charity.

**children's trusts:** Trusts created to benefit grantor's children. Often used to provide the grantor with the ability to control children's inheritances even after death. Sometimes distributable as a child reaches a certain age.

**churn:** To buy and sell securities frequently with the sole intention of earning more commissions.

**codicil:** A change to a will, executed with all the formalities of a will. Usually located with the decedent's last will.

**community property:** Property acquired by either spouse during the course of a marriage in a state whose laws recognize community property.

**common law:** Law deriving from court decisions and ancient usages and customs, as opposed to statutory law, created by legislatures.

**conservator:** Similar to a guardian, but with less-restrictive rules.

**consideration:** A benefit that must be bargained for between parties as an essential reason for the parties to enter into a contract.

**corpus:** Principal or body of the trust.

**credit shelter trust:** The trust that holds the amount of assets equal to the remaining *applicable exclusion amount.*

**Crummey trust:** A trust structured to create a brief window of time for a present interest of gifts to the trust so that no gift tax will be payable on annual exclusion gifts to the trust.

**curtesy:** The right of a widower, under common law, to a life estate in the decedent's real estate. Abolished in many states.

**CUSIP number:** The nine-digit identifier for a marketable security, issued by the Committee on Uniform Security Identification Procedures.

**death tax:** Common nickname for a tax on the value of all of the decedent's property at date of death. More properly referred to as an *estate tax*.

**decedent's estate:** The property owned by the decedent on his or her date of death. Has different meanings for both probate and estate tax purposes.

**declaration date:** The date a corporation declares (announces) it will be paying a dividend.

**delivery instructions:** The specific routing and account numbers necessary to send cash and/or securities from one bank or brokerage to another.

**depletion:** A reduction in value of an asset as that asset is used up.

**depreciation:** Recovering an asset's value ratably over its useful life.

**devise:** Term describing how real property is left by will.

**direct skip:** A transfer of property from grandparent to grandchild, bypassing the grandparent's surviving child.

**disclaim:** To refuse to accept a bequest or devise before it's received.

**domicile:** Legal home or residence.

**donee:** Person receiving a gift of property.

**donor:** Person making a gift of property.

**dower:** A provision of state law in some states that gives a widow (and sometimes a widower) a life estate in a portion of the real estate owned by the decedent, based in common law.

**dynasty trust:** A trust lasting for several generations that provides protection from both the generation-skipping transfer tax and from creditors.

**Electing Small Business Trust (ESBT):** A trust that may make an election in order to own stock in a Subchapter S corporation.

**Enrolled Agents:** Tax professionals licensed by U.S. Department of the Treasury.

**equities:** See *stocks*

**executor:** The person named in the will to carry out the decedent's wishes.

**executor's bond:** A written promise to faithfully carry out the executor's duties.

**face amount:** Amount of money a bond issuer pays a lender at maturity.

**family pot trust:** Trust where the trustee has discretion to distribute income and (in accordance with the terms of the trust) principal to any or all of the named beneficiaries — typically the decedent's spouse and descendants.

**family trust:** See *credit shelter trust*

**family trustee:** A trusted member of a grantor's family or a family friend.

**fee simple:** Absolute ownership of real property, but limited by the four basic government powers of taxation, eminent domain, police power, and escheat. May also be limited by certain obstructions or a condition in the deed.

**fiduciaries:** People to whom property is entrusted by one person for another's benefit. Includes *executors, administrators, personal representatives, trustees, guardians,* and *conservators.*

**fiscal year-end:** Ending a tax year at the end of any month except December.

**fixed income securities:** See *bill; bond; notes*

**funded trusts:** Trusts that hold assets.

**general power of appointment:** The power of the trust beneficiary to appoint all or any of the trust property to anyone he or she chooses, including himself or herself, or his or her estate, at any time during his or her lifetime, or upon his or her death.

**grantor:** The person who creates the trust. See also *settlor*

**Grantor-retained Annuity Trust (GRAT):** A trust into which the grantor transfers property and receives a scheduled and fixed payment from it based on a percentage of the initial value of the transfer for a period of years.

**Grantor-retained Income Trust (GRIT):** A trust into which the grantor transfers assets while retaining income earned by those assets for a period of years. At the end of the period, the assets either distribute to the beneficiaries or remain in trust for the beneficiaries' benefit.

**Grantor-retained Unitrust (GRUT):** A trust into which the grantor transfers assets while retaining the right to receive an annual payment from the trust for a period of years. Payment calculated is a percentage of the annual asset valuation, usually done on the second business day of each calendar year.

**gross estate:** The total value of all the decedent owned at his or her date of death.

**guardian:** A person appointed by the probate court to take care of another and his or her property when the property owner is deemed incapable of taking care of his or her own affairs because of age (in the case of a minor) or for other reasons such as mental illness, mental retardation, physical incapacity, or illness.

**guardian ad litem:** A guardian appointed by the probate court for a particular matter in order to protect the beneficiary's interest.

**heirs-at-law:** Persons who inherit a decedent's estate under state statutes of descent and distribution if the decedent died intestate.

**high yield bonds:** See *junk bonds*

**incidents of ownership:** Having the right to name or change the beneficiary of a life insurance policy, to assign the policy to another or revoke the assignment, to surrender or cancel the policy, and to pledge the policy as collateral for a loan, or to obtain a loan against the surrender value.

**income:** Everything earned by the principal of the trust other than capital gains and extraordinary dividends.

**independent trustees:** Fiduciaries who have no interest in the trust grantor, the trust beneficiaries, or the trust remaindermen.

**inheritance tax:** Tax on the amount inherited by a particular beneficiary rather than the estate as a whole.

**inventory:** A list showing a trust or estate's beginning assets, including the starting basis for each asset.

**intangibles:** Assets that you can't readily hold in your hand, such as stocks and bonds.

**intangibles tax:** A tax on certain intangible assets.

**inter vivos trust:** A trust created by trust instrument during a grantor's lifetime.

**intestate:** When a decedent dies and leaves no valid will.

**irrevocable trust:** A trust where the governing instrument may not be revoked or changed, even by the grantor.

**issue:** All persons who have descended lineally from a common ancestor.

**joint tenancy with right of survivorship:** Title passes automatically to surviving joint tenant(s) on the death of one.

**junk bonds:** Corporate or government bonds paying a high rate of interest, where the debtor may be judged to be in danger of defaulting on the debt.

**legacy:** A bequest or gift of personal property by will.

**life estate:** Right to use property and receive any income it earns for the remainder of the tenant's life.

**limited power of appointment:** The right of a trust beneficiary to designate, from a group of specified appointees (usually the grantor's children and grandchildren, or charities), who may receive trust assets either at any time or after the death or other termination of the beneficiary's interest.

**living trusts:** Trusts created (and sometimes funded) during the grantor's life.

**load:** Sales charges paid by investors to purchase mutual fund shares.

**marital trust:** A trust for the benefit of the surviving spouse, typically funded by a formula that takes full advantage of the marital deduction to avoid paying any federal estate tax at the first spouse's death.

**mean:** Average. Also your older brother when he held you down and tickled you until you almost wet your pants.

**municipal bonds:** Bonds issued by states, cities, and towns. The interest earned is typically tax exempt.

**net income:** All income (excluding capital gains and principal dividends) minus expenses (such as the trustee's and tax preparer's fees) paid from income.

**nominee trust:** A trust in name only, designed to own real estate and allow the owner of the beneficial interest in the trust to keep his or her name off the property deed, out of the local Registry of Deeds, and out of public view.

**notes:** Any loan packaged as an investment product with a maturity of more than one year but not more than ten years.

**original will:** The only signed copy of a will at any given time.

**paid-up policy:** A life insurance policy on which all the premiums have been paid. The policy remains in force until the insured's death.

**payable on death (POD) account:** See *Totten Trust*

**payment date:** Date a stock dividend is paid to shareholders of record.

**per capita:** Divided equally among the total number of persons.

**per stirpes:** When a named beneficiary predeceases the testator, that beneficiary's share divides equally among his/her children, so that the issue of a deceased child receive equally divided portions of that child's share and so on. Also known as *by right of representation*.

**personal property:** Any tangible property that can be physically moved.

**personal representative:** A general term for executor and administrator.

**power of appointment:** The power to decide who will be the ultimate owner, or have the enjoyment of, any or all of the property of a trust (and when).

**power to revoke:** The ability to alter, amend, or terminate a legal document or the enjoyment of property transferred.

**prefunded:** The issuing authority has the option of paying off the loan early.

**present interest:** Having all right, title, and interest in property when given.

**pretermitted heir:** A child, whether born before or after the testator's death, or descendant of a deceased child of the testator who is unintentionally omitted from the will.

**principal:** The assets owned by a trust. See also *corpus*

**probate:** The process by which a decedent's will is proved to be valid or invalid and the estate is administered and settled after death.

**probate estate:** Property subject to court supervision; assets held in the decedent's name alone at the date of death or payable to the estate, or held jointly only for the decedent's convenience.

**property subject to claims:** Assets available to pay the decedent's creditors.

**prospectus:** A brochure created by every mutual fund that details the fund's governing rules and lists a sample investment portfolio for the fund.

**qualified heirs:** Certain close family members, defined by state statute.

**Qualified Personal Residence Trust (QPRT):** A trust into which the grantor transfers a home while retaining the right to live there, rent free, for a period of years.

**Qualified Subchapter S Trust (QSST):** A trust that is allowed to own stock in Subchapter S corporations.

**qualified terminable interest property (QTIP):** A trust that typically pays all net income (but only a limited amount of principal) to the surviving spouse, with no power of appointment.

**quasi-community property:** Property acquired by either spouse in a non-community property state that would have been community property had the couple resided in a community-property state.

**real property:** Land and land improvements, including all buildings.

**reciprocal will:** Will written by one spouse, giving all (less bequests of specific personal property) to the other, mirroring the other spouse's will.

**record date:** Day on which stockholders must own shares to receive a dividend.

**remainderman:** The person entitled to a future interest (called a *remainder*) in property in a trust (pl. remaindermen).

**residuary devisee:** A person or entity named to receive all the real property not specifically devised.

**residuary legatee:** A person or entity named to receive all the personal property not specifically bequeathed.

**return of capital:** When payment is received that reduces an asset's acquisition costs because some part of what was originally owned no longer exists.

**reversionary interest:** The right to the return of property that the transferor has temporarily transferred to or for the benefit of another person.

**revocable trust:** A trust that can be amended, revoked, or terminated at any time prior to the grantor's death by the grantor. Also known as a *revocable living trust.*

**separate property:** Assets owned prior to marriage, inherited or received as a gift during marriage, or earned after separation in a community-property state.

**settlor:** The trust's creator. See also *grantor*

**short year:** A tax year consisting of fewer than 12 months.

**signature guarantee:** A stamp or seal from a commercial bank or stock brokerage, validating a signature.

**single premium life insurance:** A policy purchased with one premium.

**situs:** Where the property is treated as being located for legal purposes.

**small business stock:** Stock from a closely held corporation.

**socially responsible investing:** An investment strategy that integrates social or environmental criteria into financial analysis.

**special (extraordinary) dividends:** The corporation has issued a larger than ordinary slice of the corporate profits.

**special power of appointment:** Any power that can't be exercised in the manner described for a general power of appointment.

**specific devisee:** A person or entity named to receive specific real property under a will.

**specific legatee:** A person or entity named to receive designated personal property under a will.

**spendthrift trust:** A trust that gives absolute control of the income and principal to the trustee to prevent the beneficiary from squandering money.

**split interest charitable trust:** A trust where the grantor retains either a lead or remainder interest in the trust property, with the opposite interest (lead or remainder) going to charity.

**statutory share:** The share an heir is entitled to under state law if the decedent left no valid will.

**stocks (equities):** Ownership interests in corporations.

**street name:** Ownership records of marketable securities maintained by brokerage firms rather than by individual corporations. Owners receive regular statements of their holdings rather than individual certificates.

**Subchapter S corporation:** A small corporation that pays no corporate income tax but rather distributes all items of income and deduction directly to the shareholders, who then must pay applicable income taxes.

**taking against the will:** Surviving spouse's election to receive a share of estate as determined by state spousal share laws rather than by decedent's last will.

**tenancy by the entirety:** Title passes automatically to the surviving joint tenant, who can only be a surviving spouse.

**tenancy in common:** Each tenant holds property with other tenants in common but none have rights of survivorship in each others' shares.

**term insurance:** Insurance that provides coverage for a set period and builds no cash value. The premium generally increases with age.

**testamentary trust:** A trust that is contained in the decedent's will.

**testate:** When a decedent dies leaving a valid last will.

**testator:** A person who has a will.

**Totten trust:** A bank or brokerage account opened by a grantor, using specific language that transfers ownership at the grantor's death directly to a named successor. See *payable on death (POD) account*

**trust:** A legal entity that holds assets for the benefit of a person or entity.

**trust accounting income:** The net income less expenses paid from income.

**trust instrument:** The legal document (other than the Last Will) created by the grantor during life that contains all the provisions of the trust.

**trustee:** A person, bank, or trust company that holds and administers the assets of a trust for the benefit of another.

**U.S. Treasury obligations:** Loans issued by the U.S. Treasury in the form of bills, notes, or bonds. Interest is taxed federally but exempt in every state.

**unlimited marital trust:** A trust set up for the benefit of the surviving spouse, who receives the net income plus whatever principal he or she desires, and over which he or she may have a general power of appointment.

**usufruct:** The temporary right to the use and enjoyment of another's property.

**variable universal life insurance:** Similar to whole life insurance except you may invest cash value in the policy in mutual funds offered by the insurance company. The rate of return depends on success of those investments.

**whole life insurance:** A life insurance policy where the portion of premiums not used to purchase term life coverage is invested by the insurance company, providing the policy owner with a stated rate of return.

# Appendix B

# State-by-State Rules of Intestacy and Estate or Inheritance Tax

● ● ● ● ● ● ● ● ● ● ● ● ● ● ● ● ● ● ● ● ● ● ● ● ● ● ● ● ● ● ● ● ● ● ● ● ● ● ● ● ● ●

*T*he laws of *intestacy* (how a decedent's estate is distributed when no valid last will exists), as well as the wording in state statues, vary by state. We summarize a portion of these laws to give you a taste of the similarities and differences between states. However, because these laws can be quite complex, consult with a competent attorney who's an expert in estate law before you make any intestate distributions. Keep in mind that although these are the laws in effect as this book is published, they're subject to change. To look farther down the line of descent and distribution than what we provide here, refer to your individual state statute regarding intestacy.

In addition to the federal estate tax, some states impose their own version of an estate tax (where the estate is taxed on the transfer of property), others have an inheritance tax (where the beneficiary is taxed on the transfer of property), some have both, and many have neither. The following list tells you what's in place as this book goes to print, but like the laws of intestacy, bear in mind that everything can change at a moment's notice.

In states that recognize same-sex marriages, be aware that, under current law, the state probate and estate tax rules aren't the same as the federal estate tax rules. It is possible that, in these families, there may be a federal estate tax due where, for state purposes, there is a surviving spouse and thus, a marital deduction available.

## Alabama

**Rules of Intestacy**

✔ **Surviving spouse:**

- **No surviving issue or parent:** 100 percent of estate.

- **No surviving issue but surviving parents:** First $100,000 plus ½ of the remaining estate balance.

- **With issue that are all also the issue of the surviving spouse:** First $50,000 plus ½ of the remaining estate balance with the remainder distributed equally among the issue.

- **With issue that aren't all issue of the surviving spouse:** ½ of the estate with the remaining ½ distributed equally among the issue.

✔ **No surviving spouse (or portion not distributed to surviving spouse):**

- **With issue:** Estate distributes equally among the same degree of kinship. With unequal degrees of kinship, those of more remote degree take by right of representation.

- **No issue but surviving parents:** Parents share equally.

For further levels of descent and distribution, see state intestacy statute.

**State Estate Taxes:** Decedents dying after December 31, 2004, no estate tax return required. For decedents dying prior to January 1, 2005, contact the Alabama Department of Revenue, 50 North Ripley St., Montgomery, AL 36132; Phone: 334-242-1034; Website: www.ador.state.al.us for further information.

## Alaska

**Rules of Intestacy**

✔ **Surviving spouse:**

- **No surviving descendant or parent of the decedent, or all descendants of decedent are also descendants of surviving spouse and no other descendants of surviving spouse survive decedent:** All the estate.

- **No descendants but a surviving parent:** First $200,000 plus ¾ of the remaining estate with remainder distributed equally among parents.

- **All the decedent's surviving descendants are also descendants of the surviving spouse, and the surviving spouse has one or more surviving descendants who are not descendants of the decedent:** First $150,000 plus ½ of the remaining estate with the remainder of the estate to decedent's descendants by representation.

- **If one or more of the decedent's surviving descendants are not descendants of the surviving spouse:** First $100,000 plus ½ of the remaining estate with the remainder of the estate to decedent's descendants by right of representation.

✔ **No surviving spouse (or portion not distributed to surviving spouse):** Same as Alabama, but substitute "descendant" for "issue" wherever it appears in this regard.

**State Estate Taxes:** Decedents dying after December 31, 2004, no estate tax return required. For decedents dying prior to January 1, 2005, contact the Alaska Tax Division, 550 West Seventh Avenue Suite 500, Anchorage, AK 99501-3555; Phone: 907-269-6620; Website: www.tax.alaska.gov for further information.

## Arizona

**Rules of Intestacy**

*Note:* The intestate estate consists of 100 percent of separate property and 50 percent of community property.

✔ **Surviving spouse:**

- **No surviving issue or all surviving issue are also issue of surviving spouse:** 100 percent of estate.

- **Surviving issue and one or more aren't issue of surviving spouse:** 50 percent of separate property with no interest in decedent's 50 percent of community property.

✔ **No surviving spouse (or portion not distributed to surviving spouse):** Same as Alabama, but substitute "descendant" for "issue" wherever it appears in this regard.

**State Estate Taxes:** Decedents dying after December 31, 2004, no estate tax return required. For decedents dying prior to January 1, 2005, contact the Estate Tax Office, Arizona Department of Revenue, 1600 West Monroe, Phoenix, AZ 85007-2650; Phone: 602-255-3381; Website: www.azdor.gov for further information.

## Arkansas

**Rules of Intestacy**

Estate distributes first to the decedent's children and their descendants.

✔ **Surviving spouse:**

- **No descendants and married more than 3 years:** 100 percent of estate.

- **No descendants and married less than 3 years:** 50 percent of estate with remainder to surviving parents, equally, or all remainder to the survivor. Or, if no parents surviving, to decedent's brothers and sisters, in equal shares, with the descendants of any deceased brother or sister to take his or her share.

- *Note:* Surviving spouse also has rights to certain interests in property similar to dower and curtesy.

✔ **No surviving descendants or spouse:** To surviving parents equally, or all to the survivor.

✔ **Should no other heir be found**: The remaining portion of the estate distributes to surviving spouse even if marriage is of less than 3 years. If spouse is deceased, estate distributes to deceased spouse's heirs.

**State Estate Taxes:** Decedents dying after December 31, 2004, no estate tax return required. For decedents dying prior to January 1, 2005, contact the Office of State Revenue Administration, P.O. Box 1272, Little Rock, AR 72203; Phone: 501-682-7089; Website: http://www.dfa.arkansas.gov for further information.

## California
### Rules of Intestacy

Regarding community and quasi-community property:

✔ **Surviving spouse:** ½ of decedent's share of community property and ½ of decedent's share of quasi-community property.

Regarding separate property:

✔ **Either surviving spouse or domestic partner:**

- **If no surviving issue, parent, brother, sister, or issue of a deceased brother or sister:** 100 percent of intestate estate.

- **With only one child or the issue of one deceased child:** ½ of intestate estate.

- **If no issue but a parent or parents or their issue or the issue of either of them:** ½ of intestate estate.

- **If decedent leaves more than one child, one child and the issue of one or more deceased children, or issue of two or more deceased children:** ⅓ of intestate estate.

✔ **No surviving spouse or domestic partner (or portion not distributed to surviving spouse or domestic partner):**

- To the issue of the decedent, the issue taking equally if they are all of the same degree of kinship to the decedent, but if of unequal degree those of more remote degree take by right of representation.

- If no surviving issue, to the decedent's parent or parents equally.

**State Estate Taxes:** Decedents dying after December 31, 2004, no estate tax return required. For decedents dying prior to January 1, 2005, contact the California State Controller's Office, P.O. Box 942850, Sacramento, CA 94250-5872; Phone: 916-445-2636; Website: www.sco.ca.gov for further information.

## Colorado
### Rules of Intestacy

✔ **Surviving spouse:**

- **No descendant or parent of decedent or all decedent's surviving descendants are also descendants of the surviving spouse and there are no other descendants of the surviving spouse who survive decedent:** All the estate.

- **No descendant but a surviving parent:** First $200,000, plus ¾ of balance of the estate.

- **If all decedent's surviving descendants are also descendants of the surviving spouse, and the surviving spouse has one or more surviving descendants who aren't descendants of decedent or if one or more of decedent's surviving descendants aren't descendants of decedent's surviving spouse, and all such surviving descendants who are children of decedent are adults:** First $100,000 plus ½ of any balance of intestate estate.

- **If one or more of decedent's surviving descendants are not descendants of decedent's surviving spouse, and if one or more of such descendants who are children of decedent are minors:** ½ of estate.

✔ **No surviving spouse (or portion not distributed to surviving spouse):** Same as Alabama to the point described there.

**State Estate Taxes:** Decedents dying after December 31, 2004, no estate tax return is required. For decedents dying prior to January 1, 2005, contact the Colorado Department of Revenue, 1375 Sherman St., Denver, CO 80261; Phone: 303-238-7378; Website: www.colorado.gov/revenue for further information.

## Connecticut

**Rules of Intestacy**

✔ **Surviving spouse:**

- **No surviving issue or parents:** All the estate.
- **No issue but surviving parents:** First $100,000 plus ¾ of the balance.
- **With issue, all being issue of the surviving spouse:** First $100,000 plus ½ of the balance of estate.
- **With issue, and one or more aren't issue of surviving spouse:** ½ of estate.

✔ **No surviving spouse (or portion not distributed to surviving spouse):**

- To the issue of decedent.
- No issue, to decedent's parent or parents equally, but none to any parent who has abandoned decedent as a minor child and continued such abandonment until the time of death of such child.

**State Estate Taxes:** Decedents dying on or after January 1, 2011, and having estates of $2 million or more are subject to tax. Estates over $2 million are taxed on full value of estate, including first $2 million. As of April 23, 2009, Connecticut treats parties in a same-sex marriage in the same manner as parties in a heterosexual marriage for purposes of state estate and gift taxes. File **Form CT-706/709** with Department of Revenue Services, State of Connecticut, P.O. Box 2978, Hartford, CT 06104-2978; Phone: 860-297-5962; Website: www.ct.gov/DRS.

## Delaware

**Rules of Intestacy**

✔ **Surviving spouse:**

- **No surviving issue or parents:** All the estate.
- **No surviving issue but survived by a parent or parents or with surviving issue all being issue of the surviving spouse:** First $50,000 of the intestate personal estate, plus ½ of the balance of the personal estate, plus a life estate in the real estate.
- **If there are surviving issue, one or more of whom are not issue of the surviving spouse:** ½ of the personal estate, plus a life estate in the real estate.

✔ **No surviving spouse (or portion not distributed to surviving spouse):**

- **To the issue of decedent:** Per stirpes.
- **No surviving issue:** To the parent or parents equally.

**State Estate Taxes:** There was no Delaware estate tax between January 1, 2005, and June 30, 2009. Delaware reinstituted the estate tax for estates of decedents dying after June 30, 2009, and before July 1, 2013. For 2013, estates with a total value of $5.25 million are subject to tax. Contact the Division of Revenue, Thomas Collins Building, 540 S. Dupont Hwy, Dover, DE 19901; Phone: 302-577-8214; Website: www.revenue.delaware.gov for further info.

## District of Columbia

**Rules of Intestacy**

✔ **Surviving spouse or domestic partner:**

- **No surviving issue or parent:** 100 percent of estate.
- **With issue that is also issue of the surviving spouse or domestic partner and there is no other descendant of the surviving spouse or domestic partner:** ⅔ of any balance of the estate.
- **No issue but surviving parent or parents:** ¾ of any balance of estate.

- **If all decedent's surviving descendants are also descendants of the surviving spouse or domestic partner and the surviving spouse or domestic partner has one or more descendants who are not descendants of decedent or if one or more of decedent's issue are not issue of the surviving spouse or domestic partner:** ½ of estate.

✔ **No surviving spouse or domestic partner (or portion not distributed to surviving spouse or domestic partner):**

  - To decedent's surviving children and the descendants of any deceased child, by right of representation.

  - If no surviving child or descendant, equally to father and mother, or survivor.

**State Estate Taxes:** File **Form D-76** or **D-76EZ** if the gross estate is more than $1 million with the Office of Tax and Revenue, Audit Division, Estate Tax Unit, P.O. Box 556, Washington, DC 20044-0556; Phone: 202-727-4829; Website: www.otr.cfo.dc.gov.

## *Florida*

**Rules of Intestacy (Effective as of October, 2011)**

✔ **Surviving spouse:**

  - **No surviving lineal descendant:** All the estate.

  - **With surviving lineal descendants, all of whom are also lineal descendants of the surviving spouse:** All the estate.

  - **With surviving lineal descendants, one or more of whom are not lineal descendants of the surviving spouse:** ½ of estate.

✔ **No surviving spouse (or portion not distributed to surviving spouse):**

  - To decedent's surviving children and the descendants of any deceased child, by right of representation.

  - To the lineal descendants of decedent, per stirpes, or, if none, to decedent's father and mother equally, or the survivor.

**State Estate Taxes:** Decedents dying after December 31, 2004, no estate tax return required. A personal representative must file **Form DR-312, Affidavit of No Florida Estate Tax Due When Federal Return Is Not Required,** or **Form DR-313, Affidavit of No Florida Tax Due When Federal Return is Required,** to remove Florida's automatic estate tax lien. For decedents dying prior to January 1, 2005, contact Florida Department of Revenue, 5050 West Tennessee Street, Tallahassee, FL 32399-0100; Phone: 800-352-3671; Website: www.myflorida.com/dor for further information.

## *Georgia*

**Rules of Intestacy**

✔ **Surviving spouse:**

  - **No descendants:** All the estate.

  - **With descendants:** If decedent is survived by any child or other descendant, the spouse shall share equally with the children, with the descendants of any deceased child taking that child's share per stirpes; provided that the spouse's portion shall not be less than a ⅓ share.

✔ **No surviving spouse (or portion not distributed to surviving spouse):**

  - **With descendants:** Estate distributes equally to decedent's children and descendants of any deceased child, with descendants of deceased child taking per stirpes.

  - **No descendants:** Surviving parents of decedent share estate equally.

**State Estate Taxes:** Decedents dying after December 31, 2004, no estate tax return required. For decedents dying prior to January 1, 2005, contact Georgia Department of Revenue, 1800 Century Center Blvd., Room 8300, Atlanta, GA 30345-3205; Phone: 404-417-4477; Website: www.etax.dor.ga.gov for further information.

## *Hawaii*

**Rules of Intestacy**

✔ **Surviving spouse or reciprocal beneficiary:**

- The entire intestate estate if no surviving descendant or parent of decedent, or if all of decedent's descendants are also descendants of surviving spouse or reciprocal beneficiary (including a partner in a civil union) and no other descendant of surviving spouse or reciprocal beneficiary survives.

- The first $200,000 plus ¾ of any balance of intestate estate if no descendant survives but a parent survives.

- The first $150,000 plus ½ of any balance of intestate estate if all descendants of decedent are also descendants of surviving spouse or reciprocal beneficiary and surviving spouse or reciprocal beneficiary has one or more surviving descendants who are not descendants of decedent.

- The first $100,000 plus ½ of any balance of intestate estate if one or more of decedent's surviving descendants are not descendants of surviving spouse or reciprocal beneficiary.

✔ **No surviving spouse (or portion not distributed to surviving spouse):**

- **With descendants:** To decedent's descendants by right of representation.

- **No descendants:** Surviving parents of decedent share estate equally.

**State Estate Taxes:** For estates of decedents dying in 2012, a Hawaii estate tax report must be filed if the estate is more than $3.5 million. For estates of decedents dying after December 31, 2012, the exemption amount is the same as the federal estate tax exemption amount. Effective January 1, 2012, provisions that previously applied to a husband and wife in a legal marital relationship, including the availability of a marital deduction, apply to partners in a civil union. Contact Taxpayer Services Branch, P.O. Box 259, Honolulu, HI 96809-0259; Phone: 800-222-3229; Website: www.hawaii.gov/tax for further information.

## *Idaho*

**Rules of Intestacy**

✔ **Surviving spouse:**

- **No issue or surviving parents:** 100 percent of separate property and decedent's 50 percent of community property.

- **With issue or no issue and surviving parents:** 50 percent of separate property and decedent's 50 percent of community property.

✔ **No surviving spouse (or portion not distributed to surviving spouse):** Same as Alabama to the point described earlier.

**State Estate Taxes:** Decedents dying after December 31, 2004, no estate tax return required. For decedents dying prior to January 1, 2005, contact Idaho State Tax Commission, P.O. Box 36, Boise, ID 83722-0410; Phone: 800-972-7660; Website: www.tax.idaho.gov for further information.

## *Illinois*

**Rules of Intestacy**

✔ **Surviving spouse:**

- **No descendants:** All the estate.

- **With descendants:** ½ of estate.

✔ **No surviving spouse (or portion not distributed to surviving spouse):**

- **With descendants:** To decedent's descendants, per stirpes.

- **No descendants:** To the parents, brothers, and sisters of decedent in equal parts, allowing to the surviving parent if one is dead a double portion and to the descendants of a deceased brother or sister per stirpes the portion which the deceased brother or sister would have taken if living.

**State Estate Taxes:** For decedents with a date of death after December 31, 2005, and an estate exceeding $4 million in 2013, file **Form 700,** along with a federal **Form 706,** payment of all taxes, penalty, and interest to the Illinois State Treasurer's Office, Estate Tax Section, 400 W. Monroe, 4th Floor, Springfield, Il 62704; Phone: 800-252-8919. Individuals who are parties in a qualifying civil union entered into on or after June 1, 2011, are afforded the same protections and benefits under Illinois law that apply to spouses in a marriage recognized for federal estate tax purposes, including the availability of a marital deduction. Website: `www.treasurer.il.gov` for further information.

## Indiana

### Rules of Intestacy

✔ **Surviving spouse:**

- **No issue or surviving parents:** All the estate.

- **No issue but one or both surviving parents:** ¾ of estate.

- **With at least one child or issue of a deceased child:** ½ of estate.

- If the surviving spouse is a second or other subsequent spouse who did not at any time have children by decedent, and decedent left surviving a child or the descendants of a child or children by a previous spouse, the surviving second or subsequent childless spouse takes only an amount equal to ¼ of the remainder of the fair market value as of the date of death of the real property of the decedent minus the value of the liens and encumbrances on the real property of the decedent. However, a second or subsequent surviving spouse receives the same share of personal property of decedent as surviving spouses generally, as described above.

✔ **No surviving spouse (or portion not distributed to surviving spouse):**

- To issue, equally if they are all of same degree of kinship. Those of unequal degree take by representation.

- If there is a surviving spouse but no issue, to decedent's surviving parents. If no surviving spouse or issue, to surviving parents, brothers and sisters, and issue of deceased brothers and sisters by representation. Each living parent shall be treated as of the same degree as brothers and sisters, except that the share of each parent shall not be less than ¼ of the net estate.

**State Estate and Inheritance Taxes:** The Indiana inheritance tax is being phased out over 10 years, to be completely eliminated in 2022. File **Form IH-6** in the probate court of the county where the decedent was a resident or in which the estate is being administered. Contact the Indiana Department of Revenue, Inheritance Tax, Indiana Government Center North, 100 N. Senate Ave., Indianapolis, IN 46204; Phone: 317-232-2154; Website. `www.in.gov/dor/index.htm` for further information.

## Iowa

### Rules of Intestacy

✔ **Surviving spouse:**

- **No issue or issue is also that of surviving spouse:** All the estate.

- **With issue that isn't issue of surviving spouse:** ½ of estate (a minimum of $50,000) and all personal property of decedent as head of family.

✔ **No surviving spouse (or portion not distributed to surviving spouse):** Same as Alabama to the point described earlier.

**State Estate and Inheritance Taxes:** Decedents dying after December 31, 2004, no estate tax return required. For decedents dying prior to January 1, 2005, contact Iowa Department of Revenue for further information. Iowa does have an inheritance tax. File **Form IA 706** at Examination Section, Iowa Department of Revenue, P.O. Box 10467, Des Moines, Iowa 50306-0467; Phone: 515-281-3114; Website: `www.iowa.gov/tax` for further information.

### Kansas

#### Rules of Intestacy

✔ **Surviving spouse:**

- **No children or issue of a predeceased child:** All the estate.

- **With child or children or issue of a predeceased child:** ½ of estate.

- **In either case:** Under certain conditions, ½ of all real estate which decedent owned at any time during the marriage as to which surviving spouse didn't consent to disposition.

✔ **No surviving spouse (or portion not distributed to surviving spouse):** Same as Alabama, to the point described earlier.

**State Estate Taxes:** No estate or inheritance tax for decedents dying after 12/31/09. For decedents dying after 6/30/98 and before 1/1/07, estate may be liable for "pick-up" tax. For decedents dying after 12/31/06 and before 01/01/10, estate may be liable for "stand-alone" estate tax. Contact Taxpayer Assistance Center, Kansas Department of Revenue, 915 SW Harrison St., 1st Fl, Topeka, KS 66612-1588 for more information. Phone: 785-368-8222; Website: www.ksrevenue.org/.

### Kentucky

#### Rules of Intestacy

✔ **Surviving spouse:** Personal property or cash in the amount of $15,000, and ½ of each piece of real estate owned by decedent or for his or her benefit at time of death, and an estate for life in ⅓ of all real estate owned by the decedent during the marriage but no longer owned, unless the surviving spouse had relinquished this right, and ½ of decedent's personalty. If no children or their descendants or parents of decedent, the whole estate goes to the surviving spouse.

✔ **No surviving spouse (or portion not distributed to surviving spouse):**

- To children and their descendants.

- **No children or descendants:** To parents, if both are living, equally. If one parent is dead, the other, if living, shall take the whole estate.

**State Inheritance Taxes:** Kentucky does have an inheritance tax, but no tax is due and no return required if all assets pass to exempt beneficiaries (i.e., surviving spouse, parent, child, grandchild, sibling, or exempt organization). Otherwise **Form 92A201** or **92A205** must be filed. Contact Financial Tax Section, Kentucky Department of Revenue, Station 61, 501 High Street, Frankfort, KY 40601-2103; Phone: 502-564-4810; Website: www.revenue.ky.gov for further information.

### Louisiana

#### Rules of Intestacy

✔ **Community (Marital) Property:** If decedent leaves no descendants, the surviving spouse succeeds to decedent's share of community property. If descendants survive decedent, the surviving spouse has a *usufruct* over (right to use) decedent's share of community property for life or until remarriage (whichever occurs first), after which the descendants succeed to that share of the community property. If no descendants, to brothers and sisters with usufruct to surviving parents, or, if none, to nieces or nephews or their descendants, with usufruct to decedent's surviving parents.

✔ **Separate (Nonmarital) Property:** Decedent's descendants succeed to decedent's separate property. If decedent leaves no descendants but is survived by one parent, or both, and by a brother or sister, or both, or descendants from them, the brothers and sisters or their descendants succeed to the separate property of decedent, subject to a usufruct in favor of the surviving parent or parents. If both parents survive decedent, the usufruct is joint and successive. If decedent leaves neither descendants nor parents, decedent's brothers and sisters or descendants from them succeed to his separate property. Or, if none, to decedent's surviving parents, or, if none, to decedent's surviving spouse.

**State Estate Taxes:** Decedents dying after December 31, 2004, no estate tax return required. For decedents dying prior to January 1, 2005, contact Louisiana Department of

Revenue, P.O. Box 201, Baton Rouge, LA 70821; Phone: 225-219-0067; Website: www.rev. state.la.us for more information.

## Maine

### Rules of Intestacy

🗸 **Surviving spouse or registered domestic partner:**

- **No surviving issue or parent of decedent:** All the estate.

- **No surviving issue but surviving parent or parents, or surviving issue all of whom are issue of the surviving spouse or surviving registered domestic partner:** The first $50,000, plus ½ of the balance of the estate.

- **With surviving issue, one or more of whom are not issue of the surviving spouse or surviving registered domestic partner:** ½ of estate.

🗸 **No surviving spouse or registered domestic partner (or portion not distributed to such person):** Same as Alabama to the point described earlier.

**State Estate Taxes:** File **Form 706ME** for estates greater than $2 million for decedents dying after 12/31/12, and $1 million for decedents dying before 01/01/13 and mail to Maine Revenue Services, Income/Estate Tax Division, P.O. Box 1065, Augusta, ME 04332-1065. Estates that are not required to file **Form 706ME** may instead file **Form 706ME-EZ** (for decedents dying in 2012) or **Form 700-SOV** (for decedent dying in 2013) in order to request the release of the automatic statutory estate tax lien on real or tangible personal property for estates with no tax liability. As of December 29, 2012, Maine permits same-sex marriage and recognizes same-sex marriages performed in other states. Accordingly, gender-specific terms relating to family or marital relationships are to be construed as gender neutral for *all* purposes— statutory, administrative, court rule, policy or common law. Presumably, this includes the marital deduction. For further info, contact Maine Revenue Services at 207-626-8480 or Website: www.maine.gov/revenue.

## Maryland

### Rules of Intestacy

🗸 **Surviving spouse:**

- **No surviving issue or parent:** All the estate.

- **With surviving minor child:** ½ of estate.

- **No surviving minor child, but surviving issue or surviving parent:** First $15,000 plus ½ of the remainder.

🗸 **No surviving spouse (or portion not distributed to surviving spouse):** Same as Alabama to the point described earlier.

**State Estate and Inheritance Taxes:** Inheritance tax collected by the Register of Wills in the county where the decedent either lived or owned property. Tax imposed on clear value of property that passes from decedent to certain individuals. Estate tax is calculated on transfer of all property in excess of $1 million less any inheritance tax paid. Complete **Form 706** (even if no **Form 706** is required federally) first before filing Maryland **Form MET-1**. **Form MET-1** must be filed with the Register of Wills office for the county in which the estate is being administered within nine months of date of death, or may be filed (along with all payments) with Comptroller of Maryland, Revenue Administration Division — Estate Tax Section, P.O. Box 828, Annapolis, MD 21404-0828, together with **Certification of Inheritance Tax.** Although Maryland voters have approved same-sex marriage beginning in 2013, the State Comptroller has indicated that legislative or regulatory action will be required to afford same-sex couples the same tax benefits as currently available to other married couples. For further information, contact the Revenue Administration Division at 800-MD-TAXES or Website: www.marylandtaxes.com.

## Massachusetts

### Rules of Intestacy

🗸 **Surviving spouse:**

- **With descendants that are all also descendants of the surviving spouse,** or no surviving descendants or parent: 100 percent of estate.

- **No surviving descendants but surviving parents:** First $200,000 plus ¾ of the remaining estate balance.

- **With descendants that are all also the descendants of the surviving spouse, and the surviving spouse has descendants who are not descendants of the decedent:** First $100,000 plus ½ of the remaining estate balance.

- **With descendants that are not all descendants of the surviving spouse:** First $100,000 plus ½ of the estate balance.

✔ **No surviving spouse (or portion not distributed to surviving spouse):**

- **With descendants:** To the decedent's descendants per capita at each generation.

- **No descendants but surviving parents:** Parents share equally, or to the surviving parent.

**State Estate Taxes:** Decoupled from federal estate tax for deaths occurring on or after January 1, 2003. For deaths on or after January 1, 2006, first $1 million of gross estate is excludable for estate tax purposes. File **Form M-706** with Massachusetts Department of Revenue, Bureau of Desk Audit, Estate Tax Unit, P.O. Box 7023, Boston, MA 02204 within nine months after date of death. Effective May 16, 2004, Massachusetts affords same-sex married couples the same tax benefits as married opposite-sex couples. Preparation of a pro-forma federal estate tax return may be required. For further information contact the Estate Tax Unit at 617-887-6930; Website: www.mass.gov/dor.

## Michigan

**Rules of Intestacy**

✔ **Surviving spouse:**

- **No surviving descendant or parent:** All the estate.

- **No descendants but surviving parents:** The first $210,000 (for 2012), indexed

annually for cost-of-living adjustment. plus ¾ of any balance of the intestate estate.

- **If any descendants are also descendants of the surviving spouse:** The first $210,000 (for 2012), indexed annually for cost-of-living adjustment, plus ½ of any balance of the estate.

- **If none of the decedent's surviving descendants are descendants of the surviving spouse:** First $140,000 (for 2012), indexed annually for cost-of-living adjustment, plus ½ of any balance of the estate.

✔ **No surviving spouse (or portion not distributed to surviving spouse):** Same as Alabama, to the extent described earlier, but substitute "descendant" for "issue" wherever it appears in this regard.

**State Estate Taxes:** Decedents dying after December 31, 2004, no estate tax return required. For decedents dying prior to January 1, 2005, contact Michigan Department of Treasury, Lansing, MI 48922; Phone: 517-373-3200; Website: www.michigan.gov/treasury for more information.

## Minnesota

**Rules of Intestacy**

✔ **Surviving spouse:**

- **No issue or all issue are also issue of the surviving spouse and there is no other descendant of the surviving spouse who survives the decedent:** All the estate.

- **Surviving spouse has one or more surviving descendants who are not descendants of the decedent, or one or more of decedents surviving descendants are not also descendants of the surviving spouse:** First $150,000, plus ½ of any balance of the estate.

✔ **No surviving spouse (or portion not distributed to surviving spouse):** To decedent's descendants by representation, or, if none, to decedent's parents equally or all to the survivor.

**State Estate Taxes:** File **Form M706** for estates greater than $1 million ($5 million for qualifying small businesses and farms) and mail to Minnesota Department of Revenue, Estate Tax Mail Station 1315, St. Paul, MN 55146-1315 within nine months of date of death. For more information, contact Minnesota Revenue Department at 651-556-3075 or www.revenue.state.mn.us.

## Mississippi

### Rules of Intestacy

✔ **Surviving spouse:**

- **No descendants:** All the estate.
- **With descendants:** Surviving spouse shares equally with decedent's children of that or a prior marriage, and descendants of a deceased child or children take that child's share.

✔ **No surviving spouse (or portion not distributed to surviving spouse):** To decedent's descendants by right of representation, or, if none, to the brothers and sisters and father and mother of decedent, and descendants of deceased brothers and sisters, by right of representation.

**State Estate Taxes:** Decedents dying after December 31, 2004, no estate tax return required. For decedents dying prior to January 1, 2005, contact Mississippi State Tax Commission, P.O. Box 1033, Jackson, MS 39215-1033; Phone: 601-923-7000; Website: www.dor.ms.gov for further information.

## Missouri

### Rules of Intestacy

✔ **Surviving spouse:**

- **No surviving issue:** All the estate.
- **With issue, all of whom are also issue of the surviving spouse:** The first $20,000 of estate, plus ½ of the balance of estate.
- **With issue, one or more of whom are not issue of the surviving spouse:** ½ of estate.

✔ **No surviving spouse (or portion not distributed to surviving spouse):** Same as Mississippi to the extent described earlier.

**State Estate Taxes:** Decedents dying after December 31, 2004, no estate tax return required. For decedents dying prior to January 1, 2005, contact Estate Tax Division, P.O. Box 27, Jefferson City, MO 65105-0027; Phone: 573-751-1467; Website: www.dor.mo.gov for further information.

## Montana

### Rules of Intestacy

✔ **Surviving spouse:** Same as Alaska.

✔ **No surviving spouse (or portion not distributed to surviving spouse):** Same as Alabama.

**State Estate Taxes:** Decedents dying after December 31, 2004, no estate tax return required. For decedents dying prior to January 1, 2005, contact Montana Department of Revenue, P.O. Box 5805, Helena, MT 59604; Phone: 866-859-2254; Website: www.revenue.mt.gov for more information.

## Nebraska

### Rules of Intestacy

✔ **Surviving spouse:**

- **If no surviving issue or parent:** All the estate.
- **If no surviving issue but parent or parents:** First $50,000 plus ½ of the balance of the estate.
- **With issue, all of whom are also issue of the surviving spouse:** The first $50,000 of estate, plus ½ of the balance of estate.
- **With issue, one or more of whom are not issue of the surviving spouse:** ½ of estate.

✔ **No surviving spouse (or portion not distributed to surviving spouse):** Same as Alabama.

**State Inheritance Taxes:** No estate tax, but inheritance tax, which must be paid within 12 months of decedent's death. Tax is assessed as a percentage of the clear market value of property, including insurance proceeds on the decedent's life that is transferred from a Nebraska resident (or non-resident owning Nebraska property). Rate is determined by identity of beneficiary and relationship to decedent; there is no inheritance tax on interests passing to surviving spouse. Taxes are paid to the County Treasurer of the decedent's county of residence, or to the County Treasurer in the county where the property is located.

## Nevada

**Rules of Intestacy:** All community property goes to the surviving spouse and is his or her sole separate property including community property held with right of survivorship, which vests in accordance with the right of survivorship.

- ✔ **Surviving spouse:**

  - **No issue, father, mother, brother, sister, or children of any issue:** All the estate.

  - **No issue but surviving parents:** ½ to surviving spouse, ¼ to each surviving parent. If only one surviving parent, ½ of estate to that surviving parent.

  - **No issue or surviving parents but surviving siblings:** ½ to surviving spouse and remainder equally to brothers and sisters of decedent.

  - **With one child or that child's issue:** ½ to surviving spouse and ½ to child or among deceased child's issue.

  - **With more than one child or a child and the lawful issue of a deceased child:** ⅓ to surviving spouse and remainder to children in equal shares, with issue of deceased child to take by right of representation.

- ✔ **No surviving spouse (or portion not distributed to surviving spouse):** To decedent's children and lawful issue of deceased children, by right of representation.

**State Estate Taxes:** Decedents dying after December 31, 2004, no estate tax return is required for the State of Nevada. For decedents dying prior to January 1, 2005, contact Nevada Department of Taxation, 1550 East College Parkway, Suite 115, Carson City, NV 89706; Phone: 775-684-2000; Website: www.tax.state.nv.us for further information.

## New Hampshire

**Rules of Intestacy**

- ✔ **Surviving spouse:**

  - **No surviving issue or parent of the decedent:** All the estate.

  - **With issue, all of whom are also issue of the surviving spouse and there are no other issue of the surviving spouse who survive the decedent:** First $250,000, plus ½ of the balance.

  - **No surviving issue but a parent or parents:** First $250,000, plus ¾ of the balance of the estate.

  - **With issue, all of whom are issue of the surviving spouse, and the surviving spouse has one or more surviving issue who are not the issue of the decedent:** First $150,000, plus ½ of the balance of the estate.

  - **With surviving issue, one or more of whom are not issue of the surviving spouse:** First $100,000, plus ½ of the balance of the estate.

- ✔ **No surviving spouse (or portion not distributed to surviving spouse):** Same as Alabama to the extent described earlier.

**State Estate and Legacy & Succession Taxes:** The Legacy & Succession Tax was repealed effective January 1, 2003. Decedents dying after December 31, 2004, no estate tax return required. For decedents dying prior to January 1, 2005, contact Department of Revenue Administration, Audit Division, P.O. Box 457, Concord, NH 03302-0457 Phone: 603-230-5000. Website: www.nh.gov/revenue/index.htm for further information.

## New Jersey

**Rules of Intestacy**

- ✔ **Surviving spouse, surviving partner of a civil union, or domestic partner:**

  - **No descendant or surviving parent of the decedent or with descendants that are also descendants of the surviving spouse, surviving partner of a civil union, or domestic partner and there is no other descendant of the surviving spouse, surviving partner of a civil union, or domestic partner who survives the decedent:** All the estate.

  - **No descendants but a surviving parent:** First 25 percent of the estate (not less than $50,000 nor more than $200,000) plus ¾ of any balance remaining.

  - **With descendants that are also descendants of the surviving spouse, surviving partner of a civil union, or domestic partner and the surviving spouse, surviving partner of a civil union, or domestic partner has one or more surviving descendants who are not descendants of the decedent or with descendants that are not descendants of the surviving spouse, surviving partner of a civil union, or domestic partner:** First 25 percent of the estate, but not less than $50,000 nor more than $200,000, plus ½ of the balance remaining.

- ✔ **No surviving spouse, surviving partner of a civil union, or domestic partner (or portion not distributed to surviving spouse):** To the descendants by right of representation, or if none, to the parents equally, or the survivor of them.

**State Inheritance and Estate Taxes:** New Jersey has both an inheritance tax on transfers of $500 and more and an estate tax for net estates of $675,000 or more. For decedents who were partners in a civil union and who die on or after February 19, 2007, a marital deduction is allowed. For further information, contact the Division of Taxation, Individual Audit Branch, Inheritance and Estate Tax, P.O. Box 249, Trenton, NJ 08695-0249 Phone: 609-292-5033 Website: www.state.nj.us/treasury/taxation.

## New Mexico

**Rules of Intestacy**

- ✔ **Surviving spouse:**

  - **With issue:** 25 percent of separate property and the decedent's share of community property.

  - **No issue:** All the estate.

- ✔ **No surviving spouse (or portion not distributed to surviving spouse):** Same as Alabama to the point described earlier.

**State Estate Taxes:** Decedents dying after December 31, 2004, no estate tax return required. Send the federal **Form 706** and **RPD-41058**, State of New Mexico Estate Tax Return, and a certificate of no tax due will be issued. For decedents dying prior to January 1, 2005, contact New Mexico Taxation and Revenue Department, P.O. Box 25123, Santa Fe, NM 87504-5123; Phone: 505-827-0763; Website: www.tax.newmexico.gov for further information.

## New York

**Rules of Intestacy (as of July 24, 2011, under the Marriage Equality Act, the term spouse herein includes same-sex spouses)**

- ✔ **Surviving spouse:**

  - **With issue:** First $50,000 plus ½ of the remaining balance.

  - **No issue:** All the estate.

- ✔ **No surviving spouse (or portion not distributed to surviving spouse):** Same as Alabama to the point described earlier.

**State Estate Taxes:** For decedents dying on or after January 1, 2004, if the estate is greater than $1 million, file **Form ET-706** within nine months of the decedent's date of death. Federal **Form 706** must also be completed and submitted with the state return even if it is not required to be filed with the IRS. For individuals dying on or after July 24, 2011, the same deductions (including the marital deduction) and elections allowed for spouses generally are allowed for same-sex spouses, regardless of whether a federal estate tax return is filed. For decedents dying after February 1, 2000, and before January 1, 2004, and if the estate was required to file a federal estate tax return, then **Form ET-706** must be filed. Send it to NYS Estate Tax, Processing

Center, P.O. Box 15167, Albany, NY 12212-5167; Phone: 518-457-5387; Website: www.tax.ny.gov.

## North Carolina

**Rules of Intestacy**

✔ **Surviving spouse:**

- **No issue or surviving parents:** All real and personal property.

- **No issue but surviving parents:** ½ of real property and $100,000 plus one half of the balance of the personal property

- **With only one child or his or her descendants:** ½ of real property and $60,000 plus ½ of the balance of the personal property.

- **With more than one child or descendants of a deceased child:** ⅓ of real property and $60,000 plus ⅓ of the balance of the personal property.

✔ **No surviving spouse (or portion not distributed to surviving spouse):** Same as Alabama to the point described above.

**State Estate Taxes:** North Carolina imposes an estate tax only when a federal estate tax is imposed on a decedent. The North Carolina estate tax is equal to the 2001 state death tax credit for federal estate tax as it existed for estates of decedents dying before July 1, 2005. **Form A-101** must be filed within nine months of date of death if federal **Form 706 is** required. Completed return should be mailed to: North Carolina Department of Revenue, P.O. Box 25000, Raleigh, NC 27640-0100. For decedents dying prior to January 1, 2005, contact North Carolina Department of Revenue, P.O. Box 25000, Raleigh, NC 27640-0100; Phone: 877-252-3052; Website: www.dor.state.nc.us for further information.

## North Dakota

**Rules of Intestacy**

✔ **Surviving spouse:**

- **With no issue or parent or all the decedent's surviving descendants are also descendants of the surviving spouse:** All the estate.

- **With no issue but a surviving parent:** First $300,000 plus ¾ of any balance of the intestate estate.

- **With issue that is also the issue of the surviving spouse and the surviving spouse has one or more surviving descendants who are not descendants of the decedent:** First $225,000 plus ½ of any balance of the intestate estate.

- **With issue that isn't a descendant of the surviving spouse:** First $150,000 plus ½ of any balance of the intestate estate.

✔ **No surviving spouse (or portion not distributed to surviving spouse):** Same as Alabama to the point described earlier.

**State Estate Taxes:** No estate tax for decedents dying after December 31, 2004; however, **ND Form 54-91** must be filed if federal **Form 706** is required for all decedents dying on or after 01/01/1991. Contact Office of State Tax Commissioner, 600 E. Boulevard Ave., Dept 127, Bismarck, ND 58505-0599; Phone: 701-328-3158; Website: www.nd.gov/tax for further information.

## Ohio

**Rules of Intestacy**

✔ **Surviving spouse:**

- **No lineal descendants or with children or their descendants who are also descendants of the surviving spouse:** All the estate.

- **If there is one child of the decedent or the child's lineal descendants surviving and the surviving spouse is not the natural or adoptive parent of the decedent's child:** First $20,000 plus ½ of the balance.

- **If there are more than one child or their lineal descendants surviving if the spouse is the natural or adoptive parent of one, but not all, of the children:** First $60,000, or the first $20,000 if the spouse is the natural or adoptive parent of none of the children, plus ⅓ of the balance of the estate.

✔ **No surviving spouse (or portion not distributed to surviving spouse):** To the children of the decedent and their lineal descendants, per stirpes, or, if there are none, to the decedent's parents, equally, or all to the survivor.

**State Estate Taxes:** Estate tax is repealed effective 01/01/2013 for individuals dying on or after that date. For decedents dying on or after 01/01/2002 and prior to 01/01/2013, estates with net taxable value of $338,333 are exempt from estate tax; estates with gross value of $338,333 must file **Form ET 2** within nine months of date of death. For more information, contact Estate Tax Unit 4485 Northland Ridge Blvd., Columbus, OH 43229; Phone: 800-977-7711; Website: www. tax.ohio.gov.

## Oklahoma

**Rules of Intestacy**

✔ **Surviving spouse:**

- **No surviving issue, parents, or siblings:** All the estate.

- **No surviving issue but is survived by parents or siblings:** All the property acquired by the joint industry of the husband and wife during *coverture* (the state of a married woman), and an undivided ⅓ interest in the remaining estate.

- **With issue, all of whom are also issue of the surviving spouse:** An undivided ½ interest in all intestate property however acquired.

- **With issue, one or more of whom are not also issue of the surviving spouse:** An undivided ½ interest in the property acquired by the joint industry of the husband and wife during coverture, and an undivided equal part in the property of the decedent not acquired by the joint industry of the husband and wife during coverture with each of the living children of the decedent and the lawful issue of any deceased child by right of representation.

✔ **No surviving spouse (or portion not distributed to surviving spouse):** Same as Alabama to the point described earlier.

**State Estate Taxes:** The Oklahoma estate tax was phased out beginning in 2006, with the tax repealed for deaths on or after January 1, 2010. For decedents dying prior to January 1, 2010,

contact Oklahoma Tax Commission, Estate Tax Department, 2501 N. Lincoln Blvd, Oklahoma City, OK 73194-0110; Phone: 405-521-3237; Website: www.tax.ok.gov for further information.

## Oregon

**Rules of Intestacy**

✔ **Surviving spouse:**

- **No issue or with issue, all of whom are issue of the surviving spouse:** All the estate.

- **With issue, and one or more are not issue of the surviving spouse:** ½ of estate.

✔ **No surviving spouse (or portion not distributed to surviving spouse):** Same as Ohio to the point described earlier.

**State Estate Taxes:** For decedents dying after December 31, 2011, with an estate valued greater than $1 million, file **Form OR 706, Oregon Estate Transfer Tax Return.** For decedents dying before January 1, 2012, with an estate valued greater than $1 million, file **Form IT-1, Oregon Inheritance Tax Return**. If you need further information, contact the Oregon Department of Revenue, 955 Center St. NE, Salem, OR 97301-2555; Phone: 503-378-4988; Website: www.oregon.gov/DOR.

## Pennsylvania

**Rules of Intestacy**

✔ **Surviving spouse:**

- **No surviving issue or parent(s):** All the estate.

- **No surviving issue but is survived by a parent(s) or with issue, all of whom are issue of the surviving spouse:** First $30,000 plus ½ of the balance of the estate.

- Notwithstanding the foregoing, in the case of a decedent who died as a result of the terrorist attacks of September 11, 2001, a surviving spouse is entitled to 100 per cent of any compensation award paid pursuant to the Air Transportation Safety and System Stabilization Act (Public Law 107-42, 115 Stat. 230).

- **With issue, one or more of whom are not issue of the surviving spouse:** ½ of the estate.

- In case of partial intestacy, any property received by the surviving spouse under the will shall go toward satisfying the $30,000 allowance mentioned earlier.

✔ **No surviving spouse (or portion not distributed to surviving spouse):** Same as Ohio to point described earlier.

**State Inheritance Taxes:** File **Form REV-1500, Pennsylvania Inheritance Tax Return** within nine months of date of death. The return is to be filed in duplicate, with the Register of Wills of the county in which the decedent was a resident at the time of death. Effective for decedents dying after June 30, 2012, the inheritance tax is eliminated for family farms. For a list of Register of Wills, contact PA Department of Revenue, Bureau of Individual Taxes, P.O. Box 280601, Harrisburg, PA 17128-0601; Phone: 717-787-8327; Website: www.revenue.state.pa.us.

## Rhode Island

### Rules of Intestacy

✔ **Surviving spouse:**

- **Re personal property:**

  No issue: $50,000 and ½ of remaining estate.

  With issue: ½ of estate.

- **Re real estate:**

  A life estate in all real estate held in decedent's name alone, or alternatively, probate court may allow surviving spouse to fully own real estate located in Rhode Island and valued at $75,000 or less, or, if the property is worth more, the Court may order the sale of property with surviving spouse to get $75,000 of sale proceeds.

✔ **No surviving spouse (or portion not distributed to surviving spouse):** Same as Ohio to point described earlier.

**State Estate Taxes:** For a decedent dying on or after January 1, 2002, file **Form 100A, Rhode Island Estate Tax Return.** Taxable estates have gross value of $910,725 or more for decedents

dying on or after January 1, 2013, which amount is annually adjusted by the Consumer Price Index for urban consumers (CPI-U). The unified credit for estates of decedents dying in 2013 is $310,982.75, which amount is also adjusted for inflation. Effective July, 1, 2011, a marital deduction is available for property passing from a decedent to his or her same-sex partner to the same extent as property left to a surviving spouse is allowed such a deduction under federal law. The return, with payment, is due within nine months of the date of death. Mail to Rhode Island Division of Taxation, Estate Tax Section, One Capitol Hill, Providence, RI 02908-5800. You can contact the division of taxation at this address, call 401-574-8900, or visit its website at www.tax.state.ri.us for more information.

## South Carolina

### Rules of Intestacy

✔ **Surviving spouse:**

- **No issue:** All the intestate estate.
- **With issue:** ½ of the intestate estate.

✔ **No surviving spouse (or portion not distributed to surviving spouse):** Same as Ohio to the point described earlier.

**State Estate Taxes:** Decedents dying after December 31, 2004, no estate tax return required. For decedents dying prior to January 1, 2005, contact the South Carolina Department of Revenue, Estate Section, P.O. Box 125, Columbia, SC 29214-0061; Phone: 803-898-5626; Website: www.sctax.org for further information.

## South Dakota

### Rules of Intestacy

✔ **Surviving spouse:**

- No descendant or all the descendants are also descendants of the surviving spouse: All the estate.
- If one or more of the decedent's surviving descendants are not descendants of the surviving spouse: First $100,000, plus ½ of any balance of the estate.

✔ **No surviving spouse (or portion not distributed to surviving spouse):** Same as Ohio to the extent described earlier.

**State Estate Taxes:** Decedents dying after December 31, 2004, no estate tax return required. For decedents dying prior to January 1, 2005, contact South Dakota Department of Revenue, 445 East Capitol Avenue, Pierre, SD 57501-3100; Phone: 605-773-3311; Website: www.state.sd.us/ for further information.

## Tennessee

### Rules of Intestacy

✔ **Surviving spouse:**

- **No surviving issue:** All the intestate estate.

- **With surviving issue:** Either ⅓ or a child's share of the entire intestate estate, whichever is greater.

✔ **No surviving spouse (or portion not distributed to surviving spouse):** Same as Ohio to the point described earlier.

**State Inheritance Taxes:** Amounts passing to the surviving spouse are totally exempt from tax and $1,250,000 passing to all other beneficiaries is exempt in 2013, $2,000,000 in 2014 and $5,000,000 in 2015. The inheritance tax is eliminated for decedents dying in 2016 and after. File **Form INH 301, Tennessee Inheritance Tax Return,** within nine months of date of death and mail to Tennessee Department of Revenue, Andrew Jackson State Office Building, 500 Deaderick St., Nashville, TN 37242-0600. You may contact the department of revenue at the above address; call 615-253-0600; or visit www.tn.gov/revenue if you have further questions.

## Texas

### Rules of Intestacy (effective until January 1, 2014)

✔ **Surviving spouse:**

- **Re community property:**

  **No surviving descendants or descendants all of whom are also descendants of surviving spouse:** All community property.

  **Surviving descendants, not all of whom are descendants of surviving spouse:** Surviving spouse gets only his or her own ½ share of community property.

- **Re separate property:**

  **No surviving descendants:** All the personal estate and ½ of real estate, or all the real estate if the deceased has neither surviving father nor mother nor surviving brothers or sisters, or their descendants.

  **With surviving descendants:** ⅓ of personal estate and a life estate in ⅓ of real estate, with remainder equally to children or their descendants.

✔ **No surviving spouse (or portion not distributed to surviving spouse):**

- **Descendants:** All the estate.

- **No descendants:** Parents of the decedent, equally. If only one parent survives, estate to be divided into two equal portions, one of which shall pass to such survivor, and the other half shall pass to the brothers and sisters of the deceased, and to their descendants, but if there be none, then the whole estate shall be inherited by the surviving father or mother.

**State Inheritance Taxes:** Decedents dying after December 31, 2004, no inheritance tax return required. For decedents dying prior to January 1, 2005, contact the Texas Comptroller of Public Accounts, Lyndon B. Johnson State Office Building, 111 East 17th St., Austin, Texas 78774; Phone: 800-531-5441; Website: www.window.state.tx.us/taxes for further information.

## Utah

### Rules of Intestacy

✔ **Surviving spouse:**

- **No descendants or all the decedent's surviving descendants are also descendants of the surviving spouse:** All the estate.

- **If one or more of decedent's surviving descendants are not descendants of surviving spouse:** First $75,000, plus ½ of any balance of estate.

✔ **No surviving spouse (or portion not distributed to surviving spouse):** Same as Massachusetts to the extent described earlier.

**State Estate Taxes:** Decedents dying after December 31, 2004, no estate tax return required. For decedents dying prior to January 1, 2005, contact Utah State Tax Commission, 210 North 1950 West, Salt Lake City, UT 84134; Phone: 801-297-2200; Website: www.tax.utah. gov for further information.

## Vermont

**Rules of Intestacy**

✔ Surviving spouse:

- **No descendants or all the decedent's surviving descendants are also descendants of the surviving spouse:** All the estate.

- **If one or more of decedent's surviving descendants are not descendants of surviving spouse:** ½ of estate.

✔ **No surviving spouse (or portion not distributed to surviving spouse):** Same as Ohio to extent described earlier.

**State Estate Taxes:** File **Form E-1, Vermont Estate Tax Return,** within nine months of date of death and mail to Vermont Department of Taxes, 133 State Street, Montpelier, VT 05633-1401. Vermont recognizes same-sex marriage (since 9/1/09) and civil unions (since 7/1/00). You may contact Vermont Department of Taxes at the above address; call 802-828-6820; or visit www.state.vt.us/tax for more information.

## Virginia

**Rules of Intestacy (effective October 1, 2012)**

✔ Surviving spouse:

- **No descendants or descendants are also that of the surviving spouse:** All the estate.

- **With descendants, one or more of whom are not descendants of the surviving spouse:** ⅓ of estate.

✔ **No surviving spouse (or portion not distributing to surviving spouse):** To the decedent's children and their descendants,

or, if there are none, to the decedent's parents, or the surviving parent.

**State Estate Taxes:** Decedents dying after June 30, 2007, no estate tax return required. For decedents dying prior to July 1, 2007, contact Virginia Department of Taxation, Office of Customer Services, P.O. Box 1115, Richmond, VA 23218-1115; Phone: 804-367-8031; Website: www.tax.virginia.gov for more information.

## Washington

**Rules of Intestacy**

✔ Surviving spouse or state registered domestic partner:

- **No surviving issue, parents, or issue of decedent's parents:** All the net community and separate estate.

- **With issue:** All the decedent's share of net community estate and ½ of the net separate estate.

- **No surviving issue, but is survived by one or more parents or one or more issue of one or more of decedent's parents:** All the decedent's share of net community estate and ¾ of the net separate estate.

✔ **No surviving spouse or state registered domestic partner (or portion not distributed to surviving spouse or state registered domestic partner):** Same as Alabama to the point described earlier.

**State Estate Taxes:** File a **Washington State Estate and Transfer Tax Return** within nine months of date of death for estates of $2,000,000 or more. Effective January 1, 2014, Washington will accord the same tax treatment to persons in state registered domestic partnerships as to other married persons. Mail to Washington State Department of Revenue, P.O. Box 47488, Olympia, WA 98504-7488. For further information, contact the Washington State Department of Taxes at the above address; call 360-570-3265, #2; or visit them on the Web at www.dor. wa.gov.

## West Virginia

**Rules of Intestacy**

✔ Surviving spouse:

- **No descendants or all the descendants are also descendants of the surviving spouse and there is no other descendant of the surviving spouse:** All the estate.

- **If all the decedent's surviving descendants are also descendants of the surviving spouse and the surviving spouse has one or more surviving descendants who are not descendants of the decedent:** ⅗ of estate.

- **If one or more of the decedent's surviving descendants are not descendants of the surviving spouse:** ½ of the estate.

✔ **No surviving spouse (or portion not distributed to surviving spouse):** Same as Hawaii to the point described earlier.

**State Estate Taxes:** Decedents dying after December 31, 2004, no estate tax return required. For decedents dying prior to January 1, 2005, contact West Virginia State Tax Department, Taxpayer Services Division, P.O. Box 3784, Charleston, WV 25337-3784; Phone: 304-558-3333; Website: www.wva.state.wv.us/wvtax for further information.

## Wisconsin

**Rules of Intestacy**

✔ Surviving spouse or domestic partner:

- **No surviving issue, or if the surviving issue are all issue of the surviving spouse or domestic partner and the decedent:** All the estate.

- **With issue, one or more of whom are not issue of the surviving spouse or domestic partner:** ½ of decedent's property other than the following property:
  a. The decedent's interest in marital property
  b. The decedent's interest in property held equally and exclusively with the surviving spouse or domestic partner as tenants in common

✔ **No surviving spouse or domestic partner (or portion not distributed to surviving spouse or domestic partner):** Same as Delaware to the point described earlier.

**State Estate Taxes:** For deaths occurring after September 30, 2002, and before January 1, 2008, **Form W706** must be filed for every decedent whose gross estate, plus adjusted taxable gifts and specific exemption is $675,000 or more. There is no Wisconsin estate tax for deaths occurring on or after January 1, 2008. For further information, contact the Wisconsin Department of Revenue, 2135 Rimrock Road, Madison, WI 53713; Phone: 608-266-2772; Website: www.revenue.wi.gov.

## Wyoming

**Rules of Intestacy**

✔ Surviving spouse:

- **No children or descendants of children:** All the estate.

- **With children or descendants of children:** ½ of estate.

✔ **No surviving spouse (or portion not distributed to surviving spouse):**

- **With children or descendants of children:** In equal shares, by right of representation.

- **With no children or descendants of children:** To decedent's surviving father, mother, brothers, sisters, and the descendants of a deceased brother or sister by right or representation, in equal parts.

**State Estate Taxes:** Decedents dying after December 31, 2004, no estate tax return required. For decedents dying prior to January 1, 2005, contact Estate Tax Administrator, 122 West Twenty-fifth Street, Herschler Building, Cheyenne, WY 82002-0110; Phone: 307-777-5200; Website: http://revenue.wyo.gov/ for more information.

# Index

## • A •

accountant, 149, 169, 200–201, 301
acquisition costs and dates, 293–294
adeemed property, 140
administrator, 10, 95, 149–150, 349
administratrix, 10
advisors
  appraisers, 69
  attorney, 59–64
  business consultants, 70
  charitable, 70
  creating a team of, 13
  fees, 200
  for handling assets, 169
  for investments, 64, 66–69, 169, 186–187
  litigators, 70
  location for, 64
  malpractice by, 70–72
  medical, 70
  need for, 57
  tax professional, 64–66
  trustee's power to hire and fire, 166
age-based distributions, 197, 209–212
age-based trusts, 198–199
Alabama taxes/rules of intestacy, 359–360
Alaska taxes/rules of intestacy, 360
alimony, paying, 134
allowance by probate court, 151–155
allowance for surviving spouse, 24
alternative minimum tax (AMT), 306–307, 308, 327–328
amendments to trusts, 85
amortization, 349
anatomical gifts, honoring, 76
ancillary administration, 97–98, 349
annual accounts, 169–170, 221–222, 226–229, 349
annual exclusion amount, 27, 43–44
annuities, 281, 285, 349
applicable exclusion amount, 44, 246, 349
applicable federal rate (AFR), 349
appraisers, 69
appraising property, 121–125, 235
Arizona taxes/rules of intestacy, 360
Arkansas taxes/rules of intestacy, 360–361
ascertainable standard for distributions, 165
assets. *See also* marshalling assets; *specific kinds*
  advisors for handling, 169
  defined, 349
  distributing property, 140–146, 150

diversifying, 168, 188–194
frozen, 83
impact of death on decedent's, 83–84
inventory and valuing of, 223–224
jointly owned, 83
liquidating, 130–132
locating after death, 86
in probate estates, 20
proof of ownership of, 20, 172
trustee's power to buy and sell, 163
assignment of partnership interest, 176
attested will, 22
attorney
  changing, 63
  checking credentials of, 60–61
  engagement letter for, 63
  fees, 62–63, 149, 301
  finding, 59–61
  as investment advisor, 67
  knowing what you want from, 59
  litigator, 70
  location for, 64
  notification of fees, 102
  questions to ask, 61
  as trust advisor, 169
  working with, 63
audit preparations, 261–262
automobiles. *See* vehicles
autopsy, 76

## • B •

backup withholding credit, 327
bank accounts, 83, 114–115, 123
banks, as trust advisors, 169
bar associations, 60
basis, 40, 349
beneficial interest, 349
beneficiaries. *See also* remaindermen
  address and SSN for, 204
  age-based distributions to, 209–212
  assent to annual account, 228
  defined, 162, 349
  estate distributions to, 164–165
  minimizing income taxes, 317–318
  notifying of the trust, 203–205
  right to consider disclaimer, 138–139
  scheduled distributions to, 205–209
  trustee's responsibilities for, 196–199
  verifying dates of birth, 204–205

beneficiary of the present interest, 11
bequests
  defined, 349
  pecuniary, 143
  of personal property, 139, 141
  Schedule M (Form 706), 280–282
bills, 191, 349
bonds. *See also* securities
  defined, 189, 349
  laddering maturity dates of, 189
  liquidating, 131
  notes and bills versus, 191
  ratings for, 190–191
  reregistering certificates, 174–175
  Schedule B (Form 706), 265–269
  tax credits, 308
  terminology, 191
  transferring to a trust, 172–175
  at trust termination, 234
  types of, 189–190
  valuation of, 266–269
brokerages, 115, 169
business
  credits, 308
  distributions for starting, 214–215
  income, 291–292
  small, as asset, 112–113
business consultants, 70
by right of representation (per stirpes), 146, 354
bypass (credit shelter) trust, 350

• C •

C corporation, closely held, 113
calendar creation, 89
California taxes/rules of intestacy, 361
capital gain dividends, 291
capital gains, 185, 292–294, 305–306, 307
capital losses, 185, 292–294
cash
  distributions, 210
  Schedule C (Form 706), 270
  small estate procedures for, 100
  transferring to a trust, 172–175
  trust needs for, 192–193
cash flow, projecting, 106
cemetery selection, 80, 81
Certificate of Completion, 154
Certified Financial Planners, 67
Certified Public Accountant (CPA), 64–66, 67
charitable advisors, 70
charitable deductions, 282–283, 300–301
Charitable Lead Annuity Trust (CLAT), 51, 349
Charitable Lead Unitrust (CLUT), 51, 350

Charitable Remainder Annuity Trust (CRAT),
    51, 281, 350
Charitable Remainder Unitrust (CRUT),
    51, 281, 350
charitable trusts, 50–53, 281, 356
charities, qualified, 27
child support, paying, 134
children's trusts, 350
churn, 350
clergyperson for funeral, 79
closely held C corporation, 113
closing the estate, 147–156
COBRA benefits, 126
codicil, 350
collation, 81
Colorado taxes/rules of intestacy, 361–362
columbarium, 80
commissions, stockbroker, 68
common law, 350
community property, 350
Complete Estate Settlement petition, 154–155
conditional legacies and devises, 137
Connecticut taxes/rules of intestacy, 362
conservator, 10, 350
consideration, 350
contested will, 104
conventions in this book, 2
convertible bonds, 191
copyrights, valuing, 123–124
corporate bonds, 189
corporate independent trustee, 162
corpus, 350
correspondence, records of, 220–221
CPA (Certified Public Accountant), 64–66, 67
CRAT (Charitable Remainder Annuity Trust),
    51, 281, 350
credit card insurance, 127–128
credit card payment for taxes, 247–248
credit shelter trust, 350
credits, tax, 308, 327
cremation, 79–80
Crummey trusts, 47–48, 350
CRUT (Charitable Remainder Unitrust),
    51, 281, 350
curtesy, 25, 108, 350
CUSIP number, 191, 267, 350

• D •

death benefits, 125, 128–129
death certificate, 82, 250
death notice, 78
death tax, 28, 351
debts of decedent, 133–136, 274, 279

deceased spousal unused exclusion (DSUE),
244, 260–261
decedent's estate
declaring insolvent, 137–138
defined, 351
declaration date, 351
Declaration of Trust Ownership, 181
declaring the estate insolvent, 137–138
deductions
charitable, 282–283
dividing between the decedent and the estate,
314
Forms 1040 and 1041, 297–304, 314
marital, 280–282
Schedule K-1 (Form 1041), 326–327
Delaware taxes/rules of intestacy, 362
delivery instructions, 351
depletion, 351
depreciation, 351
devise, 137, 140, 141–142, 351
digital assets and info, 118–119, 124
direct skip, 351
directly apportioned deductions, 326
disclaim, defined, 351
disclaimer by beneficiaries, 138–139
discretion, exercise of, 166–167, 215
discretionary distributions, 206, 210–215
distributing property
cautions before, 140
general steps for, 140–141
intangibles, 142–143
other personal property, 143–145
residue, 145–146, 150
tangibles, 141–142
distributions to beneficiaries
age-based, 209–210
ascertainable standard for, 165
discretionary, 206, 210–215
extra payments, 210–212
income, 164–165
lump-sum, 306, 336–337
principal, 165
scheduled, 205–209
at trust termination, 232–233
trustee's power to determine, 164–165
District of Columbia taxes/rules of intestacy,
362–363
diversifying assets, 168, 188–194
dividends, 268–269, 290–291
domicile, 21, 95–96, 351
donee, 351
donors. See grantors, donors, or settlors
double-dipping rules, 298
dower, 25, 108, 351
DSUE (deceased spousal unused exclusion),
244, 260–261

dying intestate, 22–23, 95, 144
dying testate, 21–22
dynasty trust, 351

• E •

education, distributions for, 213
effective disclaimer, 138–139
electing against the will, 23, 24, 107–108, 357
Electing Small Business Trust (ESBT), 55, 319, 351
Electronic Federal Tax Payment System
(EFTPS), 247
employee benefits, valuing, 125–127
Employer Identification Number (EIN), 267,
288–289
engagement letters, 63, 65
Enrolled Agent (EA), 64–66, 67, 169, 351
equities. See stocks
errors and omissions (E&O) insurance, 72, 167
estate administration. See also marshalling
assets; probate procedure
calendar creation, 89
claiming expenses, 275–276, 278
closing the estate, 147–156
declaring the estate insolvent, 137–138
determining who can inherit, 23–30
distributing specific property, 139–145
filing a petition for, 21
funeral arrangements, 77–82
immediate concerns after death, 75–76
impact of death on assets, 83–84
locating estate-planning documents, 84–86
notifying others of death, 86–88
organizing records, 89–90
overview of steps in, 13–15
overview of tax requirements, 17–18
paying decedent's debts, 133–136
prioritizing payments, 136–137
estate income taxes, 150, 151, 345, 359–377
estate records, organizing, 89–90
estate tax closing letters, 147–148, 262
estate tax deduction, 304, 326
estate tax return. See Form 706
estate-planning documents, 84–86
estimated taxes credit, 327
eulogies, 79
excise taxes, 347
executor. See also estate administration
defined, 10, 351
fee, 149–150
first steps to take, 105–106
foreign, 97
temporary, 93–94
executor's bond, 94, 351
executrix, 10

exempt property, 107
extraordinary (special) dividends, 186, 356

# • F •

face amount, 191, 351
family allowance, 107
family pot trust, 351
family trust (credit shelter), 350
family trustees, 12–13, 162
farm income or loss, 295–296
federal gift tax, 28, 343–344
fee simple, 352
fees. *See also* payments
　accountant, 149, 200–201, 301
　attorney, 62–63, 149, 301
　deductions for, 299–300, 301
　fiduciary, 299–300
　independent trustee, 12
　investment advisor, 68
　paying final expenses, 149–150
　statutory filing, 155
　tax professional, 65–66
　terminating a trust, 233
　trustee's, 200
fiduciaries
　avoiding poor judgment, 339
　defined, 10, 92, 352
　minimizing income taxes, 317
　overview, 10
fiduciary fees, 299–300
filing system setup, 89–90, 217–222
final-year deductions, 327
financial records, 221
fiscal year-end, 312–313, 352
5/5 provision, 205
fixed amount distributions, 205
fixed-income securities. *See* bills; bonds; notes
flexible spending accounts (FSAs), 126
Florida taxes/rules of intestacy, 363
Foreign Account Tax Compliance
　Act (FATCA), 164
foreign bonds, 189–190
foreign death taxes, 285
foreign executor, 97
foreign interests, trusts with, 164
foreign tax allocations, 330
foreign tax credit, 308
foreign will, 97
Form 706. *See also specific schedules*
　alternate valuation, 255–256
　amending, 250
　applicable exclusion amount, 246
　appraisal info on, 69, 125

asking for help, 283
assets on, 110, 120
audit preparations, 261–262
continuation schedule, 252
date due, 247
deceased spousal unused exclusion, 244,
　260–261
decedent and executor, 252
double-dipping rules, 298
effective disclaimer affecting, 139
estate tax closing letters for, 147–148
for estate tax release of lien, 148
extension of time to file, 245, 249
extension of time to pay, 250
filing deadline for citizenship, 42
filing deadline for taxes, 338
general information, 257–260
installment payments, 256
options for deducting expenses, 277
pages 1–4 instructions, 252–261
payment options, 247–248
penalties, 248
person responsible for filing, 245
postponing taxes, 256–257
Publication 950, 244
recapitulation, 260
release from personal liability, 246
signature and verification, 248–249, 254
special use valuation, 256
supporting documentation, 250–252
tax computation, 252–254
for trust funded after death, 222
valuation of the estate for, 248
where and how to file, 247
who must file, 244–245, 344
Form 706-CE, 251
Form 709, 39, 179, 180, 245, 251, 344
Form 712, 179, 251, 271
Form 792, 148
Form 990-PF, 53
Form 1023, 52
Form 1040. *See also specific schedules*
　deductions, 297–304, 314
　double-dipping rules, 298
　filing annually, 225
　for grantor trusts, 53, 54
　income calculation, 290–297
　options for deducting expenses, 277
　preparing for, 288–290
　taxes owed calculation, 304–307
　trustee's fees on, 200
Form 1041. *See also specific schedules*
　credits, 308
　deductions, 297–304, 314
　double-dipping rules, 298

filing annually, 225
filing deadline, 338
household employee taxes, 309
income calculation, 290–297
options for deducting expenses, 277
page 2 questions, 309–310
preparing for, 288–290
recapture taxes, 309
Section 663(b) election, 208
tax year-end for, 289–290
taxes owed calculation, 304–307
trust accounting income on, 207
Form 1096, 331
Form 1098, 119, 120
Form 1099, 119, 120
Form 1099 for nominees, 330–331
Form 1099-B, 292, 294
Form 1099-BTC, 308
Form 1099-DIV, 291
Form 1099-S, 292
Form 1116, 308, 322
Form 1120S, 54, 113
Form 2848, 251
Form 3520, 164, 310
Form 3800, 308
Form 4255, 309
Form 4422, 148
Form 4506, 120
Form 4506-T, 120
Form 4768, 245
Form 4797, 296–297
Form 5227, 51–52
Form 5471, 164
Form 8582, 295
Form 8611, 309
Form 8801, 308
Form 8912, 308
Form 8938, 164
Form 8949, 292, 294
Form SS-4, 288
Form TD-909-22.1, 164
Form W-2, 119, 120
Form W-9, 173
fractional share, 145–146
frozen assets, 83
FSAs (flexible spending accounts), 126
funded trusts, 31–34, 222, 352
funding a trust, 171–182
funeral arrangements
    cemetery selection, 80, 81
    claiming expenses, 275–277
    clergyperson selection, 79
    collation, 81
    consulting with the family, 77, 78
    cremation versus interment, 79–80
    death notice or obituary, 77, 78
    eulogies, 79
    funeral director selection, 77
    headstone or grave marker, 80, 81
    paying for, 81–82
    planning the service, 78–79
    veterans' burial rights, 80–81

## • G •

general business credits, 308
general power of appointment, 41, 284, 352
generation-skipping transfer (GST) tax, 28–29,
    39, 45, 46, 286, 344
Georgia taxes/rules of intestacy, 363
gifts
    anatomical, 76
    annual exclusion amount for, 43–44
    estate tax requirements, 245
    federal gift tax, 28, 39, 343–344
    to irrevocable trusts, 39–40
    not considered taxable, 27
    Schedule O (Form 706), 282–283
    unified credit against tax on, 27, 43
gift-splitting, 39
grantor trusts, 32
Grantor-Retained Annuity Trust (GRAT), 48, 352
Grantor-Retained Income Trust (GRIT), 49, 352
Grantor-Retained Unitrust (GRUT), 49, 352
grantors, donors, or settlors
    defined, 11, 32, 162, 351, 352, 356
    funding a trust by, 171–181
    independent trustee use by, 11
grave marker, 80, 81
gross estate, 352
guardian, 10, 22–23, 97, 352
guardian ad litem, 103, 155–156, 353

## • H •

Hawaii taxes/rules of intestacy, 364
headstone, 80, 81
health, distributions to ensure, 212–213
heirs-at-law, 26, 86–87, 103, 353
hiding places for assets, 116–117
high yield (junk) bonds, 353
holding period, 292
holographic will, 21–22
homestead allowance, 107
house safes, 116–117
household employee taxes, 309
household property. See personal and
    household property

### • I •

icons in this book, explained, 5
Idaho taxes/rules of intestacy, 364
IDGT (intentionally defective grantor trust),
    33–34
Illinois taxes/rules of intestacy, 364–365
incidents of ownership, 353
income
    defined, 185, 353
    dividing between the decedent and the
        estate, 314
    on Forms 1040 and 1041, 290–297
    principal versus, 185–186, 224–225, 341
    Schedule K-1 (Form 1041), 325, 328–329
    taxable, balancing estate's versus
        beneficiary's, 313
    timing the receipt of, 313, 315
income distribution deduction, 302–304
income distributions, 164–165
income taxes. *See also* Form 1040; Form 1041
    beneficiary, 317–318
    federal, 29, 345, 346
    fiduciary, 317
    filing for trusts, 225
    local, 346
    short-year returns, 237
    state, 30, 316, 330, 345, 346
    at trust termination, 236–237
independent trustees, 11–12, 13, 162, 353
Indiana taxes/rules of intestacy, 365
individual independent trustee, 162
individual retirement accounts (IRAs), 128–129
inheritance tax, 29, 353
inheriting under the will, 24
insolvent estate, declaring, 137–138
insurance
    credit card, 127–128
    errors and omissions, 72, 167
    executor on policy, 105–106
    life, 178–180, 270–271, 281
    loan, 127–128
    locating and collecting proceeds, 127–128
    locating policies after death, 86
    mortgage, 127–128
    Schedule D (Form 706), 270–271
    Schedule F (Form 706), 270, 274
    traditional life, 127
    transferring to a trust, 178–180
insurance trusts, 46
intangible property, 122–124, 142–143, 353
intangibles tax, 30, 353
intellectual property, valuing, 123–124

intentional omission from will, 25–26, 139
intentionally defective grantor trust (IDGT),
    33–34
inter vivos trusts, 34–35, 223, 353
interest deductions, 298–299
interest income, 269, 290
interment, 79
Internet streaming of funeral, 79
intestacy rules, by state, 359–377
intestate
    defined, 22, 353
    dying, 22–23, 95, 144
intestate share, 107
inventory
    defined, 110, 353
    probate, filing, 129–130
    of trust assets, 223–224
investment advisors, 64, 66–69, 169, 186–187
investments to minimize taxes, 315–318
Iowa taxes/rules of intestacy, 365
IRAs (individual retirement accounts), 128–129
irrevocable trusts
    common aspects of, 38–39
    credit shelter, 43–44, 350
    Crummey, 47–48, 350
    defined, 353
    grandchildren's, 46
    grantor-retained interest, 48–49
    insurance, 46
    living trusts at grantor's death, 36, 85
    making gifts to, 39–40
    marital, 40–42, 354
    personal and household property in, 180
IRS, avoiding phoning, 58
IRS Publication 559, 58
issue date, 191
issue, defined, 353

### • J •

joint revocable living trusts, 37
joint tenancy with right of survivorship, 353
joint ventures, 274
jointly owned property, 83, 271–273
junk bonds, 353

### • K •

Kansas taxes/rules of intestacy, 366
Kentucky taxes/rules of intestacy, 366
Kiddie Tax, 205

## • L •

lawsuits, ongoing at death, 129
lease on decedent's residence, 134
leasehold, 274
legacy, 26, 137, 353
legatees, 339
letters of intent, 85, 144
letters testamentary, 251
liability insurance, 72
liens, in Schedule K (Form 706), 279
life estate, 353
life insurance, 178–180, 270–271, 281
limited liability company (LLC), 111
limited power of appointment, 41, 353
line of succession for trustees, 12
liquidating assets, 130–131
litigators, 70
living trusts, 36–37, 85, 354
load, defined, 354
loan insurance, 127–128
local taxes, 346–347
Louisiana taxes/rules of intestacy, 366–367
lump-sum distributions, 306, 336–337

## • M •

Maine taxes/rules of intestacy, 367
malfeasance, 188
malpractice, 70–72, 115
marital deduction, 280–282
marital estate trust, 42
marital trusts, 40–42, 354, 357
marshalling assets
    appraising property, 121–125
    bank statement info for, 114–115
    brokerage statement info for, 115
    checking the mail, 114–115
    defined, 109
    digital assets and info, 118–119
    employee benefits, 125–127
    finding hiding places, 116–117
    insurance proceeds, 127–128
    need for, 110
    from ongoing lawsuits, 129
    other death benefits, 128–129
    personal and household effects, 120–121
    personal papers for, 115–116
    real estate, 111
    safe-deposit box info for, 117–118
    small businesses, 112–113
    tax return info for, 119–120
    vehicles, 112

Martindale-Hubbell database, 60
Maryland taxes/rules of intestacy, 367
Massachusetts taxes/rules of intestacy, 367–368
maturity date, 189, 191
mean, defined, 354
Medicaid claims, 136
medical advisors, 70
medical expenses, as gift not taxable, 27
Michigan taxes/rules of intestacy, 368
military affidavit, 156
military funeral honors, 81
Minnesota taxes/rules of intestacy, 368–369
Mississippi taxes/rules of intestacy, 369
Missouri taxes/rules of intestacy, 369
Montana taxes/rules of intestacy, 369
Moody's, 190–191
mortgage insurance, 127–128
mortgages
    Schedule C (Form 706), 269–270
    Schedule K (Form 706), 279
    settling the debt on, 135
    at trust termination, 235
municipal bonds, 190, 354
mutual funds, 192

## • N •

Nebraska taxes/rules of intestacy, 369–370
net income, 354
net losses on Schedule L, 279–280
Nevada taxes/rules of intestacy, 370
New Hampshire taxes/rules of intestacy, 370
New Jersey taxes/rules of intestacy, 371
New Mexico taxes/rules of intestacy, 371
New York taxes/rules of intestacy, 371–372
nominee Form 1099s, 330–331
nominee trust, 38, 354
noncitizen spouse, QDOT for, 41–42
non-grantor trusts, 32–33
non-independent (family) trustees, 12–13, 162
non-operating charitable foundations, 52–53
North Carolina taxes/rules of intestacy, 372
North Dakota taxes/rules of intestacy, 372
notes, 191, 354
Notice of Appointment and Duties of Personal
    Representative, 102
Notice of Continued Administration, 103
notification of decedent's death, 86–88
notifying the surety, 156
nuncupative will, 22

## • O •

obituary, 77, 78
Ohio taxes/rules of intestacy, 372–373
Oklahoma taxes/rules of intestacy, 373
oral will, 22
Order for Complete Estate Settlement, 155
Order of Discharge, 155
ordinary gain or loss, 296–297
Oregon taxes/rules of intestacy, 373
organ donations, 76
original will, 354

## • P •

paid-up policy, 354
partnerships
    as assets, 112–113
    income from, 295
    Schedule F (Form 706), 274
    transferring to a trust, 175, 176
    at trust termination, 235
payable on death (POD) account, 83. *See also*
        Totten Trusts
payment date, 354
payments. *See also* distributions to
        beneficiaries; fees
    administration expenses, 149–150
    conditional legacies and devises, 137
    decedent's debts, 133–136
    funeral costs, 81–82
    Medicaid claims, 136
    ongoing estate expenses, 315
    prioritizing, 136–137
    timing, tax implications for, 312–315
    trust expenses, 199–201
pecuniary bequest, 143
pecuniary devise, 140
Pennsylvania taxes/rules of intestacy, 373–374
pensions, 86, 87, 126, 128–129
per capita, 146, 354
per stirpes, 146, 354
percentage, dividing residue by, 145–146
perpetuities, rule against, 50
personal and household property. *See also*
        *specific kinds*
    assets, 119–120
    bequests, 139, 141
    defined, 354
    distributing, 139–145
    do's and don'ts for splitting, 337
    Schedule F (Form 706), 273
    transferring to a trust, 180–181
    unwanted, 145
personal papers, asset info in, 115–116
personal representative, 10, 354

personalty, 143
phoning the IRS, avoiding, 58
pick-up state estate taxes, 29
pitfalls to avoid, 335–341
political organizations, gifts to, 27
politically aware investing, 196
post-mortem tax planning, 311
power of appointment, 40–41, 108, 284, 354
Power of Attorney and Declaration of
        Representative, 251
power to revoke, 354
powers of attorney, 84
prerefund dates, 191
prerefunded, defined, 191, 355
present interest, 355
Presidential Memorial Certificate, 81
pretermitted heir, 25, 104, 139, 355
principal
    age-based distribution, 198–199, 210
    defined, 184, 355
    distribution at trust termination, 210
    income versus, 185–186, 224–225, 341
    overview, 184
    unscheduled distribution, 165
prioritizing payments, 136–137
probate court
    allowance by, 151–156
    appointments by, 10, 95
    death certificate for, 82
    filing annual account with, 228–229
    filing the will with, 92
    forms and help from, 58, 98
    missing deadlines, 338
    petitioning to be administrator, 21
    state laws governing, 91–92
    statutory filing fee, 155
    Uniform Probate Code for, 99
probate estate, 355
probate procedure
    ancillary administration, 97–98
    defined, 355
    determining administration needs, 93–98
    domicile determination, 95–96
    filing the probate inventory, 129–130
    first steps, 105–106
    guardian need determination, 97
    overview, 14
    for small estates, 99–101
    special administrator for, 95
    supervised formal probate, 104–105, 154–155
    temporary executor for, 93–94
    unsupervised formal probate, 103–104, 154–155
    unsupervised informal probate, 101–103,
        153–154
promissory notes, 175–176, 235, 269–270
proof of ownership, 20, 172
property subject to claims, 355
property taxes, 347

prospectus, 355
protective claim for refund, 286
prudent man rule, 163
Publication 950, 245

# • *Q* •

qualified charities, 27
qualified conservation easement, 286
qualified dividends, 291, 305–306
qualified domestic trust (QDOT), 41–42, 261, 282
qualified heirs, 355
Qualified Personal Residence Trust (QPRT), 49, 355
Qualified Subchapter S Trust (QSST), 54, 355
qualified terminal interest property (QTIP), 42, 275, 281, 355
quasi-community property, 355

# • *R* •

ratings for bonds, 190–191
real estate
    appraising, 124–125
    assessed value of, 124–125
    devises, 141–142
    distributions to buy a home, 213–214
    failing to terminate a transaction, 335–336
    IDGTs for, 33
    local taxes, 346–347
    marshalling assets, 111
    releases of lien for, 148–149
    Schedule A (Form 706), 264–265
    Schedule A-1 (Form 706), 265
    selling, 131–132
    transferring to a trust, 176–178
    trust investment, 193–194
    at trust termination, 235
real property, 355
recapture taxes, 309
reciprocal will, 355
record date, 355
records, organizing an estate's, 89–90
records, trust. *See* trust records
reforming a trust, 163
release from personal liability, 246
remainder interests, 39, 275, 285
remaindermen
    assents of, 228, 238, 239
    defined, 11, 33, 162, 355
    paying at trust termination, 234–235
Remember icon, explained, 5
rent income, 295
reregistering stock and bond certificates, 174–175
residuary devisee, 26, 356

residuary legatee, 26, 356
residue, 144, 145–146, 150
retirement plans, 86, 87, 126, 128–129
return of capital, 185, 356
return-preparer fees, 301
reversionary interest, 274, 356
revocable trusts
    defined, 32, 35, 356
    living, 36–37, 85, 354
    nominee, 38, 354
    Totten, 37, 357
Rhode Island taxes/rules of intestacy, 374
royalty income, 295
royalty interests, 235, 274
rule against perpetuities, 50
rules of intestacy, by state, 359–377

# • *S* •

safe-deposit box, 85, 117–118
S&P (Standard & Poor's), 190–191
Schedule A (Form 706), 264–265
Schedule A (Form 1040), 117, 296, 297, 299, 301–302
Schedule A (Form 1041), 145
Schedule A-1 (Form 706), 265
Schedule B (Form 706), 265–269
Schedule B (Form 1041), 300, 302–304, 321, 322
Schedule C (Form 706), 269–270
Schedule C (Form 1040), 112, 296
Schedule D (Form 706), 270–271
Schedule D (Form 1041), 194, 292, 305–306
Schedule E (Form 706), 265, 271–273
Schedule E (Form 1040), 112, 296
Schedule E (Form 1040 or 1041), 295
Schedule F (Form 706), 265, 270, 273–275
Schedule F (Form 1040), 295–296
Schedule G (Form 706), 284
Schedule G (Form 1041), 308
Schedule H (Form 706), 284
Schedule H (Form 1040), 309
Schedule I (Form 706), 285
Schedule J (Form 706), 275–278
Schedule K (Form 706), 264, 278–279
Schedule K-1 (Form 1041)
    AMT information, 327–328
    deductions and credits, 326–327
    fiscal year-end for, 312
    general information, 322–324
    income allocation, 328–329
    income items, 325
    purpose of, 321–322
    for QSSTs, 54
    for split-interest charitable trusts, 51
    supplements to, 329–330
    for trust beneficiaries, 201
    at trust termination, 236

Schedule L (Form 706), 279–280
Schedule M (Form 706), 280–282
Schedule O (Form 706), 282–283
Schedule P (Form 706), 285
Schedule PC (Form 706), 275, 286
Schedule Q (Form 706), 285
Schedule R (Form 706), 286
Schedule SE (Form 1040), 292
Schedule U (Form 706), 286
Schedule of Beneficial Interest, 38
scheduled distributions, 205–209
Section 663(b), 208
secured debt, 135
securities. *See also* bonds; stocks
   distributing, 142–143
   liquidating, 130–131
   notes, 191, 354
   transferring to a trust, 172–175
   unmarketable, 268
   valuing, 123
Seek Advice icon, explained, 5
separate property, 356
service of process, 97
Settlement Order, 155
settlors. *See* grantors, donors, or settlors
short year, 237, 356
shortcuts, cautions for taking, 340
signature guarantee, 356
single premium life insurance, 179, 356
situs, 356
slack-tax system, 29
small business stocks, 194, 356
small estate probate procedures, 99–101
Social Security death benefits, 128
Social Security Number (SSN), 204, 288
socially responsible investing, 195–196, 356
sole proprietorship, 112, 274, 291
South Carolina taxes/rules of intestacy, 374
South Dakota taxes/rules of intestacy, 374–375
special administrator, 95
special (extraordinary) dividends, 186, 356
special power of appointment, 356
specific devisee, 26, 356
specific legatee, 26, 356
spendthrift trusts, 199, 212, 356
split-interest charitable trusts, 51–52, 356
sponge state estate taxes, 29
Standard & Poor's (S&P), 190–191
states
   estate and inheritance tax, 262, 345, 359–377
   excise taxes, 347
   help from tax departments, 58
   income taxes, 30, 316, 330, 345, 346
   intangibles tax, 347
   laws governing probate court, 91–92
   laws governing trusts, 160
   probate court governed by, 91–92
   rules of intestacy, 359–377
   transfer taxes, 29

statutory dower, 108
statutory filing fee, 155
statutory share, 23, 107–108, 357
stockbrokers, 67, 68
stocks. *See also* securities
   defined, 188, 357
   investing and diversifying, 188–189
   liquidating, 130–131
   marshalling assets, 115
   privately held, 175
   reregistering certificates, 174–175
   Schedule B (Form 706), 265–269
   small business, 194
   transferring to a trust, 172–175
   at trust termination, 234
   valuation of, 266–269
street name, 357
Subchapter S corporation, 53–55, 113, 357
subordinate bonds, 191
supervised formal probate, 104–105, 154–155
surety, notifying, 156
surviving spouse
   bequests to, 280–282
   COBRA benefits for, 126
   overview, 23–24
   rights and decisions of, 106–108
   in simultaneous death, 283
   unused exclusion (DSUE), 244, 260–261
Sworn Closing Statement, 153–154

## • T •

TAI (trust accounting income), 185, 206–208, 357
taking against the will, 23, 24, 107–108, 357
tangible property, 121–122, 141–142
tax professionals, 64–66
taxes. *See also specific forms, schedules, and
   publications*
   annual, for trusts, 169–170
   asset info in returns, 119–120
   audit preparations, 261–262
   calendar for deadlines, 89
   charitable trust consequences, 50–51
   credits, 308, 327
   death, 28, 351
   deductible, 299, 304, 326
   estate income, 150, 151, 345, 359–377
   estate tax closing letters, 147–148
   excise, 347
   federal estate, 28
   foreign death, 285
   gifts not considered taxable, 27
   on grantor trusts, 32
   GST, 28–29, 39, 45, 46, 286, 344
   on IDGTs, 33
   income, 29–30, 225
   inheritance, 353
   intangibles, 30, 347, 353

on inter vivos trusts, 34
investing to minimize, 315–318
IRS instructions for forms, 58
keeping returns, 222
Kiddie Tax, 205
local, 346–347
missing deadlines, 338
on nominee trusts, 38
on non-grantor trusts, 33
overview, 17–18, 26–30
post-mortem planning, 311
on prior transfers, 285
release from personal liability, 246
on split-interest charitable trusts, 51–52
terminating a trust, 233
transfer, 27–29
on trusts, 201, 345
types of, 343–347
UIMC, 318–320
unified credit against gift tax, 27, 43
taxpayer identification number (TIN),
    106, 172, 288
Technical Stuff icon, explained, 5
temporary executor, 93–94
tenancy by the entirety, 357
tenancy in common, 357
Tennessee taxes/rules of intestacy, 375
term insurance, 357
terminable interest, 282
terminating a trust
    calculating income distributions, 232–233
    holding funds for taxes and fees, 233
    income tax returns, 236–237
    non-probate trust, 238–239
    outliers after, 240
    paying remaindermen, 234–235
    principal distribution, 210
    probate trust, 239
    trust instrument instructions for, 231–232
testamentary capacity, 104
testamentary trusts, 35, 357
testate, 21–22, 357
testator, 357
Texas taxes/rules of intestacy, 375
Tip icon, explained, 5
total dividends, 291
Totten Trusts, 37, 357
traditional life insurance, 127
transfer taxes, 27–29
trust accounting income (TAI), 185, 206–208, 357
trust companies, 169
trust instrument
    certified copy of, 171
    defined, 159, 357
    discussing with the grantor, 160
    keeping handy, 220
    state laws governing, 160

trust records
    annual accounts, 221–222, 226–229
    correspondence, 220–221
    filing system setup, 217–222
    financial, 221
    inventory and valuing of assets, 223–224
    permanent versus temporary, 218–219
    supplies for keeping, 218
    tax returns, 222
    of transactions, 224–225
trustees
    defined, 159, 162, 357
    duties of, 15–17
    family or non-dependent, 12–13, 162
    fees, 200
    fiduciary duties and limitations, 166–167
    of grantor trusts, 32
    independent, 11–12, 13, 162, 353
    line of succession for, 12
    non-grantor trusts, 32–33
    overview, 11
    powers granted to, 163–166
trusts
    amendments to, 85
    annual tax returns and accounts, 169–170
    charitable, 50–53
    credit shelter, 43–44, 350
    Crummey, 47–48, 350
    defined, 159, 357
    with foreign interests, 164
    funded, 31–34, 352
    funding after grantor's death, 182
    funding during grantor's life, 171–181
    funeral, 82
    grandchildren's, 46
    grantor, 32
    grantor-retained interest, 48–49
    identifying the players, 161–163
    IDGTs, 33–34
    income from others, 295
    income taxes, 345
    insurance, 46
    inter vivos, 34–35, 223, 353
    irrevocable, 36, 38–44, 46–49, 353
    living, 36–37, 354
    locating agreements after death, 84–85
    marital, 40–42, 354
    marital deduction, 281
    nominee, 38, 354
    non-grantor, 32–33
    plan creation based on, 160–161
    purposes of, 197–199
    reforming, 163
    revocable, 32, 35–38, 356
    terminating, 231–240
    testamentary, 35
    Totten, 37, 357
tuition, as gift not taxable, 27

## • U •

Unearned Income Medicare Contribution (UIMC) tax, 318–320
unified credit against gift tax, 27, 43
Uniform Probate Code (UPC), 99
unlimited marital trusts, 40–41, 357
unmarketable securities, 268
unsupervised formal probate, 103–104, 154–155
unsupervised informal probate, 101–103, 153–154
U.S. flag, for veteran's funeral, 80
U.S. Government bonds, 190
U.S. Treasury bonds, 190
U.S. Treasury obligations, 357
usufruct, 358
Utah taxes/rules of intestacy, 375–376

## • V •

variable universal life insurance, 179, 358
vehicles
    marshalling assets, 112
    Schedule F (Form 706), 273
    small estate procedures for, 100
Vermont taxes/rules of intestacy, 376
Veteran's Administration, death benefits, 128
veterans' burial rights, 80–81
Virginia taxes/rules of intestacy, 376

## • W •

Warning icon, explained, 5
Washington taxes/rules of intestacy, 376
wearing apparel, small estate procedures for, 100
well-being, distributions to ensure, 212–213
West Virginia taxes/rules of intestacy, 377
whole life insurance, 179, 358
will
    attested, 22
    contested, 104
    for estate tax return, 251
    executor named in, 21
    filing with probate court, 92
    foreign, 97
    holographic, 21–22
    inheriting under, 24
    intentional omission from, 25–26, 139
    issues affecting validity of, 21–22
    locating after death, 84, 85
    oral, 22
    original, 85, 354
    in safe-deposit box, 85
    special administrator for, 95
    taking against, 23, 24, 107–108, 357
    testamentary capacity for, 104
    trusts created under, 35
    undue influence from another, 104
Wisconsin taxes/rules of intestacy, 377
Wyoming taxes/rules of intestacy, 377